W9-CSR-229

"*Putting Jesus in His Place* is a meticulously researched and brilliant book on a subject that continues to remain significant even after two thousand years. Robert Bowman and Ed Komoszewski have given readers a unique and unparalleled resource—and one with life-changing implications. I commend this volume to you with much appreciation for their work."

—RAVI ZACHARIAS
Author and speaker

"Bowman and Komoszewski do a splendid job of showing that the divine identity of Jesus is not confined to a few key texts, but presented throughout the New Testament in a wide variety of ways. Their arguments are fully based on the best of recent scholarship, and explained in a way that all serious readers of the New Testament will appreciate."

—RICHARD BAUCKHAM
Professor of New Testament Studies and Bishop Wardlaw Professor
St. Mary's College, University of St. Andrews

"An exciting, compelling, and user-friendly investigation of the full range of New Testament evidence for the unique divine identity of Jesus Christ, admirably suitable for the non-specialist reader, yet with detailed up-to-date specialist notes."

—MURRAY J. HARRIS
Professor Emeritus of New Testament
Trinity Evangelical Divinity School, Deerfield, IL

"The deity of Jesus Christ is central and foundational to the gospel. Those who have eyes to see will find it everywhere, and if your eyes are deficient this book is just the corrective you need. The work is convincing, clear, and scholarly. Most of all, the book is glorious, reminding us that Jesus is to be worshiped as our Lord, Savior, and God."

—THOMAS R. SCHREINER
James Buchanan Harrison Professor of New Testament Interpretation
The Southern Baptist Theological Seminary

"This is one of the finest pieces of readable scholarship ever written on the subject."

—GARY DEMAR
Author, speaker, and editor of *Biblical Worldview* magazine

"The authors have provided a readable and well-informed summary of a large body of scholarly work that shows a very early and very 'high' view of Jesus, not as something emerging by slow evolution, but as an explosively quick and remarkable phenomenon."

—LARRY W. HURTADO
Professor of New Testament Language, Literature, and Theology
University of Edinburgh, Scotland

"Putting Jesus in His Place is a comprehensive apologetic from the Scriptures for the person and work of Jesus Christ. From his names to his nature, from his works to his worship, this book will lead you from the descriptive affirmations to the well-deserved adoration owed to our great God and Savior, Jesus Christ. This book should be in every home and library."

—MARK L. BAILEY
President, Dallas Theological Seminary

"Putting Jesus in His Place is the finest and most comprehensive apologetic for the deity of Christ that I have yet encountered. It is my hope that this book will become a standard resource for educational institutions and for people who desire a clearer vision of the Lord Jesus."

—KENNETH BOA
President, Reflections Ministries, Atlanta, GA
President, Trinity House Publishers, Atlanta, GA

"An exceedingly readable and intelligible book on a central—and hotly debated—theme of the Christian message. It gives not only rich biblical information to the reader but also practical pastoral guidance."

—MARTIN HENGEL
Professor Emeritus of New Testament and Ancient Judaism
University of Tübingen, Germany

"Putting Jesus in His Place is a clearly written and carefully reasoned defense of the deity of Christ. Bowman and Komoszewski present a virtually comprehensive case for embracing Jesus' full and unqualified divinity. This book should be required reading in every church study group and in college and seminary classes."

—KENNETH SAMPLES
Vice President for Theological and Philosophical Apologetics, Reasons to Believe
Author, *A World of Difference*

FOREWORD BY DARRELL L. BOCK

PUTTING JESUS IN HIS PLACE

THE CASE FOR THE DEITY OF CHRIST

ROBERT M. BOWMAN JR.

J. ED KOMOSZEWSKI

Kregel
Publications

Putting Jesus in His Place: The Case for the Deity of Christ

© 2007 by Robert M. Bowman Jr. and J. Ed Komoszewski

Published by Kregel Publications, a division of Kregel, Inc.,
P.O. Box 2607, Grand Rapids, MI 49501.

Library of Congress Cataloging-in-Publication Data
Bowman, Robert J.
Putting Jesus in his place : the case for the deity of Christ /
by Robert M. Bowman, Jr. and J. Ed Komoszewski.
    p. cm.
Includes bibliographical references and index.
1. Jesus Christ—Divinity. I. Komoszewski, J. Ed. II. Title.
BT216.3.B69 2007
232'.8—dc22   2007028348

ISBN 978-0-8254-2983-5

Printed in the United States of America

07 08 09 10 11 / 5 4 3 2

Robert M. Bowman Jr. (M.A., Fuller Theological Seminary) is the manager of Apologetics and Interfaith Evangelism for the North American Mission Board (http://www.4truth.net). For five years he was a lecturer in the M.A. in Christian Apologetics program at Biola University. He is the author of eleven other books, including *Why You Should Believe in the Trinity* and the Gold Medallion Award-winning book *Faith Has Its Reasons* (with Kenneth D. Boa).

J. Ed Komoszewski (Th.M., Dallas Theological Seminary) is the founder of Christus Nexus (http://www.christusnexus.org), a non-profit organization devoted to researching, writing, and teaching on the uniqueness of Jesus Christ. He has taught biblical and theological studies at Northwestern College and currently serves as a director for Reclaiming the Mind Ministries. He is the coauthor of *Reinventing Jesus*.

Darrell L. Bock (Ph.D.) is research professor of New Testament studies at Dallas Theological Seminary. A former president of the Evangelical Theological Society, he is the author of the best-seller *Breaking the Da Vinci Code* and numerous works in New Testament studies, including *Jesus According to Scripture* and *The Missing Gospels*.

For additional resources on the subject of this book, please visit us online at http://www.deityofchrist.com.

CONTENTS

Part 4: Infinitely Qualified: Jesus Shares in the <u>D</u>eeds That God Does

Part 5: The Best Seat in the House: Jesus Shares the <u>S</u>eat of God's Throne

TABLES

FOREWORD

Putting Jesus in His Place is not a typical book. After all, it deals with a complex subject in a manner that is academically responsible *as well as* clear and memorable. Many treatments of Jesus' identity are detailed and informative, but they tend to leave a rather dry taste in one's mouth. Rarely does one get to work through the meat of biblical teaching about who Jesus was and is in the pleasant-tasting way afforded by this book. This combination of intellectual rigor and eminent readability qualifies *Putting Jesus in His Place* for a pastor's library, a sermon series, a Sunday school text, or even a required class on Christology.

The chefs for this dinner, Robert M. Bowman Jr. and J. Ed Komoszewski, have prepared a five-course meal for us. Indeed, they have presented to us five different elements in the recipe that lead to a hearty appreciation of the biblical Jesus. The savory and idiomatic manner of the meal's presentation makes the mixture of assorted and diverse—even potentially confusing—ingredients a success.

Once you've looked at this book's presentation of the honors Jesus receives, the attributes he possesses, the names by which he is identified, the deeds he performs, and the seat he occupies in heaven, you'll have a basic grasp of who Jesus is and what God has done through him. And if you're so inclined, the notes and bibliography will take you even further, all the way to the most scholarly levels of the debate.

There are many works of theology and/or apologetics on the market that are sensitive to a popular audience yet fail to reflect the state of current discussions. That is not the case here. *Putting Jesus in His Place* looks at the biblical witness to Jesus' uniqueness from a variety of well-informed angles. In a world that often tries to domesticate Jesus or bring him down to our level, it is refreshing to have a book that sets forth in a direct and appealing manner who Jesus truly is.

This is a book you should devour and digest. It will give you a deeper understanding of Jesus' true place at the center of all that exists and, most importantly, draw you closer to him. The table is set; the meal is fixed. Take a seat and enjoy a satisfying serving of the biblical witness to our unique Lord. Eat and be filled. My compliments to the chefs.

—DARRELL L. BOCK
Research Professor of New Testament Studies
Dallas Theological Seminary

KNOWING JESUS AS GOD

There's no denying it: Jesus is one of a kind.[1] He is the central figure of the world's largest religion (Christianity) and viewed as a major prophet in the world's second largest religion (Islam). Most people, in fact, regard Jesus as one of the greatest human beings who ever lived. But this remarkable consensus begs the question: Why are there so many conflicting interpretations of Jesus?

Your Own Personal Jesus

Interpretations of Jesus are fraught with bias. He's a powerful figure whom people want on their sides—and they're willing to re-create him in their image to enlist his support. Animal-rights activists imagine a vegetarian Jesus. New Agers make him an example of finding the god within. And radical feminists strip him of divinity so that Christianity doesn't appear sexist. "Frankly, it's hard to escape the feeling that our culture has taken Jesus' question 'Who do you say that I am?' and changed it to 'Who do you want me to be?'"[2]

It is an interesting irony, though, that the Jesus Seminar, a group of radically liberal scholars, warned, "Beware of finding a Jesus entirely congenial to you."[3] If only they had followed their own advice! From the start, the seminar was intent on finding a merely human Jesus who was concerned with radical equality and refused to make exclusive religious claims. In other words, they sought a Jesus who was, by today's standards, *politically correct*.[4] The seminar has been extraordinarily successful in getting publicity. In fact, their "findings" have been the cornerstone of several cover stories for *Time* magazine[5] and the thread holding together two prime-time ABC News documentaries hosted by the late Peter Jennings.[6]

Dan Brown excited interest in another way of looking at Jesus with his book-turned-movie *The Da Vinci Code*.[7] Although a novel, the book popularized a variety of misconceptions about the origins of Christianity. One especially troublesome bit of disinformation promulgated in the book is the claim that the deity of Jesus was not something embraced by his earliest followers but was, in fact, the invention of a council that convened nearly three hundred years after Jesus' time. More than one scholar has demonstrated that *The Da Vinci Code* shares more in common with conspiracy theories than with sober historical analysis,[8] yet its message continues to resonate with contemporary culture.

> Beware of finding a Jesus entirely congenial to you.
> —THE JESUS SEMINAR

These are just a few examples of the many self-serving interpretations of Jesus that circulate today. What do they share in common? An aversion to the New Testament view of Jesus as God. As attracted to Jesus as a lot of people seem to be, many are looking for a merely human Jesus—or at least a Jesus who is entirely on their side of the line between Creator and creature. Why is this?

One scholar put his finger on the problem when he explained that belief in the deity of Jesus—his unique status among human beings as God in the flesh—implies that Jesus is the only way for people to be properly related to God.

> Traditional orthodoxy says that Jesus of Nazareth was God incarnate . . . who became man to die for the sins of the world and who founded the church to proclaim this to the ends of the earth, so that all who sincerely take Jesus as their Lord and Savior are justified by his atoning death and will inherit eternal life. It follows from this that Christianity, alone among the world religions, was founded by

God in person. God came down from heaven to earth and launched the salvific movement that came to be known as Christianity. From this premise it seems obvious that God must wish all human beings to enter this stream of saved life, so that Christianity shall supersede all the other world faiths. They may perhaps have some good in them and be able to function to some extent as a preparation for the gospel, but nevertheless Christianity alone is God's own religion. . . . It is therefore divinely intended for all men and women without exception. All this follows logically from the central dogma of the deity of Jesus.[9]

It is remarkable, however, that the person who made this observation doesn't believe in the deity of Jesus. He is, in fact, a well-known opponent of that doctrine. Among his many accomplishments, John Hick served as editor for the 1977 book titled *The Myth of God Incarnate*. (By "God incarnate" is meant that God came "in the flesh" as a human being.) Hick has seen more clearly than most that if Jesus was uniquely God incarnate, then he is also uniquely the way to God.[10] And that is what really offends people today. Almost no one minds a strong affirmation of belief in Jesus. To suggest, however, that without Jesus people of other religions are missing something of eternal importance is regarded by many as an attack on the right of people to believe whatever they want. In an age when so many reject the idea that any one viewpoint is superior to another, that Jesus is regarded as uniquely God incarnate is the epitome of intolerance.

Back to the Sources

It's easy to be tempted to focus our efforts on making Jesus "relevant" to today's cosmopolitan, postmodern tastes. Non-Christians are becoming increasingly guarded—if not hostile—toward traditional Christian beliefs. By emphasizing Jesus' humanity, some Christians are, indeed, bending over backward to make Christianity—and Christ himself—more "approachable." They may not deny the deity of Jesus, but in practical terms his humanity overwhelms his deity. In the end, though, a lack of appreciation of Jesus' identity as God makes him *less* approachable. As New Testament scholar Grant Osborne warns, some of us have lost the holy reverence and awe that we should have toward Jesus:

Christians are guilty of the syndrome "Your Jesus is too small." We have made Jesus our "big brother" and "friend" to such an extent that we have lost the sense that he is also our sovereign Lord. We must recapture the realization that he too is our God and worthy of worship at the deepest level.[11]

If we are to experience a healthy relationship with God, we need to be intimately acquainted with the biblical teaching about the divine identity of Jesus. This involves more than merely knowing about, and agreeing with, the doctrine of the deity of Christ, though that is certainly essential. It must become more to us than a line we say in a creed. We need to know what it means to say that Jesus is God and why it matters. We need to see Jesus as God. We need to think about Jesus and relate to him in the full light of the truth of his identity. We need to appreciate the significance of his divine identity for our relationships with God and others.

In our quest to know who Jesus was and is, we must give careful attention to the understanding of Jesus presented in the sources closest to him: the New Testament writings. We recognize that in the early centuries of Christianity people wrote other books representing views of Jesus that differed greatly from that presented in the New Testament. In recent years much has been made of these "lost scriptures" and of the "lost Christianities" that they represent.[12] These "scriptures" all originated, however, after the New Testament writings, and none of them was written by a first-generation believer in Jesus. Even in the case of the much-heralded Gospel of Thomas, biblical scholars of all stripes agree that the apostle Thomas did not write it. In fact, almost all scholars agree that it was written at least one or two generations after the apostles.[13]

We also recognize that the New Testament writings have different ways of talking about Jesus. Several different individuals wrote the New Testament books, and they had different ways of expressing what they thought about Jesus. Nevertheless, all of them stand in that earliest stream of Christian belief that started with the original apostles. These are the writings that later came to be recognized as the primary sources of orthodox Christian teaching. Moreover, as we shall make clear, a "high" view of Jesus as deity is evident throughout the New Testament.[14]

Laying the Foundation

In this book, then, we will be examining what the New Testament writings say about Jesus' identity as God. In doing so, we will take certain things for granted.

First, we will assume that Christians should base their beliefs about Jesus on the teachings of the New Testament. For the most part, we will assume that the passages on which we are commenting are true. Only in some key instances will we seek to establish their historical accuracy. Also, we will generally not debate the inspiration of the New Testament authors' explanations of who Jesus is and what his words and deeds mean. We ourselves affirm that the New Testament is historically accurate and its teachings divinely inspired. Even if some readers do not share our convictions about the New Testament's accuracy and inspiration, those interested in what the New Testament has to say about Jesus will, nevertheless, find help here.[15]

Second, we will take as given certain historical claims about Jesus that are basic to the New Testament. We will assume that Jesus was a real human being, that he died on the cross, and that he rose bodily from the grave.[16] Our focus in this book, of course, is on the deity of Jesus. To understand all that the New Testament says on that subject, however, we also must recognize that Jesus was human—and that in the resurrection he remains a human, albeit a glorified, immortal one.[17]

Third, we take for granted that Jesus is not God the Father. Rather, Jesus is "the Son of the Father" (2 John 3 NASB). The New Testament makes a distinction between the two, sometimes as the Father and the Son and sometimes as God and the Son of God. Although it's hard to understand, the New Testament both distinguishes Jesus from God and identifies him as God— sometimes in the same breath (e.g., John 1:1; 20:28–31; Heb. 1:8–9; 2 Peter 1:1–2). It is this fact about New Testament teaching—paralleled in what it also teaches about the Holy Spirit—that led Christian theologians to formulate the doctrine of the Trinity. We will not be discussing the Trinity in this book, although Jesus' identity as God is a key part of that doctrine.[18]

What to Expect

Our aim is to provide a comprehensive case from the New Testament for the deity of Jesus Christ. Many of us were taught that the deity of Jesus can be proved using one or two verses—say, John 1:1 ("and the Word was God") or John 20:28 (where Thomas calls Jesus, "My Lord and my God"). To be sure, we will say something about these important texts. But there is much more biblical evidence for Jesus' deity. It is not limited to a few verses but includes both explicit statements that say he is "God" and implicit indications of his deity. The evidence covers a wide range of closely related truths about Jesus that are taught repeatedly in one biblical book after another. The deity of Christ is, therefore, a major theme throughout the New Testament. Recognizing that theme in all of its many expressions will not only help you in your faith in Jesus as God but also make your understanding of Scripture much richer.

Throughout this book, we will not only cite biblical passages in support of the deity of Jesus but also discuss their interpretation. Along the way, we will interact with a wide range of contemporary biblical scholarship. The endnotes provide a wealth of references to recent scholarly literature—commentaries, published doctoral dissertations, periodical articles, and specialized studies—of relevance to the subject matter. Many of the endnotes also comment on some of the more technical issues that come up in these academic discussions. Since the main points you need to know are in the body of the book, you can skip these endnotes if you wish, but the information is there if you want it.

Although biblical scholarship informs every part of the book, our subject matter is not merely the object of academic research. We try to make it clear that relating to Jesus as to God is important for every aspect of the Christian life. We hope it is obvious that understanding Jesus' identity as God is extremely relevant to how we relate to Jesus. Knowing that he is God incarnate is the only sound foundation for approaching Jesus, for coming to him in prayer, and for trusting in him for salvation. Relating to Jesus as God is also crucial to the message we take to the rest of the world. We must know whom we represent if we are to represent him faithfully. Our Christian walk, witness, and worship all must reflect a sound understanding of the identity of our Lord Jesus Christ.

Our purpose in this book is not limited to presenting the big picture of the New Testament evidence for the deity of Jesus and explaining its relevance to the Christian life. We also want to equip you to *remember* this information and be able to present it to others. To that end, we organize the biblical teaching on the deity of Jesus into five categories that will be both memorable and easy to explain. We summarize these five categories using an acronym based on the word HANDS. This acronym recalls the dramatic experience of Thomas told in John 20:24–29. Despite what the other disciples told him, Thomas doubted that Jesus had risen from the dead. But when he saw the marks in Jesus' hands left by the nails of the crucifixion, Thomas was persuaded of more than the resurrection! Amazingly, he called Jesus his Lord and his God (John 20:28). Just as an examination of the nail prints convinced Thomas he was beholding the hands of deity, a closer look at the Bible reveals that Jesus shares the HANDS of God:

Honors:	Jesus shares the *honors* due to God.
Attributes:	Jesus shares the *attributes* of God.
Names:	Jesus shares the *names* of God.
Deeds:	Jesus shares in the *deeds* that God does.
Seat:	Jesus shares the *seat* of God's throne.

This acronym is not a gimmick. It is a tested and proven device for enabling people of different backgrounds to remember and explain the biblical evidence for identifying Jesus as God.[19] Each chapter will go into detail on the biblical teaching relating to one aspect of the five-point outline. We think this method will help you much better understand the biblical teaching on the deity of Christ, as well as remember the essential elements of that teaching, so that you will be able to explain them to others.

The biblical teaching about Jesus found in his HANDS constitutes a powerful cumulative case for regarding Jesus as our Lord and God. If you do not yet believe in Jesus as God, consider the evidence presented here. If you do believe in the deity of Christ, the biblical teaching reviewed here will enrich your understanding of that truth and equip you to share it with others. After you have read this book, we invite you to find additional resources and to participate in discussions on this subject by visiting our Web site: http://www.deityofchrist.com.

Wherever you are now in your understanding of Jesus, our heartfelt prayer is that your life will be revolutionized by the realization that Jesus Christ is indeed "our great God and Savior" (Titus 2:13).

ABBREVIATIONS

Bibles

ASV	American Standard Version
ESV	English Standard Version
HCSB	Holman Christian Standard Bible
KJV	King James Version
LXX	Septuagint (ancient Greek translation of the Old Testament)
MT	Masoretic Text
NAB	New American Bible
NASB	New American Standard Bible
NEB	New English Bible
NET	New English Translation
NIV	New International Version
NKJV	New King James Version
NLT	New Living Translation
NRSV	New Revised Standard Version
NWT	New World Translation
REB	Revised English Bible
RSV	Revised Standard Version

Standard Resources

AB	Anchor Bible
AGJU	Arbeiten zur Geschichte des antiken Judentums und des Urchristentums

BECNT	Baker Exegetical Commentary on the New Testament
Bib	*Biblica*
BIOSCS	*Bulletin for the International Organization for Septuagint and Cognate Studies*
BSac	*Bibliotheca Sacra*
CBQ	*Catholic Biblical Quarterly*
EGGNT	Exegetical Guide to the Greek New Testament
ExpTim	*Expository Times*
FRLANT	Forschungen zur Religion und Literatur des Alten und Neuen Testaments
ICC	International Critical Commentary
JBL	*Journal of Biblical Literature*
JBS	*Journal of Biblical Studies*
JETS	*Journal of the Evangelical Theological Society*
JJS	*Journal of Jewish Studies*
JSJ	*Journal for the Study of Judaism in the Persian, Hellenistic, and Roman Periods*
JSNT	*Journal for the Study of the New Testament*
JSNTSup	Journal for the Study of the New Testament: Supplement Series
JTS	*Journal of Theological Studies*
NAC	New American Commentary
NICNT	New International Commentary on the New Testament
NIGTC	New International Greek Testament Commentary
NT	New Testament
NTOA	Novum Testamentum et Orbis Antiquus
NTS	*New Testament Studies*
OT	Old Testament
SNTSMS	Society for New Testament Studies Monograph Series
TNTC	Tyndale New Testament Commentaries
TrinJ	*Trinity Journal*
TynB	*Tyndale Bulletin*
UBS	United Bible Societies
WBC	Word Biblical Commentary
WUNT	Wissenschaftliche Untersuchungen zum Neuen Testament

Part 1

THE DEVOTION
REVOLUTION

Jesus Shares the H̲onors Due to God

Honors	Attributes	Names	Deeds	Seat

Chapter 1

ALL GLORY, LAUD, AND HONOR

The Christian belief that Jesus Christ is God incarnate has been around so long that many people familiar with Christianity do not realize just how astonishing such a claim was and still is. Jesus was very much a real human being. He grew up in a dusty village as the son of a carpenter. He lived during a time of political turmoil for his people. He experienced the full range of human emotions, from unbridled joy to deep sorrow. He had friends and enemies. He perspired and got tired; he slept and awoke; he got hungry and thirsty; he bled and died. Indeed, by some measures, he was not a particularly remarkable man. He led no army, held no political office, wrote no books, had no wife or children, left no estate, and never traveled even a hundred miles from home. Yet billions of people during the past two millennia all over the world have worshiped him as their Lord and their God. How did that happen?

One popular answer today among those who do not believe in Jesus as God is that the belief evolved over a period of centuries. They suggest that the earliest Christians, who were Jews, thought of Jesus as simply a rabbi or a prophet, a holy and wise man. They theorize that as Christianity spread outward and became more and more dominated by Gentile (that is, non-Jewish) believers, those Gentiles, accustomed to assigning divine honors to their heroes, did the same for Jesus.[1] Eventually, a form of Christianity emerged that explained the divinity of Jesus as a unique incarnation of God and dismissed all alternative views of Jesus as heresy. Some critics of the doctrine that Jesus is God claim that this belief did not appear until well after all of the apostles had died—perhaps, some say, as late as the fourth-century Council of Nicea.

The facts are very much otherwise. The practice of giving Jesus divine honors—of religious, spiritual devotion to Jesus—was an established, characteristic feature of the Christian movement within the first two decades of its existence. Larry Hurtado, professor of New Testament at the University of Edinburgh, described the emergence of devotion to Jesus as "a veritable 'big bang,' an explosively rapid and impressively substantial development in the earliest stage of the Christian movement."[2] According to Martin Hengel, a New Testament scholar at Tübingen University in Germany, more happened in the development of Christian beliefs about Jesus in the twenty years between his death and Paul's earliest epistles "than in the whole subsequent seven hundred years of church history."[3]

The apostles and other early Jewish Christians did not just lavish high praises on Jesus. They accorded him honors that in Jewish teaching, as authoritatively set forth in their Scriptures, were due to the Lord God of Israel and no one else. In the first of the Ten Commandments, Israel's God told them, "I am the LORD your God, who brought you out of the land of Egypt, out of the house of slavery; you shall have no other gods before me" (Exod. 20:2–3; Deut. 5:6–7).[4] Through Moses, God told the Israelites, "You shall worship no other god, because the LORD, whose name is Jealous, is a jealous God" (Exod. 34:14). The description of God as "jealous" may sound strange, but it was a forceful way of telling the Israelites that he would not "share" them with any other deity.

It was in this context of exclusive religious devotion to one God, the Lord, that the early Jewish followers of Jesus were expressing the same sort of devotion to Jesus. They worshiped him, sang hymns to him, prayed to him, and revered him in a way that believers in Judaism insisted was reserved for the Lord God alone. To make matters worse, the Christians agreed that such honors were rightly given only to God—and then proceeded to give them to Jesus anyway!

In the first part of this book, we will show that the New Testament teaches us not merely to think about Jesus as God in an abstract, theological way, but to *respond* to him as our God. We are to honor him by submitting to him as our God in worship and spiritual service. We are to honor him by our words, by speaking to him as our God in praise and prayer. Moreover, we are to honor him as God with our whole lives, living for him in faith, reverence, love, and obedience.

An Honor Roll of One

We have already repeatedly used the word *honor* in reference to how the Bible teaches us to respond to Jesus Christ. Honor was an important cultural value in the ancient Mediterranean world, including the Jewish culture. To give people honor was to acknowledge their place in the scheme of things— to speak about them and to behave toward them in a manner appropriate to their status and position. In the monotheistic Jewish culture, to honor God meant to confess and live in the light of his exclusive status as the maker, sustainer, and sovereign King of all creation. To honor any creature, no matter how wonderful, as a deity was to detract from the honor due to God. As Philo of Alexandria, a first-century Jewish philosopher, put it, "They who deify mortal things neglect the honour due to God."[5] New Testament scholar Jerome Neyrey explains, "When someone achieved honor, it was thought to be at the expense of others. Philo, for example, condemns polytheism, because in honoring others as deities, the honor due to the true God is diminished."[6]

It is in this cultural setting that Jesus asserted that it was God the Father's purpose "that all may honor the Son just as they honor the Father." By "the Son," of course, Jesus meant himself. Jesus went on to say that anyone failing to accord him such honor actually dishonors the Father: "Anyone who does not honor the Son does not honor the Father who sent him" (John 5:23). Linking the honor due God with the honor due anyone else in this way was unprecedented in the Jewish Scriptures. That Jesus is here claiming *divine* honor is evident from the immediate context. Jesus has just claimed that he does whatever the Father does (v. 19) and that he "gives life to whomever he wishes" (v. 21). The Father even has entrusted to the Son (v. 22) the responsibility of rendering eternal judgment over all people. According to Jesus, the Father did so precisely so that everyone would honor him, the Son, as they honor the Father (v. 23). In short, we are to honor Jesus as the one who holds our eternal future in his hands—as the one who has the power of life and death. We can assign no higher honor or status to someone than that of our ultimate, final Judge.

Just how much honor should we give to Jesus? There really is no limit. The book of Hebrews[7] asserts that Jesus "is worthy of more glory than Moses, just as the builder of a house has more honor than the house itself" (3:3). Think about what the author is saying. Moses is to Jesus as a house is to the builder of the house! In other words, Moses is part of the creation, the "house," and Jesus is being described as the "builder of the house," or the one responsible for the creation. "For every house is built by someone, but the builder of all things is God" (v. 4). Hebrews is telling us to honor Jesus as we would the "builder" of creation—God.

To Him Be the Glory

Hebrews 3:3 uses another term that expresses a concept closely related to that of honor: "glory." The word *glory* in the Bible (Hebrew, *k-bōd*; Greek, *doxa*) has two related meanings. As an attribute of God, glory refers to God's beautiful, shining nature—the bright, overpowering light in which God appears when he manifests his presence to human beings (e.g., Exod. 33:18–23; Luke 2:9).[8] Glory is also the proper response of praise and adulation to God's dazzling nature (not just the bright light, but all aspects of his nature) and in this sense is a synonym for honor. One of the proper responses to God, then, is to *glorify* him (Ps. 29:1–3; Matt. 5:16; Rom. 15:6–9).

A typical way in which the biblical writers summon God's people to glorify him is in a liturgical form called a *doxology* (from *doxa*, the Greek word for "glory"). Doxologies are stylized prayers of praise to God, acknowledging the glory and honor that God deserves. Sometimes a biblical writer will burst into a spontaneous doxology, but most often one finds them at the beginning or the end of a psalm, or at the end of a sermon or letter. Here are some examples of doxologies directing glory to God:

Blessed are you, O LORD, the God of our ancestor Israel, forever and ever. Yours, O LORD, are the greatness, the power, the glory, the victory, and the majesty; for all that is in the heavens and on the earth is yours; yours is the kingdom, O LORD, and you are exalted as head above all. (1 Chron. 29:10–11)

Blessed be the LORD, the God of Israel,
who alone does wondrous things.
Blessed be his glorious name forever;
may his glory fill the whole earth.
Amen and Amen.

(Ps. 72:18–19)[9]

For from him and through him and to him are all things. To him be the glory forever. Amen. (Rom. 11:36)

. . . according to the will of our God and Father, to whom be the glory forever and ever. Amen. (Gal. 1:4b–5)

Now to our God and Father be the glory forever and ever. Amen. (Phil. 4:20 NASB)

What is surprising is that the New Testament contains doxologies just like these in which the glory goes to Jesus Christ:

Now may the God of peace, who brought back from the dead our Lord Jesus, the great shepherd of the sheep, by the blood of the eternal covenant, make you complete in everything good so that you may do his will, working among us that which is pleasing in his sight, through Jesus Christ, to whom be the glory forever and ever. Amen. (Heb. 13:20–21)

. . . so that in all things God may be glorified through Jesus Christ, to whom belongs the glory and dominion forever and ever. Amen. (1 Peter 4:11b NASB)

These doxologies clearly are not ascribing glory to Jesus Christ *instead of* to God. First Peter 4:11 explicitly states that God is to be glorified *through* Jesus Christ, so that glorifying Christ is done in a way that glorifies God (see also Rom. 16:27; Jude 25). Nevertheless, both of these passages ascribe glory forever to Jesus Christ in language identical to other biblical doxologies assigning eternal glory to God.[10] One later New Testament book even contains a doxology assigning eternal glory to Christ with no direct mention of God or the Father:

But grow in the grace and knowledge of our Lord and Savior Jesus Christ. To him be the glory both now and to the day of eternity. Amen. (2 Peter 3:18)

The book of Revelation also contains doxological songs or hymns in praise of Jesus Christ, there represented by the Lamb, paralleling its own doxological hymns to God. These doxologies show that "the Lamb is appropriately worshipped on equal terms with God."[11]

> Worthy are You, our Lord and our God, to receive glory and honor and power; for You created all things, and because of Your will they existed, and were created. (Rev. 4:11 NASB)

> "Worthy is the Lamb that was slain to receive power and riches and wisdom and might and honor and glory and blessing." . . . "To Him who sits on the throne, and to the Lamb, be blessing and honor and glory and dominion forever and ever." (Rev. 5:12–13 NASB)

Here again, the doxology does not praise Jesus to the exclusion of God, but includes the giving of eternal honor and glory to Jesus Christ within the monotheistic Jewish practice of ascribing such glory to God (note the similarity of these doxologies to the one in 1 Chron. 29:10–11). We should not "underestimate the boldness that was necessary to alter these traditional Jewish forms."[12]

If we go through the entire book of Revelation and examine all of its doxological material, we find an almost complete overlap in the honorific language directed to God and that directed to the Lamb (see table). The overlap is not artificially perfect—"wealth" is directed to the Lamb and not to God, "thanksgiving" to God and not to the Lamb—but these differences seem inconsequential in light of the big picture. Matthias Hoffmann, in his dissertation on the Lamb in the book of Revelation, rightly concludes, "Most of the predicates within the doxologies do not seem to distinguish God and the Lamb from each other, but rather express an equal status of both of them in general."[13]

By constructing such doxologies to God and Christ together, or even to Christ alone, the New Testament writers were exalting Jesus Christ to the very level of God.

DOXOLOGIES TO GOD AND THE LAMB IN REVELATION

	God/One on the Throne	The Lamb	1 Chron. 29:11–12
Worthy (*axios*)	4:11	5:9, 12	
Blessing/Praise (*eulogia*)	5:13; 7:12	5:12, 13	
Honor (*timē*)	4:9, 11; 5:13; 7:12	5:12, 13	
Glory (*doxa*)	4:9, 11; 5:13; 7:12; 19:1b	1:6; 5:12, 13	1 Chron. 29:12
Dominion (*kratos*)	5:13	1:6; 5:13	
Power (*dunamis*)	4:11; 7:12; 19:1b	5:12	1 Chron. 29:11
Might (*ischus*)	7:12	5:12	1 Chron. 29:11–12
Wealth (*ploutos*)		5:12	1 Chron. 29:12
Wisdom (*sophia*)	7:12	5:12	
Thanksgiving (*eucharistia*)	4:9; 7:12		
Salvation (*sōtēria*)	7:10; 19:1b	7:10	

Chapter 2

THE WORSHIP OF
THE CARPENTER

When we think of giving God the honor due him, we naturally think of worship. Does the Bible teach us to worship Jesus Christ? Most definitely. Acknowledging the deity of Christ is not merely a matter of referring to him as "God" but more importantly is a matter of responding to him in worship. As New Testament scholar R. T. France has put it, "The basic fact which lies behind all the theological terms and titles is the worship of the carpenter."[1]

It is important here to distinguish between the word *worship* and the concept that the word (or the equivalent in other languages) may be used to express. In contemporary Christianity, worship often refers to religious music and other elements of church services focused on communing with God (such as corporate prayer, expressions of praise to God, or, in some traditions, the use of liturgy). In the Bible, however, the words usually translated "worship" do not refer to such religious acts. The biblical words (Heb., *shachah*; Greek, *proskuneō*) generally refer to an act of bowing low to the ground or prostrating oneself or, more generally, falling on the ground with or toward someone. The biblical writers express the same idea in other ways, such as stating that a person fell on his face before someone, that he bent or bowed his knee to someone, or that he fell at someone's feet. Such an act, whether bowing low or prostrating oneself, was an expression of respect or reverence toward a superior such as a king. In a religious or spiritual context, however, when performed toward a supernatural being (or an image representing such a being), the act is an acknowledgment of that being's deity. This action is typically, although not always, expressed using the words *shachah* or *proskuneō*.

In short, not all occurrences of the words *shachah* or *proskuneō* refer to the worship of a deity, and there are other ways of describing worship of a deity than using those words. As always, the contexts in which words appear are crucial to understanding their meaning. By *contexts* we mean not only the immediate situation described in a passage but also the larger context of the entire book in which that passage appears.

Disciples Worship Jesus

Consider, for example, the various accounts in the Gospel of Matthew of people "worshiping" or bowing down before Jesus. In some passages the act of bowing down (*proskuneō*) does not, in the immediate context, express any inkling on the part of the one bowing down that Jesus was a divine person. On one occasion, a leper bowed down before Jesus and asked for healing (8:2). On another occasion, a synagogue official bowed before Jesus and asked him to heal his daughter (9:18). When the mother of James and John bowed before Jesus before asking him a favor (20:20), she was certainly not revering him as deity. In these and other situations, human beings bowed before Jesus according to the common custom of showing extreme humility and respect toward someone whose assistance they wanted.

Should we conclude, then, that Matthew's reports of various persons bowing before Jesus imply nothing more than that he was a respected teacher? Actually, no. Such a conclusion misses the "big picture" of the larger context of the Gospel as a whole. A key to understanding Matthew's perspective is his report of the Devil's three temptations of Jesus in the wilderness. In Matthew, the climactic third temptation[2] is the Devil's offer to give Jesus "all the kingdoms of the world and their splendor" if he would "fall down and worship" (*proskunēsēs*) him (4:8–9). Surprisingly, Jesus did not respond by denying that Satan was personally worthy of any show of respect or honor (although that would seem to be true enough). Instead, Jesus responded by quoting the Old Testament: "Worship the Lord your God, and serve only him" (Matt. 4:10, quoting Deut. 6:13).[3] After it is made clear in Matthew that Jesus regarded God as the only proper object of worship (*proskuneō*), it is striking that Jesus appears so frequently in the same Gospel to be the object of worship (2:2, 11; 8:2; 9:18; 14:33; 15:25; 20:20; 28:9, 17)—even if in the immediate situation the act is sometimes only a token of humble respect.[4]

Moreover, on at least two occasions the act of bowing down before Jesus is evidently more than a sign of respect. About halfway through the Gospel, Matthew reports that the disciples were in a boat, fishing on the Sea of Galilee at night, when they saw Jesus walking toward them on the sea. After Jesus assured them that it was he, Peter tried to walk on the sea to Jesus—but frightened by the wind, he started to sink and Jesus had to rescue him. When the two got into the boat, the wind stopped, and the disciples worshiped Jesus and said, "Truly you are the Son of God" (Matt. 14:24–33). Here it is difficult to avoid the conclusion that the disciples were viewing Jesus as more than a man.[5] He has just walked on the sea and calmed the wind and waves, displaying supernatural power and a numinous presence, which elicits from them a confession that he is God's Son. According to Jason BeDuhn in his critique of modern Bible translations, "Most translations add to the text the false idea that the disciples are depicted worshipping Jesus, when in fact, in this particular episode, they merely are reacting to his evident powers with awe."[6] What does BeDuhn think worship means? Falling down before a being with supernatural power and attributing to him a divine status of any kind is by definition an act of worship.

The other telling incident comes at the very end of the Gospel, when the disciples meet Jesus on a mountain in Galilee after his resurrection from the dead. "When they saw him, they worshiped him; but some doubted" (Matt. 28:17).[7] One might suppose that what "some doubted" was that they were really seeing Jesus alive from the dead. Jesus did not respond, however, as he did on other occasions when his resurrection was in doubt, by assuring them of his identity or by pointing to his hands or inviting the doubters to touch him (Luke 24:36–43; John 20:20, 27). Instead, Jesus responded to their doubts by assuring them of his universal authority: "All authority in heaven and on earth has been given to me" (Matt. 28:18). Evidently, Jesus was assuring them that the act of worship was quite appropriate.[8] If you don't worship the one who has authority throughout the entire universe, whom do you worship?

If we compare this passage at the very end of Matthew's Gospel with his report of Satan's third temptation of Jesus, we find further confirmation that what the disciples were doing was, indeed, worship. The Devil had offered to "give" to Jesus "all the kingdoms of the world and their splendor" if Jesus would "worship" him—an offer Jesus refused. After his resurrection, when the disciples "worshiped" him, Jesus stated that "all authority in heaven and on earth" had been "given" to him (by the Father, of course). What Jesus refused to take from the Devil, he received from the Father; and instead of giving worship to the Devil, Jesus received worship from his disciples.

It is worth noting that these two incidents—Jesus' walking on the sea and appearing as the risen Lord on the mountain—are the only two incidents in Matthew in which Jesus' disciples "worshiped" him. In both instances—once before his resurrection and once after it—the disciples were responding to Jesus as to a powerful supernatural being, not as a mere rabbi or prophet. These are also the only two places in Matthew's Gospel where the word "doubted" (*edistasan*) occurs. It is not surprising that on both occasions—when the disciples experienced an encounter with Jesus as a supernatural, divine being and responded with worship—some of those present felt doubt in the midst of their responses of faith in Jesus. Discipleship is a process of learning in which doubts are overcome as we come to know Jesus better. Since Matthew's Gospel ends with Jesus' commanding his disciples to make disciples from all nations (Matt. 28:19–20), we are clearly supposed to view the original disciples' worship of Jesus as a model for us to follow. We also should understand the other occasions in which people bowed before Jesus in this light. It turns out that their bowing before Jesus was more appropriate than they could have known.[9]

Angels Worship Jesus

Not only did human beings worship Jesus when he was here on earth, but all of God's angels are required to worship him. According to the book of Hebrews, "And again, when he brings the firstborn into the world, he says, 'Let all God's angels worship him'" (1:6). This statement is very difficult to explain away as meaning something less than worship given to God.

First, angels, not human beings, offer this worship to Jesus. Given that human beings in the ancient Mediterranean world were accustomed to bowing down before dignitaries and powerful leaders, it is possible to rationalize the practice of bowing before Jesus as reflecting that custom. (We have seen, though, that such explanations do not fit at least some of the historical accounts.) Angels, on the other hand, have no such custom.[10]

Second, God commanded angels to worship Jesus. Hebrews 1:6 is not saying that angels happened to worship Jesus, rightly or wrongly, but that God *told* them to worship Jesus.

Third, the directive for angels to worship Jesus is a quotation from the Old Testament that in its original context refers to the worship of the Lord God himself. We know this to be the case even though there is some slight uncertainty about which of two texts the book of Hebrews is quoting. While some scholars trace the quotation to Psalm 97:7 (96:7 in the Greek Old Testament or "Septuagint," abbreviated LXX),[11] a majority now think the quotation derives from a particular version of Deuteronomy 32:43. Here are the texts:[12]

> Worship him, all his angels. (Ps. 96:7 LXX; 97:7 English Versions)
> *proskunēsate autō pantes hoi angeloi autou*

> And let all God's sons worship him. (Deut. 32:43 LXX)[13]
> *kai proskunēsatōsan autō pantes huioi theou*

> And let all God's angels worship him. (Odes 2:43)
> *kai proskunēsatōsan autō pantes angeloi theou*

> And let all God's angels worship him. (Heb. 1:6b)
> *kai proskunēsatōsan autō pantes angeloi theou*

The form of Deuteronomy 32:43 that is identical to the quotation in Hebrews 1:6 is found in the Odes (numbered there as 2:43), a liturgical collection appended to the Psalms, and also in some later Greek versions of Deuteronomy.[14] The tendency to treat the Song of Moses in Deuteronomy 32 as a psalm may explain why the author of Hebrews would quote from it in a collection of proof texts drawn almost entirely from the Psalms.[15] Moreover, the author clearly quotes from the Song of Moses later in the book (Heb. 10:30, quoting Deut. 32:35–36).

Regardless of whether Psalm 97:7 or Deuteronomy 32:43 (or Odes 2:43) is the text quoted in Hebrews 1:6, the text refers to the worship of the Lord God. In Psalm 97:7–9 the psalmist is shaming those who worship idols and telling the "gods" to worship the Lord who is exalted far above them. The Septuagint substituted "angels" in place of the Hebrew "gods," reflecting the understanding that pagan religions sometimes wrongly deified angelic beings. In Deuteronomy 32:34–43 the Lord is claiming that he alone is God (vv. 37, 39; see also vv. 12, 17, 21) and that he will take vengeance on his enemies and rescue his people. The broader theme of the Song of Moses is a warning to Israel not to abandon the Lord for any other god (see the introduction of the song in Deut. 31:24–30). Since both texts in context are speaking of angels as giving worship to the Lord God, the writer of Hebrews, in applying his quotation to Jesus, is affirming that God commanded his angels to worship Jesus.[16]

Everyone Will Worship Jesus

If angels, who are supernatural beings vastly more powerful than we are, worship Jesus Christ, then certainly we human beings should worship him as well. Indeed, eventually everyone *will* worship him: "At the name of Jesus every knee should bend, in heaven and on earth and under the earth, and every tongue should confess that Jesus Christ is Lord, to the glory of God the Father" (Phil. 2:10–11). As Paul says, giving Jesus this divine honor in no way detracts from the glory of God. Indeed, to withhold such worship, when God has commanded it, is to disrespect God. John R. W. Stott rightly said, "Nobody can call himself a Christian who does not worship Jesus. To worship him, if he is not God, is idolatry; to withhold worship from him, if he is, is apostasy."[17]

In chapter 1 we saw that the book of Revelation contains doxologies exalting "the Lamb" (Jesus Christ) alongside "Him who sits on the throne" (God, the Father).

> "Worthy is the Lamb that was slain to receive power and riches and wisdom and might and honor and glory and blessing. . . . To Him who sits on the throne, and to the Lamb, be blessing and honor and glory and dominion forever and ever." (Rev. 5:12–13 NASB)

Revelation 5 concludes with the following statement:

> And the four living creatures kept saying, "Amen." And the elders fell down and worshiped. (Rev. 5:14 NASB)

The elders directed their worship, naturally, toward the object of their doxology, which in this passage is God the Father and Jesus Christ. The action of the elders in worshiping God and Christ is representative of all of those assembled and participating in the doxology—which was "every created thing which is in heaven and on the earth and under the earth and on the sea, and all things in them" (v. 13 NASB). The passage thus envisions heavenly and earthly creatures, by the myriads (v. 11), bowing down before God and Christ. The Lamb receives worship along with God, shares his throne, and is sharply distinguished from all of God's creatures as the only one worthy of such adoration. The idea is not that Jesus is a second object of worship. Rather, as Peter Carrell notes in his dissertation on Jesus and angels in the book of Revelation, "Jesus is bound with God in such a manner that together they form a single object of worship. . . . No encouragement is given to those inclined to believe Jesus to be a second god. Rather, there is a strict adherence to monotheism—but a monotheism which allows for Jesus to be included with God as the object of worship and which envisages Jesus sharing the divine throne with God."[18]

Twice toward the end of the book of Revelation, John fell at the feet of the angel who was speaking to him so as to worship him. The angel responded by reproving John: "Do not do that; I am a fellow servant . . . worship God" (Rev. 19:10 NASB; cf. 22:8–9). These statements by the angel refute the claim that it was acceptable to worship or bow before an angel who was acting as a representative of God.

The idea that even powerful, supernatural beings such as angels were not appropriate objects of worship would have struck almost everyone in the ancient world as peculiar—*except Jews*. The prevailing view in Judaism across the various parties or schools of thought (Pharisee, Sadducee, Qumran, etc.) was that the Lord God was the only supernatural power whom humans ought to worship. There does not seem to have been any segment of first-century Judaism engaged in corporate or regular worship of angels. Paul's reference to the "worship of angels" (Col. 2:18) probably is a reference to the claim some religious enthusiasts were making that they were participating with the angels in their worship of God (i.e., worship done *by* angels, not worship done *to* angels).[19] At most, one may say that in some segments of Judaism angels were objects of fascination and speculative interest. Loren Stuckenbruck in his published dissertation has documented from Jewish and Jewish-Christian sources examples of angels being asked to help or intervene, regarded as exemplary or model worshipers of God, and even thanked for the things they do.[20] Yet even these religious acts with respect to angels (for which we have no *biblical* examples) fall far short of actually worshiping angels. The Alexandrian Jewish philosopher Philo, whose views were not always so traditional or conservative, was quite typical in opposing the practice of worshiping angels.

So just as anyone who rendered to the subordinate satraps the hon-
ours due to the Great King would have seemed to reach the height
not only of unwisdom but of foolhardiness, by bestowing on servants what belonged to their master, in the same way anyone who
pays the same tribute to the creatures as to their Master may be assured that he is the most senseless and unjust of men in that he gives
equal measure to those who are not equal. . . . Let us then reject all
such imposture and refrain from worshipping [*proskunōthen*] those
who by nature are our brothers, even though they have been given a
substance purer and more immortal than ours.[21]

WORSHIP OF JESUS VS. WORSHIP OF AN ANGEL IN REVELATION

Worship Received: Christ in Revelation 1:12–20	Worship Rejected: The Angel in Revelation 19–22
Described in detail in glorious imagery (1:13–16).	No description of the angel is given at all—but after the first time the angel refuses worship a similar description is given of Christ (19:12–16).
John fell at Jesus' feet as a dead man (1:17a).	John fell at the angel's feet to worship him (19:10a; 22:8).
Jesus said, "Don't be afraid" (1:17b).	The angel said, "Don't do that" (19:10b; 22:9a).
Jesus claimed to be "the first and the last" and to "have the keys of death and Hades" (1:17–18).	The angel said that he was merely a fellow servant of John and his brethren (19:10b; 22:9b).
Jesus does nothing to redirect worship away from himself.	The angel tells John to worship God (19:10c; 22:9c).

The repudiation of giving angels worship in Revelation, then, reflects the
broader first-century Jewish cultural norm. "The reprimand, put into the
mouth of the angel himself, serves to define the devotion to the one God of
Israel more precisely: even allied beings who serve God's purposes must not
be worshiped."[22] By rejecting the practice of worshiping angels, the book of
Revelation makes it even clearer that the practice of worshiping Jesus puts

him on a par with God. The book presents, in fact, a striking contrast between John's act of worshiping Christ at the beginning of the book and his attempt to worship the angel toward the end of the book. Whereas the angel rejected John's worship and professed merely to be a fellow servant of God, Jesus accepted John's worship and claimed to have divine power over life and death.

The message of the New Testament seems quite clear: offering worship to Jesus, of the sort reserved for the Lord God alone, is perfectly appropriate. Jesus' disciples worshiped him, the angels worship him (while refusing such worship when offered to them), and eventually everyone will worship him.

Chapter 3

WHAT A FRIEND WE HAVE IN JESUS

There are many ways of defining the terms *deity, god,* or *God.* One basic functional definition is that a deity is *an object of prayer.* Any being (real or imagined) perceived to have a supernatural or spiritual nature and to whom devotion is expressed and requests are made is in practical terms one's deity.

The Old Testament everywhere assumes that the Lord God is the only proper object of prayer. He is the one who answers prayer (Ps. 65:2). Isaiah makes fun of the idolater who makes a god for himself out of a piece of wood and then "prays to it and says, 'Save me, for you are my god!'" (Isa. 44:17). They are foolish because, of course, they are "praying to a god that cannot save" (Isa. 45:20). There is a close, natural link in biblical thought between prayer and salvation. Prayer is essentially an appeal to one's deity for rescue, deliverance, or salvation in some situation of need or danger. Only the transcendent, omniscient, omnipotent God can hear the prayers of all people and respond to them as he chooses. God may choose to answer prayers through creatures acting as his agents, but that is for him to decide. *God* is the Savior; *God* is the one who answers prayer. He is therefore the only one to whom we should turn in prayer.

> Turn to me and be saved,
>   all the ends of the earth!
> For I am God, and there is no other.
>   (Isa. 45:22)

Despite the fact that the Bible recognizes angels as real and powerful supernatural beings, it never reports or in any way encourages prayer to angels. One does not ask angels for help; rather, one asks God for help, and if he chooses to do so through angels, that is up to him. They are "sent out" by God "to render service for the sake of those who will inherit salvation" (Heb. 1:14 NASB).

The First Recorded Prayer to Jesus

With regard to prayer, then, the Bible is thoroughly monotheistic: it is the Lord, the God of Israel, to whom human beings must pray. Yet the New Testament frequently presents Jesus, within that monotheistic context, as appropriately addressed in prayer. According to the book of Acts, believers in Jesus were, indeed, addressing prayers to him from the very beginning of the Christian movement, just days after his ascension. Luke reports that before choosing a new apostle to replace Judas Iscariot, the disciples in the Upper Room, "prayed" as follows:

> Lord, you know everyone's heart. Show us which one of these two you have chosen to take the place in this ministry and apostleship from which Judas turned aside to go to his own place. (Acts 1:24–25)

Luke's word "prayed" is a form of the verb *proseuchomai*, which was "a religious technical term for talking to a deity in order to ask for help."[1] We can be reasonably sure that the "Lord" to whom the disciples prayed was the Lord Jesus, for three reasons (which are to be considered cumulatively). First, like the other New Testament writers, Luke most frequently used "Lord" (*kurios*) to refer to Jesus.[2] Second, Peter had just referred to "the Lord Jesus" (Acts 1:21) prior to the group's addressing the "Lord" in prayer. Third, Jesus personally chose the men who served as his apostles, including Paul and any others chosen after Jesus' resurrection. The verb Luke uses in Acts 1:24 for "have chosen" (*exelexō*) is the same verb that appears in another form earlier in the chapter in reference to Jesus having "chosen" his apostles (*exelexato*, 1:2).[3] In his Gospel, Luke uses another form of the same verb in reference to Jesus' choosing the twelve apostles (*eklexamenos*, Luke 6:13) and uses the related noun form in reference to the Lord Jesus' "choice" of Paul as an apostle (*eklogēs*, Acts 9:15). Thus, when the disciples prayed that the "Lord" would show them whom he had "chosen" to be an apostle, we should understand this Lord to be Jesus himself.[4]

Who Ya Gonna Call?

As Stephen, the first Christian martyr, was being stoned to death, he prayed to Jesus.

> He prayed, "Lord Jesus, receive my spirit." Then he knelt down and cried out in a loud voice, "Lord, do not hold this sin against them." When he had said this, he died. (Acts 7:59–60)

The word translated "prayed" in the NRSV (likewise the NIV) is a form of *epikaleō*, which literally means to "call on" someone. When used in religious contexts of appealing to a heavenly or supernatural being for help, *epikaleō* is another technical term for prayer.[5] Thus, it is undeniable that in this context Stephen was praying to Jesus. The significance of this act of invoking Jesus is only heightened by the occasion: the heavenly being on whom one calls at the moment of death for spiritual repose is quite simply one's God. Stephen entrusted the "Lord Jesus" with his spirit. The same writer, Luke, is the only Gospel writer to report that Jesus had entrusted his spirit to the Father at the moment of his death (Luke 23:46; cf. Ps. 31:5). Clearly, Luke understands Jesus to be performing a function of deity by receiving Stephen's spirit—and in this context Stephen's calling on Jesus is as significant an act of prayer as one could imagine. As the late Yale theologian and historian Jaroslav Pelikan pointed out, "For Stephen to commit his spirit to the Lord Jesus when the Lord Jesus himself had committed his spirit to the Father was either an act of blatant idolatry or the acknowledgment of the *kurios 'Iēsous* [Lord Jesus] as the fitting recipient of the dying prayer of Stephen."[6]

The apostle Paul, as a young man named Saul, had stood by and watched in support as Stephen was stoned to death (Acts 7:58; 8:1). He had heard Stephen "call on" the Lord Jesus to receive his spirit. Saul evidently was incensed by Stephen's devotion to Jesus and by what Saul considered Stephen's disrespect for the traditions of the Jews, and he got himself a commission to go to Damascus to arrest Christians there and take them to Jerusalem. On his way there, the Lord Jesus revealed himself to Saul (Acts 9:1–9). Then the Lord spoke to a Christian named Ananias in a vision and told him to go and meet Saul. Ananias's response is highly informative: "He has come here with authority from the chief priests to arrest all who call on your name" (Acts 9:14 NIV). Stephen's act of "calling on" Jesus, then, was not an isolated occurrence. It was, rather, the practice of all believers in Jesus (see also v. 21) and appears to have been a focal point for Saul's hostility toward Christians. Years later, Paul described his conversion and act of commitment to Jesus Christ in baptism as involving "calling on" the name of Jesus.

> A certain Ananias . . . said, "The God of our ancestors has chosen you to know his will, to see the Righteous One and to hear his own voice; for you will be his witness to all the world of what you have seen and heard. And now why do you delay? Get up, be baptized, and have your sins washed away, calling on his name." (Acts 22:12, 14–16)

In his epistles, the apostle Paul also describes Christians as "those who in every place call on the name of our Lord Jesus Christ, both their Lord and ours" (1 Cor. 1:2). This statement, written about A.D. 54 (just over twenty years after Jesus' death), in effect defines believers in Christ (what we would call Christians) as those who pray to him as Lord (see also Rom. 10:12–14). As R. T. France has pointed out, the description of Christians as those who call on the name of the Lord Jesus shows that they thought of him not only as the proper recipient of prayer but also as God himself.

> Not only does the phrase in itself indicate that prayer to Jesus was a normal and distinguishing characteristic of Christians in the 50s, but "to call on the name of the Lord" is a regular Old Testament formula for worship and prayer offered to God (Gn. 4:26; 13:4; Ps. 105:1; Je. 10:25; Joel 2:32; etc.).[7]

Take It to the Lord in Prayer

The apostles' prayers to Jesus were not limited to special occasions like baptism or the moment of death (although those are highly significant). They felt free to pray to Jesus about anything. Paul tells us about an occasion in which he prayed to Jesus to deliver him from a physical infirmity:

> Three times I appealed to the Lord about this, that it would leave me, but he said to me, "My grace is sufficient for you, for power is made perfect in weakness." So, I will boast all the more gladly of my weaknesses, so that the power of Christ may dwell in me. (2 Cor. 12:8–9)

That "the Lord" here is Jesus is, as commentator Murray Harris points out, "scarcely open to question."[8] In response to Paul's prayer, the Lord assures him that, by *his* (the Lord's) grace, Paul's weakness will provide an opportunity for a greater power to be realized. This promise clearly assumes that the power comes from the Lord. Paul then expresses gladness in his weaknesses because through them "the power *of Christ*" is manifested in his life. The power of the Lord is thus the power of Christ—and since Paul routinely uses both titles for Jesus, he is quite clearly doing so here as well. Elsewhere, Paul speaks of Christ's "grace" as providing riches in place of poverty (2 Cor. 8:9), a contrast that parallels the power/weakness contrast (see 2 Cor. 13:4) and confirms that this understanding of the passage is correct. As Larry Hurtado points out, "Paul's easy recounting of his prayer actions here suggests that he knew that his readers would be familiar with direct prayer-appeals to Jesus as a communally accepted feature of Christian devotional practice."[9]

According to the Gospel of John, Jesus himself encouraged his earliest followers to pray to him: "Whatever you ask me in my name, I will do" (John 14:14, authors' translation). It sounds strange to some readers to speak of praying to Jesus in his own name, but the Greek Old Testament also occasionally speaks this way (e.g., 1 Chron. 16:8, "call on him in his name"; Ps. 54:1, "save me in your name," translating literally).[10] Christian readers are more familiar with the practice of addressing prayer to the Father in the name of Jesus, a practice mentioned elsewhere in the same section of the Gospel (John 15:16; 16:23–24).

It turns out that some Greek manuscripts of the Gospel of John omit the word "me" (which happens to be spelled the same way in Greek, *me*) in John 14:14. The best explanation for this omission is that some copyists indeed thought it odd that Jesus should speak about addressing prayer to him in his own name, so they omitted *me*. When modern commentators agree with the variants that omit the word, this is usually the reason given.[11] There is not much question that the original wording of the passage included the word *me*, because the manuscripts supporting that wording are generally older, are from a broader range of manuscripts, and are from more diverse geographical origins than those manuscripts that omit the word.[12]

Even if the word "me" were not in the text, John 14:14 would still be speaking about praying to Jesus. Suppose Jesus said, "Whatever you ask in my name I will do." The natural inference is that the person who does *what* we ask is the person *whom* we ask. Again, the qualifying phrase "in my name" has Old Testament precedent. To ask (or do anything) in someone's name means to do it on his authority, with his backing, in fidelity to that person. Thus, Jesus is saying that whatever we ask, if we ask out of faithfulness and loyalty to him, he will do it. In context, Jesus is telling his disciples that they may do this after he has gone to be with the Father in heaven (v. 12). Properly understood, then, with or without "me," Jesus in John 14:14 is inviting us to pray to him. That we may address our prayers to either the Father or the Son is quite consistent with the immediate context. After all, Jesus has just said, "Whoever has seen me has seen the Father. . . . Believe me that I am in the Father and the Father is in me" (John 14:9, 11).[13]

Maranatha!

We will mention just one more New Testament example of prayer addressed to Jesus. Two of the books of the New Testament close with a prayer to Jesus as Lord, asking him to come back soon. This is easily seen in the book of Revelation, which closes as follows:

> The one who testifies to these things says, "Surely I am coming soon." Amen. Come, Lord Jesus! The grace of the Lord Jesus be with all the saints. Amen. (22:20–21)

This appeal to the Lord Jesus to come really expresses the hope of the entire book, which is that Jesus will return in glory to bring judgment on the wicked—especially those who persecute the saints—as well as bring complete salvation for the redeemed. That John addresses the petition to the Lord Jesus shows just how "Christ-centered" the Christian hope really is.

The same prayer was a regular part of Christian public devotion to Jesus in the early Jewish church. Paul's first epistle to the Corinthians closes as follows:

> If anyone does not love the Lord, let him be *anathema*. *Maranatha!* The grace of the Lord Jesus be with you. My love to all of you in Christ Jesus. (16:22–24, authors' translation)

In these closing comments, Paul uses two Aramaic expressions. The first, *anathema*, means "accursed." The second, *maranatha*, which is really two words, means, "Our Lord, come!" (or possibly "O Lord, come!"). Some older studies suggested that *maranatha* should be translated "Our Lord comes" or the like (construing the expression as *maran atha* instead of *marana tha*), thus avoiding the implication that the early church prayed to the Lord Jesus.[14] Joseph A. Fitzmyer has shown, however, from a comparison with some of the Dead Sea Scrolls (from Cave 4 at Qumran) that *maranatha* means, "Our Lord, come."[15]

That Paul uses this Aramaic expression in a letter to the Corinthian Christians (most of whom were Gentile converts and did not speak Aramaic) shows that *maranatha* was already widely established in Christian use in the mid-fifties, when Paul wrote the epistle. We see here evidence that the early church viewed Jesus as far more than a great teacher or prophet. As New Testament scholar Ben Witherington III dryly observes, "One does not pray to a deceased rabbi or revered master teacher to come."[16] R. T. France helpfully compares the Corinthian church's familiarity with *maranatha* to our easy use of such Hebrew prayers as *hosanna* and *hallelujah*.[17] Thus, we are looking at an expression that the early, Aramaic-speaking church was using as a prayer to Jesus—probably in some sort of corporate Christian worship setting.[18] The epistle of 1 Corinthians, therefore, begins (1:2) and ends (16:22) with indications that the early church prayed to Jesus.

The church continued to use *maranatha* in its public worship, as can be seen from the late first-century Christian writing known as the Didache (Greek for "Teaching"): "If any one is holy let him come; if any one is not, let him repent. *Maranatha*. Amen" (Didache 10:6). The invitation to "come" echoes the invitation to salvation at the end of the book of Revelation:

> The Spirit and the bride say, "Come."
> And let everyone who hears say, "Come."
> And let everyone who is thirsty come.
> Let anyone who wishes take the water of life as a gift.
> (22:17)

Shortly after this invitation, John asks Jesus to "come," bringing the full realization of that salvation: "Come, Lord Jesus!" (v. 20). These close parallels between Revelation and the Didache[19] confirm that *maranatha* is a prayer to Jesus asking him to come soon.

Chapter 4

SING TO THE LORD

O ne of the most interesting aspects of the early church's devotion to Jesus Christ was their practice of singing hymns about him. Although the New Testament does not include a collection of the church's early hymns, we have three lines of evidence from the New Testament for this practice.

When the Song Comes from the Heart

First, at least one passage explicitly directs Christians to sing hymns to Jesus Christ:

> Do not get drunk with wine, for that is debauchery; but be filled with the Spirit, as you sing psalms and hymns and spiritual songs among yourselves, *singing and making melody to the Lord in your hearts*, giving thanks to God the Father at all times and for everything in the name of our Lord Jesus Christ. (Eph. 5:18–20, emphasis added)

Paul not only tells Christians to sing songs to the Lord Jesus, but he also urges them to sing to the Lord in their "hearts." In other words, song and music in honor of Jesus are to be such a part of our lives that we find ourselves humming such hymns to ourselves or hearing them in our minds as we go about our daily routines.

For Jews steeped in the faith of the Old Testament, to "sing to the Lord" meant to sing to Yahweh, the Lord God (Exod. 15:21; Judg. 5:3; 1 Chron. 16:23; Pss. 7:17; 9:11; 92:1; 95:1; 96:2; 104:33; Isa. 42:10). Yet, in context, Paul is speaking of singing to the Lord Jesus. Verse 20 refers to him as "our Lord

Jesus Christ," and the whole passage follows a Trinitarian pattern: "be filled with the Spirit . . . singing and making melody to the Lord in your hearts . . . giving thanks to God the Father" (vv. 18–20).[1] Paul again calls Jesus "the Lord" in verse 22. So Ephesians 5 testifies to the fact that, less than thirty years after Jesus' death and resurrection,[2] singing to Christ—as "the Lord"—was an expected, uncontroversial part of the Christian life.

In the parallel passage in Colossians, probably written a year or two earlier than Ephesians, Paul urges the Colossian believers "with gratitude in your hearts sing psalms, hymns, and spiritual songs to God" (3:16). Evidently for Paul there is no real difference between singing to Jesus and singing to God. Both are acts of spiritual devotion.

Paul's statement in Ephesians 5:19 calls into question the frequent assertion that early devotion to Christ consisted "more of hymns *about* Christ than hymns *to* Christ."[3] Both were part of first-century Christian devotion to Jesus. Furthermore, we shall see that hymns *about* Christ are quite potent evidence of devotion to Jesus as God.

It's Time for Choir Practice

The second piece of evidence from the New Testament for the practice of singing to the Lord Jesus comes from the book of Revelation. Its visions include a scene in which various creatures (representing both angels and redeemed human beings) sing a song to Jesus in heaven.

> They sing a new song: "You are worthy to take the scroll and to open its seals, for you were slaughtered and by your blood you ransomed for God saints from every tribe and language and people and nation; you have made them to be a kingdom and priests serving our God, and they will reign on earth." (5:9–10)

G. K. Beale in his impressive commentary on Revelation notes, "In the OT a 'new song' is always an expression of praise for God's victory over the enemy, sometimes including thanksgiving for God's work of creation."[4] Here, the victory is ascribed to the Lamb, a symbolic representation of Jesus Christ, without in any way treating Jesus as a second or independent deity. Picturing angels and saints in heaven singing a new song in praise to Jesus implies, of course, that we should be singing praises to Jesus now.[5]

The Earliest Christian Hymns

The third line of evidence we have from the New Testament for the practice of honoring Jesus Christ in song is the presence of apparent remnants of songs in the epistles. Modern biblical scholars have given intense study to the possibility that various passages in the New Testament incorporate elements of the early church's songs, hymns, or psalms about Christ. We should be cautious about trying too hard to find such elements. As Martin Hengel points out, "all of the so-called 'hymns' and 'fragments of hymns,' which have been 'discovered,' are strictly speaking hypothetical," since the number and boundaries of these hymnic remnants are widely disputed and since none of them survived in the early church's liturgy.[6] Nevertheless, this sort of evidence is important because it comes from several books of the New Testament and appears to reflect Christian practice even before the writing of Paul's epistles.

Perhaps the clearest example of a "psalm" or "hymn" to Christ is Philippians 2:6–11. Although there are some dissenters, Pauline scholars in general agree that Paul is quoting a Christian hymn—perhaps even one that he himself wrote. The most convincing analysis of the passage's hymnic structure is that proposed by Ernst Lohmeyer. He showed that the passage forms two groups (which scholars sometimes call *strophes*) of three stanzas, with each stanza containing three lines. The only line that does not "fit" into this arrangement is the line "death on a cross," which comes at the juncture of the two strophes (and thus receives special emphasis).[7] We may set out the hymn in verse form as follows (authors' translation):

> Who existing in God's form,
> > did not think it something to exploit
> > > to be equal to God,
> But emptied himself,
> > having taken a servant's form
> > > and having become in the likeness of men.
> And being found in appearance as a man
> > he humbled himself,
> > > having become obedient to the point of death—
> > > *death on a cross.*

And therefore God highly exalted him
   and bestowed on him
      the name, the one above every name,
So that in the name of Jesus
   every knee should bow
      in heaven and in earth and the underworld
And every tongue should confess
   that Jesus Christ is Lord
      to the glory of God the Father.

Once one recognizes the poetic, hymnic structure of the passage, it is difficult to resist the conclusion that Paul is quoting an early Christian hymn. Its content is striking in that it is all about Christ—and yet in a way that preserves the Jewish monotheistic insistence on the exclusive glory due to God alone. The only action that the passage attributes to God (as distinct from Christ) is God's act of *exalting* Christ. Yet the hymn concludes that the universal acclaim that Jesus is to receive will redound "to the glory of God the Father."

The evidence for early Christian hymns to Christ extends beyond the pages of the New Testament—and not just from other early Christian writers, but from non-Christian observers as well. Around A.D. 111–115, Pliny described Christians as gathering "on a certain day before sunrise" in order to sing "hymns to Christ as to God" (Latin, *carmenque christo quasi deo*; Pliny, *Epistles* 10.96.7).[8] Evidently Pliny is referring here to the church's practice of meeting weekly early Sunday mornings, which from an early period they were doing to commemorate Jesus' resurrection from the dead.[9] Thus the very time of the church's meetings, as well as the content of their songs, focused on Christ. As Larry Hurtado points out, the political context of Pliny's remarks sheds further light on their significance for our understanding of the early church's devotion to Jesus in song:

A sophisticated Roman such as Pliny was quite ready to accept religious diversity, and was well aware that a variety of gods and heroes were reverenced in various religious circles. Nor did recognizing another new deity present a difficulty. What caused Pliny's concern about the Christians in Bithynia was that their reverence of Jesus as divine was accompanied by *a refusal to reverence images of 'the gods' and the emperor.* This religious exclusivity created a major (indeed, sometimes a mortal) social and political problem for Christians, and it made their worship of Jesus pointedly offensive to pagan outsiders. . . . But this exclusivity of devotion also signals the religious significance that worshiping Jesus had for Christians. They gave the sort of reverence to Jesus that they otherwise reserved for 'God the Father' alone, regarding it as apostasy to give such reverence to any of the other deities touted in their culture.[10]

Pliny's statement is supported by a comment made by an unknown Christian writer around A.D. 200 and quoted in the fourth-century church history written by Eusebius: "How many psalms and how many songs, which from the beginning were written by pious brothers, *sing about Christ as the Logos of God and confess his godhood.*"[11] The word translated "confess his godhood" (*theologountes*, literally, "saying God") also could be translated "confessing that he is God" or, more idiomatically in English, "confessing his deity." Notice that the statement refers to such songs as having been written "from the beginning," meaning from the beginning of the church.

The First Christian Hymnbook

We may usefully contrast the early Christian practice of composing and singing hymns about Christ to the lack of any such hymnody in the Old Testament with regard to its greatest human figures. Moses led the Israelites out of Egypt and mediated God's law covenant with them. Yet, other than the title attributing Psalm 90 to Moses, there are only seven scant references to Moses in all of the Psalms, and none of the Psalms could possibly be described as written in praise or celebration or honor of Moses (Pss. 77:20; 99:6; 103:7; 105:26; 106:16, 23, 32). Or consider Abraham, the father of the Jewish people. The Psalms mention Abraham only four times, never in a context of giving any honor to him at all (Pss. 47:9; 105:6, 9, 42). What about David, Israel's greatest king? He is, of course, mentioned in the titles of about eighty-five psalms as their author, but within the Psalms themselves he is mentioned only eleven times (Pss. 18:50; 78:70; 89:3, 20, 35, 49; 122:5; 132:10, 11, 17; 144:10). These references speak of God's choice of David, God's covenant with David, and of God's mercy and faithfulness toward David, but they say absolutely nothing about any of David's accomplishments. And Solomon, Israel's wisest man, is mentioned only as the author of two of the Psalms (72 and 127).

One could say, of course, that, indirectly, many of the psalms are about David, since so many of them are by David and in them he talks about himself. In this regard, we should notice the way in which the early church viewed the Psalter. In his work *On the Flesh of Christ,* the church father Tertullian had this to say about the psalms of David: "He sings to us about Christ, and through him Christ sings about himself."[12] Tertullian's statement is firmly rooted in what the risen Jesus himself said (Luke 24:44). Hengel points out that the most important titles given to Jesus in the New Testament "were already given or prefigured in the hymnbook of Israel."[13] He cites "Son (of God)" (Ps. 2:7), "firstborn" (Ps. 89:27), "Lord" (Ps. 110:1), and even "God" (Ps. 45:6), to which we may add "Messiah" or "Christ" (Ps. 2:2) and "Son of Man" (Ps. 8:4), although the primary Old Testament source for the Son of Man is Daniel 7:13–14.

In short, the New Testament does not contain a songbook, but that is because from a Christian perspective *they already had one*: the book of Psalms. For the early Christians, the Psalms were about their Lord and Savior Jesus Christ. Any songs or hymns or psalms that the early Christians might have composed about Christ or to Christ merely supplemented the inspired hymnbook of Israel, now appropriated by the church as its own collection of hymns about Christ. Then, as now, Jesus Christ was the center of the religious music of the church—yet in a way that never detracted from the glory of God or compromised biblical monotheism.

·····

Chapter 5

THE ULTIMATE
REVERENCE PACKAGE

Jesus once said that everyone should "honor the Son just as they honor the Father" (John 5:23). As we saw in chapter 1, Jesus here was making what would have to be regarded as an outrageous claim for any mere human being—or even for an angel. Jesus was claiming the honor due to the one who holds the power of life and death over all humanity.

If Jesus was claiming the honor due God, we would expect to find the Bible explicitly according him most, if not all, of the forms of honor that it accords to God. We already have seen that the Bible teaches us to honor Jesus by glorifying him, by worshiping him, by praying to him, and even by singing hymns to and about him. In this concluding chapter on the honors due to Jesus, we will see that in virtually every other way that the Bible teaches us to honor God it also teaches us to honor the Lord Jesus.

The Focus of Our Faith

In the Old Testament, the Lord God is the primary object of faith. The first mention of faith or belief in the Bible is a model example: Abraham "believed the LORD" (Gen. 15:6). The Hebrew word *ʾāman* here means to believe or trust in someone; it expresses an act of putting one's confidence in someone. Abraham chose to depend on the Lord to fulfill his promise, to do what he said he would do. Other persons are to be trusted or believed inasmuch as they are God's faithful servants. When Israel saw the Egyptian army destroyed in the Red Sea, "the people feared the LORD and believed in the LORD

·····

and in his servant Moses" (Exod. 14:31). The Israelites were to believe Moses because God spoke and acted through him. The Old Testament never speaks of Moses as a proper object of belief or faith except as God's imperfect but commissioned servant. When Moses failed to be faithful to God, the people, of course, were not supposed to follow him (Num. 20:8–13; 27:12–14). Thus, God was their primary object of faith, the one in whom they were to place absolute trust. Through Isaiah, the Lord told Israel that he had chosen them "so that you may know and believe me and understand that I am he" (Isa. 43:10).

In the New Testament, God is still the primary object of faith. Jesus himself told his disciples, "Have faith in God" (Mark 11:22). One of the fundamentals of the Christian religion is "faith toward God" (Heb. 6:1). A person of faith "must believe that [God] exists and that he rewards those who seek him" (Heb. 11:6).

Yet throughout the New Testament, Jesus is repeatedly presented as the object of faith in a way that treats him as far more than a spokesman for God, like Moses was. When blind men came to Jesus, he asked them, "Do you believe that I am able to do this?" (Matt. 9:28). What we would have expected a mere servant of God to have asked was whether the person believed that *God* was able to do it. Instead, Jesus unabashedly summons people to put their faith in him.

Faith in Jesus Christ is a major theme of the Gospel of John. The Gospel was written "so that you may believe that Jesus is the Christ, the Son of God; and that believing you may have life in His name" (John 20:31 NASB). Those "who believed in his name"—in the name of Jesus—became God's children (John 1:12; see also 1 John 3:23; 5:1, 10, 13). God sent Jesus to die so that whoever "believes in him may have eternal life" (John 3:15; see also 3:16, 36; 6:40). "Those who believe in him are not condemned; but those who do not believe are condemned already, because they have not believed in the name of the only Son of God" (John 3:18). These statements go beyond anything ever said about Moses or anyone else in the Bible. John teaches his readers to believe *in the name* of Jesus Christ, the Son of God. What this means is that faith in Christ is a confidence placed directly in him *because of his own identity*, not because of a merely functional role that he filled.

On the basis of his divine identity, Jesus made promises to his followers and expected them to place their faith unconditionally in him. While Martha's brother Lazarus lay dead, Jesus assured her, "I am the resurrection and the life. Those who believe in me, even though they die, will live, and everyone who lives and believes in me will never die" (John 11:25–26). To those who were spiritually thirsty, Jesus promised, "Whoever believes in me will never be thirsty" (John 6:35; see also 7:37–39). To those who rejected him, Jesus warned, "You will die in your sins unless you believe that I am he" (John 8:24). Moses never spoke like this!

Again, belief in Jesus is not *in place of* belief in God. The person who accepts his teachings, Jesus said, "believes him who sent me" (John 5:24). This is what Jesus meant when he said, "Whoever believes in me believes not in me but in him who sent me" (John 12:44). Jesus made it clear that he was not inviting faith in him apart from, or in place of, faith in God. On the other hand, he made the claim—audacious for any creature to make—that he was just as trustworthy an object of faith as God himself: "Do not let your hearts be troubled. Believe in God, believe also in me" (John 14:1). Jesus' call here for the disciples to believe in him as they believed in God "links Jesus with the Father as the supreme object of faith."[1]

The apostles taught and exemplified this faith in Jesus after his resurrection and ascension. After the lame man at the temple gate had been healed through Peter and John, Peter explicitly denied that the man had been healed by their "own power or piety" (Acts 3:12). Rather, "by faith in his name, his name itself has made this man strong" (v. 16). Peter later told Cornelius and his family, "All the prophets testify about him that everyone who believes in him receives forgiveness of sins through his name" (Acts 10:43). Paul, who had once "imprisoned and beat those who believed in" Jesus (Acts 22:19), after becoming Jesus' apostle preached the same message of salvation: "Believe on the Lord Jesus, and you will be saved, you and your household" (Acts 16:31; see also 20:21; 24:24; 26:18). In his epistle to the Romans, Paul acknowledged that Jesus was a stumbling block or offense to many of his fellow Jews, but he confidently applied the words of Isaiah 28:16 to Jesus: "No one who believes in him will be put to shame" (Rom. 10:11; cf. 9:33; similarly 1 Peter 2:6). Just as the apostle John would teach in his writings, Paul taught that Christians "are all sons of God through faith in Christ Jesus" (Gal. 3:26 NASB).[2]

The Fear Factor

It is basic to biblical religion that there is only one deity whom human beings should fear or reverence. "You shall fear the LORD your God" (Deut.

10:20; cf. 6:13). The fear of the Lord is a major theme of the book of Proverbs: "The fear of the LORD is the beginning of wisdom" (Prov. 9:10; see also 1:7; 2:5; etc.). The prophets sounded the same theme: "Do not call conspiracy all that this people calls conspiracy, and do not fear what it fears, or be in dread. But the LORD of hosts, him you shall regard as holy; let him be your fear, and let him be your dread" (Isa. 8:12–13).

In the New Testament, the apostles enjoin followers of Jesus to fear him as their divine "Lord," in language that clearly treats him as God. Consider the following passage from one of Paul's epistles:

> For all of us must appear before the judgment seat of Christ, so that each may receive recompense for what has been done in the body, whether good or evil. Therefore, knowing the fear of the Lord, we try to persuade others; but we ourselves are well known to God, and I hope that we are also well known to your consciences. (2 Cor. 5:10–11)

The plain meaning of these statements is that we fear the Lord because we must appear before him (Christ, who is the Lord) on the Day of Judgment. In other words, "the Lord" in verse 11 is clearly the same as "Christ" in verse 10.

If that were not plain enough, elsewhere Paul tells Christians to "be subject to one another in the fear of Christ" (Eph. 5:21 NASB). Even slaves are to render service as if they were serving the Lord, not people, remembering "that the Lord will reward each one of us for the good we do" (Eph. 6:7–8 NLT). The motivation for fearing Christ here is the same as in 2 Corinthians 5: we will be facing him on Judgment Day. Paul makes the same point in similar language in Colossians:

> Slaves, in all things obey those who are your masters on earth, not with external service, as those who *merely* please men, but with sincerity of heart, fearing the Lord. Whatever you do, do your work heartily, as for the Lord rather than for men, knowing that from the Lord you will receive the reward of the inheritance. It is the Lord Christ whom you serve. For he who does wrong will receive the consequences of the wrong which he has done, and that without partiality. (3:22–25 NASB, emphasis added)

If it is not immediately clear in verse 22 that "the Lord" is Jesus, this is made rather explicit in verse 24, where Paul states, "It is the Lord Christ whom you serve." Once again, the motivation for doing one's work responsibly even when not being supervised is that the Lord is watching and will one day be our Judge. In Ephesians, Paul emphasizes that the Lord Jesus will reward the good that we do; in Colossians, he emphasizes that the Lord will punish the wrong that we do. Both are reasons to "fear" him, that is, to behave in ways that respect his awesome authority and power as our ultimate, eternal Judge.

The apostle Peter also taught that Christians should fear Christ as Lord:

> But even if you do suffer for doing what is right, you are blessed. Do not fear what they fear, and do not be intimidated, but in your hearts sanctify Christ as Lord. Always be ready to make your defense to anyone who demands from you an accounting for the hope that is in you; yet do it with gentleness and reverence. (1 Peter 3:14–16a)

As exegetical commentators routinely point out,[3] Peter is here applying to Christ the words from Isaiah 8:12–13 (which we quoted earlier), which speak about fearing the Lord. Given this application, we should consider the possibility that the "fear" with which Peter says we should make a defense for what we believe is the fear of the "Lord," that is, Christ.

In some translations (e.g., the NIV) the word *phobos* at the end of verse 15 is translated "respect," and this is understood to refer to the attitude we should have toward others when we are explaining our reasons for being a Christian. Although this is good advice, it is almost certainly not what Peter meant. Peter has just said, quoting Isaiah 8:12, that we should not "fear" (*phobēthēte*) the people around us. It would be strange if in the next breath he were to say, using the related noun, that we should defend our beliefs in an attitude of "fear" (*phobou*), meaning "respect," toward those who ask.

By far the better interpretation is that "gentleness" describes the attitude we should have toward those who ask us about our beliefs while "fear" (or "reverence") describes our attitude toward the "Lord" while defending our beliefs. We conclude that here Peter is telling believers to conduct their defense of the faith in a spirit of gentleness toward others and of reverential fear toward the Lord Christ.

Serve the Savior

When the Devil tempted Jesus to worship him, Jesus replied by quoting Scripture: "Worship the Lord your God, and serve only him" (Matt. 4:10, quoting Deut. 6:13). The Greek word translated "serve" is *latreuō*, a synonym for worship that the Bible uses to refer to performing religious rites or rituals. Such "service" was to be done toward the Lord only, as Deuteronomy 6:13 indicates, because he alone is the true God.

We already have seen that the Gospel of Matthew itself teaches followers of Jesus (his disciples) to worship Jesus. But should we also "serve" Jesus Christ?

The answer is yes. The New Testament teaches Christians to perform religious rites that honor Jesus Christ. The two primary rites are baptism and the Lord's Supper. Baptism is a religious rite of initiation, while the Lord's Supper is a religious rite of remembrance. In baptism, the new believer expresses in a dramatic, religious rite his commitment to Jesus Christ. This is what it means when the book of Acts reports that the early Christians were baptized in the name of Jesus (Acts 2:38; 8:16; 10:48; 19:5).[4]

The Lord's Supper (1 Cor. 11:20) is also a religious rite focused on Jesus Christ. Jesus himself instituted the Lord's Supper on the Passover (Matt. 26:2, 18, 26–29; Mark 14:12–16, 22–25; Luke 22:8–20), the Jewish rite memorializing the Lord God's deliverance of Israel from their bondage in Egypt (Exod. 12:21–27, 42–49; Deut. 16:1–8). The apostle Paul spoke of Jesus as "the Lord" honored in the rite that the Lord himself instituted.

> The cup of blessing that we bless, is it not a sharing in the blood of Christ? The bread that we break, is it not a sharing in the body of Christ? Because there is one bread, we who are many are one body, for we all partake of the one bread. Consider the people of Israel; are not those who eat the sacrifices partners in the altar? What do I imply then? That food sacrificed to idols is anything, or that an idol is anything? No, I imply that what pagans sacrifice, they sacrifice to demons and not to God. I do not want you to be partners with demons. You cannot drink the cup of the Lord and the cup of demons. You cannot partake of the table of the Lord and the table of demons. Or are we provoking the Lord to jealousy? Are we stronger than he? (1 Cor. 10:16–22)

While the Lord's Supper was instituted by Jesus and has its own religious background in the traditions of Judaism concerning the Passover, the Corinthians were for the most part converts from paganism who had yet to break free entirely from the temptations of idolatry in their polytheistic culture. Paul therefore sharply contrasts the rite of the Lord's Supper with pagan rites that were superficially similar enough that some immature believers apparently were participating in both. In drawing these contrasts (see table), Paul contrasts the Lord Jesus with the deities worshiped in the pagan rites (which Paul calls "demons"). Paul thus makes it clear that the Lord's Supper is a religious rite in which the Lord Jesus is the presiding deity, the object of religious devotion or "service" for Christians.[5]

PAUL'S CONTRAST OF THE LORD'S SUPPER WITH PAGAN RITUAL MEALS

Lord's Supper	Pagan Ritual Meals
Sharing in the Lord's blood and body (10:16; 11:27)	Sharing in demons (10:20)
The cup of the Lord (10:21a; 11:27)	The cup of demons (10:21a)
The table of the Lord (10:21b)	The table of demons (10:21b)
Likened to eating sacrifices to God (10:18)	Eating sacrifices to demons (10:20)

We should note that there is at least one biblical text that speaks explicitly of people "serving" Jesus Christ. The book of Daniel contains a vision in which people of all nations, tribes, and languages "serve" someone who is "like a Son of Man" (Dan. 7:13 NASB). In the New Testament we learn that Jesus Christ, of course, is that Son of Man (e.g., John 9:35–38; Rev. 1:12–18). In the Septuagint version of Daniel, the word translated "serve" is *latreuō*, which is also used in the Rahlfs edition of the Septuagint and in other critical editions of the Greek Old Testament. In the Greek version of Daniel produced in the late second century A.D. by Theodotion, the word translated "serve" is *douloō*, a far more common Greek word that has a broader range of meanings.

Whichever Greek translation one chooses to follow, the underlying Aramaic word (Daniel 2:4–7:28 was originally written in Aramaic, not Hebrew) is *pelach*, a word that is always used to refer to rendering religious service or performing religious rituals in honor of a deity.[6] In other words, *latreuō* is an excellent Greek translation of *pelach*. That is why all extant ancient Greek versions of Daniel usually use *latreuō* elsewhere in Daniel to translate *pelach* (Dan. 3:12, 14, 18, 28; 6:16, 20 [6:17, 21 in Greek]).[7] In the earlier chapters of the book, Daniel and his Jewish friends had refused to "serve" the image of Nebuchadnezzar or to "serve" Darius, identifying themselves as those who "serve" only their God, the living God (3:12, 14, 17, 18, 28; 6:16, 20). In this setting, the vision of people from all nations "serving" the Son of Man presents a startling contrast. The "service" that Daniel and his friends refused to give to Nebuchadnezzar's image or to Darius, Daniel envisions all nations giving to the heavenly Son of Man.

Daniel's reference to the Son of Man being "served" implies a divine status for the Son of Man, not merely because of the use of that one word, but because of the context in which it is used. The universal sovereignty attributed to the Son of Man is earlier attributed to Daniel's God by the Babylonian and Persian kings.

> The signs and wonders that the Most High God has worked for me I am pleased to recount. How great are his signs, how mighty his wonders! *His kingdom is an everlasting kingdom, and his sovereignty is from generation to generation.* (4:2–3, emphasis added)

> When that period was over, I, Nebuchadnezzar, lifted my eyes to heaven, and my reason returned to me. I blessed the Most High, and praised and honored the one who lives forever. For *his sovereignty is an everlasting sovereignty, and his kingdom endures from generation to generation.* (4:34, emphasis added)

> I make a decree, that in all my royal dominion people should tremble and fear before the God of Daniel: For he is the living God, enduring forever. *His kingdom shall never be destroyed, and his dominion has no end.* (6:26, emphasis added)

This language of a kingdom that will not be destroyed and that will endure forever is then applied to the kingdom of the Son of Man.

To him was given dominion and glory and kingship, that all peoples, nations, and languages should serve him. *His dominion is an everlasting dominion that shall not pass away, and his kingship is one that shall never be destroyed.* (7:14, emphasis added)

Within this larger context, the reference to all peoples "serving" the Son of Man is confirmed as an expression of religious devotion. The One whom you regard as the Ruler of your entire universe for all time is by definition your God, and it would be the height of folly *not* to render religious devotion or service to him.[8]

Love the Lord—and Obey Him

Jesus said it himself: the greatest commandment is the command to "love the Lord your God with all your heart, and with all your soul, and with all your mind" (Matt. 22:37, quoting Deut. 6:5). Although God expects us to love people as well—our family, other believers, our neighbors, and even our enemies (Matt. 5:43–48)—only God deserves our *absolute* devotion. That is what "love" usually means in the Bible. It is not just a feeling, though feelings are often involved. Rather, love is commitment to the good of another; it is synonymous with loyalty.

That is why the Old Testament closely links love for God and obedience to his commandments. In the Ten Commandments, the Lord told Israel that he expected them to "love me and keep my commandments" (Exod. 20:6; Deut. 5:10). The Lord "maintains covenant loyalty with those who love him and keep his commandments" (Deut. 7:9). "You shall love the LORD your God, therefore, and keep his charge, his decrees, his ordinances, and his commandments always" (Deut. 11:1; see also 11:13, 22; 19:9; 30:6–8, 16, 20; Josh. 22:5; Neh. 1:5; Dan. 9:4). Israelites were to put loyalty to the Lord above everything else, even loyalty to their families (Deut. 13:6–11; 33:9).

Yet Jesus expected to be given the same kind of absolute devotion—the same unqualified commitment of the heart and life—that we ought to give to God. Jesus put love for him above family ties: "Whoever loves father or mother more than me is not worthy of me; and whoever loves son or daughter more than me is not worthy of me" (Matt. 10:37). A similar statement in Luke puts it more starkly: "If anyone comes to Me, and does not hate his own father and mother and wife and children and brothers and sisters, yes, and even his own life, he cannot be My disciple" (Luke 14:26 NASB). As most commentators have noted, Jesus' use of the word "hate" here is an example of hyperbole. It is a forceful, dramatic way of saying that their love and commitment to their closest family members should be less than their love and commitment to Jesus—so much so that they must be willing to choose Jesus over their families if it comes to that. Craig Keener points out that Jesus' listeners would know that "no [mere] teacher would speak of 'hating' one's parents by comparison" to their love for that teacher, since "God alone was worthy of that role."[9]

In the Gospel of John, Jesus repeatedly associates love for him with obedience to his commandments: "If you love me, you will keep my commandments" (14:15); "He who has My commandments and keeps them is the one who loves Me" (14:21 NASB); "If you keep my commandments, you will abide in my love, just as I have kept my Father's commandments and abide in his love" (15:10). As Keener has noted, "When Jesus connects obedience with love, biblically literate Jewish hearers would immediately think of the associations between obeying God's commandments and loving God."[10]

In different language, the apostle Paul also spoke of this highest kind of love for Jesus Christ. At the end of his epistle to the Ephesians, he wrote, "Grace be with all who have an undying love for our Lord Jesus Christ" (Eph. 6:24). Paul's word translated here "undying" is *aphtharsia*, which means "incorruptible." The point is, Jesus Christ comes first in our lives—our love for him is our highest priority, and nothing will interfere with, or stop us from, loving him forever. That is what it means to know Jesus as our Lord and God.

Part 2

LIKE FATHER, LIKE SON

Jesus Shares the Attributes of God

Honors	Attributes	Names	Deeds	Seat

Chapter 6

BEYOND RESEMBLANCE

The story is told of a grandmother who was observing her granddaughter drawing a picture. She asked, "Honey, what are you drawing?" Her granddaughter replied, "I'm drawing a picture of God." The grandmother gently reminded her, "But, honey, nobody knows what God looks like." The little girl stated confidently, "They will now!"

The New Testament tells us that, although no human being has ever seen God, we now know "what God looks like" through his revelation in his Son, Jesus Christ (John 1:14, 18). We have seen already that the Bible teaches us to respond to Jesus Christ as we would to God, by giving him the honors that are due God. We are to honor, glorify, worship, pray to, sing to and about, believe in, fear or reverence, religiously serve, love, and obey Jesus as we would God. Such responses to Jesus are ways in which we appreciate Jesus for who and what he is. As John Piper has pointed out, nothing is more important for the Christian: "There is no more important issue in life than seeing Jesus for who he really is and savoring what we see above all else."[1]

Honoring Jesus in these ways would be odd—and blasphemous—if he were merely a man. No matter how great a human being he might have been, no matter how wise or kind or influential we consider him to have been, it would be wrong to honor Jesus as God if he were fundamentally and in essence no more than a man.

In fact, he was—and is—much, much more than a man. Although he is completely, thoroughly human, Jesus also is fully divine. It staggers the imagination and stretches the mind, but somehow Jesus has characteristics and abilities properly associated with God. In his essence and nature, Jesus is exactly like God. He possesses what theologians call the *attributes* of God.

What Do You Mean by God's "Attributes"?

What do we mean when we speak of God's "attributes"? Drew University theologian Thomas C. Oden offers a helpful definition: "Attributes of God are qualities that belong to God's essential nature and that are found wherever God becomes self-revealed. They are those reliable character patterns that belong to God as God."[2] Our source of information about these qualities or attributes of God is, of course, the Bible.

When theologians discuss the attributes of God, they frequently distinguish between the communicable and incommunicable attributes of God. *Communicable* attributes are those attributes that God shares in some way with creatures (particularly human beings), such as love, holiness, and faithfulness. *Incommunicable* attributes are those attributes that God does not and cannot share with creatures, such as being all-knowing, all-powerful, and eternal. To say that Jesus is exactly, perfectly like God is to say that he possesses both the communicable and the incommunicable attributes of God.

We should acknowledge, though, that this distinction is not as hard and fast as one might suppose. Is goodness, for example, a communicable or incommunicable attribute of God? Since Jesus said that we are supposed to be good and to do good things (Luke 6:33, 35, 45), it would seem that goodness is communicable. On the other hand, Jesus also said that only God is good (Matt. 19:16–17; Luke 18:18–19), which would seem to make goodness an incommunicable attribute of God. Jesus may have been simply contrasting the goodness of God with the sinfulness of human beings, or he may have been asserting that goodness is ultimately found in God alone: "God alone defines the good because he is the good."[3] If the latter is Jesus' meaning, then rather than speaking of goodness being "communicable" or "incommunicable" we would do better to say that while creatures can be "good," they can never be good *in the same way that God is good*. Creatures can be good insofar as they act as God intended for them to act, but God is the source and standard of all goodness.[4]

The point is important because if we are to establish that Jesus has God's attributes, we must show that certain descriptions of God are not only also applied to Jesus but that they are applied to him *with the same meaning*. We will show that Jesus possesses the attributes of God and possesses them in the same sense and to the same extent that God possesses them. The point we are making may be stated as a paradox: No one is exactly like God; yet Jesus is exactly like God.

That no one is like God is a major theme of the Old Testament (Exod. 8:10; 9:14; 15:11; 2 Sam. 7:22; 1 Kings 8:23; 1 Chron. 17:20; Ps. 86:8; Isa. 40:18, 25; 44:7; 46:5, 9; Jer. 10:6–7; Mic. 7:18). Most of these passages in context are arguing that there are no gods like the Lord God. (That no human beings are like God is occasionally mentioned as well, but it is always assumed.) They point out that no other gods have the capabilities that God has. None of them can do the kinds of miracles that God does; none can demonstrate mastery over the forces of nature or predict and control the flow of history. There is no one as great and awesome as God, and nothing in creation looks like God or is his equal. No one can even come close to rivaling God's faithfulness, mercy, and forgiveness. And yet the New Testament confidently affirms that in all these ways Jesus Christ is exactly like God!

In order to do this topic justice, we must make two further clarifications. First, it is helpful to distinguish attributes from what theologians have sometimes called properties. In Christian theology *property* "is a technical term that has been used to speak of the characteristics of the interior relations of the persons of the Godhead."[5] For example, being the Son of the Father is a property that applies to the Son, not to the Father (or the Holy Spirit). Being the one who sent the Son into the world is a property of the Father, not of the Son (i.e., the Son did not send himself). When we say that Jesus has all the attributes of God, we do not mean that he has all the "properties" of God the Father.

Second, the thesis we are putting forth is not that all of Jesus Christ's attributes are those of God, but that Jesus Christ has all the attributes of God. The difference in wording is subtle, but the difference in meaning is highly significant. Jesus Christ, especially when he was living as a mortal on the earth, obviously had attributes that are not those of God. He was mortal (and in fact died), he got tired and fell asleep, he got hungry and thirsty, he was able to be tempted, and so forth. These are all attributes of human beings. According to the New Testament, Jesus Christ was not originally like us in any of these ways, but "he had to be *made* like his brothers in every way, in order that he might become a merciful and faithful high priest in service to God" (Heb. 2:17 NIV, emphasis added). The result is that Jesus Christ has, as it were, two sets of attributes—those of human beings and those of God.

One cannot validly object to this conclusion by pointing to biblical passages in which Jesus had human attributes.

God in a Body

We begin with one of the clearest and most emphatic statements in the Bible about Christ's divine nature. In his letter to the Colossians, Paul wrote, "For in him the whole fullness of deity dwells bodily" (Col. 2:9). The word translated "deity" (*theotēs*) means "the nature or state of being God."[6] The King James Version translates the word as "Godhead," which was accurate in the English of Shakespeare's day but is somewhat misleading today. Many people use the term "the Godhead" to refer to the Father, Son, and Holy Spirit considered collectively. The suffix -*head* in English, however, usually meant status, state, or nature, and in modern English has been largely displaced by -*hood* (e.g., *bachelorhood* is the status or state of being a bachelor; *womanhood* is the status, state, or nature of being a woman).[7] Thus, the equivalent word for "Godhead" today would be *Godhood*—and this word is about as exact a translation of *theotēs* as one could want.

Just in case someone might misconstrue "deity" here as meaning the nature or state of being *a god*—as though Christ were simply one of a group of deities or gods—Paul states that "the *fullness* of deity" dwells in Christ.[8] The use of the word "fullness" makes it explicit that nothing of deity is missing in Christ. To put it another way, he has deity in its fullness dwelling in him. The statement recalls and expands an earlier statement in the same epistle: "because in him all the fullness was pleased to dwell" (Col. 1:19, literal translation).[9] The point is that God in his fullness chose to dwell in the incarnate Son. In both passages Paul says that *all* of the fullness dwells in him—which in a sense is redundant (if it's the fullness, then it's all of the fullness!), but Paul wants to emphasize the point in the strongest way possible. Murray Harris's paraphrase nicely expresses Paul's use of redundancy for emphasis: "It is in Christ, and Christ alone, that the sum total of the fullness of the Godhead, no part or aspect excepted, permanently resides in bodily form."[10]

The Old Testament background to these sayings focuses on Mount Zion and the temple that eventually stood there.[11] In one of his psalms, David spoke of Zion as "the mountain which God was pleased to dwell in it" (Ps. 68:16, translating the Greek version literally). The language here is remarkably similar to Colossians 1:19:

eudokēsen ho theos **katoikein en autō** (Ps. 67:16 LXX)

en autō eudokēsen pan to plērōma **katoikēsai** (Col. 1:19)

While the language is very similar, what Paul says about Christ goes far beyond what the Old Testament said about Mount Zion or the temple. Although the temple was spoken of as a place for God to "dwell" (e.g., Pss. 9:11; 76:2; 132:13), from the very beginning Solomon, at the temple dedication, acknowledged that God's true dwelling place was heaven (1 Kings 8:12–13, 27, 30, 39, 43, 49; 2 Chron. 6:18, 21, 30, 33, 39). What Paul says about Christ, on the other hand, is that all the fullness of what constitutes God dwells bodily in Christ. The presence and nature of God is totally or *wholly* ("all" or "whole") found in Christ; it is *fully* ("fullness") found in Christ; it is found in him *personally* ("in him"); and it is found in him *bodily*. It is difficult to imagine a more forceful, emphatic affirmation that Jesus Christ literally embodies God's very being.

Some argue that Colossians 2:10 ("and you have come to fullness in him") shows that the "fullness" of verse 9 does not mean that Jesus has God's very nature. The reasoning seems simple enough: Paul says that we have the fullness, but we're not God by nature; therefore, saying that Jesus has the fullness doesn't make him God by nature, either.[12] But this argument misconstrues the relationship between the two statements. Paul is not saying that believers have the fullness of the deity dwelling in them bodily as well! Rather, he is saying that because God's fullness is found in Christ personally, those who are united to Christ (who are "in him") have the fullness of God's power and love working in their lives. In both cases it is God's fullness, but in the case of Christ it resides in him personally and bodily, whereas in our case that fullness is mediated to us through our relationship with Christ.

Finally, we should comment on the argument that Paul's statement in Colossians 1:19—that God "was pleased" for all his fullness to dwell in Christ—proves that Christ was not always deity.[13] In context, Paul is referring to the incarnation. He is saying that God was pleased to be fully incarnated in the human Jesus of Nazareth.[14] "It is the same Jesus, crucified and buried but risen again, and now alive for evermore as Christ the Lord, in whom the totality resides."[15] Colossians 1:19 and 2:9 on their own do not address directly the question of the nature of the Son prior to his incarnation. We will see in the next chapter, though, that in the immediate context of these statements

Paul also affirms that the Son existed not only before his human life but prior to the whole created order (Col. 1:16–17).

The Spitting Image of His Father

One of the most basic descriptions of Jesus in the New Testament is that he is the Son of God (e.g., Mark 1:1; 15:39; Luke 1:35; John 20:31; Rom. 1:3–4; Heb. 4:14; 1 John 4:15). Although the title *Son* as applied to Jesus has more than one connotation in Scripture (see part 3), here we want to focus attention on the New Testament teaching that Jesus, the Son of God, had the very nature of God.

Consider, for example, the following exchange between Jesus and his disciple Philip:

> "If you really knew me, you would know my Father as well. From now on, you do know him and have seen him." Philip said, "Lord, show us the Father and that will be enough for us." Jesus answered: "Don't you know me, Philip, even after I have been among you such a long time? Anyone who has seen me has seen the Father. How can you say, 'Show us the Father'? Don't you believe that I am in the Father, and that the Father is in me?" (John 14:7–10a NIV)

Jesus claims to be such a perfect revelation of the Father that anyone who has seen him has seen the Father (v. 9). This statement is so strong, some people have misunderstood it to mean that Jesus was claiming that he *was* the Father. That is incorrect, of course: Jesus distinguishes himself from the Father throughout the passage and states not that he is the Father but that he is *in* the Father and the Father is *in* him (v. 10a).[16] Nevertheless, what Jesus claims is astonishing. *If you want to see the Father, you cannot do any better than seeing Jesus.* Seeing Jesus the Son is as good as seeing the Father; in a sense it *is* seeing the Father because the Father is perfectly revealed in the Son. Jesus had said essentially the same thing earlier, but it obviously had not fully registered with Philip (or any of the other disciples): "Whoever sees me sees him who sent me" (John 12:45). Every word that Jesus spoke, everything that Jesus did, was the Father speaking and working through him: "The words that I say to you I do not speak on my own; but the Father who dwells in me does his works" (John 14:10b).

The same idea is expressed in various ways throughout the New Testament.

Paul says that the Father's "beloved Son . . . is the image of the invisible God" (Col. 1:13, 15a; cf. 2 Cor. 4:4). The application of the term "image" (*eikōn*) to the Father's "Son" makes it clear that Paul is speaking of Christ's likeness to the Father. Whereas God *created* and *made* human beings *in* his image (Gen. 1:26–27), Jesus Christ, God's beloved Son, *is* the image of God. In the Incarnation, Jesus Christ shows us perfectly what the invisible God is really like. Now he is the original "image," and redeemed human beings are destined to be what we might call "copies." Thus, Paul says that God's purpose is to conform us "to the image of his Son" (Rom. 8:29; see also 1 Cor. 15:49; 2 Cor. 3:18). The Son's likeness to God the Father is therefore in some sense or respect "communicable," yet his likeness to God is on a whole different level than ours is or ever will be.

Very similar is a statement found at the beginning of the book of Hebrews, which says that God's Son "is the reflection of God's glory and the exact imprint of God's very being" (1:3). The language of sonship combined with the metaphors of being the reflection and imprint of the father (God) again express in very strong terms the essential likeness of the Son to God. Although this much is clear, it will be helpful to examine the language used. The word *apaugasma* could mean either "reflection" (NRSV) or "radiance" (NASB, NIV). Both meanings fit the context and both end up affirming that the Son perfectly embodies the glorious nature of God.[17] If we take the word in the passive sense of reflection, the meaning is that looking at Jesus is like holding up to God a mirror that allows the glory of the otherwise invisible Creator to be seen. If we take the word in the active sense of radiance, the meaning is that everything we see coming from Jesus is an expression of the glorious nature of God. An equivalent modern English idiom would be to describe a son as "the spitting image of his father."

Hebrews 1:3 also describes the Son as the "exact imprint" (*charactēr*) of God's being. The Greek word literally referred to the mark or imprint reproducing the likeness of something (such as letters or a person's face), typically by a metal stamp or seal (say, on a coin or in wax) or by engraving or carving (e.g., in wood). This meaning carried over into English with the use of the word *character* to refer to a letter or mark stamped out by moveable type or other imprinting devices. Here again we should interpret the metaphor in the context of sonship: like father, like son. "The notion of a parent imprinting his or her essence and accident (likeness both of mind and of form) upon the child is certainly an apt resonance for the relationship between the Son and God."[18] Using a metaphor derived from what is now somewhat obsolete technology, we might say that the son is a "carbon copy" of his father.

By combining these two descriptions of the Son as the reflection or radiance of God's glory and the exact imprint of God's being, the book of Hebrews states emphatically the essential likeness of the Son to God. As we shall see in the rest of this section, that general statement is supported by what the rest of the New Testament teaches concerning the specific attributes of God.

Chapter 7

JESUS EXISTED BEFORE HE WAS BORN!

If Jesus, the Son, really is just like his Father—if he is the perfect revelation of the Father and the exact representation of the very being of God—then in key respects Jesus is like the Father and *unlike* any of us.

Some biblical scholars, however, interpret Jesus' likeness to God in a very different way. They interpret the New Testament teaching about Jesus' likeness to God as meaning in essence that Jesus is the perfect man. The basis for this idea is that the Bible speaks of human beings as created in "the image of God" (Gen. 1:26–27; 1 Cor. 11:7). Taking this to mean that God intends human beings to be like God in certain ways (perhaps especially in their moral attributes, such as love, goodness, compassion, and the like), some scholars argue that descriptions of Jesus as "the image of the invisible God" (Col. 1:15; cf. 2 Cor. 4:4) are representing him simply as the perfect, ideal man. This interpretation is correlated with the apostle Paul's theme of Jesus Christ as the second or last Adam (e.g., Rom. 5:14–19; 1 Cor. 15:22, 45–49).

James D. G. Dunn is perhaps the leading New Testament scholar who interprets most of the New Testament as teaching that Christ was merely the perfect man. According to Dunn, "Only in the post-Pauline period did a clear understanding of Christ as having preexisted with God before his ministry on earth emerge, and *only in the Fourth Gospel can we speak of a doctrine of the incarnation.*"[1]

As Dunn's statement implies, the crucial issue in this regard is whether Christ "preexisted" his human life on earth. The questions of Christ's preexistence and his divine nature or attributes are bound up together. If Christ existed as a divine person before his human life, then he is the definitive revelation of the nature of God because his nature *is,* in fact, the nature of God. On the other hand, if Christ did not exist before his human life, then he is a revelation of the nature of God only in the sense that in his words and actions we see how God wants us to live. We may put the question this way: Was Jesus a man through whom God was revealing himself, or was he God revealing himself as a man?

It is worth noting that even Dunn acknowledges that the Gospel of John teaches that Jesus was God revealing himself as a man. He simply views John's presentation of Jesus as one of many formulations in the New Testament and urges that it not be treated as the only correct formulation.[2] Similarly, Karl-Josef Kuschel, in his lengthy book critiquing the doctrine of Christ's preexistence, asserts, "There is no doubt that the Gospel of John, in contrast to the Synoptic Gospels and Paul, contains a series of statements about pre-existence."[3] Even if we assume, solely for the sake of argument, that none of the earlier New Testament authors spoke of Christ's preexistence, unless they *denied* it we should still accept John's clear witness on the matter and add it to what we learn about Christ from the rest of the New Testament.

In actuality, John is hardly alone in teaching that Jesus Christ existed as a divine person prior to his becoming a human being. This is, in fact, precisely what the apostle Paul taught.

Christ Existed "in the Form of God"

One of the most important biblical passages for our understanding of the person of Jesus Christ is Philippians 2:6–11. In these six verses, Paul taught that Christ was a preexistent person who was fully God and yet humbled himself by becoming human and dying on a cross (vv. 6–8). Then, in Christ's resurrection, God the Father exalted him in order that he might be honored by all creation as their divine Lord (vv. 9–11). Although this understanding of the passage has come under criticism, the evidence is decisive that Paul was, indeed, affirming the divine preexistence of Christ.

In verse 6, Paul says that Christ, "though he was in the form of God, did not regard equality with God as something to be exploited." The natural way of understanding this statement—and the way that the vast majority of Christian interpreters historically have understood it—is that Christ existed "in the form of God" in heaven before he became a man. Thus, Paul goes on immediately to say that Christ "emptied himself, taking the form of a slave, being born in human likeness," and that he was "found in human form" (v. 7).

Even Dunn, who denies that Paul taught the preexistence of Christ, admits that it is "almost inevitable" that the passage should be understood as speaking of the preexistent Christ choosing to become a man. According to Dunn, though, what Paul meant was that "preexistent" Wisdom became embodied in the human person of Christ.[4] The problem, of course, is that Paul says that *Christ* "existed in God's form" and that it was Christ who took a slave's form, was born in human likeness, and found himself to be a human being.

Dunn also argues that the dominant motif in Philippians 2:6–11 is Adam Christology, in which Jesus functions as the "last" or eschatological Adam. There is no doubt that the Adam/Christ typology is a significant motif in Pauline theology (Rom. 5:12–19; 1 Cor. 15:20–22, 45–49; see also Rom. 6:4–11; 2 Cor. 5:17; Gal. 6:15; Eph. 2:10, 15; 4:22, 24; Col. 1:18; 3:10). It is also likely that some contrast with Adam is implicit in Philippians 2. In his essay on the subject, Pauline scholar Lincoln D. Hurst makes the following important observation: "The central issue to be decided is whether the act of Adam is contrasted with the act of the *heavenly* Christ or with that of the *human* Jesus."[5] The traditional understanding has been stated this way: "Adam, who grasped at a dignity to which he had not right, should be contrasted with Christ, who renounced a status to which he had every right."[6] As New Testament scholar N. T. Wright put it in his influential article on the passage, "Adam, in arrogance, thought to become like God: Christ, in humility, became man."[7] Thus, an acknowledgment of a contrast between Adam and Christ in Philippians 2 in no way precludes the passage's clear teaching that Christ preexisted in divine form before becoming a human being.

We should set aside, then, Dunn's suggestion that Christ's existing "in the form of God" (*en morphē theou*) is another way of saying that he existed in the image of God, as did Adam (Gen. 1:26–27).[8] It would be better to draw a *contrast* between Adam, who existed in God's image, and Christ, who existed in God's form. The contrast should be understood in the light of Paul's contrast between Christ's existence "in the form of God" and his subsequent act of becoming a human being when he took "the form of a slave" (v. 7). The "image of God" in human beings refers to their role as earthly, physical representatives of God's rule (Gen. 1:26–30). The "form of God" in which Christ existed refers to his being the heavenly reflection of God's nature and glory.[9]

Most of the scholarly debate regarding Philippians 2:6 focuses on the meaning of the Greek word *harpagmos*.[10] Since the word occurs only once in the Greek Bible and is rare in extrabiblical literature, scholars have limited lexical data on which to base their understandings of Paul's intended meaning here. Some understand Paul to be saying that Jesus did not consider it "robbery" to be equal with God" (NKJV, following the KJV); others assert that Jesus did not consider equality with God something "to be grasped" (NASB, NIV, NET, ESV). Still others maintain a more nuanced view, namely, that Jesus did not think of equality with God as "something to be exploited" (NRSV).

Although the technical discussions of the meaning of *harpagmos* can be complex and confusing, this does not mean that we cannot really know what Paul is saying in Philippians 2:6. However *harpagmos* is translated, Paul is still affirming the divine preexistence of Christ. The rendering "did not consider it robbery to be equal with God" (NKJV, following the KJV), which has the least support among biblical scholars today, would mean that Christ was equal with God and did not think that he had taken that status wrongfully. The more common rendering "did not regard equality with God a thing to be grasped" (NASB; cf. NIV, NET, ESV) would mean that the preexistent divine Christ did not try to seize recognition of his rightful status of equality with God, but chose to put the glory of the Father and the salvation of sinners ahead of his own glory. The rendering "did not regard equality with God as something to be exploited" (NRSV), now favored by many and possibly a majority of commentators, would mean that Christ was equal with God but did not seek to take advantage of that status for his own personal comfort or gain.

Although these ways of translating *harpagmos* are very different, the resulting ways of understanding the overarching thrust of the passage are essentially the same. Paul is saying that Christ was divine in his nature or glorious form but did not act in the self-serving manner one might have expected an omnipotent deity to act, taking whatever he wanted and demanding to be treated as superior. This understanding fits the context well. Paul's point is that although Christ was in God's form and was (at least by right) God's equal, he did not demand his divine rights but humbly took a servant's form and became a human being.

Clearly, Philippians 2 does, indeed, speak of Christ as a preexistent divine person who humbled himself by becoming a human being. We have here, then, dating from less than twenty-five years after Jesus' death and resurrection, an apostolic writing affirming the belief in Christ's divine preexistence.

God Cared Enough to Send His Very Best

Throughout the New Testament, Jesus is described as the Son whom God sent and as the Son who came from God. We will look at samplings of the more provocative examples of such statements from three parts of the New Testament: sayings of Jesus in the Synoptics (Matthew, Mark, and Luke), statements by the apostle Paul, and statements in the writings of John.[11]

Jesus "Coming" and Being "Sent" in the Synoptic Gospels

First, then, consider the following statements by Jesus in the Synoptic Gospels:

> For I *have come* to call not the righteous but sinners. (Matt. 9:13; cf. Mark 2:17; Luke 5:32)

> The Son of Man *came* not to be served but to serve, and to give his life a ransom for many. (Matt. 20:28; Mark 10:45)

> I must proclaim the good news of the kingdom of God to the other cities also; for I *was sent* for this purpose. (Luke 4:43; cf. Mark 1:38)

> I *came* to bring fire to the earth, and how I wish it were already kindled! (Luke 12:49)

> Do you think that I *have come* to bring peace to the earth? No, I tell you, but rather division! (Luke 12:51; cf. Matt. 10:34)

> For the Son of Man *came* to seek out and to save the lost. (Luke 19:10)[12]

Although these statements by Jesus about being sent by the Father and about his having "come" do not explicitly affirm his preexistence, they strongly imply it. For one thing, Jesus links his having been sent, or his coming, with works of divine significance (about which we will have more to say in part 4). He came to bring salvation to some and judgment to others. An excellent example is Jesus' saying in Luke 19:10, which echoes what God said through Ezekiel that he, God, would do: "For thus says the Lord GOD: I myself will search for my sheep, and will seek them out. . . . I will save my flock"

(Ezek. 34:11, 22). As Douglas McCready points out in his excellent overview of the subject of Christ's preexistence, "When the language of 'having come' is linked with what Jesus came to accomplish—the salvation of the world or its judgment—something more than an earthly origin seems necessary."[13]

Second, in two of these sayings Jesus speaks of his having "come" in relation to "the earth": he came to bring fire to the earth (Luke 12:49), and to bring not peace but division to the earth (Matt. 10:34–35; Luke 12:51). Again, this does not say *explicitly* that he came from somewhere other than the earth, but such is by far the most natural way of understanding his words.

Third, the use of the title "the Son of Man" suggests a heavenly origin for the one whom God sent. The Old Testament source of this title is Daniel 7:13–14, where "one like a son of man" (NIV) is a heavenly figure to whom God gives universal dominion and all peoples will one day serve. Keying off the passage in Daniel, Jesus states that as that heavenly Son of Man he "came" not to be "served" but to serve by giving "his life" for many (Matt. 20:28; Mark 10:45). Jesus first comes to serve us, after which we are to serve him (cf. Matt. 28:16–20).

Fourth, Jesus' language about sending and coming is always "absolute." By that we mean it is never tied to an event in Jesus' life or in any way dated. Jesus simply states, "I have come," "I came," "The Son of Man came." These sayings are not referring to specific acts of "coming" from one physical place to another but of the purpose of Christ's whole human life.

It is often argued that such language is also used of John the Baptist,[14] but it is never, in fact, used of him in a way comparable to the kinds of statements we find made about Jesus. In Matthew 21:32, when Jesus says, "John came to you," the use of "came" here is dictated and explained by Jesus' preceding parable of the father who "came" to his two sons with instructions (21:28–30). In Mark 9:11–13, Jesus responds to the disciples' question about why Elijah had to "come" by saying, rather enigmatically, that "Elijah" had already "come," referring to John the Baptist. Neither the disciples nor Jesus even hinted that John preexisted as Elijah; the disciples were asking about Elijah's "coming" in relation to the final resurrection of the dead (vv. 9–10). Jesus' response amounts to saying that Malachi's apocalyptic prophecy about God's sending Elijah (Mal. 4:5–6) refers not to a literal resurrected Elijah but to John in his Elijah-like ministry (see also Luke 1:17). Thus, the language is applied to John in a very specific context that does not imply preexistence. Neither passage uses Jesus' characteristic speech pattern of having "come" or being "sent" in order to accomplish a specific end (typically "I have come" followed by an infinitive of purpose, such as "to seek out and to save the lost").

Finally, Simon Gathercole, in his impressive recent study of evidence found in the Synoptic Gospels for the preexistence of Christ, has shown that Jesus' "I have come" sayings most closely reflect sayings attributed to angels in the Old Testament and other Jewish literature in regard to their purpose for coming to the earth from heaven. The following are just two of the two dozen examples cited by Gathercole:

> Gabriel: "Daniel, I have now come out to give you wisdom and understanding" (Dan. 9:22).

> An unnamed angel: "[I] have come to help you understand what is to happen to your people at the end of days" (Dan. 10:14).

What these and many other examples show is not that Jesus is also an angel, but that, like the angels, he came from heaven for a specific purpose.[15] That Jesus is not an angel is evident in that he did not come simply to bring a message (although he did, of course, teach). Rather, Jesus described his mission as bringing redemption for some and judgment for others and as being cosmic or worldwide in scope. The way he expresses this mission makes it clear that he understood himself to have come from heaven, and therefore that he preexisted in heaven before becoming a man.[16]

Was Jesus "Sent" at His Baptism?

The one event in Jesus' life that is sometimes suggested as the event of Jesus' "commission" is his baptism. The Synoptics, however, which all report Jesus' baptism, give no indication that the Father "sent" Jesus at the time of his baptism or that when Jesus said that he had "come" he was looking back to his baptism. All three Synoptic Gospels, in fact, report that the Father simply acknowledged Jesus as his "beloved Son" in whom he was "well-pleased" (Matt. 3:17; Mark 1:11; Luke 3:22).

James Dunn understands the Father's statement as an allusion to Psalm 2:7, "You are my Son; today I have become your Father" (NIV), and thus as being at least "open to the interpretation that Jesus first *became* Son of God at the beginning of his ministry."[17] The question, though, is whether this is the *best* interpretation. The Father's statement at most reflects Psalm 2:7 only in part. It does echo, however, another Old Testament passage of messianic significance: God's description of Isaac as Abraham's "beloved" (in the Greek Old Testament, *agapētos*) son, when he instructed Abraham to sacrifice Isaac on an altar (Gen. 22:2, 12, 16). Dunn acknowledges this allusion as only "possible,"[18] but it seems instead more than likely.[19] In Genesis 22 Isaac, of course, was already Abraham's beloved son before being described as such. Furthermore, Mark (as well as Matthew and Luke) reports the Father's saying essentially the same thing at Jesus' transfiguration: "This is my Son, the Beloved; listen to him!" (Mark 9:7; cf. Matt. 17:5; Luke 9:35). How many times did Jesus have to become the Son of God?[20]

If the Father's statement at Jesus' baptism implied that Jesus had become the Son of God at that moment, this subtle implication was missed by both Matthew and Luke. Both of them report the same statement at Jesus' baptism, yet both agree that Jesus did not become the Son of God at that time. Matthew quotes Hosea 11:1 in his infancy narrative, "Out of Egypt I have called my son," and applies it to the infant Jesus (Matt. 2:15). Luke states that Jesus would be *called* God's Son because he was conceived by the Holy Spirit (Luke 1:35). (This is not the same thing as saying that he would *be* God's Son only as a result of that virginal conception.) Thus, there is no basis in the Synoptics for the idea that Jesus was "sent" at his baptism. The Father's remark actually sounds like an affirmation that Jesus was *already* his Son. It is much more like "I love you, son, you're doing great" and not at all like "You're doing so well, from now on you're my son."

Paul: God Sent His Son and His Spirit

Next, let's look at two of Paul's statements on the matter:

> But when the fullness of the time came, God sent forth His Son, born of a woman, born under the Law, so that He might redeem those who were under the Law, that we might receive the adoption as sons. Because you are sons, God has sent forth the Spirit of His Son into our hearts, crying, "Abba! Father!" (Gal. 4:4–6 NASB)

> For God has done what the law, weakened by the flesh, could not do: by sending his own Son in the likeness of sinful flesh, and to deal with sin, he condemned sin in the flesh. (Rom. 8:3)

The most natural way of understanding these statements is that God's Son existed before becoming a human being. This is especially clear in Galatians 4:4–6, where four elements converge to express this idea: (1) the statement that "God sent forth His Son"; (2) the description of this Son as "born of a woman"; (3) the contrast between Jesus as God's (apparently natural) "Son" and believers as those who have received "adoption as sons"; (4) the parallel statement that "God has sent forth the Spirit of His Son." Dunn's approach to this passage is to argue that neither of the first two elements on its own proves preexistence.[21] This argument, however, does not take adequate stock of how the two elements work *together*: "God sent forth His Son, born of a woman."[22] The third element—the contrast between Jesus as God's Son and believers as God's adopted sons—combined with these other elements further suggests a heavenly origin for Jesus.

What really clinches the conclusion that the Son is being spoken of as a preexistent person is the fourth element—the parallel statement in verse 6 that "God has sent forth the Spirit of His Son."[23] The implication is clear: first God sent his Son from heaven to redeem his people, and then he sent the Spirit of his Son from heaven to dwell within them. This is practically the theology of the Gospel of John in a nutshell, and it appears in one of Paul's earlier epistles! Kuschel takes no notice at all of the parallel between Paul's two "sending" statements,[24] and Dunn comments on it only in relation to the suggestion, which he rejects, that Paul's statement about the Son being sent echoes a similar statement about wisdom in the apocryphal book of Wisdom.[25]

The same pattern emerges in Romans 8:3, where we have (1) the statement of "God . . . sending his own Son," (2) the qualification that the "sending" was "in the likeness of sinful flesh," and (3) the contrast between the Son who comes in our likeness and the mass of (mere) human beings whom he saves by doing so (see v. 4).[26]

The first element includes the seemingly redundant "own," indicating that this was not a member of a larger class of "sons of God" but someone to whom that designation applied uniquely. As commentator John Murray noted, "In the language of Paul this corresponds to the title 'only begotten' as it appears in John (John 1:14, 18; 3:16, 18; 1 John 4:9),"[27] and, we may add, to the description "beloved" in the Synoptic Gospels.

The second element, "in the likeness of sinful flesh," involves a cumbersome locution if Jesus was no more than a human being. Nor is this the only

place where Paul seems constrained to qualify Jesus' humanity by such a cir-
cumlocution. In Philippians he says that Christ was "born in human likeness"
and "found in human form" (2:7). The former statement seems unnecessarily awkward and the latter statement unnecessarily redundant if Jesus began
his existence as a human being. In Romans the apostle comments that the
Christ is from the Jews "according to the flesh" (Rom. 9:5), again suggesting
that Christ's human ancestry is not a complete explanation for his existence.

The third element, the contrast between God's Son and his other "sons,"
is immediately apparent from the second element and receives extensive
elaboration in the rest of Romans 8, including a discussion of the status of
believers as adopted sons of God (vv. 14–17), just as in Galatians 4. The convergence of these elements results in a statement that presupposes that God's
Son existed as other than a person of flesh before he came in our likeness to
redeem us as adopted sons of God. It is true that Paul is not articulating or
defending a doctrine of the preexistence of the Son. Rather, he presupposes
the Son's preexistence as he articulates his message of what this divine Son
has done for us by becoming a man and suffering death on our account.[28]

John: The Son Came, the Son Returned

The Gospel of John contains numerous statements about the Son being
"sent" and that imply his preexistence. The following may be noted (see also
John 7:29, 33; 8:14; 9:39; 12:45; 17:8):

> If God were your Father, you would love me, for I came from God
> and now I am here. I did not come on my own, but he sent me.
> (8:42)

> Can you say that the one whom the Father has sanctified and sent
> into the world is blaspheming because I said, "I am God's Son"?
> (10:36)

> Jesus, knowing that the Father had given all things into his hands,
> and that he had come from God and was going to God . . . (13:3)

> I came from the Father and have come into the world; again, I am
> leaving the world and am going to the Father. (16:28)

As McCready says in his study of the preexistence of Christ, "These statements from John differ from similar ones in the Synoptics only in being more explicit."[29] John 13:3 and 16:28, which frame the Upper Room Discourse (John 13–16) prior to Jesus' prayer, are especially significant. In these statements John (in 13:3) and Jesus (in 16:28) assert that Jesus came from God the Father into the world and was about to leave the world and go to God the Father. The verbal contrast between "coming" and "going" makes it clear that Jesus was returning to the Father's side from where he had come.[30]

If Jesus existed in heaven before he was born as a human being on earth, how long had he preexisted? As we will see in the next chapter, his preexistence stretches back indefinitely into the past, even beyond the creation of the universe.

Chapter 8

JESUS HAS ALWAYS BEEN THERE

S ome religious groups today acknowledge that Jesus existed before his physical birth and life here on earth, but they deny that he is God. They argue that he existed as one of many created spirits in heaven, although perhaps as the greatest of those spirits. Such a statement might be made about Michael or Gabriel or any other angel. In this chapter, we will see that such an understanding of Jesus' preexistence misses the point. When the New Testament speaks of Christ's preexistence, it does so in a way that shows that he has *always* existed and that he is a preexistent, even eternal, divine person. We already have seen some evidence for this conclusion in Philippians 2:6, but the idea is present throughout the New Testament.

They Knew Him When

Consistent with the evidence we have seen so far, the New Testament speaks of Jesus Christ as being present and involved in Israel's history as recorded in the Old Testament. We will look at four statements reflecting this understanding—one from the Synoptics, one from Paul, one from John, and one from the epistle of Jude.

Jesus' Long History with Jerusalem

Both Matthew and Luke report Jesus saying the following:

O Jerusalem, Jerusalem, the one who kills the prophets and stones those who are sent to her! How often I wanted to gather your children together, as a hen gathers her chicks under her wings, but you were not willing! (Matt. 23:37; Luke 13:34 NKJV)

At first glance this saying might not seem to imply Jesus' preexistence, but in context it does. The statement that the people of Jerusalem "were not willing" refers to the times in the past when, instead of accepting the divine protection they were offered, they killed the prophets sent to warn them of impending judgment. In other words, Jesus is saying that he often tried in the past to protect them from judgment by sending them prophets, but they rejected the offer of help. The only alternative view with any plausibility is that Jesus is referring to several previous visits to Jerusalem during his human life. The saying appears to refer to past occasions, however, when the city's refusal resulted in its judgment—something that occurred repeatedly in Jerusalem's long history but not in the three or four years prior to Jesus' death. Furthermore, although the Gospel of John indicates that Jesus had visited Jerusalem three times previously during his human ministry (John 2:13; 5:1; 7:10), Matthew says nothing about such previous visits. As Gathercole points out, "Within the narrative of Matthew's Gospel, Jesus has neither been to Jerusalem, nor expressed any feeling about the city in his ministry up to this point."[1]

That Jesus is claiming to be the one who sent prophets and other emissaries is confirmed in his earlier statement in the same passage in Matthew: "I send you prophets, sages, and scribes, some of whom you will kill and crucify, and some you will flog in your synagogues and pursue from town to town" (Matt. 23:34).[2] Jesus is here referring to the messengers from among his disciples who will later suffer for their testimony to him, but when read together with verse 37, it appears that Jesus is claiming to be the one who also sent such messengers in the past. In the Old Testament and in other ancient Jewish literature it was, of course, *God* who sent prophets. Jesus' lament that the Jews would not heed his repeated warnings through prophets and other messengers especially recalls the judgment expressed at the end of the books of Chronicles:

The LORD, the God of their fathers, sent word to them through his messengers again and again, because he had pity on his people and on his dwelling place. But they mocked God's messengers, despised his words and scoffed at his prophets until the wrath of the LORD was aroused against his people and there was no remedy. (2 Chron. 36:15–16 NIV)

Furthermore, the metaphor that Jesus uses, comparing himself to a mother hen seeking to shelter her chicks under her wings, is familiar from the Old Testament and other ancient Jewish sources as descriptive of God's offer of protection to his people (Deut. 32:11; Ruth 2:12; Pss. 17:8; 36:7; 57:1; 61:4; 63:7; 91:4).[3] We have good reason, then, to understand Jesus to be making a divine claim here. He is claiming not only to have been around during Old Testament times but also to have been the one who protected Israel when they were faithful and sent them prophets and other messengers whom they all too often rejected.[4]

Paul: The Israelites and Christ in the Wilderness

Paul's rather enigmatic statement about the Israelites in the wilderness probably refers to Christ as having been involved in its earliest history: "For they drank from the spiritual rock that followed them, and the rock was Christ" (1 Cor. 10:4). This statement appears to be a reference to Christ's real preexistence, although some interpreters think Paul meant that the "rock" is a *type* of Christ. The latter view, however, does not easily fit Paul's statement that "the rock *was* Christ."[5] A few sentences later, Paul warns the Corinthian Christians, "We must not put Christ to the test, as some of them did, and were destroyed by serpents" (v. 9). Here, Paul states that some of the Israelites in the wilderness "put Christ to the test," and he warns the Corinthians not to make the same mistake. Although some ancient Greek manuscripts have the reading "Lord," the NRSV is almost certainly correct here in following the reading "Christ."[6] Therefore, we should understand Paul to have been affirming that Christ existed during the time of the Israelites' wandering in the wilderness. Moreover, what Paul says here about Christ is what the Old Testament said about the Lord God: that the Israelites had put him to the test (Num. 14:22; 21:5–6; Pss. 78:18–20; 95:9). Once again, the New Testament affirms not only Christ's preexistence but also his *divine* preexistence.

John: Jesus, Abraham, and Isaiah

In two passages in the Gospel of John in contexts that equate him with God, Jesus claims to have been around in the days of the Old Testament. In the first of these passages, Jesus claims to have antedated Abraham in a way that connotes eternal, divine preexistence:

> "Your ancestor Abraham rejoiced that he would see my day; he saw it and was glad." Then the Jews said to him, "You are not yet fifty years old, and have you seen Abraham?" Jesus said to them, "Very truly, I tell you, before Abraham was, I am." So they picked up stones to throw at him, but Jesus hid himself and went out of the temple. (8:56–59)

At a bare minimum, and beyond any reasonable doubt, Jesus here claims to have existed before Abraham was born. English versions that are designed to give smooth, highly readable English renderings often translate Jesus' statement in verse 58 to express this undeniable point very clearly: "The truth is, I existed before Abraham was even born!" (NLT). A few biblical scholars have argued that something along these lines is the most accurate translation. K. L. McKay, a Greek grammarian, has asserted that the most natural translation is "I have been in existence since before Abraham was born." McKay rightly notes that "the claim to have been in existence for so long is in itself a staggering one."[7]

Most biblical scholars agree, but go farther: Jesus' statement in John 8:58 expresses not only existence prior to Abraham but also existence of a different order than that of Abraham. That is, they understand Jesus to be affirming that his existence antecedent to that of Abraham was the eternal preexistence of deity. John 8:58 contrasts Abraham, who "came into being" (*genesthai*, translated "was" in the NRSV), with Jesus, who simply *is* (which Jesus states in the first person, "I am," *egō eimi*). The statement recalls a classic affirmation of the eternal being of God in the Old Testament: "Before the mountains came into being [*genēthēnai*, the passive form of *genesthai*] and the earth and the world were formed, even from age to age, you are [*su ei*, the second-person equivalent of *egō eimi*]" (Ps. 90:2 [89:2 in LXX]).[8] The Greek sentence here reflects the same grammatical structure as John 8:58 and uses the same verbs to make the same contrast between that which is created and temporal and the one who is uncreated and eternal.[9]

The reaction of Jesus' critics to his statement—attempting to stone him (John 8:59)—confirms that they thought he was making a divine claim. Had Jesus stated only that he had been alive longer than Abraham, they might have regarded such a claim as crazy (as they apparently did with regard to his earlier comments, vv. 48–57), but not as an offense meriting stoning. Of the offenses for which Jews practiced stoning, the only one that seems to fit the context here is blasphemy. Claiming to be older than Abraham might have been judged crazy, but it would not have been judged as blasphemy. Speaking as if one were Abraham's eternal God, on the other hand, would be quickly deemed blasphemous by Jesus' critics, who of course did not recognize his divine claims as valid.

In another passage in his Gospel, John comments on the failure of many of the people to believe in Jesus despite the many miracles they had witnessed him perform.

> Although he had performed so many signs in their presence, they did not believe in him. . . . And so they could not believe, because Isaiah also said, "He has blinded their eyes and hardened their heart, so that they might not look with their eyes, and understand with their heart and turn—and I would heal them." Isaiah said this because he saw his glory and spoke about him. (12:37, 39–41)

The quotation in this passage is from Isaiah 6:10, part of the passage in which Isaiah recounts his call to the prophetic ministry. When John says that Isaiah "saw his glory," he means the glory of Jesus as the context makes clear (vv. 36–38; see also 1:14). But in the context of Isaiah 6, the glory that Isaiah saw was the glory of the Lord.

> In the year that King Uzziah died, *I saw the Lord* sitting on a throne, high and lofty; and the hem of his robe filled the temple. Seraphs were in attendance above him; each had six wings: with two they covered their faces, and with two they covered their feet, and with two they flew. And one called to another and said: "Holy, holy, holy is the LORD of hosts; the whole earth is full of *his glory*." (vv. 1–3, emphasis added)

Here again, John speaks of Jesus not only as having existed during Old

Testament times but also as having been the glorious Lord who spoke to and through the prophets. Thus this passage is another affirmation in the New Testament of the divine preexistence of Jesus Christ.

Jude: Jesus Saved Israel and Destroyed the Unbelievers

A similar statement often overlooked in these discussions comes in the short epistle of Jude. Jude warns his readers about those "who pervert the grace of our God into licentiousness and deny our only Master and Lord, Jesus Christ" (Jude 4). Immediately after that warning, he starts giving examples from Jewish history, beginning with the Israelites' apostasy in the wilderness.

> Now I desire to remind you, though you are fully informed, that the Lord, who once for all saved a people out of the land of Egypt, afterward destroyed those who did not believe. (v. 5)

After speaking of Jesus Christ as "our only Master and Lord," Jude could hardly have proceeded in the very next sentence to refer to someone other than Jesus as "the Lord." The Lord who delivered his people out of Egypt, then, must be the Lord Jesus.

In fact, this is probably what the original text of Jude explicitly said. Many of the earliest manuscripts actually say "Jesus" instead of "the Lord" in verse 5, and this is most likely the original reading.[10] There are three principles of the discipline of textual criticism that, when considered together, point to this conclusion.

The first principle concerns the external evidence of the origins of the manuscripts. All other things being equal, the earlier and more widely attested reading is to be preferred. In this case both "Lord" and "Jesus" are among the earliest readings,[11] but "Jesus" is more widely attested. The Vaticanus and Alexandrinus uncials (fourth and fifth centuries, respectively) both have "Jesus," while the Sinaiticus and C uncials (also of the fourth and fifth centuries) are the major witnesses for "Lord." The reading "Jesus," though, has much greater support from the early translations of the New Testament into other languages (such as Coptic, Ethiopic, and Latin) and better support from the early church's leading biblical scholars, including Jerome (early fifth century) and possibly the third-century Origen.[12] The reading "Jesus," then, clearly has the edge in terms of external evidence.

The second principle is that, all other things being equal, the harder or more difficult reading—the one that sounds the strangest, to put it crudely—is more likely to be original (since a scribe is more likely to change a text from something that sounds strange to something that doesn't, rather than the other way around). Here, the reading "Jesus" obviously has the edge. Three of the five members of the editorial committee for the United Bible Societies' Greek New Testament thought, in fact, "that the reading was difficult to the point of impossibility."[13] The other two committee members, Bruce Metzger and Allen Wikgren, agreed it was difficult but not impossible, and concluded that it was the correct reading.

The third and most general principle is that whatever reading is more likely to have given rise to the others as alterations is probably the original reading. The answer to this question is much disputed, but we agree with those who argue that "Jesus" is probably original because it is more likely that scribes would change "Jesus" (the admittedly harder reading) to "Lord" (or, in a few other manuscripts, "God") but not vice versa.

Whichever reading we follow, though, Jude's immediately preceding reference to Jesus as "Lord" at the end of verse 4 makes it clear that he is the subject of verse 5. According to Jude, the Lord Jesus not only existed during the time of the Exodus but was the one who both delivered Israel from Egypt and then destroyed the unbelieving Israelites in the wilderness.

Jesus: Older Than Dirt—Literally!

The New Testament pushes the existence of the Son of God back long before the days of Israel. It teaches that Christ was around—and involved—in the creation of the world! We will explore this point fully in part 4 when we discuss the deeds or works of God that Christ performs, but we should take some notice of the main biblical statements now. Paul wrote that "in him [God's Son] all things in heaven and on earth were created, things visible and invisible, whether thrones or dominions or rulers or powers—all things have been created through him and for him" (Col. 1:16). Paul's statement here clearly means that the Son existed before all things were created. What Paul says, of course, also distinguishes God's Son from the entire realm of all creation. The apostle John agreed: "All things came into being through him, and without him not one thing came into being. . . . He was in the world, and the world came into being through him; yet the world did not know him" (John 1:3, 10). The book of Hebrews says that God "has spoken to us by a Son, whom he appointed heir of all things, through whom he also created the worlds" (1:2). The logic is simple enough: "If indeed everything came into being through Christ, then there is no option other than that he existed before that creation."[14]

In all three of these passages, the authors make other statements that confirm their meaning—the person known as Jesus Christ preexisted creation. After saying that all things were created in, through, and for the Son, Paul adds, "He himself is before all things, and in him all things hold together" (Col. 1:17). Paul here states emphatically that the Son exists prior to all creation.[15] Since the creation of the universe is also the beginning of time (Heb. 1:2),[16] to say that Christ exists "before" creation is to say in effect that he has always existed—that his existence had no beginning. Paul's statement in an earlier epistle that Christians believe in "one Lord, Jesus Christ, through whom are all things and through whom we exist" (1 Cor. 8:6) should likewise be understood to entail his existence before creation.

Just before John states that all things came into existence through Christ—whom he calls the "Word" (*logos*)—John says, "In the beginning was the Word" (John 1:1). Here, John asserts that the Word already existed "in the beginning," hearkening back to the beginning of creation (cf. Gen. 1:1). That "the Word" was a person, and not some abstraction, is made clear by John's next statement, "and the Word was with God" (*pros ton theon*, 1:1). The word *pros* (here translated "with") in this context denotes personal association with someone else, as is confirmed later in the same Gospel when John says that Jesus was going "to depart from this world and go to the Father [*pros ton patera*]" and that he "had come from God and was going to God [*pros ton theon*]" (John 13:1, 3; see also John 7:33; 14:12, 28; 16:5, 10, 17, 28; 20:17). The one who was close to God the Father in the very beginning had come from him and was about to depart and go back to be close to him again.

The Gospel of John also reports that Jesus referred to his preexistence before creation in his majestic prayer to the Father: "So now, Father, glorify me in your own presence with the glory that I had in your presence before the world existed" (John 17:5). It is difficult to imagine a more explicit affirmation of Christ's existence before creation. To these statements we may add Jesus' statement, "Before Abraham came into being, I am" (John 8:58, literal translation), which we discussed earlier.

The book of Hebrews accentuates and confirms the preexistence of the Son in another way. In backing up his opening statements about the Son from Old Testament Scriptures, the writer quotes Psalm 102:25–27, which in its original context is speaking about the Lord God, and applies it to the Son:

> In the beginning, Lord, you founded the earth,
>   and the heavens are the work of your hands;
> they will perish, but you remain;
>   they will all wear out like clothing;
> like a cloak you will roll them up,
>   and like clothing they will be changed.
> But you are the same,
>   and your years will never end.
>   (Heb. 1:10–12)

Here once again we see that the New Testament is not content with affirming that Jesus merely preexisted; it affirms his preexistence in a way that equates him with the Lord God himself.[17]

Chapter 9

JESUS: THE RIGHT STUFF

In our discussion of Christ's divine attributes, we have seen that he is described in general terms as having the nature of God. Indeed, Scripture states that he is exactly like God (or the Father) and that the "fullness" of what it means to be God dwells in him (John 14:9–10; Col. 1:15, 19; 2:9; Heb. 1:3). We also have seen that these statements do not refer to Jesus merely as a man through whom we learn what God "is really like"; rather they refer to someone who existed as a heavenly, divine being before coming to earth as a human being. We saw that Christ, in fact, has *always* existed, even before creation (Matt. 20:28; 23:34, 37; John 1:1–3; 8:56–59; 12:39–41; 16:28; 17:5; Rom. 8:3; 1 Cor. 8:6; 10:4, 9; Gal. 4:4–6; Phil. 2:6; Col. 1:16–17; Heb. 1:2, 10–12; Jude 5). In this chapter and the next, we will show that the Son of God possesses a wide array of specific attributes of God.

He Wasn't Made: Christ Is Uncreated

Perhaps the most fundamental specific attribute of God that separates him from everything that is not God is that he is *uncreated*. If this attribute is true of Christ, and he is a real, existent being, then he is by definition God. On the other hand, if Christ were by nature a created being, then it would not make much sense to speak of him as God.

The very fact that Christ has always existed implies, of course, that he is uncreated. His being uncreated has even more direct support from Scripture. In the previous chapter we drew attention to various biblical statements affirming that creation came into existence in and through the Son (John 1:3, 10; 1 Cor. 8:6; Col. 1:16; Heb. 1:2, 10–12). Some of these statements emphasize in the strongest terms that not just part, but the totality of creation owes its existence to him. "For in him *all things* in heaven and on earth were created, things visible and invisible, whether thrones or dominions or rulers or powers—*all things* have been created through him and for him" (Col. 1:16, emphasis added). Here, the apostle Paul states explicitly that the totality of all created things, including both heavenly, invisible beings and earthly, visible beings, was created through the Son. Speaking of the preexistent Son under the designation of the Word (*Logos*), the apostle John asserts, "*All things* came into being through him, and without him *not one thing* came into being" (John 1:3, emphasis added). The second clause states explicitly and emphatically that there is no exception to the universal statement of the first clause: not so much as one thing came into being except through Christ, the Word. No more sweeping, explicit statements can be imagined. Absolutely everything that was created, that "came into being," did so in and through Christ. If every created thing owes its existence to the Son, then the Son himself cannot be a created being.[1]

"Firstborn of All Creation": First Created Being?

As clear, explicit, and emphatic as these statements are, not everyone is convinced. Some religious groups, notably the Jehovah's Witnesses, argue that God created the Son as the very first of his creatures and then gave him the power to participate in the work of bringing the rest of creation into existence. They routinely cite three biblical texts in support of this claim, the first of which is adjacent to one of the texts we have just cited to prove the contrary. In Colossians 1:15, Paul calls God's Son "the firstborn of all creation." Like the Arians in the fourth century, Jehovah's Witnesses contend that this phrase means that the Son was the first and greatest of all creatures, but just a created being nonetheless.

Although the Arian interpretation of "the firstborn of all creation" has some surface plausibility if one takes it out of context, the evidence of the context is decisively against it. First, as we have already pointed out, verse 16 asserts in the strongest and most explicit terms possible that all created things were created in, through, and for the Son. If verse 15 were to mean that the Son was the first thing created, Paul would be flatly contradicting himself from one sentence to the next. He would be saying, "The Son is the first thing created, because everything was created in, through, and for him."

As commentator Murray Harris has pointed out, "If Paul had believed that Jesus was the first of God's creatures to be formed," verse 16 "would have continued 'for all other things were created in him.'"[2] Notoriously, the Jehovah's Witnesses have fixed the problem by adding the word *other* four times to Colossians 1:16–17. Paul is thus made to say,

> By means of him all [other] things were created in the heavens and upon the earth, the things visible and the things invisible, no matter whether they are thrones or lordships or governments or authorities. All [other] things have been created through him and for him. Also, he is before all [other] things and by means of him all [other] things were made to exist. (Col. 1:16–17 NWT, brackets in the original)

In an article that appeared the same year as the New World Translation, the publishers explained the reasoning behind their addition of the word *other* to the passage:

> But now trinitarians confront you with Paul's words at Colossians 1:15–20 according to the *King James Version*. They argue that, if Jesus Christ was before all things and all things consist by him and were created by him and for him, then he must be the very same as the Almighty, Most High God, or be one person with God. But we must harmonize these verses with all the other scriptures that Jesus Christ was God's Son and a creation of His. So the Greek word here must be rendered in the sense of "all other." Note, then, how the *New World Translation* blasts the trinitarian argument.[3]

One could not ask for a more candid explanation: the translators added the word *other* to make Colossians 1:16–17 cohere with their theological assumptions. Read the passage (even in the NWT) without adding *other* and the text clearly affirms that absolutely every created thing was created in, through, and for the Son.[4]

Second, the description "firstborn of all creation" is best understood to mean that the Son is the principal heir of all creation. Notice how this interpretation makes perfect sense in the immediate context: the Son is the principal heir of all creation (v. 15) because everything was created in, through, and for him (v. 16). The Son's inheritance, which the Father has graciously qualified us to share, is the subject in the broader context of the passage (vv.

12–14). The Old Testament background for this use of the term *firstborn* is found in a messianic passage describing David, the royal figure who anticipates the coming Messiah, as "the firstborn, the highest of the kings of the earth" (Ps. 89:27).[5] This statement did not mean, of course, that David (or Christ) was the first one born among all the kings of the earth. Rather, it refers to David (as a type of the Messiah) as the preeminent ruler, God's heir, the one who rules as his son in his stead (see also Ps. 2:2, 6–8).[6] Paul's description of the Son as "firstborn of all creation" is thus equivalent to the description in Hebrews of the Son as "heir of all things" (Heb. 1:2; cf. Heb. 1:6).[7]

Jehovah's Witnesses argue that the expression "of all creation" (*pasēs ktiseōs*) is a partitive genitive, meaning that the "firstborn" is being classified as part of "all creation." Such an interpretation is grammatically possible but contextually very unlikely. In context "all creation" is the inheritance or the estate to which the Son is the primary heir because, as Paul puts it, "all things have been created through him and *for* him" (v. 16). The word *for* (*eis*) indicates that all creation was created to belong to the Son.[8]

Finally, it is possible to interpret the expression "firstborn of all creation" as a partitive genitive without concluding that the Son was the first creature God made. Some exegetes have suggested that the expression means that the Son, by virtue of becoming a man in the Incarnation, *became* part of creation and as such is its "firstborn" or most honored member. The logic of Paul's reasoning from verse 15 to verse 16 (the Son is the firstborn of all creation *because* everything was created in, through, and for him) really requires, though, that in this context the Son be distinguished from "all creation." In any case, then, Colossians 1:15 does not teach that the Son was the first creature whom God made.

Is Christ a Created Wisdom?

A second proof-text that Jehovah's Witnesses and others claim as proof that Christ was created is a statement about wisdom that appears in the book of Proverbs. The statement in question reads as follows in the NRSV: "The LORD created me at the beginning of his work, the first of his acts of long ago" (8:22). Jehovah's Witnesses reason as follows: If this "wisdom" was created, then it cannot be God's intrinsic attribute of wisdom but must refer to a created being called Wisdom; and since the New Testament speaks of Christ as wisdom (e.g., 1 Cor. 1:30), the created being called Wisdom in Proverbs 8 must be Christ.

The translation "created" in Proverbs 8:22 originates with the Greek Septuagint, which used the word *ektisen*, meaning "created" or "made." There are good reasons to think, however, that this is a mistranslation. The Hebrew word in question, *qanah*, occurs fifteen times in the book of Proverbs, always (unless 8:22 is the sole exception) with the meaning "get" or "acquire." In fact, Proverbs uses *qanah* several times in exhortations to human beings to get or acquire wisdom (Prov. 4:5a, 7a; 16:16a; 17:16; 19:8) and, in other texts, to get counsel, understanding, knowledge, and truth (Prov. 1:5; 4:5b, 7b; 15:32; 16:16b; 18:15; 23:23).[9] It would be odd if, after stating several times that people should "get" wisdom, the book were to speak of God "getting" wisdom and mean rather that he created it.[10]

God did not, of course, literally "get" or "acquire" his attribute of wisdom; he has always "had" it. There are two possible ways of understanding Proverbs 8:22. First, it might be saying that God established the "wisdom" of the created order before he actually made anything in the physical universe. This understanding fits the NRSV translation (even, in a way, the use of "created"): "The LORD created me at the beginning of his work, *the first of his acts of long ago*" (emphasis added). In other words, if this interpretation is correct, Proverbs 8:22 is not talking about God's own attribute of wisdom but about the wisdom that God incorporated into his creation. Second, Proverbs 8:22 might be a poetic way of saying that God has always "had" wisdom. This understanding fits other translations: "The LORD possessed me at the beginning of His way, *Before His works of old*" (NASB, emphasis added).[11]

Either way, the text is not speaking of the creation of a personal being, whether the preexistent Christ or anyone else. In the context of the book of Proverbs, this one verse is part of a larger unit in which the writer personifies wisdom as a dignified woman who cries out in the city and urges people to listen to her counsel (Prov. 8:1–36; see also 1:20–33; 9:1–6). In this context Proverbs 8:22 is simply a highly poetic way of saying that God created the world with wisdom.[12] To the extent that what Proverbs says about wisdom also is true about Christ, we may draw some comparisons between Christ and wisdom; but we should not make the mistake of treating an Old Testament poetic statement about wisdom as if it were a doctrinal proposition about Christ.

"The Beginning of God's Creation": The First Being God Created?

The third and last major proof-text commonly used to support the

doctrine that God created Christ is Jesus' self-description in the book of
Revelation as "The Amen, the faithful and true Witness, the Beginning of
the creation of God" (Rev. 3:14 NASB). The issue here is the meaning of the
Greek word *archē*, which the NASB and other versions (e.g., NKJV, ESV) translate "Beginning." Other translations render the word as "origin" (NRSV) or
"source" (NAB), or as "ruler" (NIV).

It is fair to say that any of these translations is possible; the question is,
Which is most likely to be correct? In the Arian controversy of the fourth century, Revelation 3:14 apparently was not one of the Arian proof-texts for their
belief that Christ was a created being.[13] The church fathers from as early as
the second-century apologist Justin Martyr generally understood the verse to
mean that Christ was the "origin" of creation, meaning not that Christ himself
had an origin (which would make him a creature) but that creation originated
in and through him. Until recently, this view seems to have been held by the
majority of those who have written commentaries on the book of Revelation.
Modern commentaries advocating this interpretation include (to name just a
few) George Ladd, Leon Morris, and Robert Mounce.[14] The meaning "origin"
or "source" fits the use of *archē* for God in Revelation, "the beginning and the
end" (21:6; 22:13), making this interpretation quite possible.

An alternative interpretation with much to commend it is that *archē* in
Revelation 3:14 means "ruler." In most, if not all, other New Testament texts
referring to persons, *archē* is used to mean ruler in both the singular (1 Cor.
15:24; Eph. 1:21; Col. 2:10; and possibly Col. 1:18) and plural (Luke 12:11;
Rom. 8:38; Eph. 3:10; 6:12; Col. 1:16; 2:15; Titus 3:1). Moreover, the context offers some support for the meaning to be "ruler." Jesus' statement in Revelation
3:14 comes at the beginning of his message to the Laodicean church (3:14–
22). At the end of that message, Jesus promises a place on his throne to those
who conquer (3:21). Two of the three descriptions of Jesus in Revelation 3:14
also strongly echo two of the descriptions of Jesus in Revelation 1:5. This
suggests that *archē* in Revelation 3:14 may have a meaning similar to *archōn*
in Revelation 1:5 ("the *ruler* of the kings of the earth").[15]

Jehovah's Witnesses insist that both of these explanations are wrong and
that the text must mean that Christ is the "beginning," that is, the chronologically first member of God's creation. Greg Stafford defends this claim, arguing that *archē* followed by a genitive expression (such as "of God's creation,"
tēs ktiseōs tou theou) normally means "beginning" and the genitive is normally partitive.[16] We encountered a similar argument before in Colossians

1:15 with regard to "firstborn" (*prōtotokos*) followed by a genitive expression. Here as well, the generalization does not hold up. There are texts that fit the generalization—although their relevance to Revelation 3:14 is tenuous at best[17]—and other texts that do not.[18] At most, the Jehovah's Witnesses' view of Revelation 3:14 is possible, but it is not the most likely.

On close examination, then, these three proof-texts for the belief that Christ is a created being (Col. 1:15; Prov. 8:22; Rev. 3:14) do not teach that doctrine. They cannot overturn the clear, explicit teaching of the New Testament that the whole of creation, and indeed every created thing, owes its existence to Jesus Christ (John 1:3, 10; 1 Cor. 8:6; Col. 1:16; Heb. 1:2, 10–12). That fact sets him apart from all creation and demonstrates that he is uncreated.

He Won't Change: Christ Is Immutable

Immutability is an important but often misunderstood attribute of God. When we say that God is immutable, we mean that God is unchangeable in his essential nature, character, and purposes. We do not mean that God is static, lifeless, unresponsive, or unaffected by what happens in his creation. God's immutability has to do with "the divine reliability, the constancy of God's purpose, the trustworthiness of the divine nature."[19] If God says he is going to do something, we can rely on him to keep his word (Num. 23:19). Although we live in a world marred by evil, we can trust confidently in God's absolute goodness, knowing that he is not even tempted to do evil and that in his case "there is no variation or shadow due to change" (James 1:17).[20]

One of the last statements that God made in the Old Testament was a ringing affirmation of his immutability: "For I the LORD do not change" (Mal. 3:6). In context, God is assuring the Jews that he will both follow through on his warnings of judgment against the unrepentant and yet keep his promises to the Jews to preserve them as a people. That God declares his unchangeable character right at the close of the Old Testament era is a striking reminder that for all of the differences between the Old and New Testaments, they reveal one unchanging God.

Other than Malachi 3:6, perhaps the best-known statement of divine immutability in the Bible comes from the Psalms:

> Long ago you laid the foundation of the earth,
>   and the heavens are the work of your hands.
> They will perish, but you endure;

> they will all wear out like a garment.
> You change them like clothing, and they pass away;
> but you are the same, and your years have no end.
> (Ps. 102:25–27)

The physical universe is the most enduring, permanent reality we can see; yet in comparison to God it is ever changing.

For first-century Judaism, the contrast between the mutable, changeable universe and the immutable, changeless God was basic to their worldview. It was a revolutionary thought, then, to apply the description of God's immutability in Psalm 102 to Jesus Christ. This is exactly what the book of Hebrews does (Heb. 1:10–12). It quotes Psalm 102:25–27 verbatim as a statement about "the Son" (see vv. 8, 10).[21] This is just one of a series of Old Testament quotations that the author, in the first chapter of Hebrews, applies to the Son to demonstrate his superiority to the angels. The book of Hebrews also climaxes with an affirmation of Christ's immutability: "Jesus Christ is the same yesterday and today and forever" (13:8).

Clearly, the New Testament does not understand divine immutability to be a limitation on God's ability to interact with and in his creation. In this regard, Christianity goes beyond Judaism without contradicting it. On the other hand, it is on this point that Christianity and Islam stand in sharpest contrast theologically. Islam views God's immutability and transcendence to be incompatible with the idea of God becoming incarnate. New Testament Christianity, however, declares that God can and has done just that.

Paradoxically, it is in the Incarnation that we learn just how constant and dependable God is in his essential character. On the one hand, Jesus experienced ordinary human growth and development from infancy to childhood to adulthood (Luke 2:7, 21, 40, 52; 3:23). On the other hand, even from his youth Jesus manifested a constancy and single-mindedness of purpose that he carried to the very end of his mortal life and beyond (Luke 2:49; 19:45–48; 23:46; 24:46–49). As Paul points out, in Christ we see the fulfillment of God's promises: "For in him every one of God's promises is a 'Yes'" (2 Cor. 1:20). Gordon Lewis and Bruce Demarest, in their textbook on systematic theology, make the following observation:

> The meaning of immutability is vividly illustrated throughout Christ's past active ministry on earth. While moving from weddings

to funerals, from greedy tax collectors to the poor and powerless, from harlots to self-righteous Pharisees, from the ill to the demonized, he changelessly remained just, loving, and wise. Deeply moved by experiences of caring, temptations, and tragedies, Christ never lost his integrity.[22]

You Can't Out-give Him: Christ Is Loving

If there is one thing that virtually everyone who has ever heard of Christ acknowledges about him, it is that he was a person of unparalleled love. What most people miss, though, is that Jesus' love demonstrates that he is more than a great human being. Consider Paul's prayer for Christians to know "the love of Christ":

> . . . that you, being rooted and grounded in love, may be able to comprehend with all the saints what is the breadth and length and height and depth, and to know the love of Christ which surpasses knowledge, that you may be filled up to all the fullness of God. (Eph. 3:17b–19 NASB)

Can anyone imagine speaking this way about the love of any other human being? Think of anyone else in history renowned for being a loving person. Would anyone speak of the love of Mother Teresa, for example, as surpassing knowledge? Would anyone imagine that by coming to know her love, one would have the fullness of God in one's life? From what we know of Mother Teresa, she would be the first to protest against viewing her in that way.

Yet not only did Paul view Jesus in that way (see also Rom. 8:35–39; Gal. 2:20; Eph. 5:2), Jesus himself instructed his disciples to look to him as the supreme example of love.

> I give you a new commandment, that you love one another. Just as I have loved you, you also should love one another. . . . This is my commandment, that you love one another as I have loved you. No one has greater love than this, to lay down one's life for one's friends. (John 13:34; 15:12–13)

In claiming to be the supreme example of love, Jesus was not elevating himself above the Father. He did explicitly claim, however, to have loved his disciples with the same love that the Father had toward him: "As the Father has loved me, so I have loved you; abide in my love" (John 15:9). This would be quite a daring, even outrageous, claim on the part of any mere creature, no matter how grand. Yet Jesus' claim strikes almost no one as brash or overstated. Jesus is like this on practically every page of the Gospels. He calmly makes claims that would seem arrogant—if not megalomaniacal—coming from anyone else, yet somehow at the same time he conveys the deepest sincerity and even humility.

For the New Testament Christians, the love of Christ was not the love of the greatest man who ever lived, although he was that as well: it was the love of God himself, expressed in and through Christ.

> For God so loved the world that he gave his only Son, so that everyone who believes in him may not perish but may have eternal life. (John 3:16)

> But God proves his love for us in that while we still were sinners Christ died for us. (Rom. 5:8)

> Who will separate us from the love of Christ? Will hardship, or distress, or persecution, or famine, or nakedness, or peril, or sword? As it is written, "For your sake we are being killed all day long; we are accounted as sheep to be slaughtered." No, in all these things we are more than conquerors through him who loved us. For I am convinced that neither death, nor life, nor angels, nor rulers, nor things present, nor things to come, nor powers, nor height, nor depth, nor anything else in all creation, will be able to separate us from the love of God in Christ Jesus our Lord. (Rom. 8:35–39)

> To him who loves us and freed us from our sins by his blood, and made us to be a kingdom, priests serving his God and Father, to him be glory and dominion forever and ever. Amen. (Rev. 1:5b–6)

Truly, recognizing the love of Jesus Christ as the very love of God for us ought to move us to give Christ glory forever. That is what it means to honor Jesus as God.

Chapter 10

HE'S GOT WHAT IT TAKES

When we think of attributes of God that are exclusively his (the "incommunicable" attributes), we are likely to think especially of the three famous "omni" attributes: omnipotence (God is all-powerful), omnipresence (God is present everywhere), and omniscience (God is all-knowing). As we shall see, all three of these attributes belong to Jesus Christ, although in a paradoxical way due to his having assumed human nature to accomplish our salvation.

He Can: Christ Is Omnipotent

Omnipotence is the divine attribute of being all-powerful. It does not mean that God can do anything that is self-contradictory (like the old saw about God making a rock so big he cannot lift it) or contrary to his perfect character. For example, when the Bible says that God cannot lie (Titus 1:2; Heb. 6:18), it is not denying his omnipotence. Omnipotence also does not obligate God to do everything he can do. It does not, for example, obligate him to intervene and prevent the specific occurrences of evil that take place in the world. In keeping with his own purposes for creation, he chooses to allow bad things to happen and to allow the consequences of evil actions to unfold, intervening (miraculously) only in select situations for purposes of revealing himself and bringing redemption to the world. When, for example, Job confessed, "I know that you can do all things, and that no purpose of yours can be thwarted" (Job 42:2), he was acknowledging that his suffering was not due to any lack of power on God's part. God *could* have prevented

Job's suffering or intervened sooner; he simply chose not to do so, in keeping with his own good purposes.

The New Testament teaches that Jesus Christ, God's Son, is omnipotent. Before we look at the evidence for this claim, we should reflect for a moment on how absurd it must have seemed to people in the first century. Jesus was a man, and human life is a constant experience of limitations. Like all people, Jesus got tired and weary (John 4:6); he slept (Mark 4:38); and, of course, he died. Death seems obviously incompatible with omnipotence—especially the kind of horrific, torturous, shameful death that Jesus suffered on the cross.

Nevertheless, the New Testament presents Jesus as the definitive revelation of God's omnipotence. That revelation began even before Jesus was born. Zacharias and Elizabeth, relatives of Mary, conceived their first child in their old age. Then the angel Gabriel told Mary, a betrothed young woman barely old enough to have a child, that something even more remarkable would happen: she would have a child without a human father, and that child would be the Son of God. "For nothing will be impossible with God" (Luke 1:37), the angel said. Thus, the Incarnation itself is a demonstration of God's omnipotence.

Jesus' earthly, mortal life was a demonstration of humble omnipotence. Despite his glorious divine form, Christ "emptied himself" and "humbled himself" in order to live a life of servitude (Phil. 2:6–8).[1] He used his power to minister to others and reveal God's purpose to rescue human beings from their spiritual weakness. He refused to turn stones into bread in order to satisfy his own hunger (Matt. 4:3–4), but he turned five loaves of bread into enough bread to feed five thousand men and their families with plenty to spare (Matt. 14:15–21; John 6:1–14). He performed that miracle, not to show off, but to reveal himself as "the bread of life," the source of eternal life to those who come to him (John 6:26–58).

Jesus offered himself as the Bread of Life for the world by dying on the cross (cf. John 6:51). If his life had been forcibly taken from him against his will, that would have contradicted belief in his omnipotence; but that isn't the way it happened. Rather, Jesus voluntarily laid down his life, allowing the authorities to arrest and crucify him. "No one takes [my life] from me, but I lay it down of my own accord" (John 10:18a), he said. The proof that his death was not a sign of defeat or incapacity was that Jesus also took back the life he laid down: "I lay down my life in order to take it up again. . . . I have power to lay it down, and I have power to take it up again" (vv. 17–18b). Jesus actually claimed that he would raise himself from the dead. He said, "Destroy this temple, and in three days I will raise it up" (John 2:19). John explained that Jesus was here "speaking of the temple of his body" (v. 21) and that his prediction was fulfilled when he rose from the dead (v. 22).

The apostle Paul viewed Christ's death on the cross and his resurrection from the dead as the supreme display of God's power at work for our benefit: "We proclaim Christ crucified . . . Christ the power of God" (1 Cor. 1:23–24). Paul prayed for Christians to know "the immeasurable greatness of his power for us who believe. . . . God put this power to work in Christ when he raised him from the dead and seated him at his right hand in the heavenly places" (Eph. 1:19–20). Here is a countercultural, revolutionary message for the ages: real power is found not in armies or courts but in the resurrection of the crucified Jesus.

The resurrected and exalted Son of God now reigns supreme over all powers and authorities in creation (Eph. 1:21; Col. 2:10; 1 Peter 3:22). He continues to exercise his omnipotence contrary to what human beings might expect. After he rose from the dead, Jesus told his disciples, "All authority in heaven and on earth has been given to me" (Matt. 28:18).[2] How does Christ exert this universal authority? By sending missionaries! "Go therefore and make disciples of all nations, baptizing them in the name of the Father and of the Son and of the Holy Spirit, and teaching them to obey everything that I have commanded you" (Matt. 28:19–20).

In retrospect, the New Testament affirms that the power by which Christ is working to bring all creation into submission (1 Cor. 15:24; Phil. 2:9–11) is the same power by which he made and sustains the universe (Col. 1:16–17; Heb. 1:2–3). Therefore we can be confident that Jesus Christ will never fail us and that he will enable us to accomplish whatever he calls us to do. "So, I will boast all the more gladly of my weaknesses, so that the power of Christ may dwell in me" (2 Cor. 12:9).

He's Here: Christ Is Omnipresent

The Bible teaches that God is in some sense *omnipresent*, meaning that he is personally present everywhere or, to put it negatively, that his presence is not limited spatially. This does not mean that God is everything (pantheism) or that God is in everything (panentheism). Nor does it mean that God's presence is diffused or spread out throughout the cosmos, or that God is partially present everywhere. In some unfathomable way, God is personally, immediately present at every location simultaneously, able to act and communicate directly or indirectly as he chooses at any time and at any place. This divine presence is a spiritual presence, not a physical one. A classic passage of Scripture that speaks of God's omnipresence is the following from one of David's longest and most famous psalms:

> Where can I go from your Spirit?
> Where can I flee from your presence?
> If I go up to the heavens, you are there;
> if I make my bed in the depths, you are there.
> If I rise on the wings of the dawn,
> if I settle on the far side of the sea,
> even there your hand will guide me,
> your right hand will hold me fast.
>   (Ps. 139:7–10 NIV)

Since God is omnipresent, religions that treat God as a tribal deity ruling over one group of people or one geographical area are false. God is the God of heaven and earth. Even religions originating from biblical revelation can easily stray from the truth by looking for God only in a particular location. Solomon understood this. When he dedicated the temple in Jerusalem, he acknowledged to God in prayer, "But will God indeed dwell on the earth? Even heaven and the highest heaven cannot contain you, much less this house that I have built!" (1 Kings 8:27). Centuries later, though, Jews and Samaritans were debating on which mountain people should worship God (John 4:20). Jesus told a Samaritan woman, "Woman, believe me, the hour is coming when you will worship the Father neither on this mountain nor in Jerusalem. . . . God is spirit, and those who worship him must worship in spirit and truth" (John 4:21, 24).

As a human being Jesus possessed, of course, a physical body that always had a specific location. It took time for Jesus to walk from one town to another. Yet he also displayed an ability to act in places distant from his own physical location. On at least one occasion,[3] Jesus told a man that his sick servant at home was healed, although Jesus never went to the man's home (Matt. 8:5–13; Luke 7:1–10; cf. John 4:46–54).[4] On another occasion, a woman asked Jesus to cast a demon out of her daughter, and Jesus told her that the demon had left the girl; when the mother returned home, she found her daughter free of the demon (Mark 7:24–30).[5]

The Gospel of John reports a rather odd conversation between Jesus and a man named Nathanael, whom he had never physically met before.

> When Jesus saw Nathanael coming toward him, he said of him, "Here is truly an Israelite in whom there is no deceit!" Nathanael asked him, "Where did you get to know me?" Jesus answered, "I saw you under the fig tree before Philip called you." Nathanael replied, "Rabbi, you are the Son of God! You are the King of Israel!" (John 1:47–49)

Apparently, Nathanael was alone under the fig tree, with no one else in sight, before Philip came by himself to fetch him. Thus Nathanael was astonished when Jesus said that he had seen him under a fig tree (a fact that Philip presumably had not been able to convey to Jesus). We do not know what Nathanael was doing under the fig tree, but it would seem that Jesus' comment about Nathanael's lack of deceit convinced him that Jesus was no ordinary man.

In the Gospel of Matthew, Jesus promised his disciples that after his departure to heaven he would be present with them wherever they went on earth: "For where two or three have gathered together in My name, I am there in their midst" (Matt. 18:20 NASB). In the immediate context, Jesus was speaking of disciples coming together in groups of two or three to confront a fellow believer about his sin, resulting in either his restoration or his removal from the community (vv. 15–19). His promise to be present in their midst implies his omnipresence, since only an omnipresent spirit could be in the midst of every gathering of believers. "The tiniest possible assembly, united in prayer, gains divine ratification of their decisions because they gather in the divine presence of the Son."[6] That Jesus is claiming divine omnipresence is clear when we consider a rabbinical saying preserved in the Mishnah (a collection of rabbinical material that later formed the nucleus of the Talmud). The Mishnah quotes a rabbi named Hananiah as saying, "Two that sit together without words of Torah are a session of scorners, for it is said, 'Nor sits in the seat of the scornful' [Ps. 1:1]; but two that sit together and are occupied in words of Torah have the Shekinah among them."[7] The *Shekinah* is the manifest presence of God—his special, glorious presence to guide, bless, and (if necessary) judge. The rabbi's point was that God would be especially, graciously present wherever even two persons sat together to study the Torah, God's Law. In his similar saying, Jesus was claiming that he would be especially present whenever two or more gather in his name. "Here Jesus himself fills the role of the Shekinah, God's presence, in the traditional Jewish saying."[8] Such a claim implies that Jesus is omnipresent and amounts to a strong claim to deity.

At the end of the same Gospel, Jesus makes a similar statement. After commissioning his disciples to "go" make disciples of all the nations (Matt. 28:19), Jesus promises them, "And behold, I am with you always, to the end of the age" (28:20 ESV). To be present with his disciples as they go to all nations requires that Jesus be spiritually present everywhere. Jesus' promise echoes a number of Old Testament sayings of God promising his presence, but especially his assurance to Jacob: "Behold, I am with you and will keep you wherever you go" (Gen. 28:15 ESV).[9] When we remember that the Gospel of Matthew begins with a description of Jesus as Immanuel, "God with us" (Matt. 1:23 ESV), Jesus' closing statement can only be understood as a claim that his presence with the disciples will be the very presence of God.

We get an idea of the significance of Christ's divine omnipresence for the life of the church from Paul's epistle to the Ephesians. In that epistle, Paul stated that Christ "ascended far above all the heavens, so that he might fill all things" (Eph. 4:10), and then he gave gifts to the church, giving some people to be apostles, prophets, evangelists, and teachers (v. 11). As Harold Hoehner observes in his magisterial commentary on Ephesians, "The object of Christ's ascension was to allow him to enter into a sovereign relationship with the whole world, and in that position he has the right to bestow gifts as he wills."[10] Far from passively sitting in heaven, Christ is actively engaged in raising up gifted people throughout the world to equip the saints and build up the body of Christ to unity and maturity in both truth and love (Eph. 4:12–16).

He Knows: Christ Is Omniscient

One attribute of God that can bring great comfort and assurance—or great anxiety and consternation—is the omniscience of God. The Bible states explicitly that God "knows everything" (1 John 3:20). This knowledge is extremely detailed, including such minutiae as the number of hairs on one's head (Matt. 10:30). God knows what will happen from now until the end of history (Isa. 46:9–10). He knows what we will say before we say it (Ps. 139:4) because he knows what is in our hearts (Ps. 139:1–3). This is something that is true only of God, as Solomon acknowledged in prayer: "For you, you only, know the hearts of all the children of mankind" (1 Kings 8:39 ESV).

The New Testament attributes this same omniscience to Jesus Christ. In the first recorded corporate prayer addressed to Jesus, the apostles and other believers confessed, "Lord, you know everyone's heart" (Acts 1:24).[11] For Jesus even to be able to hear prayers essentially implies, of course, unlimited knowledge. Elsewhere, the Gospels report that Jesus knew what other people were thinking (Matt. 9:4; 12:25; Mark 2:6–8; Luke 6:8). Jesus claimed to know what the ancient peoples of Tyre, Sidon, and even Sodom would have done under different circumstances (Matt. 11:21–23; Luke 10:13–15). He would have to know people's hearts in this way in order to sit in judgment on all humanity at the end of history (Matt. 25:31–46; John 5:22–23; Acts 17:31; 2 Cor. 5:10).[12] As Paul says, the Lord (Jesus) "will bring to light the things now hidden in darkness and will disclose the purposes of the heart" (1 Cor. 4:5). In the book of Revelation, Jesus asserts that when they see his warnings fulfilled "all the churches will know that I am the one who searches minds and hearts, and I will give to each of you as your works deserve" (2:23).

Jesus also displayed knowledge of past events of which he could not (humanly speaking) have any knowledge, as well as knowledge of future actions of human beings. He knew that the woman at the well in Samaria, whom he had not previously met (physically), had been married to five different men and that the man she was with at the time was not her husband (John 4:16–18). He knew that Lazarus had died before they received any word of his passing (John 11:11–15). He knew that Judas Iscariot, one of his disciples, would betray him, even before Judas tipped his hand—probably even before Judas knew it (Matt. 26:20–25; Mark 14:17–21; Luke 22:21–23; John 6:70–71; 13:10–11, 21–29). He warned Peter that he would betray him three times, and despite protesting his loyalty, Peter did exactly that (Matt. 26:31–35; Mark 14:27–31; Luke 22:31–34; John 13:36–38). Jesus knew that when he went to Jerusalem he would be arrested, tortured, and killed, and he also knew that he would rise from the dead on the third day (Matt. 16:21; 17:9–12, 22–23; 20:18–19; 26:1–2; Mark 8:31–32; etc.). He knew that the Romans were going to destroy the temple before a generation had passed (Matt. 23:36–39; 24:2, 34; Mark 13:1–2, 30; Luke 21:20–24, 32).[13] No more than forty years later, Jesus' warning proved true, as the Romans destroyed the temple in A.D. 70. Jesus also foretold that his disciples would proclaim the gospel and make new disciples from people of all nations (Matt. 24:14; 28:19), an audacious claim in the early first century, considering how parochial and insignificant Judaism (let alone Jesus' small following) seemed at the time.

Toward the end of the Gospel of John, Christ's disciples confessed on two different occasions that he knew everything. The first occasion was shortly before his arrest and crucifixion, when his disciples said, "Now we know that you know all things" (John 16:30). Jesus' response—"Do you now believe?" (v. 31)—does not deny such knowledge but shows that, at that point, he recognized that the disciples still did not *trust* him as deeply as they should. After Jesus' resurrection, he asked Peter repeatedly if he loved him; after the third time Peter answered, "Lord, you know everything; you know that I love you" (John 21:17). If we truly believe that Jesus knows everything, we ought to love and trust him with every fiber of our being.

As with all the other divine attributes of the Son of God, there is another side that results in paradox. We saw that the Son is uncreated and yet became a human being; that he is immutable and yet grew up from infancy to adulthood; that he is omnipotent and yet experienced weariness, sleep, and even death; that he is omnipresent and yet walked from place to place like any ordinary human being. His divine attributes are his by virtue of his eternal identity as the Son of God; his finite, human limitations are normal human attributes that he has by virtue of his becoming a man in the Incarnation. A similar paradox pertains to his omniscience. By virtue of being the divine Son, Jesus was in some sense omniscient, knowing the hearts of the people around him; yet, by virtue of his incarnation, Jesus also experienced the normal limitations of human knowledge. The New Testament states that Jesus grew in wisdom (Luke 2:40, 52) and that he "learned obedience" through his sufferings (Heb. 5:8).[14] Most famously, although Jesus predicted that the destruction of Jerusalem and the temple would occur within the lifetime of his generation, he denied knowing the day or hour of the end of the age.[15]

> Truly I tell you, this generation will not pass away until all these things have taken place. Heaven and earth will pass away, but my words will not pass away. But about that day or hour no one knows, neither the angels of heaven, nor the Son, but only the Father. (Matt. 24:34–36; Mark 13:30–32)

Christians who affirm the deity of Christ take different approaches to resolving this paradox. Some Christians suggest that Christ gave up omniscience and other infinite attributes of deity in order to become a human being. For example, Kris Udd, in an article on Mark 13:32, suggests that omniscience is a normal, but not an essential, attribute of God. Thus, during his earthly life the Son could have ceased to be omniscient without ceasing to be God.[16] The principal difficulty with this explanation is that it seems to be incompatible with the immutability of God. Furthermore, if Christ could not be omniscient and also be human, then it would seem that, on this view, Christ is *still* not omniscient, since according to the New Testament the risen Christ is human (Luke 24:39; Acts 17:31; 1 Cor. 15:47; 1 Tim. 2:5).

A second approach is to attribute Jesus' lack of knowledge strictly to his human nature alone. Jesus is simultaneously omniscient with respect to his divine nature and not omniscient with respect to his human nature. When he says that "the Son" does not know, he uses this divine title merely as a self-designation, and not to mean that what he says applies to himself in his divine nature.[17] This is a possible explanation, but it can be charged with implying that natures know or do not know, whereas knowing and not knowing are properties of persons, not natures. To put it more simply, Jesus did not say, "My human nature does not know," but rather said that *he* did not know.

A third approach agrees that distinguishing the two natures is a key to resolving the paradox but suggests a different way of framing the resolution. According to this approach, the divine Son of God knew everything, yet chose in his earthly life not to have that knowledge as part of his conscious, human awareness in regards to such matters as the timing of his future return. Some theologians put it this way: the Son had the knowledge available to him by virtue of his divine nature but chose not to *use* that knowledge in his human life. This explanation allows Christ to know what is in people's hearts, to know that he will die and then rise from the dead on the third day, and the like, while not knowing things he did not need to know to accomplish his mission. Richard Swinburne, a Christian philosopher, explains it this way: "God, in becoming incarnate, will not have limited his powers, but he will have taken on a way of operating which is limited and feels limited."[18]

The chief difficulty with this approach is that we do not really understand what it would be like to be omniscient and choose to experience a lack of knowledge. Then again, we are hardly likely to understand what it would be like to be God incarnate in the first place.

However we resolve the difficulty of his lack of knowledge of certain matters during his earthly life, Jesus has no deficiency of knowledge now. The limitations on his knowledge were aspects of his self-imposed act of humbling himself to share in our mortal human nature (Phil. 2:6–7; 2 Cor. 8:9). Now, following his resurrection and ascension, in Christ "are hidden all the treasures of wisdom and knowledge. . . . For in him the whole fullness of deity dwells bodily" (Col. 2:3, 9).[19]

He's Beyond Us: Christ Is Incomprehensible

The fact that it is difficult to understand how Christ can be omniscient while experiencing human growth and limitations in knowledge gives us insight into another of his divine attributes. One of the attributes of God is that he is *incomprehensible*. This does not mean that we cannot know anything about God or that we cannot know him in the sense of having a personal relationship with him. What it does mean is that a full, complete, definitive understanding of God is beyond our capacity. This is so simply because God is a unique kind of being. "To whom then will you liken God? Or what likeness will you compare with Him?" (Isa. 40:18 NASB).

Likewise, although we may know something about Jesus Christ, he remains to some extent inscrutable and incomprehensible. Jesus himself once said, "No one knows the Son except the Father" (Matt. 11:27; cf. Luke 10:22). Peter would not have recognized Jesus' identity as the Son of God had the Father not revealed it to him (Matt. 16:16–17), and even after grasping that much, Peter obviously was a long way from really understanding Jesus. The more we learn about Jesus, the more surprising and paradoxical we find him to be.

THE PARADOXICAL PERSON

God . . .	But Christ . . .	And Yet He . . .
Is eternal (Ps. 90:2; Isa. 43:10)	Was born (Matt. 1:18)	Always existed (John 8:58; Col. 1:17)
Is immutable (Ps. 102:26–27)	Grew (Luke 2:40, 52)	Is also immutable (Heb. 1:10–12)
Is omnipresent (Ps. 139:7–10)	Was one place at a time (John 11:21, 32)	Could act from afar (John 4:46–54)
Knows all things (Isa. 41:22–23)	Did not know the day or hour (Mark 13:32)	Knew all things (John 16:30; 21:17)

Is incorporeal (John 4:24)	Has a body (John 2:21; Col. 2:9)	Cannot be seen (1 Tim. 6:16)
Is not a man (Num. 23:19)	Is a man (1 Tim. 2:5)	Is also God (John 20:28)
Cannot be tempted (James 1:13)	Was tempted (Heb. 4:15)	Could not sin (John 5:19)
Does not get tired (Isa. 40:28)	Got tired (John 4:6)	Did all God's will (John 17:4)
Cannot die (1 Tim. 1:17)	Died (Phil. 2:8)	Could not have his life taken (John 10:18)

Think about it this way: suppose the infinite Creator of the universe assumed finite, human nature, grew from infancy to adulthood, and shared in our normal human experiences of working and playing, waking and sleeping, eating and drinking, learning and growing. Would we expect to understand how he could experience our humanity to the full and still be God? Of course not. We would *expect* paradoxes or mysteries, all down the line, with respect to his attributes. And that is exactly what we find (see the accompanying table). On the other hand, if Jesus were merely a great human being or even an angel who somehow became a human being, we would not expect him to have been a fundamentally incomprehensible individual. Precisely because Jesus is both God and man, he is the preeminent, paradoxical person.

Part 3

NAME ABOVE ALL NAMES

Jesus Shares the Names of God

Honors	Attributes	Names	Deeds	Seat

Chapter 11

....

NAME ONE

S o far, we have seen from the Bible that Jesus Christ is entitled to the *honors* that are due to God (such as worship, prayer, song, faith, and reverence) and that he possesses the essential *attributes* of God (such as being eternal, uncreated, immutable, omnipotent, omnipresent, omniscient, and incomprehensible). We will now consider what Scripture says about the names of Jesus Christ. What we will find is that the Bible gives Jesus a wide array of names that properly belong to God—and that it gives him these names in contexts that confirm that they describe or identify him as God.

What's a Name?

In this current volume, unless stated otherwise, we use the word *name* to refer to both proper names (like *Jesus*) and titles (like *Savior*). We have a couple of reasons for doing this. First, the Hebrew and Greek words customarily translated "name" can refer to titles or other descriptive terms as well as to proper names. Examples of titles or descriptions that the Bible explicitly calls names include the following:

- *Jealous* (a "name" for God, Exod. 34:14)
- *Wonderful Counselor, Mighty God, Everlasting Father, Prince of Peace* (the fourfold "name" of the Messiah, Isa. 9:6)
- *Holy* (apparently a "name" for God, Isa. 57:15)
- *Redeemer* (Isa. 63:16)
- *The Christ* (Matt. 24:5, implied; 1 Peter 4:14)
- *Christian* (1 Peter 4:16)

- *The Word of God* (Rev. 19:13)
- *King of kings and Lord of lords* (Rev. 19:16)

Second, the distinction between (proper) names and titles, although legitimate, is not always hard and fast.[1] A good example is the word *God* (and its counterparts in Hebrew and Greek). Is *God* a name or a title? One could argue that *God* is a title that the Bible often uses as a name. When the Bible refers to *God* with qualifiers (such as "our God" or "the God of Israel") it is clearly using the word as a title. When it appears without such qualifiers, however, one can make a good case that it often functions just like a proper name. An even clearer example is *Christ*. In some passages, it is certain that "the Christ" is a title, the Greek equivalent of "Messiah" (e.g., Matt. 16:16; Luke 24:46; John 1:41). In many if not most instances, though, especially in the epistles, *Christ* (with or without the article "the") functions just like a proper name.

What's in a Name?

Before going farther, it is crucial to clear away a misconception that often confuses the issue of whether a name refers to deity. We are *not* saying that if the Bible uses a particular name for God, then anyone else given that name in the Bible must also be God. The Hebrew and Greek words for *god* and *lord*, as well as for *savior, shepherd, rock*, and the like, all apply in certain contexts to beings who are neither divine nor objects of religious devotion. Like virtually all words, these words have different meanings in different contexts. Even proper names can have different meanings depending on context. For example, *Rube Goldberg* is the proper name of a twentieth-century cartoonist, but it is also a term for an absurdly complicated machine, device, or plan (such as those humorously depicted in Goldberg's cartoons).

The Bible's use of various names for Jesus proves that he is God *because of their contexts*. There are at least three contextual factors to keep in mind as we examine Jesus' divine names. The first is that the application to Jesus of so many of these descriptive names for God confirms their significance as designations of deity. It is not just that the New Testament happens to call Jesus "Savior" a few times, but that the New Testament calls Jesus "God," "Lord," *and* "Savior," sometimes separately, and sometimes together (e.g., "My Lord and my God," John 20:28; "God and Savior," Titus 2:13; 2 Peter 1:1; "Lord and Savior," 2 Peter 1:11). One can find a few texts here and there in the Bible that refer to some men over here as "saviors," or to a man over there as a "rock," but one cannot find texts referring to the same mere human being as god, lord, savior, shepherd, rock, first and last, and king of kings and lord of lords! The application of all these designations to the one person, Jesus Christ, often with two or more in the same immediate context, is highly significant.

Second, when the New Testament uses these designations for Jesus, it very often does so by quoting from, or alluding to, Old Testament texts about God or by applying to Jesus characteristic Old Testament motifs and expressions that refer to God. It is one thing to call someone "lord"; it is another thing altogether to do so while saying that we "call on the name of the Lord" or that we are waiting for "the day of the Lord." As we shall see, names of God applied to Jesus in the New Testament occur in such contexts literally dozens—perhaps hundreds—of times.

Third, the New Testament calls Jesus by such names as God, Lord, and the like in the context of saying things about Jesus that connote deity. This happens when Jesus receives these designations in reference to the divine *honors* he receives, the divine *attributes* he exhibits, the divine *deeds* that he does, or the divine *seat* or position he occupies (the other four points in our "HANDS" outline). It also happens when the Bible applies these names to Jesus in relation to all creation. Again, it is one thing to call someone "lord," but another thing altogether to say that all creatures in heaven and earth must acknowledge him as "Lord"!

These three contextual factors—that Jesus receives an array of divine names, often in the same passage; that Jesus often receives these divine names in allusions to, or quotations from, Old Testament texts speaking about God; that Jesus receives these designations in reference to his divine honors, attributes, works, and position, in relation to all creation—are closely related. They converge in such a way as to prove that when the Bible calls Jesus by such names as God and Lord, it is applying those names to him in their highest possible sense.

One way that English Bibles often mark a particular name as a designation of deity is by capitalizing the name. Thus, *God* and *Lord* refer to the Supreme Being, whereas *god* and *lord* do not. This is a handy feature of the English language, but it does not reflect anything inherent in the biblical languages. The use of uppercase and lowercase lettering arose after biblical times. The two types of lettering do not occur in all languages, and those languages that have two types of lettering do not utilize them in the same way.[2] The original readers of the Bible could understand whether a name in a particular text referred to deity, but they did so based on context, not capitalization.

The Name of Jesus

Although we will soon focus on the Bible's use of such names as *God* and *Lord* for Jesus, we start by considering the significance of the proper name *Jesus*. According to the Gospels, an angel or angels told Joseph and Mary separately that they were to call Mary's son "Jesus." The angel who spoke to Joseph explained why: "for he will save his people from their sins" (Matt. 1:21; cf. Luke 1:31). The name Jesus means "Jehovah saves," and the angel's comment assumes an awareness of this meaning. Since the angel said that "he," meaning in context Jesus, would save his people, the implication is that Jesus somehow *is* Jehovah.[3]

To say that the name Jesus has a special place in the New Testament would be a gross understatement. The focus of the New Testament on this name is so intense and so persistent as to be extraordinary.

In the Old Testament, the central name, the divine name *par excellence*, was the name Yahweh, or Jehovah.[4]

> And God said moreover unto Moses, Thus shalt thou say unto the children of Israel, Jehovah, the God of your fathers, the God of Abraham, the God of Isaac, and the God of Jacob, hath sent me unto you: this is my name forever, and this is my memorial unto all generations. (Exod. 3:15 ASV)

> Thou shalt not take the name of Jehovah thy God in vain: for Jehovah will not hold him guiltless that taketh his name in vain. (Exod. 20:7; Deut. 5:11 ASV)

> If thou wilt not observe to do all the words of this law that are written in this book, that thou mayest fear this glorious and fearful name, JEHOVAH THY GOD. (Deut. 28:58 ASV)

> O Jehovah, our Lord, How excellent is thy name in all the earth. (Ps. 8:1, 9 ASV)

We could fill many pages, multiplying such examples from the Old

Testament. The New Testament assumes the same perspective on revering God's name while shifting the focus away from the name Jehovah, which is essentially absent.[5] God's name is still holy (Luke 1:49), and people should fear his name (Rev. 11:18; 15:4) and not blaspheme it (Rom. 2:24; 1 Tim. 6:1; Rev. 13:6; 16:9).[6] Jesus revealed to his followers the name of the Father (John 17:6, 11–12, 26) and taught his disciples to pray that the Father's name would be hallowed, or treated as holy (Matt. 6:9; Luke 11:2).[7]

Although these names *God* and *Father* (usually referring to the same person) occur numerous times in the New Testament, "the name" that is the focus of attention is the name *Jesus.* This focus on Jesus' name is consistent with the fact that the *person* of Jesus Christ is clearly the focus of the New Testament, even more than is God the Father.[8] According to Paul, Jesus has been exalted "above every name that is named, not only in this age but also in the age to come" (Eph. 1:21). God "highly exalted him and gave him the name that is above every name, so that at the name of Jesus every knee should bend . . . and every tongue should confess that Jesus Christ is Lord, to the glory of God the Father" (Phil. 2:9–11).

Doing the Extraordinary in Jesus' Name

The New Testament draws attention to Jesus' name in many ways. Jesus' disciples performed miracles, including healings and exorcisms, in Jesus' name (Mark 9:38–39; Luke 10:17; Acts 3:6, 16; 4:7, 10, 30; 16:18). On one occasion, some Jewish exorcists in Ephesus tried using Jesus' name to command evil spirits to leave a man.[9] Although the evil spirit refused to leave—the possessed man started beating up the exorcists, and they ran away!—the result was that among the people in Ephesus "the name [*onoma*] of the Lord [*kuriou*] Jesus was being glorified [*emegaluneto*]" (Acts 19:13–18). Luke's comment here echoes with regard to Jesus what David had said about Jehovah, the Lord God: "We will glory [*megalunthēsometha*] in the name [*onomati*] of the LORD [*kuriou*] our God" (Ps. 20:7 [19:8 Greek]).[10] F. F. Bruce comments that Jesus' name "had proved itself to be a name of unsurpassed power, a name with which it was dangerous to operate irresponsibly."[11]

Jesus himself had warned that false prophets would claim to follow him as "Lord, Lord," and that they would claim to prophesy, cast out demons, and perform many miracles in his name (Matt. 7:22). The reason, of course, false prophets make such claims is that the apostles (Christ's true prophets) really did those things in Jesus' name. Jesus' warning echoes the warning about false prophets that the Lord God had given to the Jews six centuries earlier: "They are prophesying falsely in my name" (Jer. 27:15; see also 29:9; Zech. 13:3).

Baptizing "into" Jesus' Name

Another activity that the early Christians performed in Jesus' name was baptism. The book of Acts states repeatedly that new believers were baptized in the name of Jesus Christ (Acts 2:38; 8:16; 10:48; 19:5; cf. 22:16). Paul pointed out to the Corinthians who were dividing themselves into factions that they were baptized in Jesus' name, not in Paul's (1 Cor. 1:13–15). By the ritual act of baptism in the name of Jesus, believers were identifying themselves as religious devotees of Jesus.

The most common wording the New Testament uses to express this idea is that the early Christians baptized "into" (*eis*) the name of Jesus (Acts 8:16; 19:5; 1 Cor. 1:13–15; cf. Rom. 6:3; Gal. 3:27).[12] The phrase "into the name of" (*eis tō onoma*) used in these baptismal texts has no precedent in the Old Testament and appears to reflect a rabbinical expression used with reference to religious rites or rituals. In his monograph on the subject, Lars Hartman explains, "The rites are performed 'into the name' of the god, to whose cult the rite belongs or who is otherwise associated with the rite in question. This god is the fundamental referent of the rite; he/she is the one whom the worshipper 'has in mind' or 'with regard to' whom the rite is performed and who thus makes it meaningful."[13] This sense of the expression clearly fits the New Testament usage with regard to Christian baptism.[14] It also fits the similar expressions of baptizing "in" (*en*) or "on" (*epi*) the name of Jesus Christ (Acts 2:38; 10:48).[15]

Salvation in Jesus' Name

The practice of baptizing people in Jesus' name correlates closely with the New Testament teaching that salvation and its blessings come in or through the name of Jesus. The correlation is explicit in Peter's summons for the Jewish people to repent and to be baptized "in the name of Jesus Christ for the forgiveness of your sins" (Acts 2:38 NASB). In making this summons, Peter was following through on Jesus' own instructions that the apostles were to proclaim repentance and forgiveness of sins "in his name to all nations" (Luke 24:47). Later, Peter recognized that Jesus indeed wanted this message taken to "all nations," meaning the Gentiles as well as the Jews. Hence, he told

Cornelius and his household that "everyone who believes in him receives forgiveness of sins through his name" (Acts 10:43). Likewise, the apostle John wrote years later that our "sins are forgiven on account of his name" (1 John 2:12).

Elsewhere the New Testament expands on this association of salvation with the name of Jesus. If we go back to Peter's first Christian sermon, one of the Old Testament texts he quoted states that "everyone who calls on the name of the Lord shall be saved" (Acts 2:21, quoting Joel 2:32). There is reason to think that Peter interpreted the "Lord" here to be Jesus. Later in the same sermon, Peter concluded that God had made Jesus "both Lord and Messiah" (v. 36). On another occasion, Peter made the following statement about Jesus: "And there is salvation in no one else; for there is no other name under heaven that has been given among men by which we must be saved" (Acts 4:12 NASB). Here, Peter asserts not only that we are saved by Jesus' name but also that his is the *only* name by which we can be saved. Assuming Peter did not forget his own quotation from Joel 2:32, he appears to be equating the name that Jesus has with the "name of the Lord" on whom we must call to be saved. Paul had the same perspective, because he quoted the same Old Testament text, "Everyone who calls on the name of the Lord shall be saved" (Rom. 10:13), in context clearly referring to the Lord Jesus (vv. 9–12).[16]

The apostle John's Gospel begins and climaxes with the affirmation of salvation through faith in Jesus' name. To those who believe in his name, Jesus (identified at this point as the Word) gives the right to become children of God (John 1:12; see vv. 1, 14). At the climax of the book, John explains that he wrote it "so that you may come to believe that Jesus is the Messiah, the Son of God, and that through believing you may have life in his name" (20:31; see also 1 John 3:23; 5:13).

For the Name

The apostles and other early Christians were willing to suffer and die for the sake of the name of Jesus. Jesus had, in fact, warned them that they would be hated and persecuted for his name's sake (Matt. 10:22; 24:9; Mark 13:13; Luke 21:12, 17; John 15:21). He promised, though, that those who experienced such suffering, who lost property or family for the sake of his name, would receive a hundredfold back and eternal life (Matt. 19:29).

It did not take long for Jesus' warnings to come true. Shortly after the resurrection, the religious establishment in Jerusalem opposed the followers of

Jesus and tried to suppress their message. The authorities told the apostles not to speak to anyone in the name of Jesus (Acts 4:17–18; 5:28, 40). The apostles, though, rejoiced in suffering dishonor "for the sake of the name" (Acts 5:41) or, as some translations put it, "the Name" (ASV, NIV). Years later, John mentioned in one of his epistles the itinerant evangelists who went out "for the sake of the Name" (3 John 7 NASB, NIV). This expression is a startling indicator of the preeminence the apostles attached to Jesus' name.

One of the most aggressive enemies of the Christian church in its first years was Saul of Tarsus. He had authority from the chief priests to bind all who called on Jesus' name (Acts 9:14, 21). As he acknowledged after his conversion, he had tried "to do many things against the name of Jesus of Nazareth" (Acts 26:9). These statements reveal that, for Saul, the place of the name of Jesus in the early Christian movement was especially troubling to his rabbinical, Pharisaic mind-set.[17] But Jesus, the Lord, had chosen Saul to take his name before Gentiles, kings, and the people of Israel, even though it meant that he would suffer for the sake of Jesus' name (Acts 9:15–16). Saul, better known to us as Paul, was soon speaking boldly in the name of Jesus (Acts 9:27–28). Paul and his ministry partner Barnabas "risked their lives for the name of our Lord Jesus Christ" (Acts 15:26 NASB, NIV). Paul was ready to go to prison and even to die "for the name of the Lord Jesus" (Acts 21:13).

Clearly, for the early Christians the belief in Jesus' deity was not just a doctrinal affirmation but was the crux of their entire value system. Peter encouraged Christians to consider themselves blessed if they were "reviled for the name of Christ" (1 Peter 4:14). In the book of Revelation, Jesus measures the faithfulness of the churches by their adherence to his name (2:3, 13; 3:8). Recognizing Jesus' divine claims on our lives, and the astounding, eternal blessings he promises us, ought to motivate us to live as if the only thing that matters to us is "the name." As Paul put it, we should "do everything in the name of the Lord Jesus" (Col. 3:17).[18]

Chapter 12

IMMANUEL: GOD WITH US

The New Testament does not often call Jesus "God." Contrary, though, to what some people argue, it does assign that name to Jesus several times. In this chapter, we will examine several key texts that are the subject of much debate. We shall see that in most of these texts the evidence is decisively in support of the conclusion that Jesus Christ is indeed God.

The Messiah as God in Isaiah

The belief that Jesus Christ is God has some precedent in the Old Testament, especially in the book of Isaiah, which affirms more than once that the future Messiah would be God. The most explicit of these affirmations are in the same section of the book, in chapters 7–12, that focuses on the judgment about to come on the northern kingdom of Israel and on what this judgment would mean to Jerusalem and the southern kingdom of Judah. Although the immediate concern was the Assyrian Empire and its conquest of Israel— events that took place during Isaiah's lifetime—the issue of the future of the Davidic line in Jerusalem broadened Isaiah's prophetic vision far beyond his own day. This is the context of Isaiah's most controversial prophecy.

> Therefore the Lord Himself will give you a sign: Behold, a virgin will be with child and bear a son, and she will call His name Immanuel. (7:14 NASB)

In the immediate context, Immanuel apparently was a child born during the reign of Ahaz (the king to whom Isaiah was speaking). The short time it took for Immanuel to reach maturity was to be the measure of the time Ahaz's two enemy kings had left (7:1–9, 15–16; see also 8:8). Other considerations, though, point to a future child. Perhaps a child named Immanuel born in Isaiah's time was a precursor to the future child.

Most of the debate over Isaiah 7:14 centers on the Hebrew *almah*, translated "virgin" (Greek, *parthenos*) in the Septuagint and in Matthew 1:23. Critics of Matthew 1:23, which cites Isaiah 7:14 in reference to the virginal conception of Jesus in the womb of Mary, routinely assert that *almah* meant simply "young woman" and not necessarily a virgin, which, they say, would have been better denoted using the word *bethulah*. But this objection to the traditional interpretation is mistaken. The word *almah* never refers to a married woman, and usually it is clear or implied that the woman is unmarried and a virgin (Gen. 24:43; Exod. 2:8; Ps. 68:25; Prov. 30:19; Song 1:3; 6:8). In one of these texts the Septuagint translated *almah* as "virgin" (*parthenos*, Gen. 24:43), just as it did in Isaiah 7:14. In the other texts, the Septuagint used forms of the word *neanis*, "young girl," a translation that also includes the idea of virginity. An *almah* is neither a child nor a mature woman, but a young woman who is unmarried but old enough to become married. The old-fashioned word "maiden" might be the best one-word substitute. As the *Theological Wordbook of the Old Testament* correctly concludes, *almah* "represents a young woman, one of whose characteristics is virginity."[1]

Another reason for thinking that the prophecy has a more profound meaning is that before Isaiah predicted the birth of the child, he told Ahaz to ask for a sign "deep as Sheol or high as heaven" (Isa. 7:11), that is, a miraculous sign to assure him of God's purpose to preserve the Davidic royal house (7:10–14a). The implication is that the birth was to be truly miraculous (cf. Isa. 38:7–8).[2]

A third reason for understanding Isaiah's prophecy as referring to something beyond the ordinary birth of a boy in the eighth century B.C. is that Isaiah soon gave another, similar prophecy that is clearly messianic:

> For to us a child is born, to us a son is given, and the government will be on his shoulders. And he will be called Wonderful Counselor, Mighty God, Everlasting Father, Prince of Peace. Of the increase of his government and peace there will be no end. He will reign on David's throne and over his kingdom, establishing and upholding it with justice and righteousness from that time on and forever. (9:6–7 NIV)

The context is still the same: assurance that God will fulfill his promise of an everlasting Davidic kingdom despite the impending judgment that is coming on Israel through Assyria and the subsequent judgment on Judah. Both texts speak of a "child" and "son" whom God will "give"; both say that "his name will be called" something that gives assurance of God's presence. In context, then, we should interpret this prophecy as a further revelation about the Immanuel child of Isaiah 7:14. Yet this child is indisputably a Davidic Messiah, since he will reign on David's throne forever (9:7). In retrospect, Matthew's interpretation of Isaiah 7:14 holds up very well.

Now, in both prophecies Isaiah appears to call this wonder-child God. In Isaiah 7:14 he calls the child *Immanuel*, which, as Matthew points out, means "God is with us" (1:23). If there was an eighth-century boy named Immanuel, he was not, of course, God incarnate; then again, neither was he born of a virgin nor did he come to be the Messiah and Savior of the world. That eighth-century boy was a *type* or foreshadowing figure of Jesus, the real Immanuel, who really is God with us.

In Isaiah 9:6, Isaiah calls the future Messiah "Wonderful Counselor, Mighty God, Everlasting Father, Prince of Peace." The question is whether these titles are descriptive of the Messiah himself or simply express affirmations about the God he represents. There are good reasons to think they describe the Messiah. Isaiah goes on to credit the Messiah with doing just what the titles express: he establishes peace and rules forever over an everlasting kingdom (v. 7). Another prophecy of Isaiah about the Messiah later in the same section describes him as imbued with the Spirit of counsel (11:1–2). In short, Isaiah indicates that the child will live up to his name.

Isaiah, then, refers to the future Messiah as Immanuel, meaning "God is with us," and as "Mighty God" (cf. Isa. 10:21). These are not the only statements in Isaiah that suggest that the Messiah will be God. Later in the book, Isaiah[3] states repeatedly that *God* is coming to redeem, restore, and rule over his people (Isa. 40:9–11; 43:10–13; 59:15–20). Perhaps the most famous such statement in Isaiah is the following:

> The voice of one crying in the wilderness:
>   "Prepare the way of the LORD;
>   Make straight in the desert
>   A highway for our God."
>
> (40:3 NKJV)

The Synoptic Gospels quote this passage and apply it to John the Baptist preparing the way for the Lord Jesus (Matt. 3:3; Mark 1:3; Luke 3:4–6). The New Testament teaching that Jesus is God, then, has significant precedent in Isaiah.

Jesus as God in the Gospel of John

The Gospel of John contains at least two, and probably three, statements explicitly identifying Jesus Christ as God. The first of these statements comes in the very first sentence of the book: "In the beginning was the Word, and the Word was with God, and the Word was God" (1:1). "Word" (Greek, *logos*) is a name for Jesus Christ, referring here to Christ in his existence prior to becoming a human being. Thus, verse 14 says, "And the Word became flesh and lived among us," and verse 17 identifies this incarnate Word as "Jesus Christ" (see also 1 John 1:1; Rev. 19:13). The second reference is in verse 18, which apparently also calls Jesus "God": "No one has ever seen God. It is God the only Son, who is close to the Father's heart, who has made him known." There is a textual question here, since some manuscripts do not call Jesus "God" in verse 18; we will return to this question later. The third reference to Jesus as God in the Gospel is also the most emphatic, and it comes at the climax of the book. The apostle Thomas, confronted by the risen Jesus, responds to him by saying, "My Lord and my God!" (20:28).

Jesus as God in John's Prologue (John 1:1–18)

We begin with the first two references to Christ as God (John 1:1, 18). These statements function like bookmarks indicating the beginning and the ending of the introduction of what is commonly called the prologue to the Gospel of John (John 1:1–18). Between these two statements that call Jesus "God" is a rich tapestry of affirmations about Jesus that confirm his identity as God.[4]

John says that the Word was already existing[5] "in the beginning" (vv. 1–2). The opening words of the Gospel, "In the beginning" (Greek, *en archē*), are the same as the opening words of the Old Testament, "In the beginning" (Gen. 1:1). This is not mere coincidence, since both passages go on immediately to talk about creation and light (Gen. 1:1, 3–5; John 1:3–5, 9). John states that everything that came into existence—the world itself—did so through the Word (vv. 3, 10). These statements affirming the Word's existence before creation and his involvement in bringing about the existence of all creation reveal him to be eternal and uncreated—two essential attributes of God, as we saw in part 2. John concludes this part of the prologue with a call for people to "believe in His name" (v. 12 NASB)—one of the divine honors that the New Testament often indicates we are to extend toward Christ.

The identity of this Word starts to become clear when John writes, "The Word became flesh and made his dwelling among us" (v. 14 NIV). The word that the NIV translates "made his dwelling" (*eskēnōsen*) literally meant to pitch one's tent in a place, and it alludes in this context to God's dwelling among the Israelites in the tabernacle. The tabernacle essentially was a tent where God made his presence known to the Israelites and met with them. Before the Israelites constructed the tabernacle, Moses would pitch an ordinary tent away from the camp and meet God there (Exod. 33:7–11). When the tabernacle was finished, "the glory of the LORD filled the tabernacle" (Exod. 40:35).[6] Later, the temple served the same purpose as the tabernacle (cf. Ps. 74:7).[7]

John says that the Word that made his dwelling among us has the "glory as of the only Son from the Father" (v. 14 ESV). This statement is a way of saying that the Son is just like his Father when it comes to glory (a "chip off the old block," some people still say).

John then gets specific: the Son's glory is "full of grace and truth" (v. 14). This description of the Son echoes God's description of himself to Moses, who had asked at the tent of meeting to see God's "glory" (Exod. 33:18). God's response was to descend in a cloud and to proclaim that he is "abounding in lovingkindness and truth" (Exod. 34:6 NASB). What John says here must have been startling to Jews in his day in a couple of ways. First, John is implying that the revelation of God's loving-kindness, or grace, and truth that came through Jesus superseded the revelation that came to and through Moses. John makes that plain two sentences later: "The law indeed was given through Moses; grace and truth came through Jesus Christ" (v. 17). John also makes explicit the second, even more startling implication: the revelation that Moses received of God's glory, of God himself, was only an anticipation of the revelation of God that came through his incarnate Son. John's statement, "No one has ever seen God" (v. 18a), clearly recalls the Lord's statement to Moses, "No man can see Me and live" (Exod. 33:20 NASB).[8] John concludes, "It is God the only Son, who is close to the Father's heart, who has made him known" (v. 18b).

Jesus as God in John 1:1

Now that we have looked at these two affirmations of Jesus as "God" in the prologue, we want to address the most important questions or difficulties that commentators raise about them. The primary issue of controversy in John 1:1 is how best to translate the last part of the verse (usually translated "and the Word was God"). Some translators have rendered the last clause to say that the Word was "divine" (e.g., Moffatt, Goodspeed) rather than "God."[9] The Revised English Bible (1989) translates, "and what God was, the Word was." The New World Translation (NWT), published by the Jehovah's Witnesses, is notorious for its rendering, "and the Word was a god." The NWT was not the first version to adopt this rendering, but it is by far the best known.[10]

Since an adequate treatment of this controversial question would be rather lengthy, we will be content to summarize our conclusion as simply as we can and refer the interested reader to works that explore the question in more detail.[11]

There are really two issues here. The first is how John can say that the Word was *with* God and yet also that the Word *was* God. The second question has to do with the well-known fact that the Greek article (the word we often translate as "the") is present before "God" in the second clause but not before "God" in the third clause. In order to understand the issue, it will be helpful to set out the whole verse in interlinear fashion:

> *en archē ēn ho logos*
> in beginning was the word (first clause)
>
> *kai ho logos ēn pros ton theon*
> and the word was with the god (second clause)
>
> *kai theos ēn ho logos*
> and god was the word (third clause)

Advocates of the alternate translations argue that the absence of the article "the" (Greek, *ho*, which appears in front of *logos*) in front of *theos* avoids the problem of the second and third clauses contradicting each other. The second clause says that the Word was with "the God"; the third clause says that the Word was "God," not "the God."

Up to this point, the critics of the conventional translation are more or less correct. John's statement is not an outright contradiction because he does not say that the Word was *with* "the God" and yet *was* "the God." If they stopped there (and some do), there would be no problem. They would simply be pointing out a subtlety of the Greek that does not translate well into English. If we used the article in the same way as John (which we do not), we could translate the last two clauses like this: "and the Word was with the God, and the Word was God." Many go farther, however, and argue that what John meant was that the Word was a *lesser* divine being since John did not call him "*the* God" (like the divine being in the second clause). There simply is no basis in the text for this claim, however.

The translation "a god" is especially erroneous, for this very reason. Variations in the biblical writings, including those of John, between *theos* (God) and *ho theos* (the God) have no affect whatsoever on the meaning of the word *theos*.[12] If John had meant to signal that *ho theos* meant "God" and *theos* meant "a god," his wording in the rest of the prologue (John 1:1–18) is very strange. After verse 2, which summarizes the first two clauses of verse 1, *theos* appears five times in the prologue, each time without the article, and in the first four occurrences everyone agrees it means "God" (vv. 6, 12, 13, 18a, 18b).

Jesus as God in John 1:18

The final occurrence of *theos* in John's prologue also refers to Christ: "No one has ever seen God [*theon*]. It is God [*theos*] the only Son, who is close to the Father's heart, who has made him known." In this verse, the first occurrence of "God" (*theon*) refers to the Father. The second occurrence of "God" (*theos*) refers to the Son.

We should point out that the Greek manuscripts do not all read the same way here. In fact, the majority of Greek manuscripts say "unique Son" (*monogenēs huios*), which is why the King James Version reads "the only begotten Son."[13] There is significant early manuscript support, however, for the reading "unique [Son], God" (*monogenēs theos*).[14] Two very old papyri, P[66] and P[75], have been discovered in which Jesus is called *theos* in John 1:18, and which shift the weight of evidence decidedly over to that reading as most likely to be original.[15]

It is interesting to note that both *theon* and *theos* in verse 18 occur without the article.[16] In verse 1, *ton theon* (with the article) refers to the Father and *theos* refers to the Son (called the Word). If it were true that John used the article with *theon* but not with *theos* in verse 1 in order to indicate that the Son was a lesser type of deity than the Father, it is very strange that he did not maintain this same distinction in verse 18.

The affirmation that the "only Son" is himself "God" is a fitting conclusion to the prologue to the Gospel of John. It makes it clear that the one who was God before creation (1:1) was still God when he came to make God the Father known to us through the Incarnation. Murray Harris has observed, "Inasmuch as the only Son is God by nature and intimately acquainted with the Father by experience, he is uniquely qualified to reveal the nature and character of God."[17]

Jesus as "My God" in the Climax of John's Gospel (John 20:28)

Although the Gospel of John has 21 chapters, the climax of the Gospel comes at the end of chapter 20, when the apostle Thomas confesses Jesus as his Lord and God (v. 28) and John states that the purpose of his Gospel is that people might have life through believing in Jesus as the Son of God (vv. 30–31).[18] We see here the same pattern of thought as in the prologue: Jesus is the Son of God the Father (1:14, 18) and yet he is also himself God (1:1, 18).

There is essentially no controversy among biblical scholars that in John 20:28 Thomas is referring to and addressing Jesus when he says, "My Lord and my God!" As Harris says in his lengthy study on Jesus as God in the New Testament, "This view prevails among grammarians, lexicographers, commentators and English versions."[19] Indeed, it is difficult to find any contemporary exegetical commentary or academic study that argues that Thomas's words in John 20:28 apply in context to the Father rather than to Jesus. The reason is simple: John prefaces what Thomas said with the words, "Thomas answered and said to Him" (v. 28a NASB). This seemingly redundant wording reflects a Hebrew idiomatic way of introducing someone's response to the previous speaker. John uses it especially frequently, always with the speaker's words directed to the person or persons who have just spoken previously in the narrative (John 1:48, 50; 2:18–19; 3:3, 9–10, 27; 4:10, 13, 17; 5:11; 6:26, 29, 43; 7:16, 21, 52; 8:14, 39, 48; 9:11, 20, 30, 34, 36; 12:30; 13:7; 14:23; 18:30; 20:28).[20] It is therefore certain that Thomas was directing his words to Jesus, not to the Father. No one, of course, would ever have questioned this obvious conclusion if Thomas had said simply "My Lord!" It is the addition of the words "and my God" that have sparked some creative but untenable interpretations of the text.[21]

Thomas's words echo statements addressed in the Psalms to the Lord (Jehovah), especially the following: "Wake up! Bestir yourself for my defense, for my cause, my God and my Lord [*ho theos mou kai ho kurios mou*]!" (Ps. 35:23). These words parallel those in John 20:28 exactly except for reversing "God" and "Lord."[22] More broadly, in biblical language "my God" (on the lips of a faithful believer) can refer only to the Lord God of Israel. The language is as definite as it could be and identifies Jesus Christ as God himself.

In identifying Jesus as God, Thomas, of course, was not identifying him as the Father. Earlier in the same passage, Jesus had referred to the Father as *his* God. It is interesting to compare Jesus' wording with the wording of Thomas. Jesus told Mary Magdalene, "I am ascending to my Father and your Father, to my God and your God" (*theon mou kai theon humōn*, John 20:17). As in John 1:1 and John 1:18, the Father is called "God" in close proximity to a statement affirming that Jesus is also "God." Here again, as in John 1:18, we do not see the apostle John distinguishing between the Father as "the God" (*ho theos*) and Jesus the Son as only "God" (*theos* without the article). In fact, whereas Jesus calls the Father "my God" without the article (*theon mou*, 20:17), Thomas calls Jesus "my God" with the article (*ho theos mou*, 20:28)! One could not ask for any clearer evidence that the use or nonuse of the article is irrelevant to the meaning of the word *theos*. What matters is how the word is used in context. In John 20:28, the apostle reports the most skeptical of disciples making the most exalted of confessions about Jesus. John expects his readers to view Thomas's confession as a model for them to follow.[23] Recognizing Jesus as the One who has conquered death itself for us, we too are to respond to Jesus and confess that he is our Lord and our God.

John's conclusion, at which he wants his readers also to arrive, that Jesus is the Son of God (20:30–31) is not at odds with understanding Thomas's statement in John 20:28 as a model confession of Jesus as Lord and God. In the prologue as well, John insists that Jesus is both God (1:1, 18) and the Son of God (1:14, 18). As D. A. Carson has observed, "This tension between unqualified statements affirming the full deity of the Word or of the Son, and those which distinguish the Word or the Son from the Father, are typical of the Fourth Gospel from the very first verse."[24] Those who find these descriptions of Jesus impossible to reconcile without denying or diminishing one in favor of the other are laboring under the assumption or presupposition of a unitarian view of God (i.e., the view that God can only be a solitary person).

To summarize, the Gospel of John explicitly refers to Jesus Christ as "God" three times: at the beginning and end of the prologue (1:1, 18) and at the climax of the book (20:28). These three strategically placed affirmations make it clear that Jesus is and always has been God. As Murray Harris puts it, "In his preincarnate state (1:1), in his incarnate state (1:18), and in his postresurrection state (20:28), Jesus is God. For John, recognition of Christ's deity is the hallmark of the Christian."[25]

Jesus as God in the Rest of the New Testament

The Gospel of John is the only book in the New Testament to refer to Jesus as God more than once. However, several other references to Jesus as God appear in the rest of the New Testament—some heavily disputed,[26] others beyond reasonable doubt.

Critics of the doctrine of the deity of Jesus often ask why, if Jesus is God, the New Testament does not refer to him more often as God. The answer is twofold. First, the New Testament writers were generally very careful to avoid making statements that would have implied that Jesus was the Father. While affirming Jesus' divine status in many ways, they maintained a clear distinction between the persons of the Father and the Son. Since they commonly applied the name "God" to the Father, they tended not to use that name for Jesus except in ways that did not confuse the two persons. The second reason is that the theological and religious roots of the New Testament were deeply monotheistic, and its authors sought to affirm Jesus' deity in ways that people would not perceive as undermining their Jewish monotheistic heritage. R. T. France makes a trenchant observation in this regard about statements that call Jesus "God" in such a cultural context.

> It was such shocking language that, even when the beliefs underlying it were firmly established, it was easier, and perhaps more politic, to express those beliefs in less direct terms. The wonder is not that the NT so seldom describes Jesus as God, but that in such a milieu it does so at all.[27]

God's Own Blood (Acts 20:28)

Among New Testament references or apparent references to Jesus as God, Acts 20:28 is one of the most disputed. It comes at the high point of Paul's farewell speech to the elders from the church of Ephesus with whom he met at Miletus (Acts 20:17–35). Consider the following two translations:

The church of God which He purchased with His own blood. (NASB)

The church of God that he obtained with the blood of his own Son. (NRSV)

Although most contemporary English versions render the last part of the verse in the same way as the NASB (ESV, NIV, NKJV, HCSB, and others), many scholars and commentators in recent decades have preferred the rendering found in the NRSV (and also in the REB).[28] There is no doubt as to the reason for this preference: those who dispute the conventional translation find the language, which expresses the idea of God's having "blood," difficult if not impossible to entertain.

A little lesson in grammar is unavoidable in order to understand the problem with the NRSV interpretation. The disputed words usually translated "his own blood" but translated "the blood of his own Son" in the NRSV are *tou haimatos tou idiou* (word for word, "the blood, the his-own"). The word *idiou* ("his own") is an adjective, which normally we would understand as modifying the noun *haimatos* ("blood"). The word order here, with the adjective following the noun with a second article between them, is perfectly normal and common in Greek.[29] Another example of this construction appears in the very same verse: "the Holy Spirit" (*to pneuma to hagion*, word for word, "the Spirit, the Holy"). It was not until the latter half of the nineteenth century[30] that anyone proposed that the words here in question did not mean "his own blood."

The basis for the alternate translation "the blood of his own Son" is that Greek can also use adjectives as if they were nouns (the technical term is *substantivally*). Many modern scholars argue that *tou idiou* is such a substantival use of the adjective, and therefore means "of his Own," comparable to the use of the adjective "the Beloved" (Eph. 1:6) as a kind of term of endearment for Christ.

This reinterpretation of the text is grammatically possible and difficult to disprove absolutely, but it is hardly the most natural understanding. As we mentioned, eighteen centuries went by before anyone came up with it.[31] The New Testament nowhere else calls Jesus "his Own" (*ho idios*), nor was this term ever picked up in the early church as a designation for Jesus. The substantival use of *ho idios* (or any grammatical variation, such as *ton idion*) is, in fact, rare in the New Testament, and in the singular occurs only once—and even then not in reference to a specific person (John 15:19).[32] On the other hand, *ho idios* functions as an adjective following the noun—just as in Acts 20:28—in several New Testament texts (John 1:41; 5:43; 7:18; Acts 1:25).

We are inclined to agree with Nigel Turner, a twentieth-century scholar of Greek grammar, who called the alternate translation of Acts 20:28 "a theological expedient, foisting imaginary distinctions into a spontaneous affirmation, and is not the natural way to take the Greek."[33] As Catholic scholar Charles DeVine commented sixty years ago, it is nothing more than an attempt "to avoid at all costs the full force of the expression 'God's own blood.'"[34]

God over All (Romans 9:5)

Romans 9:5 is another apparent affirmation of Jesus as God that can be translated in different ways. Consider the following translations:

. . . whose are the fathers, and from whom is the Christ according to the flesh, who is over all, God blessed forever. Amen. (NASB)

. . . to whom the forefathers belong and from whom the Christ [sprang] according to the flesh: God, who is over all, [be] blessed forever. Amen. (NWT)

According to the NASB and most recent major English versions, Paul refers to the Christ as "God," whereas in the NWT and some other (mostly older) translations, he does not. In other texts that apparently call Jesus "God," we have encountered various textual and translation disputes. Here, the difference comes down to punctuation.

If we break up the verse into lines and translate it word for word in order without punctuation, it will help us see what the issues are:

a.   whose [are] the fathers
b.   and from whom [is] the Christ according to the flesh
c.   the one who is over all
d.   God blessed unto the ages amen

Put very simply, the main options[35] for punctuating the verse boil down to three: (1) Put a period at the end of line *b*, so that lines *c* and *d* are a separate sentence. This would mean that the verse does not say that Christ is "over all" or that he is God.[36] (2) Put a period at the end of line *c*, so that line *d* is a separate sentence. This would mean that the verse says that Christ is "over all" but does not call him God.[37] (3) Treat all four lines as part of the same sentence (which may start in verse 3). This would mean that the verse says that Christ is "over all" and also calls him God.[38]

Two considerations lead most translators to choose the third option. First, grammatically, "who is over all" most naturally modifies "the Christ" in the preceding part of the verse: "and from whom is the Christ according to the flesh, the one who is over all" (translating literally). In addition, "who is" or "the one who is" (*ho ōn*) agrees grammatically with "the Christ" (*ho Christos*), leading the reader to understand that "who is over all" is continuing to say something about the Christ. Paul's wording here closely parallels a similar outburst of praise directed to God the Father in another of Paul's epistles: "The God and Father of the Lord Jesus knows, the one who is [*ho ōn*] blessed forever, that I am not lying" (2 Cor. 11:31, authors' translation). This means that the third line of Romans 9:5 most likely is part of the sentence that begins in verse 3. The thought that the Messiah is "over all" is certainly consistent with Paul's teaching; in fact, the idea is repeated just one chapter later (Rom. 10:12).

The second consideration is the position of the word for "blessed" (*eulogētos*), which in Greek follows the word for "God" (*theos*). In biblical doxologies that stand as separate sentences and that use *blessed*, it always precedes the divine name or title (God, YHWH, etc.) in the sentence. Here are some typical examples.

Blessed be God . . . (Pss. 66:20; 68:35)

Blessed be the LORD . . . (Exod. 18:10; Ruth 4:14; Pss. 28:6; 31:21)

Blessed be the LORD forever. (Ps. 89:52)

Blessed be the LORD the God of Israel . . . (1 Sam. 25:32; Pss. 41:13; 106:48; cf. Luke 1:68)

Blessed be the God and Father of our Lord Jesus Christ . . . (2 Cor. 1:3; Eph. 1:3; 1 Peter 1:3)

The fact that Romans 9:5 does not follow this standard biblical pattern for a doxology that stands as a separate sentence (which Paul himself uses elsewhere) makes it reasonably certain that "God blessed forever" is part of the same sentence as the preceding lines. Paul uses this sentence structure in other places in his writings, including earlier in the same epistle.

> They exchanged the truth about God for a lie and worshiped and served the creature rather than the Creator, who is [*hos estin*] blessed forever! Amen. (Rom. 1:25).

> The God and Father of the Lord Jesus, He who is [*ho ōn*] blessed forever. . . . (2 Cor. 11:31 NASB)

For these reasons, we can be quite confident that Romans 9:5 does, indeed, call Jesus "God."[39] This text is all the more significant when we consider that it is the earliest New Testament writing that calls Jesus "God" (dating to about A.D. 57, about a quarter-century after Jesus' death and resurrection).[40] Moreover, in Romans 9:5 we see three of the five elements we are discussing in this book pertaining to the deity of Jesus: he receives the divine *honor* of eternal praise; he has the divine *name* "God"; he shares God's *seat*, holding the highest position of ruling over all creation.

God's Throne (Hebrews 1:8)

The first chapter of the book of Hebrews presents an extended argument for the superiority of Jesus Christ over angels. In doing so, it quotes from a psalm that the author says refers to God's Son as "God" while also distinguishing him from God.

> But of the Son he says,
> "Your throne, O God, is forever and ever,
>   and the righteous scepter is the scepter of your kingdom.
> You have loved righteousness and hated wickedness;
> therefore God, your God, has anointed you
>   with the oil of gladness beyond your companions."
>   (Heb. 1:8–9)

The writer's quotation comes from Psalm 45:6–7, which reads essentially the same way in the Old Testament Hebrew text and in the Greek Septuagint. In the original context, the psalmist is addressing the King of Israel (Ps. 45:1–

5). Disturbed that the psalm would refer to the Israelite king as "God," some scholars have proposed a wide array of corrections to the Hebrew text, which they suspect was corrupted. These emendations, as textual scholars call them, include "your throne will be eternal," "God has established your throne forever," "Your throne is forever and ever," and the like. As Murray Harris properly notes, proposing to fix the text instead of accepting it as given is "an ill-advised counsel of despair."[41]

The reason so many scholars have proposed emendations to the text is, of course, that in its natural reading the text addresses the king as God. Not surprisingly, many other scholars have proposed different translations of the text, such as "your divine throne" or "God is your throne" or "your throne is like God's throne." The translation "Your throne, O God," however, besides being the best reading of the Hebrew, finds support in the ancient Greek Old Testament.[42]

The Israelite king was not, of course, literally God. Like Isaiah's prophecy about a boy named Immanuel who prefigured the Messiah, who really would be "God with us" (Isa. 7:14; Matt. 1:22–23), the psalm speaks in the immediate "horizon" about the Jerusalem king who also prefigured the Messiah, the ultimate descendant of David and the true eternal King. We should note that the psalm does not identify the specific king, and the whole psalm may be interpreted messianically. The king is fairer than other human beings (v. 2), addressed as "mighty one" (*gibbôr*, v. 3a; cf. Isa. 9:6), attributed glory and majesty (v. 3b), esteemed as the champion of truth and righteousness (vv. 4–7), and assured of an everlasting throne (v. 6). The nuptial imagery that dominates the second half of the psalm (vv. 8–15) is window dressing (likely occasioned by an actual wedding of the king) for a messianic vision of the future. The richest representatives of the nations of the world will attend to and bow before the Davidic king, and the peoples of the world will all praise him (note especially vv. 9–12, 17). Language about the king that would be hyperbolic in reference to any of Israel's merely human kings ultimately applies to the Messiah.[43] Thus, although none of those kings was literally God, Psalm 45 points forward to a coming king who really would be God.

This is exactly what the writer of the book of Hebrews claims—that the psalmist was, indeed, speaking "of the Son" (Heb. 1:8a). David, Solomon, and the other kings who ruled from Jerusalem merely anticipated God's true Son reigning from God's throne (Heb. 1:2–3), the one whom angels worship (v. 6), the Lord who made the heavens and the earth (v. 10) and will outlast them all (vv. 11–12). In a passage that makes all of these astounding statements about Jesus Christ and asserts that his name is superior to that of all the angels (v. 4), the claim that the name "God" also belongs to him (v. 8) should be given its full force.

One common objection to understanding verse 8 to mean that Jesus is God is that verse 9 (also a quotation from Psalm 45) calls someone else (presumably the Father) *his* God: "Therefore God, your God." This objection is no more valid here than the similar objection we considered earlier against understanding the Son of God in the Gospel of John to be God (John 1:1, 14, 18; 20:28, 31). In Hebrews, as in John, affirmations of Jesus as God and of the Father as Jesus' God are placed side by side (John 20:17, 28; Heb. 1:8, 9) with no sense of contradiction. By virtue of the Incarnation, Jesus became a human being, part of the created order (John 1:14; Phil. 2:6–7), and as such he properly honors the Father as his God (see also Rev. 3:12). At the same time, by virtue of his original, uncreated divine nature, Jesus was and still is God.

Our God and Savior (Titus 2:13; 2 Peter 1:1)

Two of the shortest books of the New Testament contain similar—and very strong—affirmations of Jesus Christ as God. In his epistle to Titus, the apostle Paul[44] states that Christians "wait for the blessed hope and the manifestation of the glory of our great God and Savior, Jesus Christ" (Titus 2:13). The equally short epistle of 2 Peter opens by describing its readers as "those who have received a faith as precious as ours through the righteousness of our God and Savior Jesus Christ" (1:1). Both of these texts describe Jesus using the two titles God and Savior.

Not everyone agrees that these verses call Jesus "God." Jehovah's Witnesses, for example, translate Titus 2:13 "of the great God and of [the] Savior of us, Christ Jesus" and 2 Peter 1:1 "of our God and [the] Savior Jesus Christ" (NWT, brackets in the original). The bracketed insertions of the word *the* make a significant difference. Read these verses without the bracketed insertions—especially 2 Peter 1:1—and they sound like they are referring to Jesus as both God and Savior.[45]

Several factors, taken together, prove beyond reasonable doubt that both of these verses call Jesus "God." One of these factors is the way the sentences use the article *the* in the construction or word arrangement that both sentences share.

tou megalou theou kai sōtēros hēmōn ꞌIēsou Cristou
the great God and Savior our Jesus Christ (Titus 2:13)

tou theou hēmōn kai sōtēros ꞌIēsou Cristou
the God our and Savior Jesus Christ (2 Peter 1:1)

Both of these texts use a construction that fits the following pattern:

Article + Noun + *kai* + Noun
the   God   and   Savior

The most natural way of understanding this particular construction is that both nouns refer to the same person. (In this construction, it does not matter whether the phrase includes a pronoun or where the pronoun appears.) When this construction occurs in ancient Greek using singular personal nouns that are not proper names (that is, nouns like *father, Lord, king,* not *Jesus, Peter,* or *Paul*), the two nouns normally refer to the same person. The first writer to analyze this construction in a formal way did so in the late eighteenth century. He was an English Christian abolitionist named Granville Sharp; for that reason, the analysis of this construction is commonly known as Sharp's rule.[46]

The New Testament contains plenty of examples supporting Sharp's rule. The epistles of Paul, for example, refer to "our God and Father" (e.g., Gal. 1:4; Phil. 4:20; 1 Thess. 1:3; 3:11, 13) and "the God and Father" (Rom. 15:6; 1 Cor. 15:24), which certainly refer to one person by both titles God and Father. There are numerous additional examples, many of little or no theological concern (see table on Sharp's rule).

EXAMPLES OF SHARP'S RULE[47]

Mark 6:3	"the carpenter, the *son* of Mary and *brother* of James"
Luke 20:37	"the Lord the *God* of Abraham and *God* of Isaac and *God* of Jacob"
John 20:17	"my *Father* and your *Father* and my *God* and your *God*"
Acts 3:14	"the *Holy* and *Righteous* One"

Eph. 6:21	"Tychicus, the beloved *brother* and faithful *minister* in the Lord"
Col. 4:7	"Tychicus, the beloved *brother* and faithful *servant* and *fellow-slave* in the Lord"
1 Thess. 3:2	"Timothy, our *brother* and God's *servant*"
1 Tim. 6:15	"the *King* of kings and *Lord* of lords"
Philem. 1	"our *dear friend* and *coworker*"
Heb. 3:1	"the *apostle* and *high priest* of our confession, Jesus"
Heb. 12:2	"the *author* and *finisher* of faith"
James 3:9	"the *Lord* and *Father*"
1 Peter 2:25	"the *Shepherd* and *Overseer* of your souls"
1 Peter 5:1	"as the *fellow-elder* and *witness* of Christ's sufferings"
Rev. 1:9	"John, your *brother* and *fellow-partaker*"
Rev. 1:6	"his *God* and *Father*"
Gal. 1:4; Phil. 4:20; 1 Thess. 1:3; 3:11, 13	"our *God* and *Father*"
Rom. 15:6; 1 Cor. 15:24; 2 Cor. 1:3a	"the *God* and *Father*" (also Eph. 1:3; 5:20; James 1:27; 1 Peter 1:3)
2 Cor. 1:3b	"the *Father* of mercies and *God* of all comfort"
2 Peter 1:11; 2:20; 3:18	"our *Lord* and *Savior*, Jesus Christ"
2 Peter 3:2	"the *Lord* and *Savior*"
Jude 4	"our only *Master* and *Lord* Jesus Christ"

The evidence that Titus 2:13 and 2 Peter 1:1 call Jesus God goes beyond Sharp's rule.[48] In Titus, the expression "our Savior" (*sōtēros hēmōn*) occurs six times. In five of those six occurrences, the article "the" (*tou*) immediately precedes "our Savior" (1:3, 4; 2:10; 3:4, 6); the one exception is Titus 2:13. The obvious and only good explanation for this variation is that "our Savior" is governed by the same article that governs "great God."

Another piece of evidence in the context of Titus 2:13 is Paul's use of the word *epiphaneia* ("manifestation" [NRSV], "appearing" [NASB]), from which we derive the word *epiphany*. In the Bible this word occurs only in Paul's writings, mostly in the Pastoral Epistles (2 Thess. 2:8; 1 Tim. 6:14; 2 Tim. 1:10; 4:1, 8; Titus 2:13), and always referring to the manifestation or appearing of Jesus Christ, unless Titus 2:13 is the sole exception. The close parallel between Titus 2:13 and 2 Timothy 1:10 ("the appearing of our Savior Christ Jesus") effectively rules out the possibility that Titus 2:13 is an exception. So when Paul says that Christians are awaiting "the appearing of the glory of our great God and Savior, Jesus Christ" (Titus 2:13 NASB), we can be sure that the one who will be "appearing" will indeed be Jesus Christ.

An alternative understanding of Titus 2:13, recently defended by evangelical Pauline scholar Gordon Fee, merits some attention. Fee agrees that Sharp's rule applies to Titus 2:13, so that "our great God and Savior" refers to one divine person. He argues, however, that the person called "our great God and Savior" is the Father, not Christ. His view is that Jesus Christ is called "*the glory of* our great God and Savior." In other words, he understands Paul to be saying that Christians are "awaiting the blessed hope and manifestation of the glory of our great God and Savior, [which glory is] Jesus Christ."[49]

If Fee is correct, what Paul says about Jesus Christ still implies his deity, since he would be affirming that the climactic, ultimate revelation of God's glory will be the appearing of Jesus Christ at his second coming. There are, however, some strong reasons to dispute Fee's interpretation. All of his arguments in support of that view boil down to the claim that it would be out of keeping with Paul's way of speaking for him to call Jesus "God." Yet it is clear that Paul departs from his usual terminology for Jesus in the epistle to Titus, since in this epistle alone he never refers to Jesus as "Lord" (*kurios*) and refers to Jesus at least twice as "Savior" (*sōtēr*, Titus 1:4; 3:6), a term he rarely uses for Jesus.[50] Murray Harris rightly warns against "an ever-present danger in literary research in making a writer's 'habitual usage' so normative that he is disallowed the privilege of creating the exception that proves the rule."[51]

At least eight factors cumulatively offer strong support for understanding "Jesus Christ" to be identifying "our great God and Savior," not "the glory," in Titus 2:13.

1. "Our great God and Savior" is immediately adjacent to "Jesus Christ."[52]

2. It would be odd to speak of the manifestation of God's glory and *not* mean that the one who is manifest is God.

3. Paul never refers to Jesus as God's "glory" (although 2 Cor. 4:4, 6 comes close).

4. All other things being equal, a personal designation like "our great God and Savior" is more likely to be identified as a person ("Jesus Christ") than is an abstraction ("the glory").

5. Elsewhere in the Pastoral Epistles (1 and 2 Timothy, Titus), whenever Paul uses the word *epiphaneia* ("manifestation" or "appearing"), it refers to the manifestation of Jesus Christ (1 Tim. 6:14; 2 Tim. 1:10; 4:1, 8), not of an abstract quality related to God or Christ.[53]

6. In as many as twelve out of eighteen times in his epistles that Paul uses the term "the glory" in the genitive case (*tēs doxēs*), it likely functions as a descriptive modifier of the preceding noun (Rom. 8:21; 9:23; 1 Cor. 2:8; 2 Cor. 4:4; Eph. 1:17, 18; 3:16; Phil. 3:21; Col. 1:11, 27; 1 Tim. 1:11; Titus 2:13). English translations often express this usage by the rendering "glorious" (see especially the NET and NIV).[54] Thus, Titus 2:13 may be better translated "the blessed hope and *glorious appearing* of our great God and Savior, Jesus Christ" (see, e.g., NKJV, NIV, NET).

7. Paul immediately follows his reference to Jesus Christ by speaking of his accomplishments for our salvation (Titus 2:14), confirming that in this context Jesus Christ is "our Savior."

8. The pattern of Paul's references to "our Savior" in Titus—three references to "God our Savior" each followed closely by a reference to Jesus Christ as "our Savior" (1:3, 4; 2:10, 13; 3:4, 6)—is disrupted if 2:13 does not refer to Jesus Christ as Savior.

A similar text—and one for which the exegetical issues are far simpler—is 2 Peter 1:1, which speaks of "our God and Savior Jesus Christ." Some people argue that this text cannot call Jesus "God" because "God" is clearly distinguished from "Jesus our Lord" in the very next verse (v. 2). This objection, though, assumes that the New Testament cannot affirm both that Jesus is God and that he is distinct from God. To the contrary, in at least four other New Testament texts we find such allegedly "contradictory" statements side by side (John 1:1, 18; 20:17, 28, 31; Heb. 1:8–9). Rather than mistranslate the texts to make them seem unproblematic to our minds, we should consider the possibility that these texts are revealing a paradoxical truth about the very nature of God.

As we read along in 2 Peter, we find several more references to Jesus Christ that closely parallel the wording of the first verse (see table below).

Virtually everyone acknowledges that the "Lord" in these texts is the same person as the "Savior," namely, Jesus Christ; we need offer no argument or defense of that understanding. Yet in at least two, and possibly three, of these texts the only difference between these descriptions of Christ and that in 2 Peter 1:1 is the use of *kuriou* ("Lord") instead of *theou* ("God"). Since both Lord and God were common titles of deity in both biblical usage and in the broader culture, it is difficult to see any cogent reason to deny that Jesus is called God in 2 Peter 1:1. As Richard Bauckham points out in his commentary on 2 Peter, "There is no reason why variations on the stereotyped formula should not be used."[55]

"OUR GOD/LORD AND SAVIOR JESUS CHRIST" IN 2 PETER

2 Peter	Greek Text	English Translation
1:1	*tou theou hēmōn kai sōtēros ᾿Iēsou Cristou* the God our and Savior Jesus Christ	our God and Savior Jesus Christ
1:11	*tou kuriou hēmōn kai sōtēros ᾿Iēsou Cristou* the Lord our and Savior Jesus Christ	our Lord and Savior Jesus Christ
2:20	*tou kuriou [hēmōn] kai sōtēros ᾿Iēsou Cristou* the Lord [our][56] and Savior Jesus Christ	[our] Lord and Savior Jesus Christ
3:18	*tou kuriou hēmōn kai sōtēros ᾿Iēsou Cristou* the Lord our and Savior Jesus Christ	our Lord and Savior Jesus Christ

The epistle of 2 Peter, then, opens by affirming that Jesus Christ is "our God and Savior." It closes, appropriately, with a doxology of praise to Jesus Christ: "But grow in the grace and knowledge of our Lord and Savior Jesus Christ. To him be the glory both now and to the day of eternity. Amen" (2 Peter 3:18). The verbal parallels in those opening and closing verses between "our God and Savior Jesus Christ" and "our Lord and Savior Jesus Christ," as well as the concluding doxology directing eternal glory to Jesus Christ, are stunningly clear affirmations that Jesus Christ is indeed our Lord and our God. Recognizing this is not merely an academic exercise; it is a summons to grow in our relationship with Jesus Christ and to begin living in such a way as to glorify him forever.

Chapter 13

HE IS LORD

nyone who has read the New Testament through even once knows that, although it calls Jesus "God" only occasionally, it frequently calls him "Lord"—hundreds of times, in fact. Many readers of the Bible have the mistaken impression, though, that the title *Lord* as applied to Jesus has a lesser significance than *God*—as though when the Bible calls Jesus *Lord* it means something like "almost but not quite God."

Nothing could be farther from the truth. The word *lord* had, of course, a variety of uses, and not everyone who called Jesus "Lord" meant to affirm his deity. Nevertheless, especially after Jesus' resurrection and ascension, the apostles and their associates immediately began speaking of Jesus as "Lord" in a way that strongly indicated that he was God himself.

Jehovah: The LORD

The crucial religious context of this divine sense for *Lord* was the Jewish practice of using the term (whether in Hebrew, Aramaic, or Greek) in place of the Old Testament name Yahweh, or Jehovah (YHWH).[1] (Most modern English Bibles reflect this same practice by translating YHWH in the Old Testament as "LORD," with the capitals distinguishing it from "Lord.") As almost everyone recognizes, Jehovah is the personal name of God in the Old Testament—not only the name of the God of Israel, but also of the one God of all creation. The Hebrew Bible affirms in the strongest of terms that YHWH is the one and only true God (Deut. 4:35, 39; 32:39; 2 Sam. 22:32; Isa. 37:20; 43:10; 44:6–8; 45:5, 14, 21–22; 46:9).[2] Thus, far from being a designation for a lesser deity, when used in place of the divine name YHWH, *Lord* was the highest designation a Jew could use for deity.

In the first century, it was common for Jews not to pronounce the name Yahweh aloud on most occasions in order to guard against the misuse or profaning of the name.[3] When they would read from the Hebrew scrolls of the Old Testament, they would say the Hebrew word for "Lord" (*adonai*) when they came to the name Yahweh in the text. This practice dated back to at least the second or third century B.C.

There are extant only a handful of fragments of the Old Testament in Greek from the time of the New Testament and earlier. Some of these Jewish copies of the Greek Old Testament use the four Hebrew consonants יהוה or YHWH (which scholars often call the *tetragrammaton* or *tetragram*, meaning "four letters"). Other fragments use a word in Greek that sounded like the Hebrew name (*IAŌ*). None of those discovered so far use the Greek word for "Lord" (*kurios*). This evidence has suggested to many biblical scholars that Christians around the beginning of the second century introduced the use of *kurios* in their Greek versions of the Old Testament.

On the other hand, some evidence, even from these fragments, indicate that the practice of using *Lord* or other substitutes (such as *theos*, "God") in the Greek Old Testament originated much earlier in Jewish circles. We will mention just one very interesting and easy-to-understand example. In the Greek version of Deuteronomy 31:27, "to Yahweh" (Hebrew, *ad YHWH*) is translated "to God" (Greek, *pros ton theon*). One of those early Jewish fragments of the Greek Old Testament, however, known as Rahlfs 848 and dated to the first century B.C., reads instead, "to YHWH God" (*pros* יהוה *ton theon*). How did that happen? As Albert Pietersma, a noted Septuagint scholar, has explained, the scribe was copying a Greek version of Deuteronomy that had "to God" and meant to replace "God" with the Hebrew letters for "YHWH," but accidentally left "God" in the text as well, resulting in "to YHWH God." This is just one example of the evidence that shows that these fragments were parts of *revisions* of the Greek Old Testament based on earlier copies that had *God* or *Lord* instead of the tetragram.[4]

In any case, the practice of using *Lord* in place of YHWH originated long before Christianity came on the scene and continued during and after the New Testament period. The late first-century Jewish historian Josephus, for example, expresses an unwillingness to write about God's "holy name," and when he quotes or paraphrases Old Testament statements that include the tetragram, he uses *Lord* or other titles instead.[5] The writings of the mid-first-century Jewish philosopher Philo of Alexandria exhibit the same practice, as do a wide variety of other Jewish writings from the second century B.C. through the first century A.D. A number of the Dead Sea Scrolls use the Hebrew *adonai* (Lord) or other substitutes for the tetragram.

The New Testament, written in Greek, also uses the Greek words for *Lord* and *God* and never the tetragram, not even in direct quotations from the Old Testament. We have over 5,700 Greek manuscripts of the New Testament varying in length from scraps containing a couple of verses or so to codices containing the entire New Testament. These manuscripts include papyri dating from at least the second century—possibly even the late first century—that have "Lord" (*kurios*) in direct quotations of Old Testament texts that use the name YHWH.[6] The Greek manuscripts come from various parts of the Mediterranean world and reflect different textual "traditions" or "family lines" of manuscripts that trace back to the first century.[7] In other words, there was no autocratic or organizational control forcing all of the New Testament manuscripts to read according to one ecclesiastical viewpoint.[8]

For these and other reasons outside the scope of this current volume, we should reject the theory that the New Testament originally contained the tetragram and that scribes in the second century replaced it with *Lord* or *God*. The religious group best known for advocating this is theory, of course, the Jehovah's Witnesses, whose New World Translation "restores" the name *Jehovah* to the New Testament 237 times.[9] Other "sacred name" groups (such as the Assemblies of Yahweh) make a similar claim. For years, George Howard was the one academic scholar who argued publicly for the same conclusion; recently, David Trobisch has affirmed Howard's conclusion.[10]

The question is important because those who argue that the New Testament originally contained the tetragram typically also claim that its substitution with *kurios* (Lord), as Howard puts it, "blurred the original distinction between the Lord God and the Lord Christ and, in many passages, made it impossible to tell which one was meant."[11] To the contrary, it was the New Testament writers who "blurred" such a distinction; that is, they referred to Jesus Christ as "Lord" in a way that identified him as the Lord Jehovah. In the rest of this chapter, we will demonstrate this to be the case.

Jesus as "Lord" in the Gospels

As we mentioned at the beginning of this chapter, during Jesus' lifetime other human beings were unlikely to refer to Jesus as "Lord" in a way that would identify him as YHWH. Nevertheless, the Gospels, which their authors composed after Jesus' resurrection, sometimes do speak of Jesus as Lord in this way.

A familiar example comes toward the beginning of all four Gospels, each of which states that John the Baptist's ministry of preparing the way for Jesus the Messiah was a fulfillment of Isaiah 40:3, "Prepare the way of the Lord" (Matt. 3:3; Mark 1:3; Luke 3:4; cf. Luke 1:16; John 1:23).[12]

Early in his ministry, Jesus warned that even those who said to him "Lord, Lord" (*kurie, kurie*) and claimed to do miracles in his name were condemned if they disobeyed him (Matt. 7:21–22; Luke 6:46; see also Matt. 25:11). This doubled form of address occurs repeatedly in the Septuagint in place of the Hebrew "Lord YHWH" (Deut. 3:24; 9:26; 1 Kings 8:53; Ps. 69:6; Ezek. 20:49; Amos 7:2, 5) or "YHWH Lord" (Pss. 109:21; 140:7; 141:8), but never in reference to anyone but YHWH.[13]

On one occasion, Jesus had fallen asleep while out in a fishing boat on the Sea of Galilee with some of his disciples. When a severe storm threatened to capsize the boat, the men woke Jesus up, saying, "Lord, save us!" (*kurie, sōson*, Matt. 8:25). On another occasion, Peter tried to walk on the sea after seeing Jesus do it, but when he lost faith and started to sink, he also cried out, "Lord, save me!" (*kurie, sōson me*, Matt. 14:30). They may not have intended to do so, but the disciples' cries to the Lord Jesus for help recall the words of a Psalm directed to God: "O LORD, save now" (*ō kurie, sōson dē*, Ps. 118:25, translating literally).[14]

Jesus as "Lord" in the Book of Acts

The book of Acts opens with Jesus' final appearance to his disciples and his ascension into heaven (Acts 1:1–11). As the disciples waited for the Holy Spirit to come, they prayed the first recorded prayer to Jesus, addressing him as "Lord" and acknowledging that he knows the hearts of all people (Acts 1:24).[15] The Old Testament, of course, ascribes this attribute of knowing people's hearts to Jehovah alone (1 Kings 8:39).

In the first Christian sermon, Peter quoted the prophet Joel: "Then everyone who calls on the name of the Lord shall be saved" (Acts 2:21, quoting Joel 2:32, which has YHWH). At the climax of his sermon, Peter concludes, "Therefore let the entire house of Israel know with certainty that God has made him both Lord and Messiah, this Jesus whom you crucified" (Acts 2:36). In the context of Luke's writings (Luke and Acts), this statement does not mean that Jesus was not "Lord" prior to his resurrection, since Jesus was

Lord and Messiah (Christ) even when he was born in Bethlehem (Luke 2:11). Rather, Peter means that God had exalted Jesus so that people would now recognize him for who he truly is, both Lord and Messiah. The idea is similar to Paul's statement that in the resurrection God "declared" Jesus "to be Son of God with power" (Rom. 1:4).

From the first prayer to Jesus and the first sermon about Jesus, we move to the first martyr for Jesus. As Stephen was being stoned to death, he twice "called upon" Jesus as "Lord," asking him to receive his spirit and to forgive his killers (Acts 7:59–60). As we saw when we discussed praying to Jesus, the idea of "calling upon" Jesus as Lord clearly recalls Joel 2:32, which Peter quoted in his sermon in Acts 2. Thus, simply reading these statements in the context of the whole narrative in Acts makes it clear that the early church prayed to Jesus and addressed him as the "Lord" spoken of in the Old Testament. This is consistent with the emphasis we saw in chapter 11 on the "name" of the "Lord" Jesus in Acts (8:16; 9:15, 27–28; 15:26; 19:5, 17; 21:13).

The book of Acts also refers to the message about Jesus that the apostles taught as "the word of the Lord" (Acts 8:25; 13:44, 48–49; 15:35–36; 16:32; 19:10; see also 1 Thess. 1:8; 2 Thess. 3:1).[16] This expression is common in the Old Testament in reference to the message that the Lord (YHWH) gave to his prophets (e.g., 2 Sam. 24:11; 1 Kings 13:1–2; 2 Chron. 36:21; Isa. 1:10; Jer. 1:4; Ezek. 1:3; Hos. 1:1–2; Joel 1:1; Amos 8:11–12; Jonah 1:1; 3:1; Mic. 1:1; Mal. 1:1).[17]

In Acts, then, Jesus is the Lord to whom the disciples pray. He is the one who knows the hearts of all people, on whom the disciples call in the moment of their death, whose name they live to glorify and die to serve, and whose word they believe, proclaim, and teach. In all of these ways, the identification of Jesus as "Lord" equates him with the Lord YHWH of the Old Testament.[18]

Jesus as "Lord" in Paul's Writings

Paul so often spoke of Jesus as "Lord" in contexts that equate him with YHWH that space does not permit us even to mention every such reference.[19]

Confessing That Jesus Is Lord (Romans 10:9–13)

In Romans, Paul writes, "If you confess with your mouth that Jesus is Lord and believe in your heart that God raised him from the dead, you will be saved. For with the heart one believes and is justified, and with the mouth one confesses and is saved" (Rom. 10:9–10 ESV). In this text, which Christians often use when encouraging others to come to Christ for salvation, the apostle states that the saving confession is that "Jesus is Lord" (*kurios*) and "that God raised him from the dead." As Paul does regularly in his epistles, he refers to Jesus by the divine title *Lord* while referring to the Father by the divine title *God*.[20] That these are both divine titles in Paul's usage will become clear as we proceed.

Paul then states, "For the Scripture says, 'Everyone who believes in him will not be put to shame'" (v. 11 ESV). The word "for" (Greek, *gar*) indicates that Paul is citing this Scripture reference from the Old Testament as support for the statement he has just made about believing in Jesus as the risen Lord for salvation. The reference is to Isaiah 28:16, which Paul had quoted earlier in the same passage: "They [unbelieving Israel] have stumbled over the stumbling stone, as it is written, 'Behold, I am laying in Zion a stone of stumbling, and a rock of offense; and whoever believes in him will not be put to shame'" (Rom. 9:32b–33 ESV). (This is an example of an important principle of biblical interpretation: ignore chapter divisions!) Jesus is, of course, the "stumbling stone" and the "rock of offense" in whom those Jews failed to believe for their salvation (see also Matt. 21:42–44; Mark 12:10–12; Luke 20:17–18; Acts 4:10–12; 1 Peter 2:6–8; cf. Eph. 2:20).

Next, Paul writes, "For there is no distinction between Jew and Greek; the same Lord is Lord of all, bestowing his riches on all who call on him" (Rom. 10:12 ESV). Here, Paul is explaining that belief in Jesus for salvation is not just for Jews (or just for Gentiles!) but is for anyone who calls on him for salvation. This is because "the same Lord" (*kurios*) is Lord "of all."[21] In this context, the "Lord" here must be Jesus. Paul cannot be referring to this Lord as "the same" Lord if he is a *different* Lord than the one he just mentioned! Paul states that this same Lord, Jesus, bestows his riches (cf. 2 Cor. 8:9) "on all who call on him." As we have already noted, calling on Jesus as Lord is an act of prayer, one that Paul elsewhere says characterizes Christians (1 Cor. 1:2).

Paul then backs up what he is saying with another Scripture reference: "For 'everyone who calls on the name of the Lord will be saved'" (Rom. 10:13 ESV). This reference is Joel 2:32, the same text that Peter quoted in the first Christian sermon (Acts 2:21). In context here in Romans 10, the Lord on whose name everyone calls for salvation (v. 13) must be "the same" one who is Lord "of all" and who bestows his riches of salvation on everyone who calls on him (v. 12). Since that Lord is Jesus (vv. 9–11), Paul is clearly identifying

Jesus as the "Lord" of Joel 2:32—who in the Hebrew text is called YHWH, or Jehovah.[22]

Confessing One Lord, Jesus Christ (1 Corinthians)

Paul frequently refers to Jesus as "Lord" in 1 Corinthians in such a way as to identify him as, or equate him with, the Lord Jehovah of the Old Testament.[23] Three instances appear in the opening ten verses alone. Christians, according to Paul, are "all those who in every place call on the name of our Lord Jesus Christ" (1 Cor. 1:2). The Old Testament, of course, taught that one should call on the name of the Lord YHWH (e.g., Joel 2:32, which, as we have seen, Paul also applied to Jesus in Romans 10:13). A few verses later, Paul says that Christians hope to be found "blameless on the day of our Lord Jesus Christ" (1:8; see also 5:5), whereas the Old Testament spoke of that judgment day as "the day of YHWH" (e.g., Joel 1:15; 2:1, 11, 31). The allusion to "the day of the Lord" (cf. Joel 2:31) in the same context as "calling on the name of the Lord" (cf. Joel 2:32) makes it all the more likely that Paul's language alludes directly to Joel. He refers to this future day of the Lord Jesus in several other epistles (2 Cor. 1:14; Phil. 1:6, 10; 2:16; 1 Thess. 5:2; 2 Thess. 2:1–2; 2 Tim. 1:18).[24] Paul then exhorts his readers "by the name of our Lord Jesus Christ" (1:10), again placing the focus on the name of the Lord Jesus that Judaism placed on the name of the Lord YHWH (see our earlier discussion of this point in chapter 11).[25]

Paul continues to refer to Jesus as Lord in similar ways throughout the epistle:

- After quoting the words of Jeremiah about boasting only in the Lord (Jer. 9:23–24), Paul says that his whole message to the Corinthians could be summed up as "Jesus Christ, and him crucified" (1:31; 2:2). This Jesus who was crucified, Paul says, was "the Lord of glory" (2:8). In context, then, Paul is applying the words of Jeremiah about boasting in the Lord to the Lord Jesus, as he probably does also in 2 Corinthians 10:17 (see also Gal. 6:14; Phil. 3:3).[26]
- Paul quotes the words of Isaiah 40:13, "For who has known the mind of the Lord so as to instruct him?" and then comments, "But we have the mind of Christ" (2:16). In other words, we can know the mind of the Lord only if he reveals it to us, and that is what we have in the mind of Christ.[27]

- In answer to his critics, Paul states, "The one who examines me is the Lord" (4:4 NASB). This "Lord" must be Jesus because Paul, like the rest of the New Testament writers, regards the Lord Jesus as the one who will sit in judgment (recall 1:8; see also 11:32; 2 Cor. 5:10). It is Jesus who is the "Lord" who will "come" and "bring to light the things hidden in the darkness and disclose the motives of men's hearts" (4:5 NASB). Again, this is what the Old Testament taught that the Lord (YHWH) would do (1 Kings 8:39; 1 Chron. 28:9; Ps. 96:13; 139:23–24; Prov. 16:2; 17:3; Jer. 17:10).
- Paul says that the members of the Christian church assemble "in the name of our Lord Jesus" (5:4 NASB). The "assembly" or "congregation" in the Old Testament was the congregation of YHWH; it gathered in his name. In Paul's thought, the congregations of believers are the congregations (or churches, *ekklēsiai*) of Christ (see Rom. 16:16).
- According to Paul, Christians confess that they are "justified in the name of the Lord Jesus Christ" (6:11), even though the Old Testament summons all people to be justified "in the Lord" YHWH (Isa. 45:25 NASB).
- For Paul, the directions received from the Lord are indistinguishable from those received from God: "Only, as the Lord has assigned to each one, as God has called each, in this manner let him walk" (7:17 NASB).
- Paul wants a Christian to be "anxious about the affairs of the Lord, how to please the Lord," with the ideal being "unhindered devotion to the Lord" (7:32–35). The purpose of life according to the Old Testament is, of course, to please the Lord YHWH (Exod. 15:26; Deut. 6:18; etc.). The only other use in the New Testament of any form of the verb translated in 1 Corinthians 7:35 as "devotion" (*euparedron*, also translated "service") is just a couple of chapters later in the same epistle, where Paul says that those who "serve" (*paredreuontes*) at the altar share in what is offered at the altar (9:13). Thus, Paul makes religious devotion or service to the Lord Jesus the ideal and purpose of the Christian life.
- Paul warns, "You cannot drink the cup of the Lord and the cup of demons. You cannot partake of the table of the Lord and the table of demons" (1 Cor. 10:21). Here the cup and table of the Lord refer to the rite of the "Lord's Supper" (cf. 10:16; 11:20) that the Lord Jesus

established. The expression "table of the LORD" is an Old Testament expression for the altar, which the prophet Malachi warned against defiling (Mal. 1:7, 12). Paul contrasts the observance of the Lord's Supper with pagan observances that honor the false gods of demonically inspired pagan religion (10:20; echoing Deut. 32:21). Such a contrast implicitly treats the Lord Jesus as the divine object of the religious observance. Paul then asks, "Or are we provoking the Lord to jealousy?" (10:22). This rhetorical question clearly alludes again to Deuteronomy 32:21, where Moses warned against provoking the Lord YHWH to jealousy. Paul's train of thought here makes no sense unless the "Lord" whom we should avoid provoking to jealousy (10:22) is the same "Lord" to whom belong the cup and the table (10:21). In short, Paul here assumes that the Lord Jesus is in fact the Lord YHWH.[28]

- At the end of the epistle, Paul writes, "If anyone does not love the Lord, he is to be accursed. Maranatha. The grace of the Lord Jesus be with you" (1 Cor. 16:22–23 NASB). In this short space, Paul calls for those who do not love the Lord to be cursed, prays to the Lord to come (see our earlier discussion of *maranatha* in chapter 3), and attributes divine grace or favor to the Lord Jesus. The importance attached to loving the Lord (Jesus) here is especially striking in view of the Old Testament commandment to "love the LORD your God" with all your heart, soul, and strength (Deut. 6:5; see following page).[29]

In addition to these references to Jesus as Lord in contexts that treat him as the divine Lord of the Old Testament, Paul repeatedly speaks of God (the Father) and the Lord Jesus in ways that imply the closest possible unity (see 1 Cor. 1:1–4, 24, 30–31; 3:5–6, 19–20; 4:1, 19–20; 6:13; 7:21–24, 39–40; 9:21; 10:4–5; 12:5–6, 27–28; 15:57–58).

It is in this broader context that we should read what may be the most striking reference to Jesus as Lord in 1 Corinthians. Paul states that Christians know that "there is no God but one" (1 Cor. 8:4 NIV). "For even if there are so-called gods, whether in heaven or on earth (as indeed there are many 'gods' and many 'lords'), yet for us there is but one God, the Father, from whom all things came and for whom we live; and there is but one Lord, Jesus Christ, through whom all things came and through whom we live" (vv. 5–6 NIV). Verse 6 may well be a creed or confession of faith that Paul is quoting or that he composed himself (translation ours):

One God,		One Lord,
the Father,		Jesus Christ,
from whom are all things,	and	through whom are all things,
and we from him;		and we through him.

If Judaism has a creed, it is the words of Deuteronomy 6:4–5, known as the Shema (meaning "hear," the first word of the verse): "Hear, O Israel: The LORD our God, the LORD is one. You shall love the LORD your God with all your heart and with all your soul and with all your might" (ESV). The Septuagint translated the last part of verse 4, "The Lord our God is one Lord" (*kurios heis*). In first-century Judaism, the affirmations of "one God" and "one Lord" were synonymous and referred to the same divine being, YHWH, the God of the patriarchs, of Moses, and of the prophets. Jesus affirmed the Shema as the first and greatest commandment (Matt. 22:36–38; Mark 12:28–30; cf. Luke 10:25–28),[30] and in that regard his view was in the mainstream of Judaism.

Paul and other New Testament writers echo the Shema when they affirm that God is one or that there is one God (Rom. 3:30; 1 Cor. 12:6; Gal. 3:20; Eph. 4:6; 1 Tim. 2:5; James 2:19).[31] Jews, however, would just as surely have understood Paul's affirmation of "one Lord" (particularly in the same breath as affirming "one God") as an echo of the Shema—yet with one potentially shocking twist: he identifies this "one Lord" as Jesus Christ.[32]

Confessing Jesus Christ as Lord (Philippians 2:9–11)

Although many other passages deserve attention, our study of Paul's designation of Jesus as Lord will conclude with just one more example. We have commented in previous chapters on Paul's well-known passage in Philippians about Christ's humiliation and exaltation (2:6–11). That passage concludes with stirring words about Christ's place in the cosmos:

> Therefore God also highly exalted him and gave him the name that is above every name, so that at the name of Jesus every knee should bend, in heaven and on earth and under the earth, and every tongue should confess that Jesus Christ is Lord, to the glory of God the Father. (Phil. 2:9–11)

Two factors in the immediate context make it clear that "Lord" in verse 11 stands for the divine name, YHWH. First, Paul states categorically that

Jesus has "the name that is above every name" (v. 9). In a Jewish context, that name, of course, would be YHWH, and the immediately following affirmation that Jesus is "Lord" (*kurios*) confirms that to be the name. Second, Paul's statement alludes to a passage in Isaiah about YHWH.

CONFESSING JESUS AS "LORD" IN PHILIPPIANS 2

Isaiah 45:23 LXX	Philippians 2:10–11
"to me every knee shall bend, and every tongue shall swear."[33] *kampsei pan gonu kai exomologēsetai pasa glōssa*	"that at the name of Jesus every knee should bend [*pan gonu kampsē*], in heaven and on earth and under the earth, and every tongue should confess [*kai pasa glōssa exomologēsētai*] that Jesus Christ is Lord, to the glory of God the Father."

As David Capes points out, "The claim that 'every knee shall bow' and 'every tongue confess' belongs to one of the most important monotheistic passages of the Old Testament and referred originally to Yahweh."[34]

The convergence of these two factors of the immediate context convinces most biblical scholars that, in Philippians 2:9–11, the confession that "Jesus Christ is Lord" affirms that he is in fact Jehovah. Those who object to this conclusion sometimes point out that Paul says that God "gave" Jesus this name when he "highly exalted him" (v. 9). If Jesus really is Jehovah, the eternal YHWH, how could God the Father have *given* him that name after his death and resurrection? This objection misunderstands both the nature of God's "giving" and the point of Paul's statement. Although "Lord" in verse 11 represents the divine name YHWH, Paul's point in verses 9–10 is that in exalting Jesus, God "gave" him the honor of his name being exalted above all other names. Thus, when Paul says, "that at the name of Jesus every knee should bend," he is saying that the name *Jesus* now stands as the highest, most honored name in all creation.[35] This is consistent with the way the name of Jesus is elevated throughout the New Testament (as we saw in chapter 11).

The confession "that Jesus Christ is Lord" expresses his exalted status and position definitively: God wants all creation to recognize Jesus as no one less than the Lord YHWH himself. Giving Jesus this honor does not detract from the honor that is properly due to the Father; rather, Paul insists, when we confess Jesus to have the highest name of all and to be "Lord," we do so "to the glory of God the Father" (v. 11).

Jesus as "Lord" in 1 Peter

Two passages in 1 Peter refer to Jesus as "Lord" in a way that identifies or equates him with the Lord YHWH. The first is Peter's encouragement to new believers to grow in their salvation, "if indeed you have tasted that the Lord is good" (1 Peter 2:3). This is a clear allusion to the psalmist's exhortation, "O taste and see that the LORD is good" (Ps. 34:8).[36] That the "Lord" in 1 Peter 2:3 is Jesus is evident from what follows: "As you come to him, the living Stone—rejected by men but chosen by God and precious to him" (v. 4 NIV). Peter goes on to quote a battery of Old Testament "stone" texts that the early church interpreted as referring to Jesus (vv. 6–8, quoting Isa. 28:16; Ps. 118:22; Isa. 8:14). The last of these texts, in its original context, clearly refers to YHWH as the "stone."

> Do not call conspiracy all that this people calls conspiracy, and do not fear what they fear, nor be in dread. But the LORD of hosts, him you shall regard as holy. Let him be your fear, and let him be your dread. And he will become a sanctuary and a stone of offense and a rock of stumbling to both houses of Israel, a trap and a snare to the inhabitants of Jerusalem. (Isa. 8:12–14 ESV)

When Peter applies to Jesus, then, the description "a stone of offense and a rock of stumbling" (1 Peter 2:8 ESV), he confirms that when he called Jesus the "Lord" in verse 3, he was indeed referring to him as the LORD (YHWH).

Peter returns to two of the same texts, Psalm 34 and Isaiah 8, later in his epistle, again referring to Jesus as "Lord." He begins by quoting at length from Psalm 34.

> For
> "Whoever desires to love life
> and see good days,
> let him keep his tongue from evil
> and his lips from speaking deceit;
> let him turn away from evil and do good;
> let him seek peace and pursue it.

> For the eyes of the Lord are on the righteous,
>> and his ears are open to their prayer.
> But the face of the Lord is against those who do evil."
>> (1 Peter 3:10–12; quoting Ps. 34:12–16 ESV)

This extensive quotation from Psalm 34 confirms that Peter was also quoting Psalm 34:8 earlier in the epistle (1 Peter 2:3). He then goes on to refer directly to Christ as "Lord," once again quoting from Isaiah 8:

> Now who is there to harm you if you are zealous for what is good? But even if you should suffer for righteousness' sake, you will be blessed. Have no fear of them, nor be troubled, but in your hearts regard Christ the Lord as holy, always being prepared to make a defense to anyone who asks you for a reason for the hope that is in you. (1 Peter 3:13–15 ESV)

Most English versions do not show this explicitly, but Peter here quotes from Isaiah 8:12–13, which immediately precedes the line that he quoted earlier from Isaiah 8:14 (in 1 Peter 2:8). The table below[37] makes Peter's use of the passage clear.

REVERING CHRIST AS "LORD" IN 1 PETER 3

Isaiah 8:12–13 LXX	1 Peter 3:13–15
"But do not fear what it [the people] fears, or be in dread;	"But do not fear what they fear, or be in dread;
regard as holy the Lord himself. . . ."	but regard as holy Christ the Lord . . ."
ton de phobon autou ou mē phobēthēte oude mē tarachthēte, kurion auton hagiasate	*ton de phobon autōn mē phobēthēte mēde tarachthēte, kurion de ton christon hagiasate*

The main change that Peter has made in his use of Isaiah 8:12–13 is to replace *auton* ("himself") with *ton christon* ("Christ"),[38] thereby making explicit his understanding that Christ is the Lord whom we are to "regard as holy" (*hagiasate*). Twice, then, in this short epistle, Peter draws on both Psalm

34 and Isaiah 8 and speaks of Jesus Christ as the divine Lord (YHWH) of those Old Testament texts.

Across the New Testament, then, in the Gospels, Acts, and Epistles, we find writers calling Jesus "Lord" in contexts that identify or equate him with the Lord YHWH. The basic confession of early Christianity that "Jesus is Lord" (Rom. 10:9; 1 Cor. 12:3; Phil. 2:11) turns out to entail the most astonishing and radical claim that any first-century Jew might have made: that the crucified man, Jesus of Nazareth, was Jehovah.

Chapter 14

JESUS IS IT FROM *A* TO *Ζ*

In this concluding chapter on the divine names of Jesus, we will discuss briefly a wide array of divine designations the Bible gives to Jesus. As we emphasized in chapter 11, it is not merely the use of certain words for Jesus that makes them indicative of his deity but the religious and theological contexts in which the New Testament applies them to Jesus.

Bridegroom/Husband

The Old Testament portrays YHWH, the LORD, as the bridegroom and husband of Israel.

> For your Maker is your husband,
>   the LORD of hosts is his name;
> the Holy One of Israel is your Redeemer,
>   the God of the whole earth he is called.
>   (Isa. 54:5)

> As the bridegroom rejoices over the bride,
>   so shall your God rejoice over you.
>   (Isa. 62:5)

Isaiah sets these descriptions of God's relationship with Israel in the context of Israel's gross unfaithfulness to God. Isaiah, like several other prophets, portrays Israel as an unfaithful wife, with its history of polytheism and idolatry pictured metaphorically as the immoral behavior of a wife who sells herself as a prostitute (Isa. 54:4–8; 62:4–5; Jer. 2:2; 3:1–14; Ezek 16:8–63; 23:1–49; Hos. 2:1–3:5). The prophets look beyond Israel's unfaithfulness to a time when God will bring his people into a healthy relationship with him. Notably, in Jeremiah, God promised that in the future he would make "a new covenant" with Israel, unlike the Mosaic covenant "that they broke, though I was their husband, says the LORD" (31:31–32). Hosea speaks of a day when unfaithful Israel "shall return and seek the LORD their God, and David their king" (3:5). The reference to David may, in the immediate "horizon," refer to the Israelites from the northern tribes' acknowledging the legitimacy of the Davidic royal line, but it also anticipates the greater fulfillment that came long after the Davidic dynasty had ended (v. 4), when they would seek the greater David, the Messiah.

When we turn to the New Testament, we discover that Jesus claims to be not only the Messiah but also the bridegroom! When some people challenged Jesus to explain why his disciples did not fast, he replied, "The wedding guests cannot fast while the bridegroom is with them, can they? As long as they have the bridegroom with them, they cannot fast" (Mark 2:19). Here Jesus represents himself as the bridegroom and his disciples as the bridegroom's guests.[1]

In one of his parables,[2] Jesus tells the story of foolish virgins who were not prepared for the wedding feast of the bridegroom (Matt. 25:1–13). In the context of the surrounding passage, Jesus is again the "bridegroom" (25:5, 10–13; cf. 24:42–44). In yet another parable, Jesus compared the kingdom of heaven "to a king who gave a wedding banquet for his son" (Matt. 22:2). It is likely that we should view the king as representing God the Father, while the king's son represents Jesus. It is Jesus, the Son, who is the Bridegroom in the "wedding feast" of the future kingdom of God.

John the Baptist once explained why it was appropriate that people who had been following him were leaving to follow Jesus: "He who has the bride is the bridegroom. The friend of the bridegroom, who stands and hears him, rejoices greatly at the bridegroom's voice. For this reason my joy has been fulfilled" (John 3:29). Here John compares the followers of Jesus to a bride, and Jesus to the bridegroom.

After Jesus' resurrection and ascension, the apostles in even clearer terms portrayed Jesus as the Bridegroom of the people of God. Paul expressed his concern that the believers remain faithful to Christ, using terms reminiscent of the Old Testament prophets: "I feel a divine jealousy for you, for I promised you in marriage to one husband, to present you as a chaste virgin to Christ" (2 Cor. 11:2). Elsewhere, Paul speaks of the church as Christ's bride: "For the husband is the head of the wife just as Christ is the head of the church, the body of which he is the Savior. . . . Husbands, love your wives, just as Christ loved the church and gave himself up for her, in order to make her holy by cleansing her with the washing of water by the word, so as to present the church to himself in splendor, without a spot or wrinkle or anything of the kind—yes, so that she may be holy and without blemish" (Eph. 5:23, 25–27).

The book of Revelation also uses wedding imagery in reference to Christ and the church.

> "Let us rejoice and exult and give him the glory, for the marriage of the Lamb has come, and his bride has made herself ready; to her it has been granted to be clothed with fine linen, bright and pure"— for the fine linen is the righteous deeds of the saints. And the angel said to me, "Write this: Blessed are those who are invited to the marriage supper of the Lamb." (Rev. 19:7–9)

> And I saw the holy city, the new Jerusalem, coming down out of heaven from God, prepared as a bride adorned for her husband. . . . Then one of the seven angels who had the seven bowls full of the seven last plagues came and said to me, "Come, I will show you the bride, the wife of the Lamb." (Rev. 21:2, 9)

The "new Jerusalem" in Revelation 21 is a symbolic vision of the church as a great "holy city," built on the foundation of the teaching of the twelve apostles (v. 14; cf. Eph. 2:20). The angel refers to this "city" as "the bride, the wife of the Lamb," recalling Paul's description of the church as the bride of Christ (Eph. 5:25–27).[3]

These references to Jesus as the bridegroom or husband of the church are just one of many examples of the New Testament's applying to Jesus Old Testament metaphors for God.

King of Kings and Lord of Lords

In his apocalyptic vision of the judgment and destruction of Babylon the Great (Rev. 17–18), John speaks of kings (allied with the Beast) who "will make war against the Lamb, but the Lamb will overcome them because he is Lord of lords and King of kings" (Rev. 17:14 NIV). The Lamb, of course, is John's most frequent symbolic image for Jesus Christ (see especially 5:6–14). The title "Lord of lords and King of kings" uses a familiar idiomatic way of saying that he is the greatest Lord and King. Such language appears several times throughout the Old Testament in reference to God: "God of gods and Lord of lords" (Deut. 10:17); "the God of gods . . . the Lord of lords" (Ps. 136:2, 3).[4]

John's use of the title derives from the Septuagint translation of Daniel 4:37, an expansion of a speech by Nebuchadnezzar that is not found in the original Hebrew and Aramaic version of Daniel (and thus not found in English Bibles). In this expanded speech, Nebuchadnezzar, king of Babylon, acknowledges that God, not he himself, is the greatest king.

"KING OF KINGS AND LORD OF LORDS" AS A DIVINE TITLE

Daniel 4:37 LXX	Revelation 17:14
". . . because he himself is God of gods and Lord of lords and King of kings"	". . . because he is Lord of lords and King of kings"
hoti autos esti theos tōn theōn kai kurios tōn kuriōn kai basileus tōn basileōn	*hoti kurios kuriōn estin kai basileus basileōn*

That the destruction of the old Babylonian Empire is a major theme in the book of Daniel—and that the humiliation of the Babylonian king is the immediate theme in Daniel 4—confirms that John's use of the same title for Jesus is not merely a verbal coincidence. John is deliberately applying to "the Lamb," Jesus Christ, an exalted title reserved in Judaism exclusively for God.[5] He repeats the title for Jesus in the climactic scene in which the Beast and his henchmen are finally defeated and cast into the lake of fire. The only difference in form in the title here is that John reverses the two halves: "King of kings and Lord of lords" (Rev. 19:16, 20–21).[6]

Savior

One of the more familiar titles for Jesus in the New Testament is "Savior" (Greek, *sōtēr*). The Old Testament uses this word just a few times in reference to the "judges," those heroic figures who delivered Israel from oppression during the period prior to the monarchy (Judg. 3:9, 15; 12:3; Neh. 9:27). Otherwise, the title refers consistently (at least eighteen times) to God— never to an angel or any other heavenly being.

Three aspects of the New Testament use of "Savior" for Jesus show that we are to understand its application to him in the highest possible sense. First, *the New Testament calls Jesus "Savior" in an ultimate, cosmic sense.* He is not merely a deliverer of Israel from foreign oppressors, like Othniel or Ehud in the book of Judges. He is indeed a Savior for Israel (Acts 13:23), but he is far more: he is "the Savior of the world" (John 4:42; 1 John 4:14). Jesus is our heavenly Savior (Phil. 3:20; Titus 2:13) who saves us from sin and death (Acts 5:31; 2 Tim. 1:10; Titus 2:14).

Second, *the New Testament calls Jesus "Savior" in conjunction with the divine titles "Lord" and "God."* The description of Jesus as "our Lord and Savior" (2 Peter 1:11; 2:20; 3:2, 18) is familiar to most Christians (see also Luke 2:11; Phil. 3:20). The New Testament also calls Jesus "our great God and Savior" (Titus 2:13) and "our God and Savior" (2 Peter 1:1).[7] This conjunction of the titles *God* and *Savior* is especially noteworthy, since in a majority of occurrences of the word *Savior* in the Greek Old Testament it is similarly conjoined with *God* in reference to YHWH (Deut. 32:15; Pss. 25:5; 27:9; 62:2, 6; 65:5; 79:9; 95:1; Isa. 12:2; 17:10; 45:15, 21; Mic. 7:7; Hab. 3:18). In light of this Old Testament usage, the suggestion that Paul or Peter could call Jesus "our God and Savior" and mean someone inferior to YHWH is simply untenable.

GOD AND CHRIST AS "OUR SAVIOR" IN TITUS

"the proclamation with which I have been entrusted by the command of *God our Savior*" (*tou sōtēros hēmōn theou*, 1:3)	"Grace and peace from God the Father and *Christ Jesus our Savior*" (*christou iēsou tou sōtēros hēmōn*, 1:4)
"so that in everything they may be an ornament to the doctrine of *God our Savior*" (*tou sōtēros hēmōn theou*, 2:10)	"the glory of *our great God and Savior, Jesus Christ*" (*tou megalou theou kai sōtēros hēmōn iēsou christou*, 2:13)
"But when the goodness and loving kindness of *God our Savior*" (*tou sōtēros hēmōn theou*, 3:4)	"he poured out on us richly through *Jesus Christ our Savior*" (*iēsou christou tou sōtēros hēmōn*, 3:6)

Third, *the New Testament calls Jesus our "Savior" in the same breath that it calls God our "Savior."* Three times in the short epistle to Titus, Paul calls God "our Savior" and then immediately calls Jesus "our Savior" (see table on previous page). Far from there being any suggestion of a different meaning or role, these passages equate Christ's position as Savior with that of God. The middle of these three passages refers to Jesus Christ as *both* God and Savior.

As Larry Hurtado rightly notes, in these passages "God and Jesus are both referred to as 'Savior' in such close proximity that we must infer a deliberate effort to link them through this appellative."[8]

"I Am"

In normal usage, both inside and outside the Bible, the phrase *I am* is not properly or technically classified as a *name*. It is, however, quite commonly part of an act of self-naming. So, for example, the Lord revealed himself to Abraham by saying, "I am God Almighty" (Gen. 17:1). He introduced the Ten Commandments by first introducing himself: "I am the LORD your God, who brought you out of the land of Egypt, out of the house of slavery" (Exod. 20:2). At times, God practically punctuates his instructions to Israel with the reminder, "I am the LORD" (for example, thirteen times in Lev. 19:10–37 alone).

In addition to these straightforward uses of the words *I am* in the Old Testament, God sometimes says simply, "I am he" (in Hebrew, *ʾānî hû*, literally, "I [am] he"). The Septuagint usually translates this statement as "I am" (*egō eimi*).

> See now that I, even I, am he [Gk., "that I am," *hoti egō eimi*]; there is no god besides me. (Deut. 32:39)

> I, the LORD, am the first, and with the last. I am He. (Gk., *egō eimi*; Isa. 41:4 NASB)

> . . . even to your old age I am he. (Gk., *egō eimi*; Isa. 46:4)

We may see some connections between these statements and God's declaration in Exodus 3:14, "I AM WHO I AM." The Hebrew wording of this statement, *ʾehyeh ʾasher ʾehyeh*, can be translated "I am who I am" or "I will be what I will be," both of which mean much the same thing: God is the self-determining one who is always there, or who will always be there, the one on whom all creatures may and should rely. The Septuagint translates, "I am the being," that is, "I am the one who is" (*egō eimi ho ōn*). Despite frequent criticisms of this translation, it expresses the same point reasonably well: God is the one who simply is, who depends on nothing else, and on whom all else depends.[9] The "I am (he)" statements in Deuteronomy and Isaiah make much the same point: from first to last, the Lord is the one and only God.[10]

According to a broad consensus of New Testament scholars, at least some of the "I am" sayings of Jesus in the Gospel of John echo these "I am" sayings of God, especially those in Isaiah.[11] The clearest example is a pair of such sayings in John 8, which allude strongly to a saying of God in Isaiah 43:10. Another very likely allusion is Jesus' statement to the Samaritan woman: "I am he [*egō eimi*], the one who is speaking to you" (John 4:26). On a prosaic level, one can read Jesus' statement as simply an affirmation that he is the Messiah about whom the woman had asked. It turns out, however, that Jesus' response is almost a perfect quote from Isaiah 52:6, in which God tells his people that at some point in the future they will finally realize that *he* is the one speaking to them. Other "I am" sayings of Jesus are more allusive in their relation to sayings of God in Isaiah, but in light of these clear connections, and since most of them pertain to the same passage in Isaiah 43, we should recognize these allusions as genuine as well (see table on page 178).

The reactions of those to whom Jesus spoke when he said these things change as one moves through the Gospel. In John 8 alone their reactions run the gamut from confusion to outrage (vv. 25, 27, 59). When Jesus said, "Before Abraham was born, I am" (John 8:58 NASB), his opponents attempted to stone him to death, presumably for blasphemy (v. 59). When soldiers and officials came to arrest him and said they were looking for Jesus of Nazareth, he replied, "I am he," and they promptly fell to the ground (18:5–6). John clearly expects his readers to understand that Jesus' words "I am" on these occasions were not mere self-identification, like "Yeah, it's me." They were astonishing, even numinous claims to deity that were either blasphemous or true. Jesus' resurrection from the dead proves, of course, his divine self-naming to be true (John 20:27–28).

Alpha and Omega, Beginning and End, First and Last

When we say that Jesus is it "from *A* to *Z*," we have in mind especially some of the titles of Jesus found in the last book of the Bible, the book of

"I AM" IN ISAIAH AND JOHN[12]

Isaiah (LXX)	John
"*I am* he, *the one who is speaking*" (52:6) *egō eimi autos ho lalōn*	"*I am, the one who is speaking* to you" (4:26) *egō eimi ho lalōn soi*
"When you pass through the waters. . . . *Do not be afraid*, for I *am* with you" (43:2, 5) *mē phobou hoti meta sou eimi*	"*I am; do not be afraid*" (6:20) *egō eimi mē phobeisthe* (Note: Jesus walks on the waters of the sea to meet the disciples' boat, vv. 16–19)
". . . so that *you may know* and *believe* and understand *that I am*. . . . I am God, and beside me there is no one to save. . . . But you have stood *in your sins* and in your iniquities. . . . I am, I am the one who blots out your transgressions" (43:10–11, 24–25) *hina gnōtē kai pisteusēte kai sunēte hoti egō eimi. . . . en tais hamartiais sou*	". . . for unless *you believe that I am*, you will die *in your sins* . . . then *you will know that I am*" (8:24, 28) *ean gar mē pisteusēte hoti egō eimi apothaneisthe en tais hamartiais humōn . . .* *tote gnōsesthe hoti egō eimi*
". . . my servant whom I have chosen [*exelexamēn*], *so that you may* know and *believe* and understand *that I am*" (43:10) *hina gnōtē kai pisteusēte kai sunēte hoti egō eimi*	"I am not speaking of all of you; I know the ones *I have chosen* [*exelexamēn*]. . . . I tell you this now, before it occurs, *so that you may believe* when it does occur *that I am* he" (13:18–19) *hina pisteusēte hotan genētai hoti egō eimi*

Revelation. Revelation uses three titles that mean the same thing: "the Alpha and the Omega" (*to alpha kai to ō*), referring to the first and last letters of the Greek alphabet; "the first and the last"; and "the beginning and the end." None of these titles occurs elsewhere in the New Testament.[13] The title *the first and the last* clearly originates at least in part from Isaiah, in which the Lord insists that he is the only God: "I, the LORD, the first, and with the last;

I am he. . . . I am the first and I am the last; besides me there is no god. . . . I am he; I am the first, and I am the last" (Isa. 41:4; 44:6; 48:12 ESV). In the context of Isaiah's prophecies, the Lord is asserting in these statements that he is the one in control of Israel's future and that God's people have a sure hope of restoration.

Beyond controversy, Revelation applies the title *the first and the last* to Jesus, who explicitly claims it for himself. "Don't be afraid! I am the First and the Last, and the Living One. I was dead, but look—I am alive forever and ever, and I hold the keys of death and Hades" (1:17b–18 HCSB). "The First and the Last, the One who was dead and came to life, says [this]" (2:8 HCSB). In the context of John's visions, Jesus is asserting in these statements that by his death and resurrection he has conquered death, and is assuring his people of their future resurrection and vindication in the age to come. Thus, the title *the first and the last* has a religious significance in Revelation that is parallel to that in Isaiah.

Some interpreters deny that Revelation also applies the titles *the beginning and the end* and *the Alpha and the Omega* to Jesus, noting that these titles apply explicitly in the book to the Lord God Almighty (Rev. 1:8; 21:6). Near the end of the book, however, both titles appear alongside the title *the first and the last*, which we already know belongs to Jesus.

> Look! I am coming quickly, and My reward is with Me to repay each person according to what he has done. I am the Alpha and the Omega, the First and the Last, the Beginning and the End. (Rev. 22:12–13 HCSB)

The speaker's statement, "I am coming quickly," is the second of three such declarations in the closing lines of the book (Rev. 22:7, 20). The third very clearly is Jesus speaking: "He who testifies about these things says, 'Yes, I am coming quickly.' Amen! Come Lord Jesus!" (22:20 HCSB). Jesus also had said earlier in the book that he is coming to bring judgment on the unfaithful and reward for the faithful (2:16; 3:11). Elsewhere Jesus also warns that he is the one who will repay people according to what they have done (2:23; cf. 20:13). Thus, the speaker[14] in Revelation 22:12–13 declares that he is coming quickly, that he will repay people according to what they have done, and that he is the first and the last—all of which the book explicitly says about Jesus. In view of these contextual elements, and the fact that "the Alpha and the Omega" and "the beginning and the end" are obviously synonymous with "the first and the last," we conclude that the book does assign these titles to Jesus.

If we read the first occurrence of the title *the Alpha and the Omega* in this light, we find further confirmation of its application to Jesus:

> Look! He is coming [*erchetai*] with the clouds, and every eye will see Him, including those who pierced Him. And all the families of the earth will mourn over Him. This is certain. Amen. "I am the Alpha and the Omega," says the Lord God, "the One who is, who was, and who is coming [*ho erchomenos*], the Almighty." (Rev. 1:7–8 HCSB)

Verse 7, as everyone agrees, refers to Jesus as "coming." Then God states in the next verse that *he* is the one who is "coming." In light of the later references to Jesus using the title *the Alpha and the Omega* and synonymous titles, it would seem clear enough that verse 8 is identifying Jesus as God Almighty.

There is something else about the title "the first and the last" that we should notice.[15] When John introduces this description of Jesus, it is actually a three-part title: "I am the First and the Last and the Living One" (1:17b–18a, our translation).[16] In form and meaning, this three-part title is synonymous with another title of deity in the book of Revelation: "the one who is and the one who was and the one who is to come" (Rev. 1:4, 8, authors' translation).[17] Both titles express the lordship of the one to whom they apply from three temporal perspectives: past ("the First"; "the one who was"), present ("the Living One"; "the one who is"), and future ("the Last"; "the one who is coming"). In Jesus, though, God's everlasting existence is seen not as static, unperturbed, or remote, but as fully engaged in our own life-and-death struggle: the everlasting one, the first and the last, is the living one on our behalf through his death and triumphant resurrection (1:18). The ungrammatical wording of the three-part title in Revelation 1:4, 8 (literally, "the being and the was and the coming"!) reveals such dynamic involvement in time and history to be true to the very nature of God.[18]

We also should note that the title *the one who is and the one who was and the one who is coming* is likely a covert form or interpretation of the Old Testament divine name YHWH, or Jehovah. The first part of this title, "the One who is," is identical to the Greek translation of God's explanation of his name in Exodus 3:14 (see table).

"I AM THE ONE WHO IS"	
Exodus 3:14	**Revelation 1:8**
"I am the One who is [*egō eimi ho ōn*]."	"I am . . . the one who is [*egō eimi . . . ho ōn*], and the one who was, and the one who is coming."

Also suggesting that God's self-description in Revelation 1:8 is a self-description of Jesus Christ is the third element, "the one who is coming." This Greek expression, *ho erchomenos*, is a messianic title found in all four Gospels (Matt. 11:3; 21:9; 23:39; Mark 11:9; Luke 7:19, 20; 13:35; 19:38; John 6:14; 12:13; see also Heb. 10:37).[19]

The evident application to Jesus of this three-part title of God in Revelation 1:8, and the parallel three-part divine title of Jesus in Revelation 1:17–18, recalls another threefold description of Jesus: "Jesus Christ is the same yesterday and today and forever" (Heb. 13:8). This description of Jesus would seem to be yet another affirmation of his unchanging, divine presence throughout time, and in which we hear another echo of God's self-description in Exodus.

He's Got the Names!

When Christians affirm that Jesus is God, they are simply being faithful to the explicit teaching of the Bible. After all, the New Testament does, indeed, call Jesus Christ "God," not once, but several times. It also affirms that Jesus is "Lord," repeatedly doing so in contexts that equate Jesus with YHWH, the God of the Old Testament. In addition, the New Testament assigns a variety of other divine names or titles to Jesus (such as Bridegroom, Savior, and the first and the last). It gives Jesus all these names in the broader setting of a pervasive attitude of exalting the name of Jesus above every other name. If we are to be faithful to the teaching of the Bible, we must acknowledge Jesus Christ as our great God and Savior.

Part 4

INFINITELY QUALIFIED

Jesus Shares in the <u>D</u>eeds
That God Does

Honors	Attributes	Names	Deeds	Seat

Chapter 15

....

MEET YOUR MAKER

Belief in the deity of Jesus is not merely a matter of assigning to him the label "God" or any of the other divine names. As we saw in parts 1 and 2, to affirm that Jesus is God is to acknowledge that he is worthy of receiving all divine honors and that he possesses the divine attributes. Why is any of this important to us? The answer is that Jesus *does everything for us that God does*. Although it is proper to accord Jesus divine honors in view of his divine attributes, in the Bible the primary impetus to the unlimited worship, reverence, praise, faith, and obedience that we owe to God is what God has done for us. Likewise, the New Testament summons us to acknowledge and honor Jesus Christ as God primarily because of what *he* has done for us.

It is not surprising that the focus of most of the New Testament is on what Jesus did for us in his death and resurrection. These redemptive acts are the core of the "good news," or gospel, "of first importance" in the teaching of the apostles (1 Cor. 15:1–5). Yet the New Testament also tells us that Jesus Christ, the Son of God, was performing divine acts on our behalf long before he became a man.

Pop Quiz: How Many Gods Did It Take to Create the Universe?

It is basic to the teaching of the Old Testament, and of Judaism, that the Lord God is the only Creator and Maker of the universe. It is the first act of God recorded in the Bible: "In the beginning God created the heavens and the earth" (Gen. 1:1 NASB). We know that the Lord is God because he is our

Maker: "Know that the LORD is God. It is he that made us, and we are his" (Ps. 100:3).

> The sea is his, for he made it,
>> and the dry land, which his hands have formed.
>
> O come, let us worship and bow down,
>> let us kneel before the LORD, our Maker!
> For he is our God,
>> and we are the people of his pasture,
>> and the sheep of his hand.
>>> (Ps. 95:5–7)

His work of creation is what identifies him alone as the Lord Jehovah: "You are the LORD, you alone; you have made heaven, the heaven of heavens, with all their host, the earth and all that is on it, the seas and all that is in them. To all of them you give life, and the host of heaven worships you" (Neh. 9:6). The God of Jacob, unlike the worthless idols that the nations worshiped, is "the one who formed all things" (Jer. 10:16; 51:19).

Jeremiah's language pictures God as forming all things as a potter forms clay with his hands. The point of this figurative language is to emphasize that God personally and directly created the universe. Such is the consistent teaching of the Old Testament. According to Genesis, God personally formed the first human being: "The LORD God formed man from the dust of the ground, and breathed into his nostrils the breath of life; and the man became a living being" (Gen. 2:7). The psalmist affirms that God personally made the entire universe: "Long ago you laid the foundation of the earth, and the heavens are the work of your hands" (Ps. 102:25).

The book of Isaiah emphasizes the uniqueness of the Lord God as the only Creator and Maker of all things: "O LORD of hosts, God of Israel, who are enthroned above the cherubim, you are God, you alone, of all the kingdoms of the earth; you have made heaven and earth" (Isa. 37:16). He "measured the waters in the hollow of his hand and marked off the heavens with a span" (40:12). God challenges idolaters to name anyone who can compare with him in light of his unique work of creation: "To whom then will you compare me, or who is my equal? says the Holy One. Lift up your eyes on high and see: Who created these?" (40:25–26a). The Lord God is the one "who created the heavens and stretched them out, who spread out the earth and what comes from it" (42:5).

Especially noteworthy is the following statement: "I am the LORD, who made all things, who alone stretched out the heavens, who by myself spread out the earth" (Isa. 44:24). It is difficult to imagine a more emphatic and explicit statement that Jehovah is the sole Creator and Maker. The Lord asserts that he "alone" and by himself did the work of stretching out the heavens and spreading out the earth (see also 40:22; 42:5; 45:12, 18; 48:13; 51:13). The point here is not necessarily that no other beings *existed* at the time that God made the physical universe,[1] but that he "alone," by himself, performed the actual work of creation. Thus, Greg Stafford misses the point when he writes, "Isaiah 44:24 does not in any way conflict with the biblical teaching that God's 'Wisdom,' His Son, was with Him when He 'stretched out the heavens.'"[2] Stafford wishes to argue that the Son is a created being who acted as God's "agent" by performing the actual work of making the universe, using power delegated to him by Jehovah. Isaiah 44:24, though, precludes the idea of any created being assisting or working alongside the Lord in the creation of the universe.

Jesus Made It All

We have spent some time emphasizing the point that God created and formed the universe entirely by himself—with no one assisting him or working with him—because it is the context in which one must understand the New Testament teaching about Christ's role in creation. As Richard Bauckham points out, "However diverse Judaism may have been in other respects, this was common: only the God of Israel is worthy of worship because he is sole Creator of all things and Ruler of all things. . . . God alone created, and no one else had any part in this activity."[3] The New Testament maintains this same monotheistic belief, affirming that God "created all things" (Rev. 4:11; see also Acts 4:24; 14:15; 17:24). Yet the New Testament also teaches that all things owe their existence to Jesus Christ, God's Son.

> All things came into being through him, and without him not one thing came into being. . . . He was in the world, and the world came into being through him; yet the world did not know him. (John 1:3, 10)

> For us there is one God, the Father, from whom are all things and for whom we exist, and one Lord, Jesus Christ, through whom are all things and through whom we exist. (1 Cor. 8:6)

> For in him all things in heaven and on earth were created, things visible and invisible, whether thrones or dominions or rulers or powers—all things have been created through him and for him. (Col. 1:16)

> In these last days [God] has spoken to us by a Son, whom he appointed heir of all things, through whom he also created the worlds. (Heb. 1:2)

Assuming these statements cohere with the Jewish doctrine that YHWH, the Lord God, is the sole Creator and Maker of all things, the clear implication is that Jesus Christ, the Son, is himself the Lord God. Francis Beckwith expressed the reasoning that leads to this conclusion as a simple syllogism:

> Yahweh is the only one who participated in creation;
> Christ is one who participated in creation;
> Therefore, Christ is Yahweh.[4]

The only way to challenge the soundness of this argument is to challenge one or both of its two premises. As we have seen, the Old and New Testaments explicitly teach the first premise, that Yahweh, the Lord God, is the only one who participated in creation (Neh. 9:6; Isa. 37:16; 40:25–26; 44:24; Rev. 4:11). The New Testament also explicitly teaches the second premise (John 1:3, 10; 1 Cor. 8:6; Col. 1:16; Heb. 1:2). The conclusion follows necessarily from the premises; and since the premises are true, the argument is sound.

God's "Junior Partner"?

One common objection to this conclusion is that the New Testament distinguishes the Son's role in creation from that of God the Father. The texts we cited say that all things were created "through" (Greek, *dia*) the Son. On the other hand, one of these texts states that all things are "from" (Greek, *ek*) God the Father (1 Cor. 8:6). Hebrews states, "God . . . has spoken to us by a Son, whom he appointed heir of all things, though whom he also created the worlds" (Heb. 1:1–2). Here the subject of the verb "created" is "God," and the phrase "through whom" indicates that God did this work of creating through the Son, who acted on his behalf. It would seem, then, that these texts indicate some kind of "division of labor" in creation. They seem to say that all things originate "from" God the Father, who creates all things "through" the Son.

It is not surprising that some interpreters have seen in this distinction evidence that the Son performed an *inferior* or lesser role in creation. New Testament scholar Robert M. Grant, for example, commenting on 1 Corinthians 8:6, had this to say: "The supreme Father resembles the supreme Zeus, while the work of the Lord Christ is like that of the various demiurgic gods to whom cosmic functions were assigned."[5] Similarly, Jehovah's Witnesses interpret 1 Corinthians 8:6 to mean that Jesus Christ was God's "junior partner, as it were," in the work of creation.[6]

If this understanding of Paul were correct, we would have to conclude that he (and other New Testament writers) had abandoned the Jewish monotheistic position that the Lord God is the sole Creator and Maker of all things. There is good evidence, however, that this way of reading 1 Corinthians 8:6 is mistaken.

First, as we saw in chapter 13, Paul has taken the words of the Shema (Deut. 6:4), the classic Jewish creedal affirmation of monotheism, and reframed it to refer to the Father and the Son. Paul has just echoed the Shema in his comment that "there is no God but one" (1 Cor. 8:4). He acknowledges that pagans revere many so-called gods and lords (v. 5), but then he reasserts Jewish monotheism in a distinctively Christian way: "The LORD our God, the LORD is one" (Deut. 6:4 ESV) becomes "for us there is one God . . . one Lord," with the Father identified as the "one God" and the Lord Jesus Christ identified as the "one Lord." As Bauckham points out, "Paul has in fact reproduced all the words of the statement about YHWH in the *Shema* . . . but Paul has rearranged the words in such a way as to produce an affirmation of both one God, the Father, and one Lord, Jesus Christ. . . . Paul is not adding to the one God of the *Shema* a 'Lord' the *Shema* does not mention. He is identifying Jesus as the 'Lord' whom the *Shema* affirms to be one."[7]

Bauckham's analysis demonstrates that Paul is not distinguishing two deities, the supreme deity and a lesser one. Rather, he is distinguishing within the identity of the one Lord God of Judaism two persons, the Father and Jesus Christ.

Second, the argument from the use of different prepositions (*ek* or *ex*, "from," the Father; *dia*, "through," the Son) fails to come to terms with the way ancient writers used these prepositions in reference to creation. Paul uses both prepositions in another passage referring simply to God: "For from [*ex*] him and through [*di'*] him and for [*eis*] him are all things" (Rom. 11:36 NAB).[8] Pauline scholar Thomas Schreiner accurately paraphrases Paul's statement: "God is the source of all things, the means by which all things are accomplished, and the goal of all things."[9] Bauckham rightly understands the three phrases to express God's causation of all things in three ways: God is the efficient cause (*ex autou*), the instrumental cause (*di' autou*), and the final cause (*eis auton*).[10] All three of the prepositional phrases in Romans 11:36 occur in 1 Corinthians 8:6, which states, "To us there is one God, the Father, from whom [*ex hou*] are all things and we for him [*eis auton*], and one Lord, Jesus Christ, through whom [*di' hou*] are all things and we through him [*di' auton*]" (literal translation). As Bauckham notes, Paul here assigns two of the causal functions of God to the Father and the third to Christ.[11]

One should not infer from 1 Corinthians 8:6 that the causal functions assigned there to God the Father are not also applicable to the Son or vice versa (see table).[12] Elsewhere, the apostle states, "In him [*en autō*] all things in heaven and on earth were created . . . all things have been created through him [*di' autou*] and for him [*eis auton*]" (Col. 1:16). Here, Paul assigns the "final cause," as Bauckham puts it, to the Son. Paul also says that all things were created "in him," that is, in the Son. This wording appears to be an alternate way of expressing instrumental cause.[13] Yet in Athens, Paul said with reference to God, "in him [*en autō*] we live and move and have our being" (Acts 17:28). The New Testament also assigns the instrumental cause specifically to the Father: "For it was fitting for Him, for whom [*di' hon*] are all things, and through whom [*di' hou*] are all things . . . " (Heb. 2:10 NASB).[14] This statement appears not long after the writer's statement that it was "through" the Son that God "created the worlds" (1:2). Since the two statements are in relatively close proximity and both contexts are about creation, it seems unlikely that "through whom" has a different meaning in 2:10 than it does in 1:2. Thus, the statement that God created the worlds "through" the Son should not be taken to imply an inferior role for the Son in creation.[15]

It is true that the New Testament never says that all things are "from" (*ek*) the Son. This particular wording occurs only a few times, however, in the entire New Testament with reference to all things in creation being from God

THE ROLES OF THE FATHER AND THE SON IN CREATION

	God (the Father)	The Lord Jesus (the Son)
ek (*ex*): "from" Efficient cause	Rom. 11:36; 1 Cor. 8:6; 11:12; 2 Cor. 5:18	
dia (*di*ᶜ) + genitive: "through" Instrumental cause	Rom. 11:36; Heb. 2:10	John 1:3, 10; 1 Cor. 8:6; Col. 1:16; Heb. 1:2
en: "in" Instrumental cause	Acts 17:28; Eph. 3:9	Col. 1:16; cf. John 1:4
eis: "to," "for" Final cause	Rom. 11:36; 1 Cor. 8:6	Col. 1:16

or the Father (Rom. 11:36; 1 Cor. 8:6; 11:12; 2 Cor. 5:18). The absence of this wording with reference to Jesus is therefore too slender an argument from silence to prove any inferiority of the Son's role in creation.[16]

"The Heavens Are the Works of Your Hands"

In the same context as its statement that God made the worlds "through" the Son (1:2), the book of Hebrews draws on an Old Testament text about God's creating the universe to assert that the Son did so: "But of the Son he says . . . 'In the beginning, Lord, you founded the earth, and the heavens are the work of your hands'" (Heb. 1:8, 10). The quotation here comes from Psalm 102:25, which is a prayer directed to God, acknowledging him as the Creator (v. 24). Indeed, the language of "founding" is standard biblical rhetoric for God's work as Creator (Job 38:4; Pss. 8:3; 24:1–2; 78:69; 89:11; 104:5; 119:90; Prov. 3:19; 8:29; Isa. 40:21; 48:13; 51:13, 16; Amos 9:6; Zech. 12:1). The parallel description of creation as "the work of [God's] hands" is also language used elsewhere of God's work in creation (Ps. 8:6; Isa. 64:8; cf. Isa. 40:12) and more broadly of all that God does (e.g., Pss. 28:5; 92:4; 111:7; 138:8; 143:5; Isa. 45:11).

Greg Stafford raises two objections to understanding Hebrews 1:10 to imply that Jesus is the Creator. First, he asserts, "Since Jesus' role in creation has already been discussed (Heb. 1:3 [i.e., 1:2]), it is not likely that in verses 10–12 the author would return to the same point he has explained earlier."[17] This is at best a weak objection; what would prevent any author from returning to and elaborating on a point mentioned earlier? A careful analysis of the first chapter of Hebrews proves, in fact, that this is exactly what the author is doing. The Old Testament quotations in verses 5–13 are proof-texts that he cites in support of his introductory affirmations about the Son in verses 1–4 (see table). The writer's citation of Psalm 102:25 in reference to the Son proves that his role in creation is not a lesser role than God's role; it *is* God's role.

AFFIRMATION AND PROOF IN HEBREWS 1

Affirmation	Old Testament Proof
"God . . . has spoken to us by a Son" (1:1–2a)	"For to which of the angels did God ever say, 'You are my Son; today I have begotten you'? Or again, 'I will be his Father, and he will be my Son'?" (v. 5; quoting Ps. 2:7; 2 Sam. 7:14)
"whom he appointed heir of all things" (1:2b)	"And again, when he brings the first-born into the world, he says, 'Let all God's angels worship him'" (v. 6; quoting Deut. 32:43; Ps. 97:7)
"through whom he also created the worlds" (1:2c)	"And, 'In the beginning, Lord, you founded the earth, and the heavens are the work of your hands'" (v. 10; quoting Ps. 102:25)
"He is the reflection of God's glory and the exact imprint of God's very being, and he sustains all things by his powerful word" (1:3a)	"they will perish, but you remain; they will all wear out like clothing; like a cloak you will roll them up, and like clothing they will be changed. But you are the same, and your years will never end" (vv. 11–12; quoting Ps. 102:26–27)
"When he had made purification for sins, he sat down at the right hand of the Majesty on high" (1:3b)	"But to which of the angels has he ever said, 'Sit at my right hand until I make your enemies a footstool for your feet'?" (v. 13; quoting Ps. 110:1)

Second, Stafford points out that Hebrews 1 also applies to Jesus Christ (Heb. 1:8–9; quoting Ps. 45:6–7) what Psalm 45 says about the Israelite king (usually identified as Solomon). He argues that if the application of Psalm 45 to Christ does not prove that he is Solomon, the application of Psalm 102 to Christ does not prove that he is God. He quotes with approval the comment of a Watchtower publication: "Although that text had its first application to Solomon, the later application of it to Jesus Christ does not mean that Solomon and Jesus are the same. Jesus is 'greater than Solomon' and carries out a work foreshadowed by Solomon."[18]

The problem with this argument is evident from the Watchtower's own observation that "Jesus is 'greater than Solomon' and carries out a work fore-shadowed by Solomon." That is quite accurate: Solomon is a type of Christ, which means that what Psalm 45 says about Solomon (or any other Israelite king) applies to him only partially or in a limited way; the one to whom its exalted language actually applies is Christ.[19] But this way of understanding the use of a Psalm quotation will not work in Hebrews 1:10–12. It makes no sense at all to treat the Lord God (Jehovah) as a type of Christ! Furthermore, while Solomon was in no way unique (being just one of many human kings), Psalm 102 is speaking about the unique God who alone founded the earth and made the heavens. The application to the Son of what Psalm 102 says about God, then, indicates that he shares in that work of creation that is uniquely the province of God.

It is best, then, to understand the New Testament as teaching that Jesus Christ shares in the very work of God in creation because he also shares in his identity as the one Lord God. This understanding preserves the Old Testament teaching that the Lord God is the sole Creator and Maker of all things (e.g., Isa. 44:24). It also, of course, makes the best sense of the fact that more than once the New Testament calls Jesus "God" or "Lord" in the same context in which it speaks of his role in making the universe (John 1:1–3; 1 Cor. 8:6; Heb. 1:8, 10). To affirm that Jesus Christ is God is to acknowledge that he made us and that we belong to him (John 1:10–11).

Chapter 16

HE'S GOT THE WHOLE WORLD IN HIS HANDS

Jesus' divine work was not finished after the initial creation of the universe. That was just the beginning. Every minute of every day, year after year, century after century, Jesus has been doing the work of God for our benefit.

He Keeps It Going and Going and Going . . .

In theology, God's ongoing activity of sustaining the universe and directing it toward the accomplishment of his purposes for it is called *providence*.[1] Paul's statement of divine providence is classic: "He himself gives to all mortals life and breath and all things. . . . In him we live and move and have our being" (Acts 17:25, 28). Our life, every move that we make, even our very existence depends at every moment on God. The same is true for all living things: not only does God create them, but they also depend on him for their daily food and for every breath that they take (Ps. 104:24–30).[2]

The New Testament ascribes this work of providence to the Son, Jesus Christ. In Colossians, Paul states not only that all things "were created" (*ektisthē*) in the Son, but also that all things "have been created" (*ektistai*) through and for him (Col. 1:16). Paul uses the same verb but in two different forms. The first form is the aorist, which typically functions as the simple past tense form. The second form is the perfect, which also refers to past activity but typically with an emphasis on present results.[3] "The change of verb tense from the aorist to the perfect form indicates creation's ongoing existence. In other words, not only were all things created but they also remain in their created existence through Christ and for Christ."[4] Verse 16, then, indicates that creation stands in an ongoing relation of dependence on the Son for its existence.

What seems implicit in verse 16, Paul states explicitly in verse 17: "in him all things hold together." The word translated "hold together" (*sunestēken*) likely expresses two closely related concepts. First, Paul is saying that everything fits together, or is united, in Christ. This meaning clearly fits the immediate context, since Paul goes on to talk about what God has done in Christ to reconcile everything to him (that is, God; vv. 18–20). Second, Paul is saying that, in Christ, everything finds its proper function or place in the scheme of things. This idea also fits the immediate context since Paul emphasizes in this passage that all other authorities find their purpose for existence in relation to him (v. 16, "all things were created through him *and for him*" ESV, emphasis added) and that Christ is to have first place "in everything" (v. 18). Paul's statement here, then, speaks of Christ's role in divine providence from the perspective of the goal or purpose of all created things.[5] We may put it another way: ultimately, everything finds its *meaning* in Christ.

Paul also seems to speak of Christ as sustaining our existence, writing that for us there is "one Lord, Jesus Christ, through whom are all things and through whom we exist" (1 Cor. 8:6). This statement appears to ascribe to Christ a role not only in the initial creation of the universe but also in the existence of everything in it, including every one of us. It is a sobering thought that even those people who reject Jesus Christ owe their very existence to his providential work (cf. John 1:10).

Perhaps the most explicit reference to Christ as Sustainer is found in Hebrews 1:3, which states that the Son "sustains all things by his powerful word." The word for "sustains" (*pherōn*) means that the Son bears, supports, or sustains all things—and in context "all things" refers to everything in creation (v. 2). Whereas in Colossians 1:17 Paul states that Christ "holds together" all things, the writer of Hebrews states that Christ "holds up" all things. The Old Testament passage the author cites in support of this point is Psalm 102:25–27. The universe is perishing and wearing out; but the Son, as the Lord who made it, remains ever the same (Heb. 1:10–12). The point, then, is that the Son sustains the universe so that it does not simply fizzle out of existence; although it is constantly changing and things are constantly falling apart and dying, what permanence and continuity it has is the result of the Son's providential care.

The book of Hebrews states that the Son performs this work "by his powerful word" (or, as some translations more literally render it, "by the word of his power"). The writer is actually saying that the Son is the one whose word keeps the universe moving along. The Jewish wisdom book Sirach, written a couple of centuries earlier, stated that "by his word," that is, by *God's* word, "all things hold together" (Sir. 43:26).[6] This, of course, was the standard Jewish position; and it is in that theological milieu that the writer of Hebrews asserts that the Son sustains all things by *his* word.

The Gospel of John also teaches that Christ sustains all things, although it does so in different language. The very term *logos*, used as a designation of the Son before he became incarnate (1:1, 14), implies such a role. In Hellenistic philosophy, the Logos was the principle of order, coherence, and rationality of the cosmos. While John's worldview assumptions derive from the Old Testament and the ministry of Christ, not from Greek philosophy, it is likely that he uses *logos* as a "cross-cultural" expression that would be intelligible to Gentiles as well as Jews and would convey the significance of the preincarnate Son. Such an interpretation certainly fits the context: John states that all things came into being through the Logos, and that life and light are in the Logos (vv. 3–4). His statement, "in him was life" (v. 4), affirms of the Logos what Paul affirms of God in Acts 17:28a ("in him we live").[7] John's description of the Logos as "the true light" that "enlightens everyone" (v. 9) is also consistent with this interpretation, since the Greeks commonly thought of the Logos as the source of illumination or knowledge of truth as well as the source of life and order in the cosmos. In contrast to the usual Greek view, though, John states that the Logos that enlightens all people was "coming into the world" (v. 9) to bring the fullness of light and life.[8]

Later in his Gospel, John records an intriguing statement from Jesus. After the Jewish leaders challenged Jesus for healing a paralytic on the Sabbath, Jesus responded to them by saying, "My Father is still working, and I also am working" (5:17). Jesus' statement alludes to the fact that although God "rested" from his work of creating the universe on the original "Sabbath" (Gen. 2:1–3), he did not cease from all work.[9] The Father continues to sustain the universe and to give life to his creatures. Likewise, the Son, incarnate in Jesus Christ, also continues doing such divine works. Jesus saw his work on earth as the completion of God's work. When he healed the paralytic, he was doing the same kind of thing the Father does whenever he extends the life of one of his creatures.

He's Got the Power!

Christ's healing of the paralytic was just one of numerous miracles he performed during his earthly ministry. Although skeptics typically dismiss the Gospel miracle narratives out of hand as myth or legend, there are good reasons to conclude that these accounts, at least in general, reflect historical fact. Non-Christian sources dated as early as the first century refer to Jesus' reputation for performing miracles—although sometimes these sources denigrate Jesus' miracles as sorcery. Although the apostle Paul does not discuss any specific miracles of Jesus, there are traces in his writings of an awareness that Jesus performed them (Rom. 15:18–19; 1 Cor. 4:20; 13:2; cf. 2 Cor. 12:12; 2 Thess. 2:9). Furthermore, all of the Gospels, and all of the source materials that biblical scholars think the Gospels incorporated, attest to Jesus' miracles. Minimally, historians can say with full confidence that the belief that Jesus performed miracles originates from his own lifetime and is not the product of later myth or legend.[10] Internally, the Gospels exhibit remarkable restraint in their miracle narratives, lacking many of the elements common to legendary tall tales.[11] In his cautious and thorough study of the historicity of the Gospel accounts of Jesus' miracles, Graham Twelftree concludes that "*there is hardly any aspect of the life of the historical Jesus which is so well attested as that he conducted unparalleled wonders.*"[12]

Jesus was not, of course, the only person in the Bible to perform miracles. In the Old Testament, the human beings with whom miracles are most associated are Moses, Elijah, and Elisha. According to the book of Acts, the apostles, especially Peter and Paul, also performed miracles. We therefore must be careful not to oversimplify the matter; miracles in and of themselves do not prove that the human agent involved is deity.

New Testament scholar Werner Kahl helpfully distinguishes three kinds of miracle workers. A person who has inherent healing power he calls a "bearer of numinous power" (BNP). He uses the term "petitioner of numinous power" (PNP) for those who ask God to perform the miracle. Between these two extremes is the category of "mediator of numinous power" (MNP), which applies to persons who mediate the numinous power of a BNP in order to produce a miracle.[13] Being a MNP or PNP clearly is not evidence of deity, whereas being a BNP could be evidence of deity.

Eric Eve, in his published dissertation *The Jewish Context of Jesus' Miracles*, observes that in the Old Testament, Yahweh is the only BNP; Moses is an example of an MNP; Elijah is an example of a PNP.[14] Eve provides a comprehensive review of miracles in the Judaism of the New Testament period. He considers beliefs about miracles in Josephus, Philo, the wisdom and apocalyptic literature of the period (e.g., Wisdom of Solomon; 1 Enoch), some Qumran texts, and in some examples of romantic, fanciful Jewish literature of the time (e.g., Tobit). He finds that with rare (and quite marginal) exceptions, Judaism in that period agreed with the Old Testament in viewing the Lord God as the only BNP.

Eve also examines the rabbinical accounts of "charismatic holy men" such as Honi the Circle-Drawer and Hanina ben Dosa, both of whom Jewish scholar Geza Vermes has argued were miracle workers similar to Jesus.[15] The rabbinical comments about Honi date from about four centuries after he lived, mention at most one miracle associated with him, and portray him as simply a pious man whose prayer was answered (at most a PNP, to use Kahl's classification). The material about Hanina is similarly late and unreliable (to the extent that it is not entirely certain in what century he lived), and even the most robust miracle reports about him characterize him as a PNP.[16] As Eve says, "Hanina is portrayed as a poor, pious rabbi, living at home with his wife and daughter, occasionally called upon to help in cases of accident, fever and venomous reptiles, and occasionally assisted by bizarre divine interventions."[17]

The closest analogue to one of Jesus' miracles is the healing of a rabbi's son for whom Hanina prayed at a distance (cf. John 4:46–54). But as Eve points out, "Whereas Jesus heals at a distance, Hanina merely prays at a distance." Hanina "apparently has no idea whether his prayer will prove efficacious until he prays it. This story does not therefore portray Hanina as a miraculously gifted healer, but rather as someone who is especially proficient in prayer."[18] Eve rightly concludes that the stories of Honi and Hanina illustrate only that Jesus' contemporaries were likely to view his miracles as evidence that he was at the very least a prophet,[19] something the Gospels also tell us (Matt. 21:11; Mark 6:15; Luke 7:16; 24:19; John 9:17).

According to Eve, the Gospel portrayals of Jesus break with Jewish tradition by characterizing Jesus as a "bearer of numinous power" (BNP) and his miracles as pointing to him as Yahweh. Although some of the miracle reports resemble accounts of prophetic miracles (notably those of Elisha), the dominant theme in the Gospel accounts of Jesus' miracles with regard to his identity is that Jesus is unlike any other human being.

A review of the Gospels confirms Eve's assessment. The Gospels rarely record Jesus uttering any sort of prayer before performing a miracle, and the exceptions are prayers of thanks or blessing, not prayers asking God to effect a miracle (Matt. 14:19; 15:36; Mark 6:41; 8:6; Luke 9:16; John 6:11; 11:41–43).[20] Thus, the Gospel evidence uniformly contradicts any notion that Jesus was a "petitioner of numinous power" (PNP). By way of contrast, the book of Acts reports both Peter and Paul praying prior to performing miracles of healing (Acts 9:40; 28:8). Furthermore, on one occasion Jesus explained to his disciples that at least some demons could not be cast out apart from prayer: "This kind can come out only through prayer" (Mark 9:29). As R. T. France explains, Jesus' statement here pertains to his followers, not to himself.

> In Jesus' encounters with demons, however threatening, a simple word of command has sufficed in every case, and the present narrative has not depicted Jesus himself as engaging in a special régime of prayer (and fasting). But the disciples' authority is always derivative, and prayer is an appropriate recognition of that fact in any encounter with spiritual evil.[21]

Jesus also never invokes anyone else's name when performing a miracle. One might have expected him to pronounce healings "in the name of my Father" or with some similar locution, but he never does. The apostles, on the other hand, healed in Jesus' name. After they came back from their first venture of preaching and healing during Jesus' earthly ministry, they joyously reported that the demons were subject to them *in Jesus' name* (Luke 10:17–20). Once, having tried and failed to cast a demon out of a boy, they informed Jesus that they had tried to stop someone outside of the apostolic circle from casting out demons in Jesus' name (Mark 9:38–40; Luke 9:49–50)!

After Pentecost, the apostles characteristically conveyed healing and exorcism to others in the name of Jesus (Acts 3:6; 16:18; cf. 19:11–17). The first time this happened, Peter emphatically explained that it was not his piety or power that produced the healing, but that Jesus had healed the man through faith in his name (Acts 3:11–16; 4:7–11). On another occasion, Peter simply stated, "Jesus Christ heals you" (Acts 9:34). When Paul performed a miracle of judgment on a magician who opposed the gospel, he told the man, "The hand of the Lord is against you" (Acts 13:11), as an explanation for the blindness with which he was immediately stricken. Jesus never spoke in such a way with regard to his miracles.

Jesus did not, of course, perform his miracles *independently* of the Father. Quite the opposite: Jesus claimed that all of his miracles—indeed all his works and deeds—were performed in union with the Father. After he healed a paralytic, Jesus asserted that his miraculous works testified that the Father had sent him (John 5:36). He later made the point that if his critics would believe his works, they would know and understand that the Father was in Jesus and that Jesus was in him (10:38). Jesus also told his disciples that the Father who abided in him was doing his works (14:10–11). These statements indicate that Jesus considered his actions to be not merely his own but joint actions performed with the Father in him. Jesus was not a mere man through whom God occasionally chose to act by performing miracles. Jesus was the incarnate Son of God, and God the Father was acting in and through him in absolutely everything that Jesus said and did.

Several statements in the Gospels indicate that Jesus was what Kahl termed a "bearer of numinous power" (BNP). On one occasion, the sick pressed around Jesus to touch him, hoping to be healed (Mark 3:10; Luke 6:19a), and Luke comments, "power was coming from him" (Luke 6:19b NIV). On another occasion, a woman was healed when she pushed her way through a crowd and in faith touched the hem of Jesus' garment. According to both Mark and Luke, Jesus felt power go out from him, and he asked who had touched him (Mark 5:30; Luke 8:46). In another passage, Luke states, "The power of the Lord was with him to heal" (Luke 5:17). By "the Lord" here Luke probably means Jesus himself: as "the Lord," Jesus had power for healing.[22]

When Jesus Talks, Nature Listens

The complete and total command that Christ exhibits over the natural realm in his miracles reveals his deity. On two separate occasions—once before his resurrection and once after it—Jesus tells his disciples precisely where to lower their nets in order to catch a large haul of fish (Luke 5:1–11; John 21:1–11). Jesus commands unclean spirits, and they immediately obey and come out of their host (Mark 1:21–28; Luke 4:31–37). He rebukes a fever, and it immediately leaves (Matt. 8:14–15; Mark 1:29–31; Luke 4:38–39). Even more astonishing, he rebukes the winds and the waters during a dangerous storm on the sea, and they immediately become calm (Matt. 8:23–27; Mark 4:35–41; Luke 8:22–25). The Gospels conclude this particular episode with the disciples' question, "Who then is this?" showing that the miracle points to Jesus' unique (and, from a human point of view, hidden) identity. The

Psalms confess to God, "You silence the roaring of the seas, the roaring of their waves" (Ps. 65:7). "You rule the raging of the sea; when its waves rise, you still them" (Ps. 89:9).

> Some went down to the sea in ships,
>   doing business on the mighty waters;
> they saw the deeds of the LORD,
>   his wondrous works in the deep.
> For he commanded and raised the stormy wind,
>   which lifted up the waves of the sea.
> They mounted up to heaven, they went down to the depths;
>   their courage melted away in their calamity;
> they reeled and staggered like drunkards,
>   and were at their wits' end.
> Then they cried to the LORD in their trouble,
>   and he brought them out from their distress;
> he made the storm be still,
>   and the waves of the sea were hushed.
> Then they were glad because they had quiet,
>   and he brought them to their desired haven.
>
> (Ps. 107:23–30)

One possible counterargument at this point might be to appeal to Jesus' saying that his apostles could do similar things. When he was in Jerusalem, Jesus saw a fruitless fig tree and cursed it, causing it to wither. When the disciples asked him how that had happened, Jesus told them that if they had faith and no doubts, they could even tell a mountain to go jump into the sea and it would obey. The traditional understanding of this passage is that Jesus was speaking hyperbolically about the performance of extraordinary miracles. Whatever type of event Jesus means here, he says it will happen in response to prayer: "And all things *you ask in prayer*, believing, you will receive" (Matt. 21:18–22 NASB, emphasis added; likewise Mark 11:12–14, 20–24).[23]

A similar qualification applies to Jesus' promise that those who believe in him will do the works that he did and even greater works (John 14:12). Jesus immediately explains, "*I* will do whatever you *ask in my name*, so that the Father may be glorified in the Son. If *in my name you ask* me for anything, *I*

will do it" (John 14:13–14, emphasis added). Jesus is the actual miracle worker; the disciples are merely the "petitioners of numinous power" (PNP), asking Jesus in his name to perform the miracles in order to glorify the Father
in the Son.

As a matter of record, the apostles do not seem to have performed any
"nature miracles" after Christ's ascension, such as walking on the sea. When
the ship taking Paul to Rome encountered heavy seas, no miracle prevented
its shipwreck, although God providentially protected Paul and his shipmates
from death (Acts 27:14–44). The miracles the apostles performed appear to
have consisted primarily of healings, exorcisms, and a couple of judgment
miracles, inflicting blindness and death. The miracles that the Gospels report
Jesus as performing go beyond anything reported of the apostles.

The mastery of Christ over nature, for example, is so complete that he
does not even need to be physically present at the location of the miracle. On
two or three occasions, Jesus healed people at a distance, without his ever seeing or touching them (Matt. 8:5–13; 15:21–28; Mark 7:24–30; Luke 7:1–10;
John 4:46–54).[24] In one amusing account, when Peter asked him whether
they should pay the temple tax, Jesus responded by telling Peter to go fishing;
the first fish Peter caught would have a shekel in its mouth, with which Peter
was to pay the temple tax (Matt. 17:24–27).

The Gospel writers themselves interpret Jesus' miracles as evidence that he
is God. Consider Luke's account of Jesus' raising from the dead a widow's son
in the town of Nain. "When the Lord saw her," Luke says, Jesus felt sorry for
her (Luke 7:11–13). (Notice Luke's use of the divine title *the Lord* for Jesus.)
He then went up to the coffin and simply said, "Young man, I say to you,
rise!" (v. 14). The dead man immediately came back to life, sat up, and started
to talk (v. 15). The people responded by glorifying God. They acknowledged
Jesus as "a great prophet" but also stated, "God has looked favorably on his
people!" (v. 16).[25] Luke then reports Jesus' response to the disciples of John
the Baptist, who wanted to know if he was "the one who is to come" (vv.
19–20). Jesus told them, "Go and tell John what you have seen and heard:
the blind receive their sight, the lame walk, the lepers are cleansed, the deaf
hear, the dead are raised, the poor have good news brought to them" (v. 22).
Jesus' response alludes to Isaiah 35:4–6 and 61:1–3, in which Isaiah says that
God will come to his people and that the blind, deaf, lame, and mute will be
healed. In Isaiah, the "good news" brought to "the poor" is that the Lord, God
himself, is coming to bring salvation (Isa. 40:9–11; 52:7–10; 61:1–3).

One of Jesus' best-known miracles was his casting out of a "legion" of demons from a violent demoniac (Mark 5:1–20; Luke 8:26–39). The demons immediately recognized Jesus as the Son of God (and called him by name!) and were ready to leave the man's body without argument. After the demons left the man, Jesus told him, "Go home to your friends, and tell them how much the Lord has done for you, and what mercy he has shown you" (Mark 5:19). Luke reports the same instructions, with Jesus' saying, "Declare how much God has done for you" (Luke 8:39). Mark and Luke then state that the man went home and began telling people "how much *Jesus* had done for him" (Mark 5:20; Luke 8:39b, emphasis added). Evidently, it's essentially the same thing: what Jesus did for him, God did for him. What is remarkable and telling is that this is true about anything and everything that Jesus did: he was God in action.

Perhaps Jesus' most dramatic miraculous demonstrations of his power over nature, other than his own resurrection (John 2:19–22; 10:17–18; 20:27–28), were his acts of feeding the multitude and of walking on the Sea of Galilee. These two miracles occurred one after the other, and both echo miracles experienced by the Israelites in the Exodus (Matt. 14:13–33; Mark 6:33–52; John 6:1–58; cf. Luke 9:12–17).

The miraculous feeding of over five thousand people (the one miracle of Jesus' earthly ministry reported in all four Gospels) has obvious associations with the feeding of the Israelites with manna in the wilderness shortly after the crossing of the Red Sea. In John's extended account of the aftermath of this miracle, Jesus explicitly compares it to the giving of manna (John 6:31–33, 49–51, 58). According to Exodus, God, not Moses, gave the Israelites the manna (Exod. 16:4, 8, 15). Rather than casting himself in the "role" of Moses, Jesus actually casts himself both as the Lord who gives the bread and as the bread itself: "I am the bread of life. Whoever comes to me will never be hungry, and whoever believes in me will never be thirsty. . . . the bread that I will give for the life of the world is my flesh" (John 6:35, 51).

As various scholars, both conservative and liberal, have observed, the Gospel accounts of Jesus walking on the sea allude rather clearly to the account in Exodus 14–15 of the Israelites' crossing of the Red Sea.[26] The Israelites walked in "the midst of the sea" (Exod. 14:16, 22, 27, 29 NASB) and crossed to the other side (Exod. 15:16). Likewise, the disciples' boat was "in the middle of the sea" (Mark 6:47 NASB) and they also "crossed over" the sea (Mark 6:53). A strong wind from the east blew across the Red Sea and, close to daybreak, the Egyptians found it increasingly difficult to drive their chariots as they attempted to follow the Israelites (Exod. 14:21, 24–25). Likewise, an adverse wind blew across the Sea of Galilee and, based on the geography, it also would have been blowing from the east; this wind also blew close to daybreak and made it difficult for the disciples to row their boat (Mark 6:48).[27] According to Mark, the disciples had the same problem as the Egyptians: their hearts were hardened (Exod. 14:4, 8, 17; Mark 6:52).

According to Eric Eve (and many other commentators), in this miracle account "Jesus is portrayed as filling the role, not of another Moses, but of Yahweh."[28] We suggest that this conclusion needs to be restated in a more nuanced way. Jesus appears, in fact, to fulfill the role of a greater Moses *and* of Yahweh. Jesus' response to the disciples' fear encompasses both roles. Moses had told the Israelites, "Take heart!" (*tharseite*, Exod. 14:13 LXX) and Jesus told the disciples the same thing: "Take heart!" (*tharseite*, Matt. 14:27; Mark 6:50). But then Jesus added, "It is I [*egō eimi*]; do not be afraid" (Matt. 14:27; Mark 6:50; John 6:20). This statement echoes statements by the Lord God in Isaiah, where he speaks of a kind of "new Exodus" when the Jews would be restored to their land:

> "Do not fear, for I have redeemed you;
>   I have called you by name, you are mine.
> When you pass through the waters, I will be with you;
>   and through the rivers, they shall not overwhelm you; . . .
> Do not fear, for I am with you; . . .
> so that you may know and believe me
>   and understand that I am he [*egō eimi*] . . .
> I am the LORD, your Holy One,
>   the Creator of Israel, your King."
> Thus says the LORD,
>   who makes a way in the sea,
>   a path in the mighty waters.
>
> (Isa. 43:1–2, 5, 10, 15–16)

The most striking aspect of the account is, of course, Jesus' actually walking on the sea. In the historical Exodus miracle, the Israelites crossed through the sea but on dry land. In later poetic reflection on this defining moment in Israel's history, biblical authors pictured God walking on the sea:

When the waters saw you, O God,
   when the waters saw you, they were afraid;
   the very deep trembled.
The clouds poured out water;
   the skies thundered;
   your arrows flashed on every side.
The crash of your thunder was in the whirlwind;
   your lightnings lit up the world;
   the earth trembled and shook.
Your way was through the sea,
   your path, through the mighty waters;
   yet your footprints were unseen.
You led your people like a flock
   by the hand of Moses and Aaron.
                                    (Ps. 77:16–20)

By walking out to the disciples' boat on the sea, Jesus demonstrated a mastery over the forces of nature unparalleled among human beings. Moses was merely the human agent through whom the Lord led the Israelites across the dry bed of the Red Sea. Jesus walked across the raging waters of the Sea of Galilee and spoke divine words of assurance and sovereign control to his disciples. No wonder, according to Matthew, the disciples responded by worshiping Jesus and affirming that he was God's Son (Matt. 14:33). They did not understand it at the time, but what they had witnessed was a display of God's own numinous power incarnate.

Chapter 17

THE WAY, THE TRUTH, AND THE LIFE

One of Jesus' most famous—and, for some people, most troubling—statements in the Gospel of John is his declaration, "I am the way, and the truth, and the life. No one comes to the Father except through me" (John 14:6). The exclusivity of Jesus' statement obviously means that he was claiming to be more than just a good and insightful teacher of moral and spiritual values, of which the world has known many. No prophet, rabbi, or priest would ever have said such a thing. As we shall see, Jesus' claim summarizes much of what the New Testament says about him and, in fact, points once again to his divine identity.

"I Am the Way"

The first part of Jesus' statement is his claim to be "the way." Since he goes on immediately to say, "No one comes *to the Father* except through me," Jesus evidently means that he is the way to the Father. Jesus is the way to his Father's "house," the way to a relationship with the Father in which we are assured of dwelling with him forever (John 14:2–4). All this presupposes, of course, that we are not naturally safe and secure in such a relationship. The human race is estranged from God and needs to be brought into that relationship with him.

The message of the New Testament is, *This is what Jesus—and he alone—does for us.* Some people reject this message while claiming to accept Jesus. In her 1875 book *Science and Health with Key to the Scriptures*, Mary Baker Eddy claims, "The Christ-element in the Messiah made him the Way-shower, Truth and Life."[1] But this subtle rewriting of Jesus' statement was outdone by an early twentieth-century book called *The Aquarian Gospel of Jesus the Christ*, a pseudo-gospel written in biblical "style" but espousing a metaphysical or mind-science philosophy, which expresses a similar point of view. It asserts, "And all the people were entranced, and would have worshiped Jesus as a God; but Jesus said, I am your brother man just come to show the way to God; you shall not worship man; praise God, the Holy One."[2] The real Jesus, of course, never said any such thing. He is not merely "the way-shower"; he *is* the way.

The evidence that Jesus made this claim to be the way to God is not confined to the Gospel of John. According to the book of Acts, the earliest Christians referred to the movement of which they were a part as "the Way" (Acts 9:2; 19:9, 23; 22:4; 24:14, 22; cf. Acts 16:17; 18:25–26).[3] To belong to the Way meant to belong to Christ; to know about the Way meant to know about Christ; and, as Paul found out, to persecute the Way meant to persecute Christ (Acts 9:2, 5). We see here strong evidence that the earliest Christians already understood Jesus to be the way of salvation, the way to God.

Those who think such a claim is narrow-minded will have to take that up with Jesus himself. The evidence is clear that he regarded the way of salvation as "narrow."

> Enter through the narrow gate; for the gate is wide and the way is broad that leads to destruction, and there are many who enter through it. For the gate is small and the way is narrow that leads to life, and there are few who find it. (Matt. 7:13–14 NASB)

Jesus' statement in John 14:6 is very similar to the following statement recorded in Matthew and Luke:

> All things have been handed over to me by my Father; and no one knows the Son except the Father, and no one knows the Father except the Son and anyone to whom the Son chooses to reveal him. (Matt. 11:27; cf. Luke 10:22)

Here, Jesus' exclusive claim to be able to bring us into a relationship with the Father is grounded on the fact that as the Son, he alone, among all humanity, knows the Father. If we are to know the Father, we must depend on the Son to reveal him to us (cf. John 1:18). Jesus is not just one of God's many sons; he is *the* Son, the one to whom the Father has handed over "all things," the one whose prerogative it is to choose who will know the Father. Reflect on that claim for just a moment: Jesus asserts that it is his prerogative to choose who among all humanity will come to know the Father, that is, who will come to enjoy that relationship with God the Father. Such a prerogative places Jesus on an entirely different level from the rest of the human race.

The uniqueness of Jesus as the way to the Father is a function not only of his unique status as the Son, but also of what he, and he alone, has done to restore human beings to a relationship with the Father. This restoration of human beings to a relationship with God as Father is, broadly speaking, what Christianity means by *salvation*.

It is basic to the New Testament that Jesus does this divine work of salvation. The angel Gabriel told Joseph that he was to name Mary's son Jesus (a name that means, "YHWH saves"), "for he will save his people from their sins" (Matt. 1:21). Jesus saw himself as the Savior, the one who brings and accomplishes salvation. "Today salvation has come to this house," he said to Zacchaeus, "for the Son of Man came to seek out and to save the lost" (Luke 19:9–10). God sent the Son into the world "in order that the world might be saved through him" (John 3:17; cf. 12:47). In a picturesque illustration, Jesus compares himself to the entrance gate to a sheep pen, saying, "Whoever enters by me will be saved" (John 10:9). After Jesus rose from the dead, the apostles asserted that "there is no other name under heaven that has been given among men by which we must be saved" (Acts 4:12 NASB). Paul could summarize his message of salvation as simply as this: "Believe on the Lord Jesus, and you will be saved" (Acts 16:31).

What did Jesus do to accomplish this salvation? He died on the cross and rose from the dead. The message that "Christ died for our sins" and "was raised" from the dead is "the good news" through which we "are being saved" (1 Cor. 15:1–4). The proof of Jesus' claim to be the way to an eternal relationship with the Father is the historical fact of his resurrection from the dead, attested by his closest friends, skeptical siblings, and a formerly hostile critic, Paul himself (1 Cor. 15:5–11).[4]

Through his death, Jesus "became the source of eternal salvation for all who obey him" (Heb. 5:9). In the context of the Old Testament religious and theological tradition, such a claim for Jesus is every bit as much an indication of deity as the claim that he made the universe. A heavenly or supernatural

being to whom one looked as the source of deliverance or salvation is by definition one's God.[5] After the crossing of the Red Sea, Moses led the Israelites
in singing this song to the Lord:

> The LORD is my strength and my might,
>   and he has become my salvation;
> this is my God, and I will praise him,
>   my father's God, and I will exalt him.
>   (Exod. 15:2; cf. Ps. 118:14, 21)

David affirmed,

> For God alone my soul waits in silence;
>   from him comes my salvation.
> He only is my rock and my salvation, . . .
> He only is my rock and my salvation,
>   my fortress; I shall not be shaken.
> On God rests my salvation and my glory;
>   my mighty rock, my refuge is God.
>   (Ps. 62:1–2, 6–7 ESV)

It is also in this context that the New Testament's frequent designation of
Jesus as the "Savior" implies his deity. As we saw in chapter 14, in religious
contexts the title "Savior" in the Greek Old Testament is nearly always paired
with the title "God" (Deut. 32:15; Pss. 24:5; 25:5; 27:9; 62:2, 6; 65:5; 79:9;
95:1; Isa. 12:2; 17:10; 45:15, 21; Mic. 7:7; Hab. 3:18; cf. 1 Sam. 10:19; Ps. 27:1;
Isa. 62:11). In the New Testament, we still find affirmations of God as Savior
(e.g., Luke 1:47), but these often come alongside affirmations of Jesus Christ
as Savior, or some equivalent statement. In Titus, for example, three times
Paul speaks of "God our Savior" and then immediately follows by referring
to Jesus as "our Savior," the second time actually calling Jesus "our great God
and Savior" (Titus 1:3, 4; 2:10, 13; 3:4, 6; cf. 2 Peter 1:1, 11; 2:20; 3:18).[6] In
his first epistle to Timothy, Paul calls God "our Savior" and then immediately
calls Jesus Christ "our hope" (1 Tim. 1:1), which in biblical patterns of speech
are parallel, essentially synonymous, affirmations (see Pss. 14:6; 61:2; 62:7;
71:5; 91:9; 142:5). A few sentences later, Paul affirms that "Christ Jesus came
into the world to save sinners" (v. 15).

Jesus' contribution to our salvation is not limited solely to his death and resurrection, as great as those redemptive acts are. Jesus actually forgives people of their sins. We pointed out earlier that Jesus decides who gets to know the Father (and by implication who does not). Likewise, Jesus decides whose sins are forgiven. It's his call (Acts 5:31; Col. 3:13).

Jesus started forgiving people even before his death on the cross. (Think of it as debt resolution in advance based on an imminent payment.) We are not talking here about Jesus forgiving people with whom he had personal grievances. We are referring to Jesus forgiving persons of every sin they had ever committed. The Gospels report at least two separate incidents when this occurred. One of these involved an immoral woman who came to Jesus, crying; she wet his feet with her tears, wiped them with her hair, and anointed his feet with perfume (Luke 7:36–38). The Pharisee who was Jesus' host was offended, but Jesus told him, "Her sins, which were many, have been forgiven; hence she has shown great love. But the one to whom little is forgiven, loves little." He then said to the woman, "Your sins are forgiven." The reaction of the others who were there is quite understandable. "Who is this who even forgives sins?" they asked (Luke 7:47–49).

On another occasion, four men brought a paralyzed man to Jesus in the hope that Jesus would heal him. The first thing Jesus did was say to the paralyzed man, "Son, your sins are forgiven" (Mark 2:5; similarly Matt. 9:2; Luke 5:20). Some scribes standing by thought what Jesus said was blasphemy; they were saying to themselves, "Who can forgive sins but God alone?" (Mark 2:7; Luke 5:21). Jesus responded by asking them a hypothetical question: "Which is easier, to say to the paralytic, 'Your sins are forgiven,' or to say, 'Stand up and take your mat and walk'?" (Mark 2:9; cf. Matt. 9:5; Luke 5:23). Hypothetically, it is easier, of course, to forgive someone's sins than to make a paralyzed man walk. Thus, if Jesus has the ability to make the man walk, his claim to have the ability to forgive the man's sins should be accepted. Jesus then backs up his claim: "'But so that you may know that the Son of Man has authority on earth to forgive sins'—he said to the paralytic—'I say to you, stand up, take your mat and go to your home'" (Mark 2:10–11; cf. Matt. 9:6; Luke 5:24).

Jesus' reference to himself here as "the Son of Man" alludes to an apocalyptic vision in the book of Daniel in which he saw "one like a son of man" presented before "the Ancient of Days" (7:13 ESV). "And to him was given dominion and glory and a kingdom, that all peoples, nations, and languages should serve him" (Dan. 7:14 ESV). The emphasis in this chapter is on the authority of the "one like a son of man" to sit in judgment on the wicked (see Dan. 7:10–12, 22, 26–27). One could argue that the authority to judge also entails the authority to forgive. Thus, Jesus' claim that the Son of Man has authority to forgive sins may simply make explicit what is already implicit in Daniel's vision.[7] This does not, however, make Jesus' claim to exercise that prerogative any less astonishing. Even Daniel affirms the traditional Jewish view, "To the Lord our God belong mercy and forgiveness" (Dan. 9:9; cf. Ps. 51:4; Isa. 43:25; 44:22; 55:7). What the Old Testament generally treats as a divine prerogative, Jesus claims (with perhaps implicit support from Dan. 7) as his own. Moreover, Jesus exercises this prerogative while living as a human being on the earth, prior to his exaltation in heaven. This may be why Jesus specifies that what he is claiming is the authority of the Son of Man to forgive sins "on earth."

If we compare the early chapters of Mark with Isaiah 40, we see from another perspective that Jesus' claim to forgive sins is a claim to deity. In Isaiah, God announces that Israel's sins have been removed and her chastisement is over (vv. 1–2). Then a voice calls for the way to be cleared for the coming of *the Lord* (vv. 3–5). His presence is once again going to inhabit the Promised Land, and his people are going to be restored to that land. The "good news" for Jerusalem is that *God* is coming with might to rule (vv. 9–10). He will begin by gathering his flock and leading them (v. 11).

Now look at the opening chapters of the Gospel of Mark. It begins with an announcement of "the good news" (1:1). Mark explicitly quotes Isaiah 40:3 (1:3), which he says is fulfilled in John the Baptist, who preaches forgiveness of sins (vv. 4–6) and announces that the one coming after him is mightier than he (vv. 7–8). Then Jesus shows up, and John baptizes him (vv. 9–11). Jesus goes out into the wilderness and returns, preaching the "good news" of God's kingdom rule (vv. 12–15). He begins by calling people to follow him (vv. 16–20) and starts demonstrating his "authority" by casting out demons, healing the sick, and cleansing the leper (vv. 21–45). It is in this context that Jesus heals the paralyzed man and forgives his sins (2:1–12). His actions are all part of the "program" of the Lord God coming to the land to rule, forgive, restore, and lead his people.[8]

The New Testament articulates Christ's role as Savior in many ways that make it clear that he is doing exactly what the Old Testament affirmed that God, and he alone, would do for his people. According to Paul, for example, it is "our great God and Savior, Jesus Christ . . . who gave himself for us that he might redeem us from all iniquity" (Titus 2:13–14). But the Psalms assert that it is the Lord God "who will redeem Israel from all its iniquities" (130:8). The psalmist confesses, "Salvation belongs to the LORD" (3:8 NASB); the multitude in the apostle John's apocalyptic vision confesses, "Salvation belongs to our God who is seated on the throne, and to the Lamb!" (Rev. 7:10). This text in Revelation is just one of several that declare that Jesus Christ deserves divine honors in view of his redeeming, sacrificial death on the cross for our sins. The following is perhaps the most forceful of those passages:

> They sing a new song: "You are worthy to take the scroll and to open its seals, for you were slaughtered and by your blood you ransomed for God saints from every tribe and language and people and nation; you have made them to be a kingdom and priests serving our God, and they will reign on earth." Then I looked, and I heard the voice of many angels surrounding the throne and the living creatures and the elders; they numbered myriads of myriads and thousands of thousands, singing with full voice, "Worthy is the Lamb that was slaughtered to receive power and wealth and wisdom and might and honor and glory and blessing!" Then I heard every creature in heaven and on earth and under the earth and in the sea, and all that is in them, singing, "To the one seated on the throne and to the Lamb be blessing and honor and glory and might forever and ever!" And the four living creatures said, "Amen!" And the elders fell down and worshiped. (Rev. 5:9–14)

"I Am . . . the Truth"

We quoted earlier Jesus' statement, "I am the way, and the truth, and the life" (John 14:6). His claim to be "the truth" grates especially hard on many postmodern ears today. If Jesus really is God incarnate, though, we would expect him to have regarded himself in just that way. The evidence from all four Gospels is unanimous and overwhelming on this point.

The Gospels recognize that in some ways Jesus fit into certain conventional categories of a religious leader. Jesus functioned as a rabbi[9] or Jewish teacher: he quoted Scripture (what we call the Old Testament), used earthly illustrations (his parables), and had students (disciples) who referred to him as rabbi and asked him theological questions (for the term *rabbi*, see Mark 9:5; 10:51; 11:21; 14:45; John 1:38, 49; 3:2; 4:31; 6:25; 9:2; 11:8; 20:16).[10] Jesus accepted this description, sometimes referring to himself as a teacher (Matt. 10:24–25; John 13:13), although he insisted that ultimately he was to be their *only* teacher (Matt. 23:8). Jesus also functioned as a prophet: he spoke the word of God, warned of a coming judgment, and referred to himself as a prophet (Matt. 21:11, 46; Luke 7:16; 13:33; 24:19; Mark 6:4; John 4:19, 44; 6:14; 7:40; 9:17). The apostle Peter referred to Jesus as the prophet whom Moses had foretold (Acts 3:22–23; cf. 7:37).

In crucial ways, though, Jesus did not speak like a rabbi or a prophet. A rabbi was a teacher or expositor of the *Torah*, or Law, the foundational books of the Old Testament (Genesis through Deuteronomy). Furthermore, the rabbis interpreted the Torah within the stream of oral tradition and rabbinical reflection on Scripture that had been going on for centuries—at least since the time of Ezra. One of the principal functions of scribes in Judaism was to write down, study, and codify the often disparate opinions that were passed down and constantly supplemented by each new generation.[11] Rabbis based their teaching on this oral tradition to such an extent that offering interpretations of the Torah without citing past rabbis or scribes was something of an outrage. A famous statement in the Jerusalem Talmud (a compilation of rabbinical opinion published centuries later) typifies the mentality. It is said that Hillel, arguably the most highly esteemed rabbi in history following the close of the Old Testament era, talked on a particular point of interpretation all day, but the other rabbis would not accept his opinion "until he said, Thus I heard from Shemaiah and Abtalion," two rabbis from an earlier era.[12]

Jesus never spoke this way. In the Sermon on the Mount, he deliberately contrasts his approach with that of "the scribes and Pharisees" (Matt. 5:20), drawing the contrast in this way: "You have heard that it was said to those of ancient times. . . . But I say to you" (vv. 21–22). The scribes claimed that their interpretations derived ultimately from God through Moses via the process of oral tradition passed down from the time of Moses to their own day. Jesus' statement, "You have heard that it was said to those of ancient times," refers to the rabbinical, scribal way of reasoning: they heard it from this rabbi, who heard it from that rabbi before him, and so on, back to the ancient source. Jesus sets aside all that and says, "but *I* say to you."[13]

Throughout the Sermon on the Mount, Jesus cites not one single rabbi or other religious authority. Instead, he says, "I say to you," thirteen times just in this one sermon (Matt. 5:18, 20, 22, 28, 32, 34, 39, 44; 6:2, 5, 16, 25, 29). At the close of his sermon, Jesus challenges his hearers to base their lives on *his* words: "Everyone then who hears these words of mine and acts on them will be like a wise man who built his house on rock. . . . And everyone who hears these words of mine and does not act on them will be like a foolish man who built his house on sand" (Matt. 7:24, 26).

Not surprisingly, Matthew reports that "the crowds were astounded at his teaching, for he taught them as one having authority, and not as their scribes" (7:28–29). The other Gospels report similar reactions to Jesus' teaching (Mark 1:22; Luke 4:32; John 7:46).

Nor did Jesus speak like a prophet. In the Old Testament, prophets did not speak in their own name or treat their own words as the word of God. Instead, when they prophesied, they would generally introduce God's message with a formula such as "thus says the Lord" (over 400 times) or "the word of the Lord came" to such-and-such prophet (about 100 times). Jesus never uses such an introductory formula. Instead, as we have just noted, Jesus typically introduced his comments by saying, "I say to you" (about 145 times).[14] While it is possible for mere humans to use those words in various contexts without implying any exalted claims for themselves, the way Jesus uses them (in deliberate contrast to the most highly respected religious authorities of Jewish tradition) does imply such claims.

Moreover, seventy-four or seventy-five times Jesus uses an introductory locution that appears to be unparalleled: "Amen I say to you" (often translated "Truly I say to you").[15] Jesus' habit of beginning a sentence with the word "Amen" has no precedent in the Old Testament, nor have scholars found any precedent in the rest of ancient Jewish literature.[16] This expression invests what Jesus is about to say with religious authority and assurance even before he says it. Jesus speaks with absolute confidence that what he says—that everything he says—is the absolute truth. "Heaven and earth will pass away, but my words will not pass away" (Matt. 24:35; Mark 13:31). No rabbi, no priest, no prophet would ever say "my words" here; they would confidently say that *God's* words will never pass away, but no pious Jew would dare claim that *his* words would never pass away. Yet Jesus made such a claim. Isaiah, one of Israel's greatest prophets, said, "The grass withers, the flower fades; but the word of our God will stand forever" (Isa. 40:8). Jesus makes the equivalent claim for his *own* words. As Ben Witherington points out, "Jesus believed he spoke not merely by inspiration and thus for God, but also with divine power and authority and for himself. . . . No ordinary or even extraordinary person, whether teacher or prophet, spoke this way."[17]

The conflict between Jesus and the Jewish religious educational establishment over his claims to divine authority is evident, especially in his handling
of the Sabbath. The rabbinical traditions of his day gave considerable attention to what was and was not "work" in order to specify what was and was
not permissible activity on the Sabbath. The regulations became more and
more detailed, to the point that scribes were needed just to keep track of all
the rules.[18] Jesus cuts through all such scribal argumentation and asks such
simple questions as, "Is it lawful to do good or to do harm on the sabbath,
to save life or to kill?" (Mark 3:4). Peter Ensor observes, "With great daring
and boldness he claims the right to 'work' on the sabbath day, to be free from
the scribal restrictions, to be able to interpret and apply scripture in his own
way without reference [to] human traditions, to determine for himself what
might be permissible on the sabbath day."[19]

The view of Jesus in the Gospel of John is fundamentally no different from
what we find in the Synoptic Gospels. Jesus does not merely speak on God's
behalf; he *is* God speaking. The opening statement of the Gospel refers to the
preincarnate Son as the *Logos*, "the Word," who was with God and was God
(John 1:1). This Word became flesh and dwelled among us (1:14); in his incarnation, God the only Son "explained" or "interpreted" God for us (1:18).
As Robert Gundry has documented, this idea of Jesus as God speaking is a
major theme throughout the rest of the Gospel.[20] Jesus told the Samaritan
woman, "I am he, the one who is speaking to you" (John 4:26), a statement
echoing the declaration of God in Isaiah 52:6. He asserted, "Very truly, I tell
you, whoever keeps my word will never see death" (John 8:51), a claim that
his hearers recognized went far beyond anything said of the patriarchs or
prophets in the Old Testament (v. 52).

Jesus denied that what he said was merely his own word: "The word that
you hear is not mine, but is from the Father who sent me" (John 14:24).
When he speaks, it is always God speaking; his words are not his alone, for
the Father is speaking in and with him, testifying together with the Son (cf.
John 5:31–32; 8:16–18).

Jesus' claim, "I am . . . the truth" (John 14:6), then, is consistent with Jesus'
view of his words evident throughout all four Gospels. He regarded himself
not as someone who merely spoke the truth, but as the very embodiment of
truth. Jesus, like the Father, is "full of grace and truth" (John 1:14).

"I Am . . . the Life"

Jesus' seemingly audacious claims for himself in John 14:6 climax with his assertion that he is "the life." Truly, he could not have made any higher claim than this. Jesus claims to be life itself for us. We are to find life in him.

The focus of Jesus' statement here is the eternal life that he alone provides as we put our faith in him. That Jesus is the source of eternal life is the dominant theme of the Gospel of John from beginning to end. Thus, the prologue states, "In him was life, and the life was the light of all people" (1:4). John's concluding explanation for the purpose of his Gospel is that "you may come to believe that Jesus is the Messiah, the Son of God, and that through believing you may have life in his name" (20:31). Between these two statements, John quotes Jesus saying repeatedly that we may have eternal life by believing in him (3:15–16; 5:24; 6:47). Those who believe in Jesus in some sense already have this eternal life, but its full realization will come when Jesus raises believers from the dead to live forever (5:28–29; 6:40, 54). His most dramatic statement on the matter comes just before he raises Lazarus from the dead: "I am the resurrection and the life. Those who believe in me, even though they die, will live, and everyone who lives and believes in me will never die" (11:25–26). Of course, Jesus is not claiming to be the source of eternal life apart from or independent of the Father. Eternal life is found in knowing the Father, who is the only true God—*and* in knowing Jesus Christ, whom the Father sent (17:3).[21]

Jesus' statement that he is "the life" is a claim not only to be the source or way of eternal life, although that is a stupendous enough assertion. It is a claim that we find the very meaning of life in a relationship with him. Jesus invites us to find a quality of life with him that we cannot find elsewhere: "I came that they may have life, and have it abundantly" (John 10:10).

The rest of the New Testament exhibits a similar understanding of Jesus. The apostle Peter spoke of Jesus as "the Author of life" (Acts 3:15), an expression that can also be translated "the Prince of life" (NASB). Paul states that "the free gift of God is eternal life in Christ Jesus our Lord" (Rom. 6:23). For Paul, the purpose of the Christian life is "that the life of Jesus also may be manifested" in our physical bodies (2 Cor. 4:10, 11 NASB). Paul states repeatedly that life is all about Christ:

> I have been crucified with Christ; and it is no longer I who live, but it is Christ who lives in me. (Gal. 2:19–20)

> For to me, living is Christ and dying is gain. (Phil. 1:21)

> For you have died, and your life is hidden with Christ in God. When Christ who is your life is revealed, then you also will be revealed with him in glory. (Col. 3:3–4)

When Paul says that Christ lives in us and that he is our life, he is identifying Christ as the source of eternal life and of all the spiritual blessings that go along with it. Two of Paul's characteristic terms for these spiritual blessings are *grace* and *peace*. *Grace* is the generous, undeserved favor by which God grants us life instead of the eternal death we deserve; *peace* is the condition of reconciliation and harmonious relationship with God that we enjoy as a result. Paul's characteristic salutation with which he begins his epistles identifies the Father and the Son as the source of these blessings: "Grace to you and peace from God our Father and the Lord Jesus Christ" (Eph. 1:2).[22] Notice that Paul says that grace and peace both come "from" (*apo*) God the Father and the Lord Jesus Christ. Immediately following this salutation in Ephesians, Paul writes, "Blessed be the God and Father of our Lord Jesus Christ, who has blessed us in Christ with every spiritual blessing in the heavenly places" (1:3). Elsewhere, Paul appeals to Jesus Christ and God the Father to comfort and strengthen believers in everything they do: "Now may our Lord Jesus Christ Himself and God our Father, who has loved us and given us eternal comfort and good hope by grace, comfort and strengthen your hearts in every good work and word" (2 Thess. 2:16–17 NASB). It takes nothing away from the honor due God the Father for us to acknowledge—as we must—that every spiritual blessing in our lives comes to us in and from Jesus Christ.

One of the most important spiritual, life-giving blessings we can receive is the presence and power of the Holy Spirit. This blessing, too, comes from Jesus Christ. After Jesus asked the woman at the well in Samaria for a drink of water, he said to her, "If you knew . . . who it is that is saying to you, 'Give me a drink,' you would have asked him, and he would have given you living water. . . . Those who drink of the water that I will give them will never be thirsty. The water that I will give will become in them a spring of water gushing up to eternal life" (John 4:10, 14). This "living water" is a symbolic description of the Spirit, as John later makes explicit: "Now he said this about the Spirit" (7:39, see vv. 37–38).

The night before his death, Jesus told his apostles about "the Advocate, the Holy Spirit, whom the Father will send in my name" (John 14:26). According to this statement, the Father will send the Spirit. Later, however, Jesus says that *he* will send the Spirit: "When the Advocate comes, whom *I will send* to you *from the Father*, the Spirit of truth who comes from the Father, he will testify on my behalf" (John 15:26, emphasis added). Notice here that the Spirit "comes from the Father," but Jesus is the one who sends the Spirit, as he says again a few sentences later: "I will send him to you" (16:7). This apparent imprecision (does the Father send the Spirit, or does Jesus?) simply demonstrates that Jesus' role in sending the Spirit is in no way inferior to the role of the Father. The Father even sends the Spirit *in Jesus' name* (14:26)!

Other New Testament writers also teach that Jesus sent the Holy Spirit. All of the Gospels report John the Baptist's announcement that the one coming after him (Jesus) "will baptize you with the Holy Spirit" (Mark 1:8; cf. Matt. 3:11; Luke 3:16; John 1:33). At the end of his Gospel, Luke reports Jesus saying, "And see, I am sending upon you what my Father promised; so stay here in the city until you have been clothed with power from on high" (24:49). What the Father promised, as Luke says explicitly in Acts, is the baptism in the Holy Spirit (Acts 1:5).

In the first Christian sermon on the Day of Pentecost, when the apostles were "filled with the Holy Spirit" (Acts 2:4), Peter stated that the event was a fulfillment of Joel's prophecy: "And it shall come to pass in the last days, says God, that I will pour out of My Spirit on all flesh" (Acts 2:17 NKJV, quoting Joel 2:28). What Joel's prophecy states that God would do, Peter says that Jesus did: "This Jesus God raised up, and of that all of us are witnesses. Being therefore exalted at the right hand of God, and having received from the Father the promise of the Holy Spirit, he has poured out this that you both see and hear" (Acts 2:32–33). Grammatically, by "he" Peter must mean the one who was exalted at the right hand of God and who received from the Father the promise; in short, Jesus poured out the manifestation of the Holy Spirit.

According to John, after Jesus rose from the dead, he gave his disciples the indwelling presence of the Spirit.[23] "When he had said this, he breathed on them and said to them, 'Receive the Holy Spirit'" (John 20:22). This is an astonishing thing for him to do. The words for "Spirit" in both Hebrew (*rûach*) and Greek (*pneuma*) also mean "breath." Thus, we can express the force of what Jesus is doing in this symbolic action by saying that he breathed on his disciples the "holy breath," the life-giving Spirit, of God. In other words, Jesus' Spirit *is* God's Holy Spirit; they are one and the same Spirit.

We find the same equation of the Spirit of God with the Spirit of Jesus elsewhere in the New Testament. Luke, reporting on the movements of Paul and his companions, writes, "They went through the region of Phrygia and Galatia, having been forbidden by *the Holy Spirit* to speak the word in Asia. When they had come opposite Mysia, they attempted to go into Bithynia, but *the Spirit of Jesus* did not allow them" (Acts 16:6–7, emphasis added). In Romans, Paul says, "But you are not in the flesh; you are in the Spirit, since *the Spirit of God* dwells in you. Anyone who does not have *the Spirit of Christ* does not belong to him" (Rom. 8:9, emphasis added). There are not two different Spirits here: to have the Spirit of Christ is to have the Spirit of God dwelling in you. Elsewhere Paul writes, "I know that through your prayers and the help of the Spirit of Jesus Christ this will turn out for my deliverance" (Phil. 1:19).

The Spirit of Christ is not a new development. The apostle Peter speaks of the Spirit of Christ inspiring the prophets of the Old Testament. They inquired about the salvation to come, "searching what, or what manner of time, the Spirit of Christ who was in them was indicating when He testified beforehand the sufferings of Christ and the glories that would follow" (1 Peter 1:11 NKJV).

The New Testament's treatment of the Spirit of God as the Spirit of Christ, and especially its teaching that Jesus Christ sent the Spirit to act on his behalf, is one of the most striking evidences that the New Testament writers thought of Jesus as God. As Max Turner has argued,

> *There is simply NO analogy for an exalted human* (or any other creature) *becoming so integrated with God that such a person may be said to 'commission' God's Spirit, and through that to extend that exalted person's own 'presence' and activity to people on earth.* For the Jew, such relationship to, and activity in or through, the Spirit appears to be necessarily, inalienably, and so distinctively, *God's.*[24]

Consistent with what we have seen already, the apostle Paul credits Jesus Christ with the gifts of the Spirit. Thus, in his discussion of the spiritual gifts, Paul states, "Now there are varieties of gifts, but the same Spirit; and there are varieties of services, but the same Lord; and there are varieties of activities, but it is the same God who activates all of them in everyone" (1 Cor. 12:4–6). "Gifts," "services," and "activities" are merely different ways of describing the same spiritually gifted functions that take place within the church. In this context, the parallel references to "the same Spirit . . . the same Lord . . . the same God" treat both the Spirit and the Lord (Jesus), along with God (the Father), as the divine source of spiritual gifts.

Mehrdad Fatehi, in his doctoral dissertation on the Spirit's relation to the risen Lord in the writings of Paul, argues that "Paul's use of the Spirit-language with reference to Christ . . . cannot be regarded as simply another case of God's delegating one of his functions or prerogatives to a chief agent." This is because "the Spirit stands not for one of God's functions but for *God himself when he directly acts to discharge such functions.*" He concludes, "It may be possible for God, and the evidence from Judaism shows that it *was* regarded to be possible for him, to delegate or share some of his prerogatives or functions, but the same evidence shows that it did not seem plausible for the Jews to think of God *delegating or sharing himself*, so to speak, as he was present and active through his Spirit."[25] The implication is that Paul thought of Christ as truly divine.

> If the Spirit-language was an exclusively God-language in Judaism, the fact that this language is used to express Christ's presence and activity in the same ways that it was used to express God's, establishes that Paul and the Pauline believers viewed Christ as "divine."[26]

The same conclusion follows from what we have seen in the rest of the apostolic writings. Everything that we look to God to do for our spiritual, eternal benefit, the New Testament in one way or another tells us to look to Jesus to do. That makes him truly our Lord and our God.

Chapter 18

HERE COMES THE JUDGE

Jesus' role in performing the works of God is not temporary. As he has been doing God's deeds from the beginning of Creation, so he will still be doing God's deeds in the consummation of all things. From beginning to end, from first to last (Rev. 1:8, 17–18; 2:8; 22:12–13), Jesus does what God does. In this chapter, we will focus on Jesus' *eschatological* deeds—that is, his works that pertain to the end of history.

Order in the Court!

One of the main difficulties many non-Christians have with the belief that Jesus is the Messiah is that when Jesus was here on earth he did not bring an end to injustice, war, and other human evils. This is clearly the main "sticking point" with followers of Judaism, for whom item number one on the Messiah's "to do" list is the establishment of worldwide peace under his benevolent rule. Members of other religions, as varied as Islam and the Unification Church, sometimes voice the same objection. They may respect Jesus as a great prophet or teacher, but they do not view him as "the last word," precisely because the world is still in obvious need of divine intervention.

This objection would have great force if it were not for one thing: *Jesus is coming back*. He came to die and rise again, but not just to leave the world to its own devices for the rest of time. His death and resurrection were the first (and crucial) stage in God's plan to bring the world into harmony with his eternal purposes. Jesus is going to return, and he is going to bring God's plan to its glorious consummation.

On what basis can we be sure that Jesus is coming back? As with so much
in Christian belief, God validated this truth for us through the resurrection
of Jesus from the dead. Keep in mind that Jesus rose physically, bodily from
the grave to immortality (Luke 24:36–43; John 2:19–22; 20:19–20; Acts 2:24–
32; Rom. 6:9–10; 8:11; 1 Cor. 15:3–8, 42–49; Phil. 3:20–21).[1] Resurrection to
glorious, and yet still human, bodily life implies that Jesus intends to live forever with other human beings in what the Bible calls the new heaven and new
earth (Rev. 21:1).[2] In short, the very nature of his resurrection implies what
the New Testament plainly affirms: Jesus is coming back to the earth.

In the Old Testament, the hope of final peace and justice in the world is the
coming of the Lord (YHWH).

> Let the field exult, and all that is in it.
>   Then all the trees of the forest will sing for joy
> Before the LORD, for He is coming,
>   For He is coming to judge the earth.
> He will judge the world in righteousness
>   And the peoples in His faithfulness.
>   (Ps. 96:12–13 NASB)

> Get you up to a high mountain,
>   O Zion, herald of good tidings;
> lift up your voice with strength,
>   O Jerusalem, herald of good tidings,
>   lift it up, do not fear;
> say to the cities of Judah,
>   "Here is your God!"
> See, the Lord GOD comes with might,
>   and his arm rules for him;
> his reward is with him,
>   and his recompense before him.
> He will feed his flock like a shepherd;
>   he will gather the lambs in his arms,
> and carry them in his bosom,
>   and gently lead the mother sheep.
>   (Isa. 40:9–11)

There is a reason why Handel's *Messiah* includes some of these lines from Isaiah 40: the church historically has recognized that these words refer to the coming of Jesus Christ. As we have seen in earlier chapters, the New Testament sees the coming of Jesus Christ into the world as a human being in the Incarnation as a fulfillment of the promise of God coming to his people in Isaiah 40 (e.g., Matt. 3:3; cf. Isa. 40:3). In John's affirmation that "the Word became flesh and lived among us" (John 1:14), Christians rightly see that God's promise of once again dwelling with humanity has begun to be fulfilled. Andrew Brunson has argued that this theme is a significant one in the Gospel of John:

> His appropriation of Yahweh's role extends beyond occasionally taking up a divine prerogative, actually covering the entire complex of restoration hope, at the core of which was a longing for the abiding presence of God. What allows this complete identification of Jesus with Yahweh . . . is John's emphasis on the incarnation: in the person of Jesus, God has indeed come to reign and dwell among his people.[3]

What began in the event Christians celebrate at Christmas—the reuniting of the human race with God—will be completed following the second coming of Christ. The Lord is indeed coming, and when he does, he will come in might, bringing reward and recompense and bringing his sheep to permanent safety and security.

Thus, the New Testament teaches believers in Jesus to look forward to his return, when he will make everything right.

> Repent therefore, and turn to God so that your sins may be wiped out, so that times of refreshing may come from the presence of the Lord, and that he may send the Messiah appointed for you, that is, Jesus, who must remain in heaven until the time of universal restoration that God announced long ago through his holy prophets. (Acts 3:19–21)

> And just as people are appointed to die once, and then to face judgment, so also, after Christ was offered once to *bear the sins of many*, to those who eagerly await him he will appear a second time, not to bear sin but to bring salvation. (Heb. 9:26–28 NET)[4]

One of the most striking references to Christ's second coming is in Paul's epistle to Titus, where he writes that we are "looking for the blessed hope and glorious appearing of our great God and Savior Jesus Christ" (Titus 2:13 NKJV). We already have shown in chapter 12 that this text does, in fact, call Jesus Christ "our great God and Savior." Here we wish to draw attention to something else that is quite significant. Paul tells us to be looking for Christ's glorious "appearing." The Greek word Paul uses, *epiphaneia*, is the word from which English derives the word *epiphany*. Unfortunately, in contemporary usage this word is most likely to evoke one of two ideas. The first is the feast day called Epiphany, observed on January 6 as a commemoration (usually) of the visit of the Magi to see the child Jesus. This usage is not especially illuminating as to the meaning of the Greek word (although at least Jesus is involved!). The second meaning of "epiphany" that many will recognize is the experience of sudden illumination or discovery—a usage that is even less "illuminating" as to what Paul meant.

The actual meaning of *epiphaneia* in religious contexts in the Greek of Paul's day is the appearance of a deity in some visible form. That Paul uses the word with this meaning is clear from the fact that he speaks of the epiphany "of our great *God* and Savior." Paul consistently uses *epiphaneia* in his writings to refer to the appearance of Christ (2 Thess. 2:8; 1 Tim. 6:14; 2 Tim. 1:10; 4:1, 8; Titus 2:13). Andrew Y. Lau, in his dissertation titled *Manifest in Flesh: The Epiphany Christology of the Pastoral Epistles*, has shown that the epistles to Timothy and Titus view Christ's future appearance or "epiphany" as the visible revelation of God. The point of Titus 2:13 is that "*at the epiphany of Christ the otherwise invisible and holy God Himself will take on a personal visible appearance.*"[5] Thus, the coming of Jesus Christ will be the visible coming of God.

All Rise!

One thing the Bible says will happen when Christ comes back is the resurrection of the dead. According to Paul, if the dead do not rise, then Christ did not rise—and if that were the case, then Christianity would be false: "If there is no resurrection of the dead, then Christ has not been raised; and if Christ has not been raised, then our proclamation has been in vain and your faith has been in vain. We are even found to be misrepresenting God, because we testified of God that he raised Christ—whom he did not raise if it is true that the dead are not raised. . . . If for this life only we have hoped in Christ, we are of all people most to be pitied" (1 Cor. 15:13–15, 19).

Our hope in Christ, then, rests on the truth of his resurrection. In a sense, Jesus' resurrection was the beginning of the eschatological resurrection from the dead for which we are still waiting. Paul describes the risen Christ as "the first fruits" of the resurrection (1 Cor. 15:20, 23), the "firstborn from the dead" (Col. 1:18; cf. Rev. 1:5). The resurrections that Jesus performed during his earthly ministry (Mark 5:21–24, 35–43; Luke 7:11–17; John 11:1–45) returned those people to their mortal lives, and eventually they died again. Those resurrections were "sneak previews" of the resurrection to come. Jesus, however, rose from the dead to immortal life, and in doing so became the one who overcomes death for all who believe in him (Rom. 6:9–10; 1 Cor. 15:42–57; Rev. 1:17–18).

Jesus' role here is not a passive one of merely being the first person raised from the dead to immortal life. It is true that the New Testament credits God the Father with raising Jesus (see especially Gal. 1:1). But it also teaches that Jesus raised himself from the dead! When challenged to produce a sign validating his claimed authority, Jesus replied, "Destroy this temple, and in three days *I* will raise it up" (John 2:19, emphasis added). Although his hearers thought Jesus was referring to the man-made building in Jerusalem, John explains, "But he was speaking of the temple of his body" (v. 21). He then comments, "When therefore he was raised from the dead, his disciples remembered that he had said this, and they believed the Scripture and the word that Jesus had spoken" (v. 22 ESV). John could not be more explicit: what Jesus meant was that after he was killed, he would "raise up" his own body from the dead.

Even in death, then, Jesus was able to exert divine power to bring himself up alive from the dead. This is because, as we saw in the previous chapter, Jesus was Life incarnate; he was, if you will, Resurrection personified (John 1:4; 11:25; 14:6). As Jesus explained, it was impossible for anyone to take his life away, and he laid it down in order to take it back up: "No one takes it from me, but I lay it down of my own accord. I have power to lay it down, and I have power to take it up again" (John 10:18). Jesus *could not* stay dead, "because it was impossible for him to be held in its power" (Acts 2:24).

Jesus' resurrection is not just a historical curiosity or an impressive display of power that proves Jesus to have been someone special (although it is that!). As the one who has overcome death on our behalf, Jesus is the "Prince" or "Author" of life (Acts 3:15). For believers in Christ, then, the future resurrection of the dead is an indispensable part of our faith in Christ. Not just believers, however, but *all* people will be raised from the dead. Paul affirmed, as did the Pharisees of his day, "that there will be a resurrection of both the righteous and the unrighteous" (Acts 24:15). The basis for this expectation is a statement near the end of the book of Daniel: "Many of those who sleep in the dust of the earth shall awake, some to everlasting life, and some to shame and everlasting contempt" (Dan. 12:2). The wicked will be raised from the dead in order to stand "whole" in the final judgment.

Jesus is the one who will raise both the righteous and the wicked from the dead. Referring to himself as the Son of Man, Jesus said, "Do not be astonished at this; for the hour is coming when all who are in their graves will hear his [the Son of Man's] voice and will come out—those who have done good, to the resurrection of life, and those who have done evil, to the resurrection of condemnation" (John 5:28–29). Who decides which people are resurrected to eternal life and which to eternal condemnation? Again, the answer is Jesus: "Indeed, just as the Father raises the dead and gives them life, so also the Son gives life to whomever he wishes" (5:21). As Jesus explains, he chooses, in agreement with the Father, to raise up to eternal life all who believe in the Son: "This is indeed the will of my Father, that all who see the Son and believe in him may have eternal life; and I will raise them up on the last day" (6:40; cf. vv. 44, 54).

The New Testament teaching that Jesus will raise the dead—and decide who lives forever and who does not—is evidence of his deity because the Old Testament ascribes this prerogative and power to God alone. "The LORD kills and brings to life; he brings down to Sheol and raises up" (1 Sam. 2:6). This point is made in one of the two most emphatic monotheistic statements in the Old Testament:

> See now that I, even I, am he;
>   there is no god besides me.
> I kill and I make alive;
>   I wound and I heal;
>   and no one can deliver from my hand.
>   (Deut. 32:39)

So Jesus not only claims the prerogative of deciding who ultimately dies in eternal condemnation and who lives in eternal life, but he does so in language that clearly echoes the words of the Lord God in Deuteronomy:

My sheep hear My voice, and I know them, and they follow Me; and I give eternal life to them, and they will never perish; *and no one will snatch them out of My hand.* (John 10:27–28 NASB, emphasis added)

It would be one thing for Jesus to claim that God has delegated one of his prerogatives or functions to him. Even that claim, generally speaking, would be remarkable, but it is altogether something else for him to claim that he exercises a prerogative of God, using language taken directly from a scriptural affirmation of monotheism. And yet this is exactly what Jesus does.[6]

Judge Jesus

To say that Jesus Christ will decide who enjoys eternal life and who suffers eternal condemnation is to say that he will be the eternal Judge of all humanity. This is precisely what the New Testament says. Jesus as judge is, in fact, a rather common portrayal of him in Scripture.

The prevailing view of the Old Testament is, of course, that God is the ultimate Judge of all human beings. Abraham, the original patriarch, recognized the Lord God as "the Judge of all the earth" (Gen. 18:25). The Psalms repeatedly affirm that God is the judge (Pss. 7:11; 50:6; 75:7).

The New Testament teaches that Jesus will be that Judge. After stating that he gives life to whomever he wishes, Jesus asserts, "The Father judges no one but has given all judgment to the Son, so that all may honor the Son just as they honor the Father" (John 5:22–23). Note what Jesus does *not* say: that the Father has merely delegated all judgment to the Son, but still expects us to honor the Father in ways that we should not honor the Son. To the contrary, the Father has deferred all judgment to the Son precisely so that all may honor the Son just as they properly honor the Father! When we stand before Jesus Christ on Judgment Day, we will not be able to appeal his decisions to his Father in the hope of getting a more lenient sentence. (Were anyone actually to try this, Jesus presumably would respond in the same words he spoke in John 14:9: "Whoever has seen me has seen the Father"!) Jesus' sentence will be final.

New Testament affirmations of Jesus as the eschatological Judge not only assign him that role but often do so (once again) in language that appears to be deliberately echoing Old Testament affirmations about the Lord God. Here are just a few examples:

- At the end of his speech in Athens, Paul warns that God "has fixed a day on which he will have the world judged in righteousness by a man whom he has appointed" (Acts 17:31). This statement recalls the psalmist's declaration that the Lord "is coming, for he is coming to judge the earth. He will judge the world with righteousness, and the peoples with his truth" (Ps. 96:13).

- Paul told the Corinthians not to pass judgment on Christ's servants "before the Lord comes, who will bring to light the things now hidden in darkness and will disclose the purposes of the heart" (1 Cor. 4:5). The reference to the Lord coming in judgment recalls Psalm 96:13, and Paul's affirmation that the Lord Jesus will expose what is in people's hearts (cf. Acts 1:24) recalls the familiar Old Testament teaching that the Lord God alone knows the hearts of all people (1 Sam. 16:7; 1 Kings 8:39; 1 Chron. 28:9; Ps. 139:23–24; Prov. 16:2; 17:3; Jer. 17:10).

- The Old Testament frequently speaks of the eschatological Day of Judgment (as well as certain historical judgments on the nations that were precursors to that day) as "the day of the LORD," that is, the day of YHWH (Isa. 13:6, 9; Ezek. 13:5; 30:3; Joel 1:15; 2:1, 11, 31; 3:14; Amos 5:18, 20; Obad. 15; Zeph. 1:7, 14). As we pointed out in chapter 13, the apostle Paul frequently referred to the eschatological Day of Judgment as the Day of the Lord Jesus Christ (1 Cor. 1:8; 5:5; 2 Cor. 1:14; Phil. 1:6, 10; 2:16; 1 Thess. 5:2; 2 Thess. 2:1–2; 2 Tim. 1:18; cf. 2 Peter 3:8–10, 12). The use of such a familiar Old Testament idiom in reference to the Lord Jesus' exercising the same function of judgment strongly identifies the Lord Jesus with the Lord YHWH.

- Jesus warns the church at Thyatira that he is going to bring disciplinary judgment on those who are compromising the faith, "and all the churches shall know that I am He who searches the minds and hearts. And I will give to each one of you according to your works" (Rev. 2:23 NKJV). The Old Testament, however, teaches that "the righteous God tests the hearts and minds" (Ps. 7:9 NKJV; cf. Prov. 24:12a; Jer. 11:20) and that the Lord God "will recompense every one according to his works" (Ps. 62:12 LXX; Prov. 24:12b).[7] Yet, Jesus himself claimed that he will perform this judgment according to each person's works (Matt. 16:27). Paul, too, alludes to the same Old Testament texts when he writes, "For all of us must appear before the judgment seat of Christ, so that each may receive recompense for what has been done in the body, whether good or evil" (2 Cor. 5:10).

According to Paul, Jesus Christ will carry out the final judgment from what he calls "the judgment seat of Christ." Just what is the significance of this "judgment seat"? In part 5 of this book, we will examine what the Bible says about Christ's exalted position. What we will find will confirm in some startling ways that Jesus Christ is, indeed, God. We already have seen that Jesus Christ does everything that God does: he creates and sustains the universe, saves people from their sins, provides them with every spiritual blessing, speaks with absolute truth and authority, raises the dead, and judges all humanity. What we will see in the concluding chapters of this book is that Jesus Christ does all of these things from the highest possible position in all existence.

Part 5

THE BEST SEAT
IN THE HOUSE

Jesus Shares the <u>S</u>eat of God's Throne

Honors	Attributes	Names	Deeds	Seat

Chapter 19

JESUS TAKES THE STAND

> Bobby was spending the weekend with his grandmother. His grandmother decided to take him to the park on Saturday morning. It had been snowing all night and everything was beautiful. His grandmother remarked . . . "Doesn't it look like an artist painted this scenery? Did you know God painted this just for you?" Bobby said, "Yes, God did it and he did it left handed." This confused his grandmother a bit, and she asked him, "What makes you say God did this with his left hand?" "Well," said Bobby, "we learned at Sunday School last week that Jesus sits on God's right hand!"[1]

We can all get a chuckle out of Bobby's obvious misunderstanding of what the Bible means when it speaks of Jesus sitting "on God's right hand." Yet the truth is that many members of adult Sunday schools and other Christians are hazy on the real significance of this biblical concept. Worse still, some scholars go out of their way, trying to explain away this remarkable aspect of the New Testament teaching about Jesus Christ.

We have seen that Jesus does all of the deeds or works of God, not the least of which is determining at the end of history who will live forever in God's loving presence and who will be consigned forever to the eternal darkness of unending separation from the presence of God. How can Jesus be the final arbiter of the eternal future of every human being who will ever live?

We won't find an answer in the revisionist theories being floated today. A Jesus who sits as Judge over all humanity defies all attempts to squeeze him into those man-sized molds. This greatest of teachers doesn't just grade our papers; he grades our *lives*. And just as he is too big to fit the molds suggested in our day, he was too big to fit the molds of his own day—even the mold of Messiah, as popularly understood.

The only possible answer is that Jesus occupies God's position, God's place. And this is exactly what the New Testament teaches. Jesus exercises God's prerogatives of judgment and salvation because he shares God's *seat*. That is, Jesus sits on God's throne, from which he rules over all creation and is the rightful arbiter to make those determinations as to our final disposition for all eternity.

Here's the point: someone sitting on God's throne and exercising God's ultimate prerogatives is, in at least a very practical sense, God. He occupies God's position and in doing so has the rightful expectation that we respond to him as to God himself.

Of the five major lines of evidence for the deity of Christ we are discussing in this book, this last category of evidence—that of Jesus' occupying the seat of God—is the least familiar to most Christians. One might make the case that sharing God's throne is one of the honors that Jesus shares with God (which we covered in part 1). We think it's better, however, to say that Jesus properly receives those honors precisely *because* he shares God's throne. For that reason, and because the concept is less familiar, we have decided to treat it separately.

From where, then, does this idea arise that Jesus shares God's throne? It turns out that Jesus himself announced this to be so at a climactic moment in his earthly life.

Who Does He Think He Is?

According to all four Gospels, before Jesus was sentenced to death by the Roman governor Pontius Pilate, he was questioned by the Sanhedrin, or Jewish council, led by the high priest Caiaphas (Matt. 26:57–66; Mark 14:53–64; Luke 22:66–71; cf. John 18:24, 28).[2] Jesus' appearance before the Sanhedrin was more like what we would call a grand jury inquisition than a formal trial. Since the Sanhedrin couldn't legally sentence Jesus to death, the intent was probably to assess charges that could be taken before Pilate.[3]

Throughout his itinerant ministry, Jesus had agitated the religious establishment by speaking and acting as someone above the religious laws and customs of Israel. In the days just prior to his arrest, Jesus had rankled the Sanhedrin by entering Jerusalem to acclamation, driving the money changers out of the temple, refusing to tell Sanhedrin members by what authority he did such things, and directing a parable of divine judgment against them (Mark 11:1–12:12). Small wonder, then, that the religious leaders in the Sanhedrin were looking for a way to have Jesus killed.

Arranging to have Jesus executed was a delicate matter. On the one hand, Israel was under the jurisdiction of Rome, and at the time only Roman magistrates could sentence someone to death (cf. John 18:31). For that reason, Caiaphas needed a *political* charge against Jesus that the Sanhedrin could take to Pilate. If Jesus would acknowledge that he believed himself to be the Messiah, the religious leaders could tell Pilate that Jesus was claiming to be a king. If there was anything Rome would not tolerate, it was a competitor with Caesar. On the other hand, the Sanhedrin would not want to hand Jesus over to Pilate for execution unless they could specify a sufficiently potent *religious* charge against him that would legitimate their actions before the people.

According to Mark,[4] the Sanhedrin initially had some difficulty finding charges that would stick. The witnesses they found to testify against Jesus were inconsistent as well as untruthful (14:55–56). One accusation that especially would have riled the priestly members of the Sanhedrin was that Jesus had threatened to destroy the temple (vv. 57–58). The Sanhedrin also was likely to see the charge as damaging to Jesus politically, because the Romans might have viewed such a threat as inciting unrest. That might have been enough (especially when combined with Jesus' action against the money changers), except that the testimonies concerning this accusation were inconsistent (v. 59), and Jesus refused to comment (vv. 60–61a).[5] For the Sanhedrin, it would be ideal for Jesus to admit to something, since this would make their case against Jesus beyond challenge. Finally, Caiaphas asked Jesus a question he was willing to answer: "Are you the Messiah, the Son of the Blessed One?" (v. 61b). Jesus' response apparently took Caiaphas somewhat by surprise:

> "I am; and 'you will see the Son of Man seated at the right hand of the Power,' and 'coming with the clouds of heaven.'" Then the high priest tore his clothes and said, "Why do we still need witnesses? You have heard his blasphemy! What is your decision?" All of them condemned him as deserving death. (vv. 62–64)

Jesus gave Caiaphas the confession he wanted: he was indeed the Messiah. A claim to be the Messiah would give the religious leaders reason to bring

Jesus before Pilate, because the conventional Jewish concept of Messiah was that of a conquering heroic king of Israel—an obvious threat to Roman rule. Assuming the Romans executed Jesus, his death would establish him as a false Messiah in the eyes of the general Jewish public. After all, most Jews thought, the Messiah is supposed to make the Romans suffer, not suffer at the hands of the Romans. So Caiaphas had the grounds he needed to make the case for Jesus to be executed by the Romans.

Caiaphas, though, responded to Jesus' statement in what seems an odd way, by rending his clothes and declaring that Jesus had committed blasphemy. What makes Caiaphas's response odd is that the claim to be the Messiah was not itself blasphemous. Evidently, Jesus' answer went beyond a simple affirmation that he was the Messiah.[6] Just what did Caiaphas mean by accusing Jesus of blasphemy? What sort of offense was it that he thought Jesus had committed?

Christ Says the Most Outrageous Things!

Although blasphemy could cover a range of possible offenses, we can learn what the Gospel writers understood the accusation to mean by examining how they use the word in context.

One common use of the word *blasphemy* reflected in the Gospels clearly does not have any direct bearing on the charge made against Jesus. In some cases, blasphemy refers to abusive or insulting comments about another person. The Gospels report that bystanders at Jesus' execution (Matt. 27:39; Mark 15:29), as well as his guards and one of the criminals crucified next to him (Luke 23:39; cf. 22:65), were "deriding" him (NRSV; cf. "hurling abuse," NASB; "blasphemed," NKJV). The Gospels may be intimating some irony in Jesus' being falsely accused of "blasphemy" and then becoming the object of "blasphemy" at his crucifixion. This particular offense, however, does not tell us the nature of Jesus' alleged blasphemy. Nothing in the account of Jesus' trial before the Sanhedrin suggests that they thought he was guilty of insulting someone.

The Synoptic Gospels also report the use of the word *blasphemy* in a dispute between Jesus and some of his religious critics who had accused him of performing exorcisms in league with the Devil (Matt. 12:22–24; Mark 3:20–22; Luke 11:14–16). According to Matthew, Jesus explained that he, in fact, cast out demons "by the Spirit of God" (Matt. 12:28; "by the finger of God," Luke 11:20). Besides refuting their criticism, Jesus warned his critics of the danger of blaspheming the Holy Spirit: "Therefore I tell you, people will be forgiven for every sin and blasphemy, but blasphemy against the Spirit will not be forgiven. Whoever speaks a word against the Son of Man will be forgiven, but whoever speaks against the Holy Spirit will not be forgiven, either in this age or in the age to come" (Matt. 12:31–32; cf. Mark 3:28–29; Luke 12:10). Here, blasphemy refers to an insult or abusive speech, directed in this case to the Son of Man and to the Holy Spirit. Again, there is no reason to think that the high priest accused Jesus of insulting God or anyone else. Nevertheless, in the context of the Gospel narrative, there is a reason why these acts are called blasphemy, as we will see.

According to the Synoptic Gospels, some scribes accused Jesus of blasphemy when he forgave a paralyzed man's sins (Matt. 9:3; Mark 2:7; Luke 5:21). Mark and Luke, in the same verses just cited, both report that the scribes viewed the act as blasphemy because, as they asked, "Who can forgive sins but God alone?" In this instance, it is clear that Jesus' alleged "blasphemy" consisted of *claiming to exercise a prerogative belonging only to God.* The scribes' rhetorical question echoes the *Shema* (Deut. 6:4) and thus indicates that they saw Jesus' act as contravening the Jewish commitment to monotheism.

In John's Gospel, opponents of Jesus threatened to stone him for blasphemy, explaining, "Because you, though only a human being, are making yourself God" (John 10:33).[7] In this instance, Jesus' opponents here state explicitly that, by "blasphemy," they mean that Jesus is in some way claiming to be God. In context, Jesus has just claimed to do his works in the name of the Father (v. 25), to be the Shepherd of the sheep (vv. 26–27), to give eternal life to them (v. 28), and to prevent anyone from snatching them out of his hand, just as the Father does (vv. 28–29; cf. Deut. 32:39). He then concludes that, in asserting these divine prerogatives, he is claiming, "The Father and I are one" (John 10:30). It is not hard to see how Jesus' opponents drew the conclusion they did. Clearly, they understood Jesus to be claiming to do things that only God[8] can do.

Elsewhere in the Gospel of John, the Jewish opponents of Jesus make it clear that this is indeed their objection to Jesus. The first time his opponents tried to kill Jesus, his claim to do what only God does also was the issue.

> But Jesus answered them, "My Father is still working, and I also am working." For this reason the Jews were seeking all the more to kill him, because he was not only breaking the sabbath, but was also

calling God his own Father, thereby making himself equal to God.
(John 5:17–18)

It is evident here that these Jewish opponents understood Jesus' statement,
"My Father is still working, and I also am working," to be claiming a prerogative or power belonging only to God. Thus, although *blasphemy* is not used
in this passage, it further confirms that the charge of blasphemy mentioned
in John 10:33 was an accusation of claiming some sort of functional equality
with God.

Jesus' opponents also tried to stone him after he said, "Very truly, I tell you,
before Abraham was, I am" (John 8:58–59). By now, it should be obvious that
they also viewed this statement as a blasphemous claim to equality with God.
This incident is unusual in that, rather than claiming to do something God
does, Jesus claimed to *be* something God is. The bottom line is the same: his
opponents understood him to be claiming some kind of equality or parity
with God.

John reports that when Pilate told the Sanhedrin that he had no grounds to
crucify Jesus, they replied, "We have a law, and according to that law he ought
to die because he has claimed to be the Son of God" (John 19:7). This statement recalls both John 5:17–18—where Jesus' claim to work on the Sabbath
just as his Father implies a claim to be uniquely God's divine Son—and John
10:28–33, where Jesus' statement that he and the Father are one provoked an
explicit accusation of blasphemy. Thus, in John 19:7, when the Jews say Jesus
claimed to be "the Son of God," they clearly mean that Jesus claimed to be
divine, God's "Son" in a sense that made him functionally on a par with God.
In short, their reason for wanting Jesus dead remained consistent from John
5 through John 8 and 10 all the way to John 19: they regarded his claim to be
God's Son—uniquely like him in his prerogatives, attributes, and works—to
be blasphemy.[9]

Let us now return to the Gospel of Mark. There are good reasons to conclude that the Sanhedrin's blasphemy charge there likewise had to do with
Jesus' claiming divine prerogatives or powers.

For one thing, it is probable that the scribes' opinion that Jesus had committed blasphemy when he forgave a man's sins—by claiming to do what
God alone can do (Mark 2:1–12)—assumes the same kind of blasphemy
as the high priest's formal accusation at Jesus' trial (Mark 14:53-65). In the
structure of Mark's Gospel, the two scenes are the first and last confronta-

tions between Jesus and his religious critics.[10] Scribes play a role in both confrontations (2:6; 14:53), and in both confrontations Jesus responds to his critics by referring to himself as the Son of Man (2:10; 14:62). So, when his critics accuse him in both instances of blasphemy (2:7; 14:64), it seems likely that both accusations have the same sort of offense in mind. Jesus' critics think he has committed blasphemy by claiming prerogatives belonging only to God.

On the other hand, when Mark describes Jesus' critics as blaspheming when they attribute his miracles to the Devil (3:28–29) or when they verbally abuse him at his crucifixion (15:29), he is indicating that it is Jesus' critics who actually are blaspheming. As Darrell Bock points out, the result is a "battle of the blasphemies" in which each side is "accusing the other of offending God by their appraisal of Jesus."[11]

Jesus gave the religious leaders more than they bargained for. Apparently, instead of simply confirming that he considered himself the Messiah, he went further and made a statement that the high priest and the other leaders thought amounted to a claim to divine prerogatives. He was the Messiah but not the kind of Messiah they had in mind. In fact, he was far *more* than Messiah. How so?

The answer clearly lies in his statement that they would "see the Son of Man seated at the right hand of the Power,' and 'coming with the clouds of heaven'" (Mark 14:62). How this statement implied that Jesus was claiming prerogatives or powers belonging to God is the subject of the next chapter.

Chapter 20

GOD'S RIGHT-HAND MAN

As we saw in the previous chapter, Jesus' answer to the question about his identity at his trial before the Sanhedrin revealed that he thought himself to be much more than Israel's king. His answer, however, contains language that even many Christians today find somewhat unfamiliar. As we unpack the meaning of Jesus' answer, we will discover that he claimed to be functioning in the very place of God.

JESUS' TRIAL STATEMENT IN LIGHT OF THE OLD TESTAMENT[1]

"I am; and 'you will see <u>the Son of Man</u> <u>seated at the right hand</u> of the Power,' and '<u>coming with the clouds of heaven</u>'" (Mark 14:62).	"The LORD says to my Lord: '<u>Sit at my right hand</u>'" (Ps. 110:1 ESV).
	"And behold, <u>with the clouds of heaven there came</u> one like a <u>son of man</u>" (Dan. 7:13 ESV).

In Mark 14:62, Jesus' answer to Caiaphas's question blended two Old Testament texts that confirmed he was the Messiah, but expanded the concept to include total authority.[2] These two texts were Psalm 110:1, in which David speaks of someone as his Lord sitting at God's "right hand," and Daniel 7:13, in which someone "like a son of man" is said to come "with the clouds of heaven."

Sitting in the Big Chair (Psalm 110:1)

Let's consider each of these Old Testament texts in turn, beginning with Psalm 110:1, in which David says,

The LORD [YHWH] says to my Lord [*'adonî*]:
"Sit at my right hand,
until I make your enemies your footstool."

(ESV)

The Hebrew makes it clear that by "the LORD" and "my Lord"two different persons are in view. Jesus identified the second person ("my Lord") as the Messiah when he applied the text to himself. Earlier in Mark, Jesus points out something peculiar about this statement. The Jews typically expected the Messiah simply to be a descendant of David who would prove to be the ultimate human warrior-king. Yet David calls the future Messiah his "Lord." How, Jesus asks, could the Messiah be David's son and also be his Lord (Mark 12:35–37)?

Some modern readers of the Bible have suggested that Jesus was here denying that the Messiah would be a descendant of David, but this really misses the point. Jesus is not denying that the Messiah would be a descendant of David but is pointing out that somehow the Messiah would be much *more* than that.[3] The Messiah would not be a mere Davidic king but would be a universal sovereign, sitting at God's right hand, honored as Lord even by his ancestor David.

A careful examination of Psalm 110:1, and Jesus' application of it (in conjunction with Daniel 7:13) to himself, reveals how remarkable Jesus' claim was and why it seemed to the Sanhedrin to be blasphemous. It was one thing to enter God's presence and yet another to sit in it. But to sit *at God's right side* was another matter altogether. In the religious and cultural milieu of Jesus' day, to claim to sit at God's right hand was tantamount to claiming equality with God.

We may illustrate the point with the story of the King of Siam and Anna, the nineteenth-century English schoolteacher hired to teach his children, most memorably told in Richard Rodgers and Oscar Hammerstein's musical *The King and I*. Anna flouts Siamese court protocol by barging into the king's throne room unannounced, by standing in the king's presence when he is sitting, or by sitting with her head as high as, or higher than, the king's. Protocol required that all subjects of the king keep their heads *lower* than his at all times. This sort of royal protocol was well understood in most cultures until the rise of democracy in modern times (the very cultural shift celebrated in *The King and I*). For Jesus to claim that he would sit at God's right hand was akin to claiming, in an "Oriental" cultural context, that he would be entitled to have his head as high as that of the king.

Jesus, then, was claiming the right to go directly into God's "throne room" and sit at his side. The temerity of such a claim for any mere human would be astonishing to the Jews of Jesus' day.[4] The priests of the Sanhedrin, to whom Jesus made this claim, could not, as a rule, even go into the inner sanctum of the temple, known as the Holy of Holies. Many of them probably had never been inside it. The Holy of Holies could be entered only on a specific day in specific ways by one specific person. Failure to follow the instructions exactly resulted in death. On the Day of Atonement, the high priest entered the Holy of Holies, carrying the blood of a bull as offering for personal purification and the blood of a ram as offering for atonement for the people. This was followed by a change of garments and ritual washings (Lev. 16). In other words, one entered into God's presence in the temple *cautiously*.

If entrance requirements to the earthly Holy of Holies were so strict, we can imagine what the Sanhedrin priests would have thought about Jesus claiming to have the right to enter God's heavenly presence. After all, the earthly temple was, according to Josephus, viewed as a model of the heavenly one.[5] Worse still, though, Jesus was claiming that he was going to enter permanently into the heavenly Holies of Holies *and sit down*. Jesus might as well have claimed that he owned the place! Indeed, that is what his statement amounted to. As Darrell Bock has put it, Jesus' claim "would be worse, in the leadership's view, than claiming the right to be able to walk into the Holy of Holies in the temple and live there!"[6]

The Heavenly Man (Daniel 7:13)

The other Old Testament text to which Jesus alludes is Daniel 7:13–14, in which Daniel says (ESV, emphasis added),

> I saw in the night visions,
>   and behold, *with the clouds of heaven*
>   *there came one like a son of man,*
> and he came to the Ancient of Days
>   and was presented before him.
> And to him was given dominion
>   and glory and a kingdom,

> that all peoples, nations, and languages
> > should serve him;
> his dominion is an everlasting dominion,
> > which shall not pass away,
> and his kingdom one
> > that shall not be destroyed.

Jesus' allusion to "the Son of Man . . . coming with the clouds of heaven" clearly would have been recognized by his learned interrogators as a reference to Daniel 7:13. Jesus was claiming to be the figure described as "one like a son of man" and to possess his kind of authority.

It is often mistakenly assumed that the title "Son of Man" refers simply to Jesus' humanity. It is true that the common phrase "son of man" is another way of saying "human being," and that when used in this sense in the Old Testament it most often stresses human frailty and dependence (see, e.g., Pss. 8:4; 80:17 NASB; nearly a hundred occurrences in Ezekiel; cf. "sons of men" in Isa. 52:14 NASB). When Daniel 7:13 speaks of "one like a son of man," however, it is to indicate that this figure has a human appearance or likeness (in contrast to the beasts of Daniel's vision) and yet is not simply or merely human. In this respect, "son of man" is more like the figure of God at the end of Ezekiel 1:

> And above the dome over their heads there was something like a throne, in appearance like sapphire; and seated above the likeness of a throne was *something that seemed like a human form.* Upward from what appeared like the loins I saw something like gleaming amber, something that looked like fire enclosed all around; and downward from what looked like the loins I saw something that looked like fire, and there was a splendor all around. Like the bow in a cloud on a rainy day, such was the appearance of the splendor all around. *This was the appearance of the likeness of the glory of the LORD.* (Ezek. 1:26–28, emphasis added)

In all likelihood, then, Daniel's description of "one like a son of man" is a symbolic, visionary description of a figure who is actually divine.[7]

In Daniel's vision, the humanlike figure possesses all judgment authority and rules over an everlasting kingdom. The notion of frailty and dependence is absent. The description of the figure as coming with the clouds also identifies him as divine, since elsewhere in the Old Testament the imagery of coming on clouds is used exclusively for divine figures:

> The image of riding the clouds is reserved for God or as a description of pagan gods in the Old Testament, outside of this text in Daniel (Exod. 14:20; 34:5; Num. 10:34; Ps. 104:3; Isa. 19:1). So the image shows how intimately the function of the Son of Man is tied to divine authority even though the description is of a human.[8]

Jesus frequently used the phrase "Son of Man" in conjunction with his messianic role, effectively giving it the force of a title.[9] That Jesus had Daniel's "one like a son of man" in mind when he used this title is evident from other places where he explicitly quotes Daniel 7:13 (e.g., Mark 13:26; see also Mark 8:38).

So, when Jesus alluded to Daniel 7:13 and Psalm 110:1 in his response to Caiaphas's question, he was making a staggering claim. Jesus was claiming to be a heavenly, divine figure who would be seated at God's right hand, exercising divine rule forever over all people everywhere. This claim to divine authority creates a great deal of irony in Jesus' hearing before the Sanhedrin. As the Son of Man who sits at God's right hand, Jesus exercises the authority of God. So while the religious leaders thought they sat in judgment over Jesus (and were seeking his death!), Jesus asserted they were actually the ones on trial.

The response of the religious leaders to Jesus' statement is not surprising. In their minds, Jesus had committed blasphemy by claiming that he belonged right alongside God. What's more, Jesus undermined the authority of the religious establishment by suggesting that their examination of him was a farce and that in the end *he* would be judging *them*. "Not only had Jesus made himself too close to God, he had also created a great, irreversible gap between himself and the leadership."[10] Indeed, he had claimed to occupy "the highest place in heaven."[11]

Messiah's Throne Is God's Throne

Jesus' claim that as the Messiah he would sit on God's throne did have some scriptural precedent, not only in Psalm 110:1 but also in other Old Testament statements. In 1 Chronicles, David stated that God had chosen his "son Solomon to sit upon the throne of the kingdom of the LORD over Israel" (28:5). As Martin Hengel points out, however, David's statement falls short of what the New Testament says about Christ: "Here it is not a question of the heavenly throne of God itself, but of the ideal kingdom of the house of David, that Yahweh as the true king of Israel established, a motif that can be traced back to 2 Sam. 7:14 in connection with 1 Sam. 8:7 and 16:1."[12] At the end of 1 Chronicles the author states, "Then Solomon sat on the throne of the LORD, succeeding his father David as king" (29:23). In light of the previously quoted statement of David, the meaning here is that the Lord is the true king of Israel (1 Sam. 8:6–7); David and his sons are simply ruling on his behalf, subject to his continued support (cf. 1 Chron. 29:25). These statements do not speak of the king as ruling from God's heavenly throne, but they do suggest that in some sense the king rules in God's place.

Psalm 2 goes a little further. It refers to Israel's king as God's "anointed" (i.e., Messiah) and as his "son" (vv. 2, 7). God promises to give the Messiah "the nations" and "the ends of the earth" (v. 8) and speaks of the Messiah's exercising judgment on them (v. 9). These statements also stop short, however, of recognizing the Messiah as exercising cosmic authority over the entire universe from God's heavenly throne. What Psalm 2 affirms the Messiah will do is, in fact, precisely what most of the Jews in Jesus' day wanted and expected: for the Messiah to bring the foreign nations that were oppressing them to their knees.

The book of Isaiah comes a bit closer to affirming the exalted place of the Messiah that Jesus explicitly claimed. One of the clearest prophecies of the coming Messiah (Isa. 11:1–10) attributes the function of judgment over the whole earth to a descendant of Jesse, David's father (vv. 3–4). It also describes the Messiah in some ways that suggest his deity. He will not judge by outward appearance (v. 3; 1 Sam. 16:7).[13] The Messiah will "strike the earth with the rod of his mouth, and with the breath of his lips he shall kill the wicked" (v. 4; see Isa. 30:27–28; 40:24; 49:2; and cf. Job 4:9). Elsewhere in Isaiah's prophecies about the "servant of the LORD," the statement that the Servant would be "exalted and lifted up" (52:13; Heb., *yārûm weʾnissāʾ*) alludes to the vision in Isaiah 6:1 in which the prophet saw the Lord seated on his throne "high and lofty" (Heb., *rām weʾnissāʾ*).[14]

The one Old Testament text that speaks about the Messiah as ruling at God's right hand is Psalm 110:1. This statement, however, does not seem to have played any significant role in Jewish thinking about the Messiah. Nor did the Jews generally understand Daniel 7 to mean that the Messiah would rule from God's throne.

There is an interesting story in the Babylonian Talmud that probably typifies Jewish opinion on this subject. According to the Talmud, Rabbi Akiba (a rabbi of the early second century A.D.) proposed the idea that Daniel 7:9 meant that the Davidic Messiah would sit on a throne alongside God. Even this interpretive suggestion from a respected rabbi was met with a sharp warning not to "profane" God. The account goes on to report that Akiba accepted an alternate interpretation, according to which the thrones represented God's attributes of justice and mercy. Even this explanation was unacceptable to some rabbis.[15]

The Old Testament anticipates, then, the idea of the Messiah as ruling on God's throne at his side, but it stops short of stating explicitly that he would sit on God's throne in heaven and exercise absolute rule over all creation. It is not surprising that such a claim shocked the sensibilities of the learned Jewish religious leaders of Jesus' day. In this light, it is interesting to consider a comment attributed in the Talmud to the late third-century Rabbi Abbahu: "If someone says to you, 'I am God,' he is lying, 'I am the son of man,' he will regret it: 'I will ascend into heaven,' he said it, but he will not carry it out."[16] It seems likely that the three parts of Abbahu's saying correspond to the three parts of Jesus' response to the high priest at his trial: "I am"; "and 'you will see the Son of Man seated at the right hand of the Power'"; "and 'coming with the clouds of heaven'" (Mark 14:62).

If this is correct, this rabbinical saying (admittedly dating from over 150 years after the fact) suggests that the Jewish leaders also understood Jesus' words "I am" to be a claim to be God. In context, the words "I am" could simply be an affirmative response to the high priest's question, "Are you the Messiah, the Son of the Blessed One?" (v. 61). This is clearly how Matthew understands it (Matt. 26:64; cf. Luke 22:70). But the Jewish leaders already knew from previous encounters with Jesus that his self-description as the Son of God entailed a claim to parity with God (John 5:17–18; 10:27–39). Thus, when Jesus answers affirmatively that he is the Son of God and then immediately adds statements claiming to sit on God's throne at his right hand, exercising divine power in heaven, his response confirms that he is, indeed, claiming to be on the same level as God. The question they had been asking, "Who do you think you are?" (John 8:53 NIV) finally had been answered.

No One Else Comes Close

Despite the judgment of the high priest and the rest of the Sanhedrin that Jesus' statement was blasphemy, some scholars today argue that Jesus' claim fits comfortably into one or another stream of Jewish religious speculation. More broadly, many scholars claim that the New Testament's view of Jesus as an exalted object of worship arose from an existing Jewish tradition concerning one or more exalted, "intermediate" figures between human beings and God. In Jewish literature of the period, similar claims supposedly can be found for various angels, including Michael, Gabriel, and angels not mentioned in the Bible (notably Yahoel and Metatron), as well as exalted human beings from the Old Testament, especially Adam, Enoch, Melchizedek, and Moses.[17]

The very multiplicity of these different figures ought to give one pause in appealing to them too quickly or easily as examples of figures exalted in a way comparable to Jesus Christ. We will not attempt to discuss each of these figures (or the many others that could be named), since such an exercise would necessarily take us beyond the limits of this chapter. Instead, we will comment on the two examples of "exalted" human figures most often cited in this connection: Moses and Enoch.

In *The Exagoge* [i.e., Exodus] *of Ezekiel*, thought to have been written in the second century B.C., Moses dreams about a throne on Mount Sinai that reaches into the sky. Sitting on the throne is "a noble man," evidently representing God (as in Ezek. 1:26–28). The figure steps aside and has Moses sit on the throne in his place. Moses looks all around at the earth, sees "a host of stars" that kneels before him, and then wakes up from his dream. His father-in-law Jethro tells him that the dream means that Moses "will raise up a great throne" from which he will "judge and lead humankind," with the ability to "see things present, past, and future."[18]

P. W. van der Horst and David Aune each assert that the dream "implies a deification of Moses," and they are hardly alone in their assertion.[19] As Hengel points out, however, such an interpretation implies that God *abdicates* his throne, which is, of course, unlikely to have been the meaning of the story.[20] Jethro's interpretation, in fact, suggests that Moses does *not* sit on God's throne, since Moses "raises up" a throne. The kneeling of the stars before Moses probably symbolizes the submission of the countless descendants of Israel to the Law of Moses, since the imagery of stars frequently refers in Genesis to the seed of Israel (Gen. 15:5; 22:17; 26:4; and especially 37:9; cf.

1 Chron. 27:23; Neh. 9:23; see also Gen. 27:29).[21] Moses' ability to see things present, past, and future most likely refers to Moses' ability as the author of the Pentateuch (according to the traditional view) to produce narratives of Israel's prehistory from creation through the patriarchs (Genesis) and to prophesy the future history of Israel (the focus of most of Deut. 28–33). Bauckham rightly says that Jethro's interpretation "clearly refers to the common Jewish understanding of Moses as an inspired prophet, who wrote in the Torah not only of things present but also of the past and of the future."[22] Thus, we disagree that the text implies that Moses possessed omniscience.[23]

All in all, we see little basis for the claim that the work teaches a deification of Moses. "Moses may have been revered as an extraordinary human being, but his alleged divinity has no devotional consequences in any extant writing."[24] There was no Jewish tradition of worshiping Moses. Nor was Moses credited with the array of divine works (creation, providence, etc.) that are basic to the identity of God. Rather, the text gives a visionary, symbolic picture of the significance of Moses' ministry in leading Israel out of Egypt and giving them the Law. As Darrell Bock puts it, "What Moses is pictured as becoming in heaven is what Moses is to be in his ministry on earth, namely, God's vice regent."[25]

Something similar is likely at work in the "Similitudes" or "Parables" of Enoch, found in Section II (chaps. 37–71) of *1 Enoch* (sometimes called *The Book of Enoch* or *The Ethiopic Apocalypse of Enoch* to distinguish it from other works bearing Enoch's name). Given the textual history of this work, one should exercise extreme caution in drawing any conclusions from it regarding Jewish beliefs held prior to the time of Jesus.[26]

What makes this part of the book of 1 Enoch of such interest is that it speaks of the Son of Man sitting on God's throne, which is called "the throne of (his) glory" (or "[his] glorious throne"). In the Gospel of Matthew, Jesus uses the same expression when he speaks of himself as the Son of Man who will sit on the throne of his glory (Matt. 19:28; 25:31). Many scholars, including Hengel, think that Matthew is dependent on Enoch for the expression.[27] The term also occurs in the book of Wisdom (9:10) and in Sirach, which says that God forgave David's sins and gave him a royal covenant and a throne of glory in Israel (Sir. 47:11). Jeremiah, too, uses the term "throne of Your glory" in reference to God's throne (Jer. 14:21 NASB; cf. 17:12). Hengel's suggestion that Matthew is dependent on Enoch here is plausible, though, in that Matthew and Enoch both say that *the Son of Man* sat on "the throne of (his) glory." That idea is unusual enough that some connection between the two seems reasonable. That connection, however, may be a "common dependence" of both on a tradition of understanding Daniel 7 to speak of the enthronement of the Son of Man as eschatological judge.[28]

In any case, what matters is what 1 Enoch and Matthew (quoting Jesus) respectively mean in their own contexts. Although the Enoch Son of Man will sit on God's throne, the text says nothing to indicate that he will sit on God's throne *alongside God.* To our knowledge, no Jewish writing from the period speaks of any human or angel sitting at God's right hand.[29] What Jesus does in fusing Psalm 110:1 with Daniel 7:13 is unique and results in a claim that goes far beyond anything said about the Son of Man in Enoch. The Enoch Son of Man also differs from the Christian Son of Man in another important respect: the Enoch Son of Man does not rule in the present but will take the throne only when it is time to carry out the final judgment.

Nothing in Enoch suggests that the Son of Man is actually divine. He is not credited with any role in creation, providence, or salvation; he is not described as possessing any divine attributes; and he is not called Lord, God, or any other distinct, divine name. In short, in Enoch the Son of Man plays at most a very limited role on the throne of God.

Finally, we have reason to believe that Enoch's vision of the Son of Man sitting on God's throne to administer the final judgment was at most a marginal, exceptional concept during Jesus' day. Bock, reporting on later writings that also focused on Enoch but with a different perspective, concludes, "The image of an exalted Enoch appears to have been countered by other Enoch traditions arguing that he only observed and recorded the judgment, was punished as Metatron-Enoch, or even failed to be among the righteous."[30] Thus, the unusual, and still only partial, parallels between the Son of Man in 1 Enoch and in Matthew do nothing to convince us that Jesus' claim to a place on God's throne at his right hand would have been widely perceived as anything other than a blasphemous assertion of divine prerogative. Again, the way Jesus brings together the claim to sit on God's throne at his right hand (something not said in 1 Enoch) with the claim to come on the clouds of heaven was by all accounts an unprecedented claim for any person to make. As Darrell Bock concludes,

> The self-made claim to sit at the right hand and ride the clouds would be read as a blasphemous utterance, a false claim that equates

Jesus in a unique way with God and that reflects an arrogant disrespect toward the one true God. . . . Only the figure of Enoch-Son of
Man seems close to this imagery, and even his access to God in this
way was controversial, despite his translation by God.[31]

Although the New Testament may well have drawn on some of the language and motifs in Jewish literature expressing "exalted" roles for various
prophets and other figures, the attempt to explain the exalted view of Jesus
Christ in the New Testament as a purely natural development from Jewish
speculations about intermediate religious figures or "divine agents" must be
judged a failure. Timo Eskola, a Finnish New Testament scholar specializing
in Christology, has aptly observed,

> These theories have been attempts to find a "missing link" between
> Jewish theology and early Christology. Scholars have attempted
> to discern a divine agent or an angelic figure that might serve as a
> prototype for the exalted Christ in Christology. According to these
> scholars, only such *typos* [type, prototype, model] could explain how
> the first Christians were able to present the resurrected Christ as a
> heavenly being. This sort of goal leads us astray, however.
>
> *In pre-Christian Judaism there is no exact typos* [type] *for Christ
> that could serve as a "missing link" for the interpretation of his exalted
> status as Lord on the heavenly throne.* It seems that such typological
> idealism has rested on an implicit "evolutionist" presupposition.[32]

If we may state the problem more bluntly, explaining the belief in a divine
Jesus as a natural development within Judaism rests on the faulty assumption
that the belief is not true. *It presupposes that Jesus was not, in fact, the exalted
figure the New Testament says that he is.* If Jesus really is the divine Son of God
incarnate, and if he really did rise from the dead, appear to his disciples, and
ascend into heaven, then *the origin of the New Testament teaching about Jesus
is Jesus himself.* The multiplicity of strained theories attempting to account
for this teaching in another way attest to the difficulty of coming up with an
explanation that is superior to the one given in the New Testament. Richard
Bauckham rightly characterizes such a research program as a mistake:

> Some recent work on New Testament Christology seems to be

working with the conviction that it is only possible to understand
how a high Christology could have developed within a Jewish
monotheistic framework if we can show that something rather like
it already existed in pre-Christian Judaism. This is a mistake. . . . The
concern of early Christology was not to conform Jesus to some pre-
existing model of an intermediate figure subordinate to God. The
concern of early Christology . . . was to understand the identification
of Jesus with God.[33]

Chapter 21

JESUS TAKES HIS SEAT

A t this point, we need to be careful that we are not led astray by trying to understand literally the metaphor of being "seated at God's right hand." That this language is metaphorical follows from the fact that God is infinite, transcendent Spirit (John 4:24) and that biblical language about God's "throne" can apply that term to heaven itself (e.g., Isa. 66:1; quoted in Acts 7:49; also Matt. 5:34). Biblical writers could and did use the metaphor of being at one's "right hand" in different ways. But the imagery of Jesus being seated at God's right hand has a very specific meaning that is made clear by the contexts in which that imagery is used. That meaning is that Jesus *shares God's very position of divine rule over all creation.* That Jesus shares this highest of positions is, in fact, a major theme of the New Testament.

On Top of the World!

That Jesus is portrayed in the New Testament as occupying the same place as God in heaven is evident from a number of considerations.

1. *Jesus is said to exercise universal rule over "all things"*—that is, over all of creation, both in heaven and on earth—using language routinely used in Judaism to express God's unique sovereignty (Matt. 11:25–27; 28:18; Luke 10:21–22; John 3:35; 13:3; 16:15; Acts 10:36; 1 Cor. 15:27–28; Eph. 1:22; Phil. 2:10; 3:21; Heb. 1:2; 2:8; Rev. 5:13). Richard Bauckham notes that "the phrase belongs to the standard rhetoric of Jewish monotheism, in which it constantly refers, quite naturally, to the whole of the created reality from which God is absolutely distinguished as its Creator and Ruler."[1]

2. ***Jesus' exaltation is described in the same spatial terms reserved for expressing the exalted location of God's throne.*** God "seated him at his right hand in the heavenly places, *far above* all rule and authority and power and dominion, and above every name that is named, not only in this age but also in the age to come" (Eph. 1:20–21). Jesus "ascended *far above all the heavens*" (Eph. 4:10); he is "exalted *above* the heavens" (Heb. 7:26; cf. 4:14). God "*highly* exalted him" with the name "*above* every name" (Phil. 2:9). Jesus "sat down at the right hand of the Majesty *on high*" (Heb. 1:3).[2] He is not only "above" every name, he is "far above" every power that can be named. He is not only in heaven, he is "far above all the heavens." Jesus is as high up as he can go!

The prevailing imagery of the heavenly court was of a single throne, high above the rest of the throne room (note Isa. 6:1), in which God sat, surrounded by his servants, all standing below him and at attention, ready to carry out his orders.[3] (Recall our illustration in chapter 20 of the King of Siam taking offense when Anna's head was not lower than his.) From this position, God rules over all creation, both angelic and human, in heaven and on earth. The New Testament repeatedly describes Jesus as having ascended to the very highest point in all existence. He is "over all" (Rom. 9:5; cf. Eph. 4:6).

The combination of these two points alone—Jesus' exercise of universal rule over all creation, and the exaltation of Jesus' position far above all creation—is enough to establish him in the place that in the Old Testament and ancient Judaism belonged to God alone. As Bauckham observes, "God's servants may be said, by his permission, to rule some things, as earthly rulers do, but only God rules over all things from a throne exalted above all things."[4]

Jesus is utterly unique in this shared position. No one else shares God's throne and rules over all creation. That is because "he with whom God shares his throne must be equal with God."[5] And he who is equal with God must be approached accordingly.

3. ***The New Testament states emphatically that Jesus is exalted above all of God's heavenly court***—that is, over the angels or other supernatural powers that attend God's presence in heaven. This point is already implicit in the previous point but is worth special attention (as

it also is given in the New Testament). Peter, for example, states that Jesus Christ "has gone into heaven and is at the right hand of God, with angels, authorities, and powers made subject to him" (1 Peter 3:22). Paul says that Christ is "far above all rule and authority and power and dominion" (Eph. 1:21), probably referring to angelic powers. His exaltation means that "at the name of Jesus every knee should bend, *in heaven*" as well as everywhere else (Phil. 2:10). The book of Hebrews argues this point at some length:

> When he had made purification for sins, *he sat down at the right hand of the Majesty on high, having become as much superior to angels* as the name he has inherited is more excellent than theirs. For to which of the angels did God ever say, "You are my Son; today I have begotten you"? Or again, "I will be his Father, and he will be my Son"? And again, when he brings the firstborn into the world, he says, "Let all God's angels worship him." . . . But *to which of the angels has he ever said, "Sit at my right hand* until I make your enemies a footstool for your feet"? (Heb. 1:3b–6, 13)

The book of Revelation teaches the same thing. John tells of a vision he had in which he "heard the voice of many angels around the throne, the living creatures, and the elders; and the number of them was ten thousand times ten thousand, and thousands of thousands" (Rev. 5:11 NKJV). All of these millions of voices were shouting, "Worthy is the Lamb" (v. 12). John then says that he "heard *every creature in heaven*" and everywhere else declaring praises "to the one seated on the throne and to the Lamb" (v. 13). The Lamb, a symbolic representation of Jesus, receives honor from every creature in heaven—and indeed every creature everywhere—along with "the one seated on the throne," that is, God.

4. **The New Testament reveals that Jesus actually sits on God's own throne.** That Jesus sits with God on his divine throne is stated explicitly and unambiguously in some places in the New Testament. In John's final vision in the book of Revelation, he records seeing the river of the water of life coming "from the throne of God and of the

Lamb" (Rev. 22:1). He goes on to say that "the throne of God and of the Lamb" will be situated in the New Jerusalem (Rev. 22:3). These statements go beyond saying that Jesus sits on God's throne; they actually refer to the throne as belonging to the Lamb right alongside God. Interestingly, in this text John says that the saints "will serve him,"[6] apparently referring to both God and the Lamb—or at least not bothering to distinguish between them in this respect.[7]

Paul taught that "all of us must appear before the judgment seat [bēma] of Christ" (2 Cor. 5:10). As Hengel points out, a few months later Paul wrote that "we will all stand before the judgment seat [bēma] of God" (Rom. 14:10).[8] There is no reason to think that by "judgment seat" Paul means anything other than God's throne, since judgment is often associated with thrones (e.g., Ps. 9:4, 7; Matt. 19:28; Luke 22:30). Most significantly, Jesus said that he would judge all humanity as the Son of Man seated "on the throne of his glory" (Matt. 25:31; cf. Rev. 20:11). Paul can say that we will all appear before the judgment seat of Christ as well as the judgment seat of God because it's the same thing: Christ sits on the judgment seat or throne of God.

The book of Hebrews repeatedly describes Jesus as occupying this exalted position. In its introductory affirmations about Jesus, it says that he "*sat down at the right hand of the Majesty on high*" (Heb. 1:3). Later, the author says that Jesus "sat down at the right hand of the throne of the Majesty in heaven" (8:1 NIV) and that he "has taken his seat at the right hand of the throne of God" (12:2). Grammatically, the language here could be taken to mean that Jesus' seat is somewhere to the right of God's throne and therefore is a separate or different throne, but such an understanding fails to account for the imagery of the throne in the heavenly sanctuary (Heb. 8:1–2). This imagery is drawn from the furnishings of the Holy of Holies, where the only place to sit is on the throne of God represented by the ark of the covenant. The meaning here, then, is that Jesus is seated to God's right on God's very own throne—that is, that Jesus exercises the universal, royal rule over all creation that is God's prerogative. Hengel suggests that it would be better to translate Hebrews 12:2 "at the right hand of God on his throne."[9]

5. ***What Jesus does from God's right hand shows that he functions as God.*** In the previous chapter, we saw that there is some limited prece-

dent in the Old Testament and other Jewish literature for the idea that the Messiah, or some other exalted human figure, would function as the eschatological judge of all humanity. Jesus, however, does other things in his position at God's right hand that transcend anything anticipated of a merely human Messiah.

For example, Jesus sends the Holy Spirit and gives spiritual gifts to his people. Before he died, Jesus told his apostles that after he went away, he would send them the Holy Spirit (John 16:7). On the Day of Pentecost, Peter told the crowd in Jerusalem, "Being therefore exalted at the right hand of God, and having received from the Father the promise of the Holy Spirit, he [Jesus] has poured out this that you both see and hear" (Acts 2:33, cf. vv. 34–36). In his letter to the Ephesians, Paul quoted Psalm 68:18: "When he ascended on high . . . he gave gifts to his people" (Eph. 4:8). In its original context, the Psalm is referring to material "gifts" that God gave to the Israelites. Paul applies this to the spiritual gifts that Christ (see v. 7) gave to the church when he "ascended far above all the heavens," including the gifts of apostles, prophets, evangelists, pastors, and teachers (vv. 10–11). Elsewhere, Paul credits all kinds of spiritual gifts to the Lord Jesus: "There are varieties of services, but the same Lord" (1 Cor. 12:5).

Stephen's death gives us insight into other functions of God that Jesus performs from God's right hand. As Stephen was dying, he asked Jesus to do two things: receive his spirit and forgive his executioners (Acts 7:59–60). These are both prerogatives of God. It is worth noting that the same author, Luke, reports that when Jesus was dying he asked the Father to receive *his* spirit (Luke 23:46). In short, from God's right hand Jesus performed at least three divine prerogatives: hearing prayer, receiving the spirit of the departed, and forgiving sinners.

Clearly, Jesus' exaltation to God's right hand is no merely "honorary" position. From that position, Jesus does what God does.

6. *Jesus receives universal worship from his position at God's right hand.* As we have just said, Jesus' position is not merely honorary, but it is indeed a position of ultimate honor. We quoted earlier the statement in Hebrews that "all God's angels worship him" in his position at God's right hand (1:6). At least five aspects to the scene depicting universal worship of Christ in Revelation 5, to which we have

already referred, demonstrate that Jesus occupies the highest possible position.

a. *The worship offered to the Son is the same kind of worship offered to the Father.* Revelation 4–5 presents three cycles of worship that culminate in chapter 5 with the worship of God and the Lamb together. First God is worshiped (4:9–11), then the Lamb (5:8–12), and finally God and the Lamb together (5:13–14). The noted commentator on Revelation, Henry Barclay Swete, with some justice concluded, "This chapter is the most powerful statement of the divinity of Christ in the New Testament, and it receives its power from the praise of God the Creator which precedes it."[10]

b. *Revelation forbids angel worship even while it encourages Christ worship.* It is striking that this same book that so powerfully exalts Jesus Christ as "worthy" of such praise, adoration, and worship (5:11–14), also contains strong prohibitions against angel worship (19:10; 22:8–9). "This combination of motifs had the effect, probably more clearly than any other Christological theme available in their world of ideas, of placing Jesus on the divine side of the line which monotheism must draw between God and creatures."[11]

c. *Christ is worshiped in the very throne room of God.* If there's any place that false worship won't be tolerated, it's in the heavenly Holy of Holies. Yet Jesus is worshiped there in the same manner as the Father. Jesus doesn't reject it, and the Father doesn't correct it. It is theorized that, even though Jesus is not really God, earth-bound humans might legitimately "worship" Jesus merely as God's visible representative. That theory crumbles, however, in the light of Revelation 5.

d. *Jesus is at God's right hand when he receives worship.* Not only is "the Lamb" in the throne room of God in heaven, but he also appears to be located right at God's side at the throne when he receives worship. John says that the Lamb "went and took the scroll from the right hand of the one who was seated on the throne" (5:7). As soon as he took the scroll, "the four living creatures and the twenty-four elders fell before the Lamb" (v. 8). The rest of creation then joins in the adulation (5:11–14).

e. *All creation worships Jesus.* As we noted earlier, John says that he saw every created being declaring the worthiness of the Lamb:

"Every creature in heaven and on earth and under the earth and in the sea, and all that is in them" (5:13a). This statement echoes the language of the second commandment, which forbids the worship of idols fashioned after anything "in heaven above, or . . . on the earth beneath" (Exod 20:4; Deut 5:8–9).[12] If Jesus were not "worthy" of the same honors as the Father, then we should expect to see him worshiping the Father along with the rest of creation, not being accorded the same worship as the Father. Yet there he is, in the brilliant light of the very throne room of God, receiving the same accolades of "blessing and honor and glory and might forever and ever" (Rev. 5:13b).

In short, John's vision draws a line between that which must worship but not be worshiped (all creatures in heaven, on earth, or anywhere else) and that which must be worshiped, and puts Christ on the "worshiped" side of the line.

Ruling the Universe as Father and Son

Despite the six lines of evidence we have just reviewed, we need to address certain objections to the conclusion that Jesus shares God's throne as his equal.

The first and perhaps most common objection is that if Jesus was exalted or elevated to the right hand of God, then he must not always have occupied such a high position. This objection ignores the larger history of which Jesus' exaltation is one part. Jesus is the divine Son of God who existed in heaven at God's side, with God's form, possessing the divine glory from before creation (John 1:14, 18; 17:5; Phil. 2:6). In order to bring glory to the Father and out of love for lost human beings, the Son humbled himself by becoming a human being (John 1:14; Phil. 2:6–7). In becoming a man, Christ put himself in a position of dependence on his Father, as *his God* (cf. John 20:17). This meant that he depended on the Father to exalt him. According to the book of Hebrews, Jesus, "for the sake of the joy that was set before him endured the cross, disregarding its shame, and has taken his seat at the right hand of the throne of God" (12:2).

Three of the most common objections appeal to the same passage of Scripture, so we will consider them together. In his discussion of the resurrection from the dead, Paul wrote the following:

> Then comes the end, when he hands over the kingdom to God the Father, after he has destroyed every ruler and every authority and power. For he must reign until he has put all his enemies under his feet. The last enemy to be destroyed is death. For "God has put all things in subjection under his feet." But when it says, "All things are put in subjection," it is plain that this does not include the one who put all things in subjection under him. When all things are subjected to him, then the Son himself will also be subjected to the one who put all things in subjection under him, so that God may be all in all. (1 Cor. 15:24–28)

From this one passage alone, three distinct objections have been made to viewing Jesus Christ as equal with God: the Son's kingdom is temporary, not eternal (vv. 24–25); even now the Son's authority does not extend over God (v. 27); in the end the Son will be subject to God (v. 28).

The first objection may be answered fairly simply. The act of the Son "handing over" the kingdom to God the Father does not mean that the Son's rule over all creation will come to an end. Paul does not say that it will, and such an inference contradicts other biblical statements that plainly affirm that "of his kingdom there will be no end" (Luke 1:33), that Christ rules over every other power "not only in this age but also in the age to come" (Eph. 1:21), and that "he will reign forever and ever" (Rev. 11:15). What Paul means is that the Son will deliver to God the Father a fully reconciled kingdom in which all of his enemies have been defeated (1 Cor. 15:24–26). Paul is speaking of a "stage" in the kingdom of God in which God's Son, Jesus Christ, is in this age focusing on bringing people redemption from sin and salvation from evil powers and death (see also Eph. 1:19–23; Col. 1:13–20). In other words Paul is referring specifically to a spiritual or mediatorial phase of the kingdom of God in which Christ's position as ruler is most prominent.

The claim that Jesus' act of handing over the kingdom to God the Father means that Jesus will no longer be ruling that kingdom clearly leads to an unacceptable conclusion. That argument implies that God is currently *not* ruling over that kingdom. If Paul were speaking of a "hand-off," in which Jesus stops ruling and God starts ruling, that would imply that God is currently not ruling. Since such an inference is clearly wrong and incompatible with Paul's own theology (e.g., Rom. 14:17), the premise that Jesus will one day cease ruling also must be wrong.

The second objection is the weakest of the three. To the best of our knowledge, no one claims that God is currently subject to the Son. Paul's observation that God is excepted from the sweeping statement that all things are subject to Christ does not make Christ inferior to God. On the understanding that Christ is on the same level as God, it obviously is still true that God the Father has not been subjected to the Son.

The third objection is widely thought to be the most difficult, but we think it poses no insuperable objection to the deity of Christ. The objection suffers from a problem similar to the first: if Paul is understood to mean that at the end the Son will change his status by subjecting himself to God, that implies that the Son is not currently subject to God. If Jesus is a creature, inferior to God, is it possible for him not to be subject to God for even a minute?

Recall the point we made earlier about the Son humbling himself to become a human being for the glory of the Father and the salvation of the lost. In his resurrection, as the "last Adam," Jesus Christ continues to be a man, retaining human nature (Acts 17:31; Rom. 8:11; 1 Cor. 15:45–47; 1 Tim. 2:5), albeit in a glorified, immortal state (1 Cor. 15:42–44; cf. Phil. 3:21). As a human being, the Son still honors and subjects himself to the Father as his God (e.g., John 20:17; 2 Cor. 1:3; Rev. 3:12). In that context, the Son, who is both fully God and fully man (cf. Col. 2:9), rightly and properly subjects himself to God the Father. But *this fact about the relationship between God the Father and the incarnate Son does not diminish the Son's exalted status over all creation.* He is still "Lord of all" (Rom 10:12).

The final objection we will consider is that Jesus' occupancy of God's throne is really not unique since the Bible says that Christians are presently seated with Christ (Eph. 2:6) and will one day share his throne (Rev. 3:21). This objection glosses over the obvious contextual differences between these statements and the many New Testament affirmations we have seen about Christ's unique status at God's right hand.

Let's look at Ephesians 2:6 in context:

> But God, who is rich in mercy, out of the great love with which he
> loved us even when we were dead through our trespasses, made us
> alive together with Christ—by grace you have been saved—and
> raised us up with him and seated us with him in the heavenly
> places in Christ Jesus, so that in the ages to come he might show the

immeasurable riches of his grace in kindness toward us in Christ
Jesus. (Eph. 2:4–7)

The only person who *actually* has been "made alive," "raised up," and
"seated in heavenly places" is Christ. Paul is not asserting that these things
have actually happened to believers. What he is saying is that Christ's death,
resurrection, and exaltation all occurred for our benefit, so that those of us
who are "in Christ Jesus" will eventually receive all the blessings of God's rich
grace. In the meantime, God graciously considers us to be "with" Christ in
his death, resurrection, and exaltation, so that our standing with God is secure. As our advocate, Christ "is at the right hand of God" and "intercedes for
us" from that privileged position (Rom. 8:34).

It is likely that a similar idea is at work in Revelation 3:21, where Jesus says,
"The one who conquers, I will grant him to sit with me on my throne, as I
also conquered and sat down with my Father on his throne" (ESV). Jesus certainly is not saying that believers who conquer through their faith will pass
judgment on all creation or receive worship from all creatures. Jesus is calling
people to conquer, or overcome, through repentance and faith so that they
may have a relationship with him (vv. 19–20). In this context, Jesus' promise that he will grant a place on his throne to those who conquer appears to
be a symbolic way of expressing a promise of *immediate access to the throne*.
Believers have someone sitting on the throne of God who represents them,
someone who is "on their side," and through whom they have immediate,
direct, intimate access to God.

In its own way, using the symbolic language of apocalyptic literature, the
book of Revelation is making a point that is probably very similar to the astonishing teaching of the book of Hebrews:

> *Let us therefore approach the throne of grace* with boldness, so that
> we may receive mercy and find grace to help in time of need. (Heb.
> 4:16)

> Therefore, my friends, since we have confidence *to enter the sanctu-
> ary* by the blood of Jesus, by the new and living way that he opened
> for us through the curtain (that is, through his flesh), and since we
> have a great priest over the house of God, *let us approach*. . . . (Heb.
> 10:19–22a)

BELIEVERS AND CHRIST IN REVELATION

Overcoming Believers	Overcoming Christ
Eat of the tree of life (2:7)	The "water" of the tree of life comes from his throne (22:1–3)
Not be hurt by the second death (2:11)	Holds the keys of death (1:18)
Will be given new manna and a new name (2:17)	*Is* the new manna (cf. John 6) and has the greatest name (22:12–13)
Will be given authority over the nations as Christ was given from his Father (2:27–28)	Has the authority of the King of kings and Lord of lords (17:14; 19:16)
Will not have name erased, but Christ will confess it before the Father (3:5)	Christ decides whose names will be confessed before the Father (3:5; cf. 1:18; 2:7; 22:12)
Will be made a pillar in God's temple (3:12)	God and the Lamb *are* the temple (21:22)
Will be given a place to sit on Christ's throne as he overcame and sat on his Father's throne (3:21)	Receives universal worship while sharing his Father's throne, which *is* the throne of God and the Lamb (5:12–14; 22:3)

The promise of full, unfettered access to God is the heart of the New Testament message. From one standpoint, Christ's sitting on God's throne is a unique, unparalleled position of authority at the right hand of God. From another standpoint, Christ's sitting on God's throne is the means by which we have direct, intimate fellowship with God. The profound blessing of this promise does not negate the vast, obvious differences in what the Bible says about Christ as compared to those who overcome through faith in Christ (see the table).

It is interesting that the Gospel of John makes no statement about Jesus sitting on God's throne or at his "right hand." The same relationship is expressed, though, from a different perspective. Instead of saying that Jesus sits at the right hand of God, John says that Jesus resides "in the bosom of the

Father" (John 1:18 NASB). This is a way of saying that Jesus, the Son, is as close to the Father as possible; he is right there with him, sharing the same "space," above which it is not possible to go. The fact that we are graciously invited into a relationship with the Father in which he will love us as he loves his own Son (John 17:26) surely should not obscure for us the fact that Jesus' position in the scheme of things is unique and far, far above all creation.

THE CASE FOR THE DEITY OF CHRIST

The case for the deity of Christ does not rest on a few proof-texts. The popular notion that some fourth-century Christians decided to impose on the church a belief in Jesus as God and wrenched isolated Bible verses from their contexts to support their agenda is a gross misrepresentation of the facts. The framers of the orthodox doctrines of the Incarnation and the Trinity did have an agenda, but it was not to replace a merely human Jesus with a divine Christ. Their agenda was to safeguard the New Testament's clear teaching of the deity of the Lord Jesus Christ in a way that did equal justice to three other clear teachings of the Bible: there is only one God; Jesus is the Son and not the Father; Jesus is also a human being. In this book, we have touched at various places on the biblical evidence for these three teachings, while our focus throughout has remained on establishing the truth of the deity of Christ.

We have examined a mass of biblical material and discussed a wide array of topics. Now we bring all the evidence together and show how it supports the case for the deity of Christ. Think of this conclusion as our "closing argument."

HANDS: The Five Indicators of Deity

We have presented the evidence for the deity of Christ under five categories or themes, arranged using the acronym HANDS.

Honors:	Jesus shares the *honors* due to God.
Attributes:	Jesus shares the *attributes* of God.
Names:	Jesus shares the *names* of God.
Deeds:	Jesus shares in the *deeds* that God does.
Seat:	Jesus shares the *seat* of God's throne.

Our contention is that the case for the deity of Christ should not rest exclusively, or even primarily, on any one of these lines of evidence. (We do not object, of course, to scholars focusing their attention on one of these lines of evidence.) There was a time, for example, when it seemed that the case for Christ's deity depended primarily on demonstrating that the New Testament calls Jesus "God." Some people still approach the subject on that assumption. The New Testament *does* call Jesus "God," as we have seen, but even if it did not, something like 99 percent of the biblical evidence for the deity of Christ would remain untouched.

Recently a great deal of attention has been lavished on the worship or religious devotion to Jesus in the New Testament. We are profoundly grateful for the work that others have done in this area, for it has brought to many people's attention the broader range of biblical material relating to the deity of Christ. We simply point out that a comprehensive understanding of the deity of Christ takes into account all five of the lines of evidence discussed in this book.

In this regard one of the most promising approaches to the subject in recent New Testament scholarship is that of Richard Bauckham. In his book *God Crucified*, Bauckham lays out briefly his argument to show that the intent of New Testament teaching about Christ "is to include Jesus in the unique divine identity as Jewish monotheism understood it." He continues,

> The writers do this deliberately and comprehensively by using precisely those characteristics of the divine identity on which Jewish monotheism focused in characterizing God as unique. They included Jesus in the unique divine sovereignty over all things, they include him in the unique divine creation of all things, they identify him by the divine name which names the unique divine identity, and they portray him as accorded the worship which, for Jewish monotheists, is recognition of the divine identity.[1]

Bauckham here specifies four of the five lines of evidence that we have been discussing. Jesus' inclusion "in the unique divine sovereignty over all things" is another way of saying that Jesus shares the *seat* of God's throne (typified in the New Testament teaching that Jesus sits at God's right hand). Bauckham gives considerable attention to the application to Jesus of this characteristic of the divine identity. His inclusion "in the unique divine creation of all things" is the primary example of the *deeds* of God that Jesus shares in doing. His identification by the divine name, of course, focuses on one of the *names* that Jesus shares with God. Finally, his inclusion in receiving the worship that expresses recognition of divine identity refers to the *honors* that Jesus shares with God.[2]

The one line of evidence that Bauckham does not include is that of the *attributes* of God that Jesus shares. Bauckham wishes to redefine the debate away from whether New Testament Christology is "functional" (in which Jesus is simply a man who acts on God's behalf) or "ontic" (in which Jesus is seen as possessing divine *nature*), and to ask instead whether it teaches a Christology of "divine identity" (in which Jesus is included in the identity of God). According to Bauckham, the New Testament is not concerned with defining Christ's nature (*what* he is) but rather with identifying Christ's person (*who* he is).[3]

It is certainly true enough to say that the New Testament does not engage in philosophical or systematic theological analysis of the nature (or natures) of Christ. It does have plenty to say, however, about his characteristics or attributes, and we would argue that these play a role in recognizing his divine identity. It is important to know, for example, whether the Son of God is eternal or a created being. Even more basic is the question of whether Christ existed prior to his human life. Given the widespread skepticism concerning Christ's preexistence (not only in modern Western scholarship but also, notably, in Islam), a defense of this truth is an important part of our case for the deity of Christ. We think that it would strengthen Bauckham's excellent contribution to Christology to take into account what the New Testament *does* say about this and other divine attributes of Christ.

In his published dissertation, Charles Gieschen expresses dissatisfaction with the view that "the criteria for distinguishing divine status should be based solely on worship or cultic veneration." He identifies what he calls five "criteria of divinity" that "may be used either individually or in combination to assert the divinity of a mediator alongside God, a mediator who usually is not completely separate from God."[4] These five criteria parallel the five lines of evidence we present in this book. The "*Divine Veneration* criterion" asks whether the figure is "the object of some form of veneration." The "*Divine Appearance* criterion" asks whether the figure has "the physical characteristics of God's visible form as depicted in various theophanies." (This is not quite the same as our "attributes" category, but it is suggestive of it.) The "*Divine Name* criterion" asks whether the figure in some way possesses "the Name of God." The "*Divine Function* criterion" considers whether the figure performs "an act, or actions, typically ascribed to God." Finally, the "*Divine Position* criterion" asks whether the figure is "positioned with or near God or his throne."[5]

The problem with these criteria is that, as Gieschen explains them, they are not truly definitive of deity. Not all acts of veneration indicate belief in the deity of the object of that veneration. Resemblances to the visible characteristics of a theophany do not prove that an actual theophany is taking place. There are ways in which a figure might be said to have or bear God's name without being God. God might delegate functions "typically ascribed to God" to one of his created servants. One might describe a figure as near God or his throne without implying his deity.

In response to Gieschen, Timo Eskola argues that these criteria "are not sufficient categories to be used as proper criteria for the divinity of a heavenly being."[6] As Gieschen has articulated them, we would agree. We maintain, however, that similar criteria, properly defined and related, *do* constitute valid criteria for identifying someone as divine.

Divine Honors

Not all acts of veneration imply deity or deification. If, however, a figure is the recipient of honors reserved *exclusively* for God, or of a *wide range* of honors normally associated with God, and if believers express such honors *in contexts of religious activity or spiritual devotion*, such honors do indicate that those according him such honors regard him as God.

By this standard, the evidence for the deity of Christ is quite compelling. The Son is to be honored just as we honor the Father (John 5:23). He is given glory in doxologies modeled on Old Testament doxologies to God (1 Peter 4:11; 2 Peter 3:18). He is the object of worship that is expressed in the words of Old Testament references to the worship of YHWH (Heb. 1:6) or in scenes in which all creation worships Christ alongside God in heaven itself (Rev.

5:8–14). He hears and answers prayers for salvation, for the safekeeping of one's spirit at the moment of death, and for other needs (John 14:14; Acts 7:59–60; Rom. 10:12–13; 2 Cor. 12:8–9). Religious songs are sung in his honor (Eph. 5:19; Rev. 5:9–10). He is as much the object of religious faith as God is (John 14:1; Rom. 10:11). We are to fear or revere him (Eph. 5:21; 1 Peter 3:14–16), serve him (Dan. 7:14), and love him (John 14:15, 21; Eph. 6:24) as we do God.

Divine Attributes

Given that angels bear some likeness to God as heavenly spirits and that human beings are created in God's image, elements of likeness or resemblance to God does not prove deity. Similarly, likeness to angels does not make one an angel. If, however, a figure possesses attributes that are *unique* to God, or if his likeness to God is *complete, total, and perfect*, those are cogent indicators that the figure is deity.

The biblical case for Christ's deity from his attributes is complicated by the fact that Christ is not merely divine, but is a divine person who became a human being. The New Testament therefore attributes characteristics to the incarnate Son that are typical of all human beings. Thus, Jesus was born; he grew (and so changed); he experienced hunger, thirst, sleep, and other physical limitations; he even acknowledged limits to what he knew (Mark 13:32).

Nevertheless, the New Testament also attributes characteristics to Christ that show him also to be something far greater than a human being; indeed, they show him to be God. The totality of what it means to be God is embodied in Jesus Christ (Col. 1:19; 2:9). The Son is completely, perfectly like God the Father (John 14:9; Col. 1:15; Heb. 1:3). He existed before all creation and is eternal, uncreated, and immutable (John 1:1–3; Col. 1:15–17; Heb. 1:2, 10–12; 13:8). His moral character, in particular his love, is perfectly that of God (Rom. 8:35–39; Rev. 1:5). His omnipotence is implicit in his work of creation and providential sustaining of the universe (Col. 1:16–17; Heb. 1:2–3), and that same power became incarnate, paradoxically humbled in weakness for our salvation (1 Cor. 1:23–24; 2 Cor. 12:9). He is omnipresent (Matt. 18:20; 28:20; Eph. 4:10–11) and even omniscient (John 16:30–31; Acts 1:24; Rev. 2:23), as someone who made the cosmos must be. Like God, he is beyond our comprehension (Matt. 11:27).

Divine Names

Many people in the Bible have what are called *theophoric* names, that is, names that include a name for God. The name Elijah, for example, includes both the names *El* (God) and *Jah* (a short form of Yahweh). Obviously (it is obvious, isn't it?), Elijah is not God. Thus, theophoric names in themselves do not imply that those so named are themselves divine.

It is popularly argued that the theophoric name "the LORD our righteousness" in Jeremiah 23:6 (NASB) connotes the deity of the Messiah. This argument is really rather weak. There is nothing in the immediate context in Jeremiah 23 to support the argument that this name connotes the Messiah's deity. One might say the same thing about the theophoric name *Immanuel* (God with us) in Isaiah 7:14; in this case, however, other contextual indicators, both in the immediate context and in the broader context of Isaiah, support the inference that the child in some unique way will be God. In addition, Matthew's use of the term, in the context of his Gospel as a whole, further supports a more direct argument from the name Immanuel to the conclusion that Jesus is himself truly "God with us." Still, we see the name Immanuel in Isaiah as merely anticipating or laying a foundation for the New Testament revelation that the Messiah Jesus is God.

We disagree, then, that divine names "cannot be regarded as a criterion of divinity," as Eskola concludes.[7] Rather, we must distinguish theophoric names from divine names, and base the case for the deity of Christ primarily on what are, properly speaking, divine names rather than the theophoric names that Christ also possesses. Moreover, the contexts in which texts apply these names to Christ must be taken into account. If a figure is affirmed to *be* God, or is called God *in a confessional or religious context*, and is given a variety of other names for God in contexts that show such names to be applied to him *in the same way they apply to God*, those are positive indicators that the figure is, indeed, God.

By this standard, the New Testament clearly teaches that Jesus is God. Despite the fact that the New Testament usually uses the name *God* with reference to the Father, it also affirms several times that Christ is God (John 1:1, 18; 20:28; Acts 20:28; Rom. 9:5; Titus 2:13; Heb. 1:8; 2 Peter 1:1). With astonishing frequency—far more often than even many scholars have noticed—Jesus is identified as the Lord (that is, YHWH) of the Old Testament (Rom. 10:9–13; 1 Cor. 8:6; Phil. 2:9–11; 1 Peter 3:13–15). He is the King of kings and Lord of lords (Rev. 17:14; 19:16), the divine Savior (Titus 2:13;

2 Peter 1:11), the one who says "I am" or "I am he" (John 8:24, 28, 58), the first and the last, the Alpha and the Omega, and the beginning and the end (Rev. 1:7–8, 17b–18; 2:8; 22:12–13). The New Testament repeatedly and in a variety of ways makes the name of Jesus the center of Christian faith; he has the name that is above every name (Eph. 1:21; Phil. 2:9–11; Col. 3:17).

Divine Deeds

Performance of functions related to God, such as judging, does not necessarily tell us what kind of being is performing those functions. It is possible for God to delegate certain functions to his creatures (serving as his agents). Eskola notes that in Jewish apocalyptic writings, "Exalted patriarchs act as heavenly judges, but their status in the heavenly hierarchy is strictly defined. Only the theme of creating the world, and probably that of absolving sins—even though this may also be a priestly function—appear to reveal certain divine aspect in heavenly functions."[8] A key question is whether the divine functions associated with a figure pertain to all time (the primeval past, the present age, and the eschatological age to come or consummation).[9] If a figure performs deeds that are the *exclusive* prerogative of God, or if he performs *all* the deeds, *or at least a wide range* of them, that are normally associated with God *throughout time*—from creation through history and right up to and including the consummation—then such deeds demonstrate that he is, in fact, God.

On this basis, we are on firm ground in identifying Jesus as God. The heavens and the earth—which is to say, the universe—are his work (Heb. 1:10–12). Nothing came into being apart from him (John 1:3). All created things exist in, through, and for him (Col. 1:16). He sustains the universe (Col. 1:16; Heb. 1:3). In his earthly ministry, he demonstrated divine sovereign control over the forces of nature (Matt. 8:23–27; 14:13–33). His word is the divine "word of the Lord" (Acts 8:25; 13:44, 48–49). He forgives sins (Mark 2:1–12; Col. 3:13). He sends the Holy Spirit and imparts spiritual gifts (John 20:22; Acts 2:33; 1 Cor. 12:4–5; Eph. 4:8–11). He gives life to whomever he chooses (John 5:21, 26). He judges all people, so that all may honor him as they honor the Father (John 5:22–23; 2 Cor. 5:10).

Divine Seat

Eskola rightly insists that enthronement is not the same thing as deification.[10] Not every reference to someone being enthroned is an expression of belief in the divinity of that figure, and not every reference to a figure being exalted to heaven and occupying a high position near God qualifies as evidence of deity. If, however, a figure *is positioned permanently in God's place,* sharing his throne, exercising the *prerogatives* of God from that position, and receiving in that position *honors* properly due to God, then he is certainly functioning as God. Note, then, that this criterion, even more so than the others, really gains its validity when applied in conjunction with one or more of the other criteria.

The New Testament teaching on this point is explicit. Jesus claimed that he would sit at God's right hand and exercise divine judgment—a claim that the Jewish religious authorities recognized as a claim to deity (Mark 14:61–64). In this position, Jesus exercises authority over all things (Matt. 28:18; 1 Cor. 15:27–28). He is exalted far above everyone and everything in created existence, including all the angels in God's heavenly court (Eph. 1:21; 4:10; Phil. 2:9–10; Heb. 1:3–6). Jesus not only sits on God's throne, it is his throne, too (Rev. 22:1, 3). From this exalted position, Jesus sends the Holy Spirit (Acts 2:33), receives the spirit of a dying man (Acts 7:59), and receives universal worship (Heb. 1:6; Rev. 5:8–14).

Beyond Reasonable Doubt

Any one of these five lines of evidence would be good support for belief in the deity of Christ. All five lines of evidence, considered together, prove beyond reasonable doubt that Jesus Christ is God.

Let us change metaphors for a moment and look at this question, not as a case to be settled in a court, but as an investigative matter from the point of view of a reporter. One of the most basic methods of journalism is to ask the five "wh" questions: who, what, when, where, and why? (Sometimes a sixth question, "how?" is also asked.) We can apply these five questions to the matter of the deity of Christ (arranged in a different order).

1. *Why?* This question asks for the significance of the person to others.
2. *When?* This question asks for the time when the person was present and involved.
3. *Who?* This question asks for a person's name.
4. *What?* This question asks for an account of the person's activity.
5. *Where?* This question asks for the place where the person lives or was active.

You can see that these five questions correspond (perhaps a bit roughly) to the five lines of evidence for the deity of Christ discussed in this book. The *honors* that Jesus shares with God are the answer to the question of *why* knowing that Jesus is God is significant. Perhaps the most basic of all Christ's divine *attributes* is that he existed *when* creation began and in fact is eternal. The *names* that Jesus shares with God, of course, tell us *who* he is. The *deeds* that Jesus does with God tell us *what* Jesus has done. Finally, that Jesus shares the *seat* of God's throne tells us *where* Jesus is.

That these five investigative questions correspond to the five categories of evidence for Christ's deity is not accidental. The information gathered from these five questions provides a complete picture of the facts pertaining to the identity of the person in question.

Suppose you meet a man who claims to be the president of the United States. The fact that military personnel greet him with a salute does not by itself prove his claim correct. The mere use of the title "president," apart from context, is ambiguous, since he might be the president of a corporation or of some other country. If all you know is that he signs bills into law, you would not necessarily infer that he was the president of the United States; after all, state governors do the same. Even the fact that he lives at the White House would not be enough by itself to prove his claim. But now put all these things together in a coherent context. If he lives in the White House at 1600 Pennsylvania Avenue, is saluted by the Joint Chiefs of Staff, regularly sits in the chair behind the president's desk in the Oval Office, responds affirmatively when addressed as "Mr. President," and from that chair signs into law federal legislation, he must be the president of the United States![11]

The situation is much the same with the New Testament evidence for the identity of Jesus Christ as God. All creatures, even the most glorious angels in heaven, are expected to worship him. He has existed forever. He exerted omnipotence in making the universe, and he continues to do so by sustaining its existence. He goes by the divine name "Lord" and also answers to "God." He lives in God's "home" (heaven) and sits in God's "chair" (his heavenly throne). From that very position he sends the Holy Spirit, reveals himself to apostles, guides the church by his divine presence as they complete his commission to tell the whole world that he is Lord, and will one day judge all creatures and give eternal life to whomever he chooses. Such a person must, in fact, be God.

The Deity of Christ in the Nicene Creed

We have emphasized throughout this book that the belief in the deity of Christ did not originate centuries after Jesus and the apostles but in fact is taught throughout the New Testament. It is worth noting, however, that the five aspects of the biblical case for Christ's deity are also evident in the creeds of the early church, especially the Nicene Creed. We reproduce that creed here, with words emphasized and with bracketed insertions to note where the five points appear:

We *believe . . . in* one Lord Jesus Christ [**honors**],
the only Son of God,
eternally [**attributes**] begotten of the Father;
God from God, Light from Light, *true God* from true God [**names**];
begotten, *not made, of one Being with the Father* [**attributes**].
Through him all things were made [**deeds**].
For us and *for our salvation* [**deeds**] he came down from heaven:
by the power of the Holy Spirit he became incarnate from the virgin Mary,
and was made man.
For our sake he was crucified under Pontius Pilate;
he suffered death and was buried.
On the third day he rose again in accordance with the Scriptures;
he ascended into heaven, and is *seated at the right hand of the Father* [**seat**].
He will come again in glory
to judge the living and the dead [**deeds**],
and his kingdom will have no end [**seat**].

The Deity of Christ: Not a Postbiblical Construct

One question possibly remains. In bringing together these five lines of evidence for the deity of Christ, are we perhaps cobbling together a composite picture of Jesus as God that is not found anywhere in the New Testament? Are we seizing upon a text in John calling him "God," another text from Hebrews crediting him with making the universe, and yet another text from Revelation about Christ sitting on God's throne, and then out of these disparate texts from different contexts forming a theory about Jesus that is not taught in any one part of the Bible?

The answer to this question is decidedly no. There are many passages in which three or more of our five lines of evidence attesting to the deity of Christ are found in one place. In fact, there are *several* passages in the New Testament in which *all five* of these lines of evidence converge in a single context. Four such passages stand out, three of which are widely regarded as among the most important Christological passages in the New Testament.

Matthew 28:16–20

In the closing verses of the Gospel of Matthew, Jesus' disciples go to a mountain to see him after he has risen from the dead. "When they saw him, they worshiped him" (Matt. 28:17). That is a rather clear example of Jesus receiving **honors** due to God.

Jesus responds by saying, "All authority in heaven and on earth has been given to me" (v. 18). This is one way of saying that Jesus shares the **seat** of God's throne; his position places him over the entire universe. (It is interesting to note that Jesus' statement alludes to Daniel 7:13–14, one of the two passages that Jesus used when he told the high priest that he would be sitting at God's right hand.)

Jesus then tells them to "make disciples of all nations, baptizing them in the *name* of the Father and of the Son and of the Holy Spirit" (v. 19). This instruction treats the Son's name as a divine **name** (one that is invoked in the religious rite of baptism).

Jesus tells his disciples, "Go . . . teaching [all nations] to obey everything that I have commanded you. And remember, I am with you always, to the end of the age" (vv. 19–20). Jesus here claims the authority to issue commandments. By itself, this statement would be consistent with Jesus claiming only to be a prophet like Moses, but in light of the rest of the Gospel (in which Jesus speaks with absolute personal authority, not as a prophet), we know that he claims an even higher, divine prerogative. Furthermore, Jesus' promise to be with his disciples indicates that he will be personally guiding the church throughout its generations as they fulfill this commission. Thus, we have here two divine **deeds** that Jesus claims to perform.

Finally, Jesus' promise to be with his disciples as they go to all nations clearly presupposes that he is omnipresent. Thus, his statement is an indication that Jesus shares in the **attributes** of God.

In just five short verses, we see elements of all five lines of evidence for the deity of Christ.

John 1:1–18

The prologue of the Gospel of John is one of the Christologically richest passages in the New Testament. Even the great prophet John the Baptist saw his purpose as to bear witness to Jesus (John 1:6–8, 15), and all people are summoned to put faith in Jesus' name (v. 12). These responses to Jesus are evidence that he deserves the **honors** that are due to God. The Gospel writer describes Christ as eternal, full of grace and truth, and sharing in the glory of his Father (vv. 1–3, 14, 17), clearly indicating that Jesus shares the **attributes** of God. He identifies him as "God" twice (vv. 1, 18), thus assigning to him one of the **names** of God. He also credits Christ with the works of creation, illumination, and revelation (vv. 3–5, 9–10, 18), all clear examples of the divine **deeds** that Jesus does. Finally, John's statement that Jesus "is in the bosom of the Father" (v. 18 NASB) reveals that Jesus shares the **seat** of God's throne, as he is positioned immediately and intimately next to the Father.

Hebrews 1:1–13

As with John 1, we have had many occasions throughout this book to turn to the exposition of the deity of Christ in the opening chapter of the book of Hebrews. Here we see that the angels of heaven all worship the Son (Heb. 1:6), exemplifying the **honors** that he shares with God. The writer informs us that the Son is eternal and immutable (vv. 11–12), showing that Jesus shares the **attributes** of God. A major emphasis in this chapter is on the superiority of Jesus' name above that of the angels (v. 4), and the author quotes Old Testament texts, calling Jesus ever more exalted titles: Son (v. 5), Firstborn (v. 6), God (v. 8), and Lord (v. 10). Clearly, Jesus shares the **names** of God. The writer credits the Son with the works of creation and providence, as well as salvation (vv. 2–3, 10), illustrating that Jesus shares in the **deeds** that God does. The author also emphasizes that Jesus sits at God's right hand (vv. 3, 13), indicating that Jesus shares the **seat** of God's throne.

Philippians 2:6–11

Philippians 2:6–11 also nicely brings together all five of the elements of the New Testament teaching on the divine identity of Jesus that we have examined in this book. We will explore this passage in a bit more depth.

Right away, we see that Jesus shares fully in God's **attributes:** he existed in God's form (v. 6) and demonstrated God's love for us by humbling himself to share in our human attributes in order to die for us (vv. 7–8). In doing so, he shared in one of God's most precious **deeds** on our behalf, namely, the work of redemption.

Paul then tells us that God's response to Jesus was that he "highly exalted" him (v. 9). This word, which we might translate "super-exalted" (*huperup-sōsen*),[12] is used of Yahweh, the Lord God, in a similar context in the Greek translation of Psalm 97:9.

JESUS THE HIGHLY EXALTED LORD

"For you, O LORD,	"Therefore God also **highly exalted** him . . .
are the Most High over all the earth;	every knee should bend, in heaven and on earth . . .
You are **exalted far** above all gods" (Ps. 97:9 NIV).	and every tongue should confess that Jesus Christ is Lord" (Phil. 2:9–11).

In the light of this Old Testament background and the context of Philippians 2:6–11, it is evident that Paul is not saying that Christ enjoyed a lesser position prior to his Incarnation than he has now as a result of his exaltation. As Bauckham puts it,

> The verb does not indicate that God has exalted Jesus to a higher status than he had previously occupied (whether in pre-existence or in mortal life), but that God has exalted him to a higher status than that of anyone or anything else, i.e., to the pre-eminent position in the whole cosmos.[13]

We see here, then, that Jesus Christ shares the **seat** of God's universal throne.

Paul also says that God gave Jesus "the name that is above every name" (v. 9). In light of the allusion to Isaiah 45:23 in verses 10–11, the title "Lord" in verse 11 almost certainly represents the name Yahweh. Here, then, we have explicit statements that Jesus shares the **names** of God.

As we just mentioned, Paul also alludes—even more directly than to Psalm 97:9—to Isaiah 45:23, where Yahweh declares, "Surely every knee will bow to me, every tongue will solemnly affirm" (NET). In Philippians 2 "every knee will bow" and "every tongue confess" (NET) that Jesus is Lord. Larry Hurtado observes that texts like these show that worship was given to the exalted Jesus, "not because early Christians felt at *liberty* to do so, but because they felt *required* to do so by God."[14] N. T. Wright notes the astonishing application of divine prerogative to Jesus:

> Paul is quoting a monotheistic text from the Old Testament. Not just any text, either. This comes from Isaiah 40–55, where we find the clearest and most sustained scriptural exposition and exaltation of the one true God over all false claimants, and at the same time the stoutest declaration of the sovereignty of the one God. . . . The whole point of the context is that the one true God does not, cannot and will not share his glory with anyone else. It is his alone. Paul, however, declares that this one God has shared his glory with—Jesus.[15]

Jesus, then, also shares the **honors** that are due to God. Moreover, he shares them *because he is due them* as the one who has God's **attributes**, who has God's **name**, whose **deeds** on our behalf include the divine work of redemption, and who has taken his **seat** as the Lord enthroned over all creation.

Here's a sobering thought. This life is short. Soon we will meet Jesus face to face. And we promise you this: none of us will extend a hand to him and tell him it's finally nice to put a face with the name! We'll fall at his feet and worship. The time to start doing that is now.

Appendix

HANDS REVIEW TABLES

The following pages provide tables that summarize most of the evidence for the deity of Christ that we have covered in this book. To understand the significance of some of this material, it will be important to read the relevant part of the book. Thus, these tables should prove useful for review purposes. They also provide a quick overview for those wanting to see the "big picture."

HONORS

	LORD GOD	Lord Jesus
Honor	Exod. 20:2–3; 34:14; Deut. 5:6–7	John 5:23; Heb. 3:3–4
Glory (glorify)	Exod. 15:2; Ps. 29:1–3; cf. Matt. 5:16; Rom. 15:6–9 *Doxologies*: 1 Chron. 29:10–11; Ps. 72:18–19; cf. Rom. 11:36; Gal. 1:4–5; Phil. 4:20; Rev. 4:11	2 Tim. 4:18; Heb. 13:20–21; 1 Peter 4:11; 2 Peter 3:18; cf. Rom. 16:27; Jude 25; Rev. 5:12–13
Worship (*proskuneō*)	Deut. 6:13; cf. Matt. 4:9–10; Ps. 97:7; Isa. 45:23; Rev. 19:10; 22:8–9	Matt. 2:2, 11; 8:2; 9:18; 14:33; 15:25; 20:20; 28:9, 17; Phil. 2:10–11; Heb. 1:6; Rev. 1:17; 5:14
Prayer	Gen. 4:26; 1 Chron. 16:8; Ps. 65:2; Isa. 44:17; 45:20–22; Joel 2:32	John 14:14; Acts 1:24–25; 7:59–60; 9:14; 22:16; Rom. 10:12–13; 1 Cor. 1:2; 16:22; 2 Cor. 12:8–9; Rev. 22:20–21

HONORS

	LORD GOD	Lord Jesus
Song	Exod. 15:21; Judg. 5:3; 1 Chron. 16:23; Pss. 7:17; 9:11; 92:1; 95:1; 96:2; 104:33; Isa. 42:10	Eph. 5:19; Rev. 5:9–10; cf. Phil. 2:6–11
Faith	Gen. 15:6; Isa. 28:16; 43:10; Mark 11:22; Heb. 6:1; 11:6; cf. Exod. 14:31 with Num. 20:8–13; 27:12–14	Matt. 9:28; John 1:12; 3:15–18, 36; 6:35, 40; 7:37–39; 8:24; 11:25–26; 14:1; 20:31; Acts 3:16; 10:43; 16:31; 20:21; 22:19; 24:24; 26:18; Rom. 9:33; 10:11; Gal. 3:26; 1 Peter 2:6; 1 John 3:23; 5:1, 10, 13
Fear	Deut. 6:13; 10:20; Prov. 1:7; 2:5; 9:10; etc.; Isa. 8:12–13	2 Cor. 5:10–11; Eph. 5:21; 6:7–8; Col. 3:22–25; 1 Peter 3:14–16
Serve (religious devotion; *latreuō*)	Deut. 6:13; cf. Matt. 4:10	Matt. 26:2, 18, 26–29; Mark 14:12–16, 22–25; Luke 22:8–20; Acts 2:38; 8:16; 10:48; 19:5; 1 Cor. 10:16–22; 11:20, 27; and see Dan. 7:14; cf. 3:12, 14, 17, 18, 28; 4:2–3, 35; 6:16, 20, 26; see also Rev. 22:3
Love	Exod. 20:6; Deut. 5:10; 6:4–5; 11:1, 13, 22; 13:6–11; 19:9; 30:6–8, 16, 20; 33:9; Josh. 22:5; Neh. 1:5; Dan. 9:4; Matt. 22:37	Matt. 10:37; Luke 14:26; John 14:15, 21; 15:10; Eph. 6:24

ATTRIBUTES

	LORD GOD	Lord Jesus
All	Exod. 8:10; 9:14; 15:11; 2 Sam. 7:22; 1 Kings 8:23; 1 Chron. 17:20; Ps. 86:8; Isa. 40:18, 25; 44:7; 46:5, 9; Jer. 10:6–7; Mic. 7:18	John 12:45; 14:7–10; Rom. 8:29; 2 Cor. 4:4; Col. 1:13, 15, 19 (cf. Ps. 68:16); 2:9; Heb. 1:3
Preexistent	*passim*	Matt. 9:13; 20:28; 23:34, 37; Mark 2:17; 10:45; Luke 4:43; 5:32; 12:49, 51; 13:34; 19:10; John 8:42; 10:36; 12:39–41; 13:3; 16:28; Rom. 8:3; 1 Cor. 10:4, 9; Gal. 4:4–6; Phil. 2:6–7; Jude 5
Eternal	Pss. 90:2; 102:25–27	John 1:1–3; 8:56–59; 17:5; Col. 1:16–17; Heb. 1:2, 10–12; 7:3
Uncreated	Gen. 1:1; Isa. 43:10	John 1:3, 10; 1 Cor. 8:6; Col. 1:15–16; Heb. 1:2, 10–12; cf. Prov. 8:22; Rev. 3:14
Immutable	Num. 23:19; Ps. 102:26–27; Mal. 3:6; James 1:17	Heb. 1:10–12; 13:8; cf. 2 Cor. 1:20
Loving	Deut. 7:8; 10:15, 18; Ps. 146:8; Prov. 3:12; Isa. 63:9; Jer. 31:3; Hos. 3:1	John 13:34; 15:9, 12–13; Rom. 8:35–39; Gal. 2:20; Eph. 3:19; 5:2; Rev. 1:5; cf. Rom. 5:8
Omnipotent	Job 42:2; Luke 1:37	Matt. 28:18; John 2:19–22; 10:17–18; 1 Cor. 1:23–24; 2 Cor. 12:9; Eph. 1:19–21; Col. 2:10; 1 Peter 3:22
Omnipresent	Gen. 28:15; 1 Kings 8:27; Ps. 139:7–10; John 4:20–24	Matt. 8:5–13; 18:20; 28:20; Mark 7:24–30; Luke 7:1–10; John 1:47–49; 4:46–54; Eph. 4:10–11

ATTRIBUTES

	LORD GOD	Lord Jesus
Omniscient	1 Kings 8:39; Ps. 139:1–4; Isa. 46:9–10; Matt. 10:30; 1 John 3:20	Matt. 9:4; 11:21–23; 12:25; Mark 2:6–8; 8:31–32 [etc.]; Luke 6:8; 10:13–15; 21:20–24; John 4:16–18; 11:11–15; 13:10–11, 21–29, 36–38 par.; 16:30–31; 21:17; Acts 1:24; 1 Cor. 4:5; Rev. 2:23; cf. Mark 13:30–32
Incomprehensible	Isa. 40:18	Matt. 11:27; cf. Luke 10:22

NAMES

	LORD GOD	Lord Jesus
Name above every name	Exod. 3:15; 20:7; Deut. 5:11; 28:58; Pss. 8:1, 9; 20:7; Isa. 45:21–23; Joel 2:32; Luke 1:49; Rom. 2:24; 1 Tim. 6:1; Rev. 11:18; 13:6; 15:4; 16:9	Matt. 7:22; 10:22; 19:29; 24:9; Mark 9:38–39; 13:13; Luke 10:17; 21:12, 17; John 1:12; 15:21; 20:31; Acts 2:21, 36, 38; 3:6, 16; 4:7, 10, 12, 17–18, 30; 5:28, 40–41; 8:16; 9:14, 21, 27–28; 10:43, 48; 15:26; 16:18; 19:5, 17; 21:13; 22:16; Rom. 10:12–13; 1 Cor. 1:13–15; 6:11; Eph. 1:21; Phil. 2:9–11; Col. 3:17; 1 Peter 4:14; 1 John 2:12; 3:23; 5:13; 3 John 7; Rev. 2:3, 13; 3:8
God	Deut. 4:35, 39; 32:39; 2 Sam. 22:32; 2 Chron. 15:3; Isa. 37:20; 43:10; 44:6–8; 45:5, 14, 21–22; 46:9; Jer. 10:10; John 5:44; 17:3; Rom. 3:30; 16:27; 1 Cor. 8:4–6; Gal. 3:20; Eph. 4:6; 1 Thess. 1:9; 1 Tim. 1:17; 2:5; James 2:19; 1 John 5:20–21; Jude 25	Isa. 7:14; 9:6; John 1:1, 18; 20:28; Acts 20:28; Rom. 9:5; Titus 2:13; Heb. 1:8; 2 Peter 1:1 (cf. 1:11; 2:20; 3:18)

NAMES

	LORD GOD	Lord Jesus
Lord (*YHWH/ Kurios*)	Gen. 2:4; Exod. 3:15– 18; Deut. 3:24 LXX [etc.]; 6:4; Pss. 34:8; 118:25; Isa. 8:12–13; 40:3, 13; 45:23; Joel 2:32	Matt. 3:3; 7:21–22; 8:25; 14:30; Mark 1:3; Luke 3:4; 6:46; Acts 1:24; 2:21, 36; 7:59–60; 8:25 [etc.]; Rom. 10:9–13; 1 Cor. 1:2, 8 [etc.], 31; 2:16; 4:4–5; 5:4; 6:11; 7:17, 32–35; 8:6; 10:21–22; 16:22–23; Phil. 2:9–11; 1 Peter 2:3; 3:13–15
Bridegroom/ Husband	Isa. 54:5; 62:5; Jer. 31:32	Matt. 22:2; 25:1–13; Mark 2:19; John 3:29; 2 Cor. 11:2; Eph. 5:25– 27; Rev. 19:7–9; 21:2, 9
King of kings and Lord of lords	Dan. 4:37; 1 Tim. 6:15; cf. Deut. 10:17; Ps. 136:2–3	Rev. 17:14; 19:16
Savior	Deut. 32:15; Pss. 25:5; 27:9; 62:2, 6; 65:5; 79:9; 95:1; Isa. 12:2; 17:10; 45:15, 21; Mic. 7:7; Hab. 3:18	Luke 2:11; John 4:42; Phil. 3:20; 2 Tim. 1:10; Titus 2:13; 2 Peter 1:11; 2:20; 3:2, 18; 1 John 4:14
I Am	Deut. 32:29; Isa. 41:4; 43:2, 5, 10–11, 25; 46:4; 52:6; cf. Exod. 3:14	John 4:26; 6:20; 8:24, 28, 58; 13:18–19; 18:5–8
First and Last/ Alpha and Omega/ Beginning and End	Isa. 41:4; 44:6; 48:12; Rev. 21:6	Rev. 1:7–8, 17b–18; 2:8; 22:12–13

DEEDS

	LORD GOD	Lord Jesus
Creating and sustaining all things	Gen. 1:1; 2:7; Neh. 9:6; Pss. 95:5–7; 102:25; 104:24–30; Isa. 44:24; Jer. 10:16; 51:19; Acts 4:24; 14:15; 17:25, 28; Rom. 11:36; Heb. 2:10; Rev. 4:11	John 1:3, 10; 1 Cor. 8:6; Col. 1:16–17; Heb. 1:2–3, 10
Sovereignly ruling over the forces of nature	Gen. 8:1; Exod. 14:21; Job 38:8–11; Pss. 33:7; 65:7; 74:13–14; 77:16–20; 89:9; 104:4–9; 107:23–30; Prov. 8:22–31; Isa. 17:12–13; 35:4–6; Jer. 5:22; 31:35	Matt. 8:23–27 (cf. Mark 4:35–41; Luke 8:22–25); Matt. 14:13–21 (cf. Mark 6:32–44; Luke 9:10–17; John 6:1–15); Matt. 14:22–33 (cf. Mark 6:45–52; John 6:16–21); Matt. 15:32–39 (cf. Mark 8:1–10); Matt. 17:24–27; Mark 5:19–20 (cf. Luke 8:39); Luke 5:1–11; 7:11–16; John 2:1–11; 21:1–14
Illumination and revelation	Gen. 40:8; 41:15–16; Ps. 119:18; Dan. 2:20–23; Amos 3:7	Matt. 11:27; Luke 10:22; John 1:4–5, 9, 18; 2 Thess. 2:8; 1 Tim. 6:14; 2 Tim. 1:10; 4:1, 8; Titus 2:13
Speaking with divine authority	Cf. "Thus says the Lord" (over 400x); Isa. 40:8; 52:6; 55:11–12	Matt. 5:20–22 [etc.]; 7:24–29; 24:35; Mark 1:22; 13:31; Luke 4:32; John 4:26; 7:46; cf. "Amen I say to you" (74x)
Word of the Lord	1 Kings 13:1, 2, 5, 32; 20:35; 2 Chron. 30:12; cf. 2 Sam. 16:23; 1 Chron. 15:15	Acts 8:25; 13:44, 48–49; 15:35–36; 16:32; 19:10, 20; 1 Thess. 4:15
Salvation	Exod. 15:2; Deut. 32:15; Pss. 3:8; 24:5; 25:5 [etc.]; 62:1–2, 6–7; 118:14, 21; 130:8; Isa. 45:15, 21; Titus 1:3; 2:10; 3:4	Matt. 1:21; Luke 19:9–10; John 3:17; 10:9; 14:6; Acts 4:12; 16:31; 1 Cor. 15:1–4; 1 Tim. 1:1, 15; Titus 1:4; 2:13–14; 3:6; Heb. 5:9; Rev. 7:10

DEEDS

	LORD GOD	Lord Jesus
Showing mercy	Pss. 6:2; 9:13; 31:9; 41:4, 10; 56:1; 86:3; 123:3; Isa. 33:2	Matt. 15:22; 20:30, 31
Forgiveness of sins	Exod. 34:6–7; Pss. 51:4; 130:4; Isa. 43:25; 44:22; 55:7; Jer. 31:34; Dan. 9:9	Matt. 9:1–8 (cf. Mark 2:1–12; Luke 5:17–26); Luke 7:47–49; Acts 5:31; Col. 3:13
Sending the Spirit and his gifts	Joel 2:28–29; John 14:26; Rom. 8:9; 1 Cor. 12:6	Matt. 3:11; Luke 24:49; John 1:33; 4:10, 15; 7:37–39; 15:26; 16:7–14; 20:22; Acts 2:33; 16:6–7; Rom. 8:9; 1 Cor. 12:5; Eph. 4:8–11; Phil. 1:19
Giving and being life	Gen. 2:7; Deut. 32:39; 1 Sam. 2:6; Ps. 36:9; Jer. 2:13	John 1:4; 3:15–16; 5:21–26; 10:10; 14:6; 17:3; 20:30–31; Acts 3:15; Rom. 6:23; 2 Cor. 4:10–11; Phil. 1:21; Gal. 2:20; Col. 3:3–4
Raising the dead	Deut. 32:39; 1 Sam. 2:6; Gal. 1:1	John 2:19–22; 5:28–29; 6:40, 54; 10:17–18, 27–28; 11:25–26; Acts 2:24
Source of all spiritual blessings	(See references to the right)	Eph. 1:2–3; 2 Thess. 2:16–17; 1 Tim. 1:2; 2 Tim. 1:2; 2 John 3; Rev. 1:4; etc.
Judging all people	Gen. 18:25; Deut. 1:17; Pss. 7:9–11; 50:4, 6; 62:12; 75:7; 96:12–13; Prov. 24:12; Isa. 40:9–11; Jer. 25:31; Joel 3:12; Rom. 2:3; 14:10	Matt. 16:27; 25:31–46; John 5:22–23; Acts 10:42; 17:31; Rom. 2:16; 1 Cor. 4:4–5; 2 Cor. 5:10; 2 Thess. 1:7–8; 2 Tim. 4:1; Rev. 2:23

SEAT

	Lord GOD	Lord Jesus
God's highest possible throne	Dan. 4:34–35; Rom. 14:10; Rev. 4:2; 5:1; 20:11; cf. 7:15	Ps. 110:1; Matt. 22:44; 25:31; 26:64; Mark 12:36; 14:62; 16:19; Luke 20:42–43; 22:69; Acts 2:33–35; 5:31; 7:55–56; Rom. 8:34; 1 Cor. 15:25; 2 Cor. 5:10; Eph. 1:20; 2:6; Col. 3:1; Heb. 1:3, 13; 8:1; 10:12–13; 12:2; 1 Peter 3:22; Rev. 3:21; 7:17; 22;1, 3
Claiming to be equal to God	Exod. 20:3, 7; Deut. 5:7, 11; cf. Ps. 110:1; Dan. 7:13–14; cf. Ezek. 1:26–28; see also Exod. 14:20; 34:5; Num. 10:34; Ps. 104:3; Isa. 19:1	Matt. 9:3 (cf. Mark 2:7); Mark 14:61–64; John 5:17–18; 8:58–59; 10:27–33; 19:7
Ruling over all things	Isa. 44:24; Jer. 10:16; 51:19	Matt. 11:25–27; 28:18; Luke 10:21–22; John 3:35; 13:3; 16:15; Acts 10:36; 1 Cor. 15:27–28; Eph. 1:22; Phil. 2:10; 3:21; Heb. 1:2; 2:8; Rev. 5:13
Ruling forever	Pss. 9:7; 45:6; 93:2; Lam. 5:19; Dan. 4:34–35; Rev. 5:13	Luke 1:33; Eph. 1:19b–21; Heb. 1:8; Rev 11:15; cf. Eph. 5:5; Rev. 22:1, 3

NOTES

Introduction: Knowing Jesus as God

1. Some deny that Jesus ever existed, but the influence of these persons is negligible. As the late British scholar F. F. Bruce noted, "The historicity of Christ is as axiomatic for an unbiased historian as the historicity of Julius Caesar. It is not historians who propagate the 'Christ-myth' theories" (F. F. Bruce, *The New Testament Documents: Are They Reliable?* 5th rev. ed. [Downers Grove, IL: InterVarsity Press, 1960], 19).

2. J. Ed Komoszewski, M. James Sawyer, and Daniel B. Wallace, *Reinventing Jesus: How Contemporary Skeptics Miss the Real Jesus and Mislead Popular Culture* (Grand Rapids: Kregel, 2006), 262.

3. Robert W. Funk, Roy W. Hoover, and the Jesus Seminar, *The Five Gospels: The Search for the Authentic Words of Jesus*, A Polebridge Press Book (New York: Macmillan, 1993), 5.

4. The Jesus Seminar is a prime example of people creating Jesus in their own image. Indeed, their revisionist Jesus "probably tells us more about various members of the Jesus Seminar than about Jesus" (Ben Witherington III, *The Jesus Quest: The Third Search for the Jew of Nazareth*, 2nd ed. [Downers Grove, IL: InterVarsity Press, 1997], 57).

5. E.g., "Jesus at 2000," *Time*, December 6, 1999; "The Search for Jesus," *Time*, April 8, 1996; "Who Was Jesus?" *Time*, August 15, 1988. Since 1996, Jesus has made the cover of *Time* in four issues—equal to the number of issues in which he did so in all the years of the magazine prior to that date.

6. Peter Jennings, *The Search for Jesus* (ABC News documentaries, 2000); and idem, *Jesus and Paul: The Word and the Witness* (ABC News documentaries, 2004). For two complementary critiques of these programs, see Darrell L. Bock, "Jesus and Paul: Looking at a Journalistic Approach to Christianity's Beginnings," *Christianity Today*, April 5, 2004 [online version only], http://www.christianitytoday.com/ct/2004/114/21.0.html (accessed July 14, 2004); and Robert M. Bowman Jr., "Peter Jennings, Jesus, and Paul" (Center for Biblical Apologetics, 2004), available at http://www.biblicalapologetics.net.

7. Dan Brown, *The Da Vinci Code: A Novel* (New York: Doubleday, 2003).

8. See, e.g., Darrell L. Bock, *Breaking the Da Vinci Code: Answers to the Questions Everyone's Asking*, rev. ed. (Nashville: Nelson, 2006); Ben Witherington III, *The Gospel Code: Novel Claims About Jesus, Mary Magdalene and Da Vinci* (Downers Grove, IL: InterVarsity Press, 2004).

9. John Hick, "A Pluralist View," in *More Than One Way? Four Views on Salvation in a Pluralistic World*, ed. Dennis L. Okholm and Timothy R. Phillips (Grand Rapids: Zondervan, 1995), 51–52.

10. See also John Hick, *Disputed Questions in Theology and the Philosophy of Religion* (New Haven, Conn.: Yale University Press, 1993), 35–101; and idem, *The Metaphor of God Incarnate*, 2nd ed. (London: SCM Press, 2005), 7, 175.

11. Grant R. Osborne, *Revelation*, BECNT (Grand Rapids: Baker, 2002), 266.

12. See, e.g., Bart D. Ehrman's two recent books, *Lost Scriptures: Books That Did Not Make It into the New Testament* (New York: Oxford University Press, 2003) and *Lost Christianities: The Battle for Scripture and the Faiths We Never Knew* (New York: Oxford University Press, 2003).

13. For informed, accessible treatments of these works, especially the "Gnostic gospels," see Darrell L. Bock, *The Missing Gospels: Unearthing the Truth Behind Alternative Christianities* (Nashville: Nelson, 2006); and Craig A. Evans, *Fabricating Jesus: How Modern Scholars Distort the Gospels* (Downers Grove, IL: InterVarsity Press, 2006). For more on their exclusion from the New Testament canon, see Komoszewski, Sawyer, and Wallace, *Reinventing Jesus*, chaps. 10–11.

14. Even Bart Ehrman, while arguing that Christianity was more diverse than the New Testament and that orthodoxy was a later development, acknowledges that the New Testament writings share a united tradition that led to orthodoxy. See Bart Ehrman, *The Orthodox Corruption of Scripture: The Effect of Early Christological Controversies on the Text of the New Testament* (New York: Oxford University Press, 1993), 33n. 11; 36nn. 25–26. Ehrman acknowledges that the New Testament writers, whom he calls "proto-orthodox," held to the same "paradoxical view of Christ" as both God and man. "These proto-orthodox Christians opposed anyone who claimed that Christ was a man but not God, and anyone who claimed that he was God but not a man, and anyone who claimed that he was two distinct beings, one divine and one human" (ibid., 13–15).

15. For a broad overview of the historical reliability of the New Testament, see Craig Blomberg, *Making Sense of the New Testament: Three Crucial Questions* (Grand Rapids: Baker, 2004), chap. 1. For a detailed treatment of the accuracy of New Testament manuscripts, see Komoszewski, Sawyer, and Wallace, *Reinventing Jesus*, chaps. 4–8.

16. For a popular-level defense of these claims, with references to supporting literature, see Kenneth D. Boa and Robert M. Bowman Jr., *20 Compelling Evidences That God Exists* (Colorado Springs: Cook Communications–RiverOak Publishing, 2002), 189–261.

17. On the New Testament teaching on the resurrection of Jesus, see especially N. T. Wright, *The Resurrection of the Son of God* (Minneapolis: Fortress Press, 2003). For a thorough, accessible, and practical treatment of historical evidence for the resurrection, see Gary R. Habermas and Michael R. Licona, *The Case for the Resurrection of Jesus* (Grand Rapids: Kregel, 2004).

18. A helpful introduction is Millard J. Erickson, *Making Sense of the Trinity: Three Crucial Questions* (Grand Rapids: Baker, 2000). See also Robert M. Bowman Jr., "The Biblical Basis of the Doctrine of the Trinity: An Outline Study" (Center for Biblical Apologetics, 2004), online at http://www.biblicalapologetics.net.

19. The acronym was originally developed by one of the authors (J. Ed Komoszewski), who has presented it to a variety of audiences in both academic and popular settings.

Chapter 1: All Glory, Laud, and Honor

1. E.g., John Hick, *The Metaphor of God Incarnate*, 2nd ed. (London: SCM Press, 2005), 4–5 (whose view is neither novel nor unique).

2. Larry W. Hurtado, *Lord Jesus Christ: Devotion to Jesus in Earliest Christianity* (Grand Rapids: Eerdmans, 2003), 135.

3. Martin Hengel, *Between Jesus and Paul* (London: SCM Press, 1983), 39–40.

4. Biblical quotations are taken from the NRSV unless otherwise noted.

5. Philo, *On Drunkenness* 110; found online at http://www .earlyjewishwritings.com/text/philo/book13.html.

6. Jerome H. Neyrey, "'Despising the Shame of the Cross': Honor and Shame in the Johannine Passion Narrative," *Semeia* 69 (1996): 113–37.

7. With virtually all biblical scholars today, we regard the author of the book of Hebrews as anonymous. The traditional view that Paul was the author does not square well with the author's distinguishing himself from the apostles (Heb. 2:3–4). On this question, see Paul Ellingworth, *The Epistle to the Hebrews: A Commentary on the Greek Text*, NIGTC (Grand Rapids: Eerdmans; Carlisle: Paternoster, 1993), 3–21.

8. See our discussion of Christ's divine attributes in part 2.

9. Except as noted, we cite Old Testament passages, according to the standard chapter and verse references in English Bibles, even when referring to the Septuagint (LXX) or Greek translation. This is important to remember primarily when looking at the Greek text of the Psalms.

10. It is just barely possible, grammatically, that "to whom" in these verses refers back to God rather than to Jesus Christ. In both passages, however, "to whom" follows immediately after the name "Jesus Christ," making it reasonably certain that the glory is being directed to him. At the very least, constructing the doxologies in this way shows that the authors are not bothered about distinguishing between glory given to Christ and glory given to God. Second Timothy 4:18 also should be understood as a doxology to Jesus, who is there called "the Lord" (a title Paul customarily reserves for Jesus).

11. David R. Carnegie, "Worthy Is the Lamb: The Hymns in Revelation," in *Christ the Lord: Studies in Christology Presented to Donald Guthrie*,

ed. Harold H. Rowdon (Leicester, UK; Downers Grove, IL: InterVarsity Press, 1982), 249.

12. James L. Bailey and Lyle D. Vander Broek, *Literary Forms in the New Testament: A Handbook* (Louisville: Westminster John Knox, 1992), 75.

13. Matthias Reinhard Hoffmann, *The Destroyer and the Lamb: The Relationship Between Angelomorphic and Lamb Christology in the Book of Revelation*, WUNT 2.1203 (Tübingen: Mohr Siebeck, 2005), 162.

Chapter 2: The Worship of the Carpenter

1. R. T. France, "The Worship of Jesus: A Neglected Factor in Christological Debate?" in *Christ the Lord: Studies in Christology Presented to Donald Guthrie*, ed. Harold H. Rowdon (Leicester, UK; Downers Grove, IL: InterVarsity Press, 1982), 35.

2. In Luke, this temptation is the second, not the third; Matthew's frequent use of *proskuneō* (more than any other NT book except Revelation) suggests that he placed this temptation last to draw attention to the contrast between the Devil's seeking worship from Jesus and the spontaneous worship of Jesus by various human beings. In Luke, the Devil's climactic temptation is that Jesus should throw himself down from the pinnacle of the temple in order to elicit angelic assistance (Luke 4:9–12). This placement may again be a matter of emphasis, since Luke gives more attention both to angelic beings (good and bad) and to the temple than does any other NT writer.

3. Both Matthew and Luke use *proskunēseis* (worship) here, in agreement with the Alexandrian Codex version of Deuteronomy 6:13 but unlike other ancient Greek versions, which have "fear" (*phobēthēsē*) instead.

4. We are here omitting Herod's feigned interest in going to bow before the infant king himself (Matt. 2:8).

5. It is true that at this point the disciples were unlikely to have fully grasped the true identity of Jesus or to have carefully reflected on the significance of their response to Jesus as an act of worship. However, by ending his account of the incident with the disciples' worshipful confession of Jesus as God's Son (Matt. 14:33), Matthew validates their response and encourages his readers to join in that worship. Moreover, the fact that Jesus does not correct the disciples or reject

their worship—after having rebuffed the Devil by pointing out that
only God should be worshiped (Matt. 4:9–10)—confirms that he
regarded their worship of him as proper. In other words, Matthew
already has linked worship with acknowledgment of the exclusive
honors due to God, and the reader is expected to see the implications
even if Jesus' disciples at that moment did not.

6.   Jason David BeDuhn, *Truth in Translation: Accuracy and Bias in
     English Translations of the New Testament* (Lanham, MD: University
     Press of America, 2003), 46.

7.   Although most translations have "some doubted" (KJV, NIV, NRSV;
     "some were doubtful," NASB), BeDuhn asserts, "there is nothing in
     the Greek from which you could get 'some'" (*Truth in Translation*,
     48). However, the words *hoi de* ("but the ones," or "while those")
     used without a noun or adjectival expression can have the sense "but
     some" or "while others," as they do just two chapters earlier in the
     same book: "Then they spat in his face and struck him; and some
     [*hoi de*] slapped him" (Matt. 26:67; "and others slapped him," NASB).
     Interpreters have understood this idiom at Matthew 28:17 in several
     ways: (1) The eleven disciples worshiped while unmentioned others
     doubted. (2) Some of the eleven worshiped while others among
     the eleven doubted. (3) The eleven worshiped, but some of those
     eleven doubted. (4) Those present (the eleven disciples plus others)
     worshiped but some of them doubted. The first two interpretations
     construe *hoi de* to refer to "others" besides those who worshiped. The
     last two interpretations construe *hoi de* to refer to a subset of those
     who worshiped. The options are discussed in John Nolland, *The
     Gospel of Matthew: A Commentary on the Greek Text*, NIGTC (Grand
     Rapids: Eerdmans; Bletchley, UK: Paternoster, 2005), 1262–63; and
     Ulrich Luz, *Matthew 21–28: A Commentary*, Hermeneia: A Critical
     and Historical Commentary on the Bible, trans. James E. Crouch,
     ed. Helmut Koester (Minneapolis: Fortress, 2005), 622–23. "In any
     case, *hoi de* refers to a subgroup of the whole group, however that is
     understood to be constituted" (Nolland, *Gospel of Matthew*, 1262).
     Thus, the one certainly wrong view (*contra* BeDuhn) is that everyone
     present doubted.
         The two exegetical issues remaining are whether others besides
     the Eleven were present and whether *hoi de* means "some" (of those

who worshiped) or "others" (differentiated from those who worshiped). Many interpreters are quick to reject the suggestion that others besides the Eleven were present (e.g., Luz, *Matthew 21–28*, 622). As Nolland (*Gospel of Matthew*, 1262) points out, however, Matthew 28:7 says that the women also went to Galilee to see Jesus; and if we know they were present although unmentioned in verses 16–17, perhaps others were as well.

When *hoi de* means "others," it usually follows a clause with *hoi men* ("On the one hand, some . . . on the other hand, others . . . ," Acts 14:4; 17:32; 28:24; Phil. 1:16–17) or a similar expression such as *tines* ("some," Acts 17:18; see also John 7:40–41). In Matthew 26:67, though, *hoi de* must mean either "some" or "others" despite the lack of a *hoi men* or similar clause preceding. Nolland acknowledges this example but asserts, "There is no other possible example of this construction [with *hoi de*] in the NT" (*Gospel of Matthew*, 1263) in which *hoi de*, not following *hoi men* or an equivalent expression, means "others." This meaning, however, also nicely fits Mark 14:45–46: Judas kissed Jesus to betray him; "then the others" [*hoi de*] arrested him. There is also at least one example in the Apocrypha (2 Macc. 8:14, "Others sold all their remaining property"; see also 2 Macc. 10:36). In neither of these texts is "some" a likely meaning for *hoi de*. We tend to agree, then, with Greek grammarian A. T. Robertson: "The reference is not to the eleven who were all now convinced after some doubt, but to the others present" (A. T. Robertson, *Word Pictures in the New Testament* [Nashville: Broadman Press, 1933], 1:244). Matthew's meaning is probably that the eleven disciples worshiped while others who were also present had doubts—answering BeDuhn's question, "How can someone worship and doubt at the same time?" (BeDuhn, *Truth in Translation*, 48).

However one translates *hoi de* in Matthew 28:17, doubt is not incompatible with worship. The lack of certainty or assurance, which we call doubt, present even when performing acts of faith is a phenomenon familiar to most people. Even if all of the disciples had doubts, then, it would not mean they were not worshiping. It would simply mean that they had doubts in the midst of their worship.

8. Craig Keener acknowledges that this interpretation "makes sense of the following context" but suggests that "it lacks sufficient clarity in

its immediate context," by which he seems to mean the immediately preceding context. See Craig Keener, *A Commentary on the Gospel of Matthew* (Grand Rapids: Eerdmans, 1999), 716n. 338. Nothing in the preceding context, however, prepares for the mention of doubt except the disciples' worship.

9.   In Matthew's account of these occurrences there is further evidence to confirm this conclusion. In the first such occurrence, for example, a leper "came to" (*proselthōn*) Jesus, "knelt before" (or worshiped) him, and addressed him as *kurie* (Matt. 8:2). All of these words have a religious meaning beyond their more prosaic uses. We can read the text as saying that the man went up to Jesus, knelt in front of him, and called him "sir"; but the language can also mean that the man came before Jesus (as one would God), worshiped him, and addressed him as "Lord." This ambiguity appears to be deliberate: Matthew is saying that the man's respectful approach to Jesus anticipates the overt religious worship that is properly his.

10.   BeDuhn takes no notice whatsoever of Hebrews 1:6 (*Truth in Translation*, 41–49).

11.   The term "Septuagint" technically refers to the original Greek translation of the Old Testament, produced in the third century B.C. In common usage, however, it refers also to ancient Greek versions that stemmed from that original translation and that became a standard part of the Christian Greek Bible. We will follow common practice and use the term (and the abbreviation *LXX*) loosely in reference to the ancient Greek Old Testament.

12.   Authors' translation.

13.   Deuteronomy 32:43 in the LXX actually has two similar lines: "And let all God's sons worship him. . . . let all God's angels be strong in him":

   kai proskunēsatōsan autō pantes huiou theou. . . .
   kai enischusatōsan autō pantes angeloi theou

It is possible that Hebrews 1:6 (and/or the Odes) deliberately conflates these lines, which would yield exactly the wording we find there, "And let all God's angels worship him":

   kai proskunēsatōsan autō pantes angeloi theou

14.   The primary witness to the text of the Odes is the Alexandrian Codex, a fifth-century Christian Greek Bible. The possibility that the reading in the Odes was made to conform to the quotation in Hebrews 1:6

cannot be definitively ruled out. On the other hand, the practice of associating the Song of Moses with the Psalms predated the fifth-century codex, and the reading may reflect a pre-Christian tradition.

15. Of the seven quotations in Hebrews 1, at least five are from the Psalms (Heb. 1:5b quotes 2 Sam. 7:14): Hebrews 1:5a = Psalm 2:7; Hebrews 1:7 = Psalm 104:4; Hebrews 1:8–9 = Psalm 45:6–7; Hebrews 1:10–12 = Psalm 102:25–27; Hebrews 1:13 = Psalm 110:1.

16. L. D. Hurst, in an essay interpreting Hebrews 1 as speaking of a man who was exalted rather than of a divine person who became a man, works hard to make this interpretation fit verse 6. Hurst admits that God is the object of worship "according to all LXX texts of Deut. 32:43" but finds some "help" in the Qumran Cave 4 fragment containing Deuteronomy 32:43 in Hebrew, where, he argues, it would have been possible to misunderstand "him" to refer to Israel rather than to God. Yet Hurst admits this misreading requires one to ignore the whole verse. Hurst concludes, in effect, that the writer of Hebrews misread Deuteronomy 32:43 as speaking of angels worshiping Israel and chose to apply this misreading to the exaltation of Jesus. Appealing to a possible misreading of an isolated Hebrew version of the text in order to avoid the natural meaning of the text is hermeneutically unjustifiable—especially when we have the Greek text that the book of Hebrews is almost certainly quoting. See L. D. Hurst, "The Christology of Hebrews 1 and 2," in *The Glory of Christ in the New Testament: Studies in Christology in Memory of George Bradford Caird*, ed. L. D. Hurst and N. T. Wright (Oxford: Clarendon Press, 1987), 158–59.

17. John R. W. Stott, *The Authentic Jesus* (London: Marshall, Morgan & Scott, 1985), 34; quoted in Murray J. Harris, *3 Crucial Questions About Jesus* (Grand Rapids: Baker, 1994), 74–75.

18. Peter R. Carrell, *Jesus and the Angels: Angelology and the Christology of the Apocalypse of John*, SNTSMS 95 (Cambridge: Cambridge University Press, 1997), 114, 128.

19. Fred O. Francis, "Humility and Angel Worship in Col 2.18," *Studia Theologica* 16 (1962): 109–34; Larry W. Hurtado, *One God, One Lord: Early Christian Doctrine and Ancient Jewish Monotheism* (London: SCM Press, 1988), 28–34; Loren T. Stuckenbruck, "An Angelic Refusal of Worship: The Tradition and Its Function in the Apocalypse of John,"

Society of Biblical Literature Seminar Papers 1994, ed. E. H. Lovering
(Atlanta: Scholars Press, 1994): 679–96; and idem, *Angel Veneration
and Christology: A Study in Early Judaism and in the Christology of
the Apocalypse of John*, WUNT 2.70 (Tübingen: Mohr, 1995), 111–19.
Stuckenbruck suggests that one perceived danger in seeking to participate in angelic worship of God was that the human participant
would become too enamored of angels and thus be tempted to revere
them.

20.   Stuckenbruck, *Angel Veneration and Christology*, 51–204; see his summary on page 201.
21.   Philo, *de Decalogo* 61, 64; in F. H. Colson and G. H. Whitaker, trans.,
Philo, Loeb Classical Library (Cambridge, MA: Harvard University
Press, 1929–1943), 7:37–39.
22.   Stuckenbruck, *Angel Veneration and Christology*, 102.

Chapter 3: What a Friend We Have in Jesus

1.   Timothy Friberg and Barbara Friberg, *Greek-English Lexicon*, s.v. *proseuchomai*, accessed in BibleWorks 5.0.
2.   The Greek word *kurios* appears about 207 times in Luke and Acts;
of these, about 143 refer explicitly or implicitly to Jesus (67 times in
Luke, 76 in Acts). In about 20 instances, *kurios* refers to God as distinguished in the context from Jesus. In part to avoid Jesus being called
"Lord" in a context that implies his identity with the "LORD" Yahweh
or Jehovah of the Old Testament, Jehovah's Witnesses translate *kurios*
237 times in the New Testament as "Jehovah," including Acts 1:24 and
7:60 (on which see below). For a critique, see chapter 13 of this book.
3.   Noted by F. F. Bruce, *The Acts of the Apostles: The Greek Text with
Introduction and Commentary*, 3rd rev. and enlarged ed. (Grand
Rapids: Eerdmans; Leicester, England: Apollos, 1990), 112.
4.   See also Joel B. Green, "Persevering Together in Prayer: The Significance
of Prayer in the Acts of the Apostles," in *Into God's Presence: Prayer
in the New Testament*, ed. Richard N. Longenecker (Grand Rapids:
Eerdmans, 2001), 187–88. Green rightly argues that, in context, Peter's
injunction to Simon Magus to "pray to the Lord" for forgiveness (Acts
8:22) also refers to the Lord Jesus.
5.   H. G. Liddell and Robert Scott's *Greek-English Lexicon* gives as its
first definition of *epikaleō* "*to call upon* a god, *invoke, appeal to*" (ac-

cessed in BibleWorks 5.0). Passive forms of the verb typically are used to say that someone is "called" by a certain name, e.g., Simon was "called" Peter (Acts 10:5, 18, 32; 11:13). The word in appropriate contexts also can mean filing a formal, legal appeal, as when Paul "appealed to Caesar" to have his case reviewed (Acts 25:11, 21, 25; 28:19). Oddly, Greg Stafford equates the use of *epikaleō* in Acts 7:59 with this latter meaning: "Thus, when Jesus became visible, Stephen made an appeal to him even as Paul appealed to Caesar." See Greg Stafford, *Jehovah's Witnesses Defended: An Answer to Scholars and Critics*, 2nd ed. (Huntington Beach, CA: Elihu Books, 2000), 585. The comparison is odd for two reasons. First, Stephen saw Jesus, but Paul did not see Caesar. Second, Stephen was not filing a legal appeal to Jesus but was asking him to receive his spirit. This is an example of choosing the meaning that fits one's theology rather than the meaning that fits the context.

6. Jaroslav Jan Pelikan, *Acts*, Brazos Theological Commentary on the Bible (Grand Rapids: Brazos, 2005), 107; see also Bruce, *Acts of the Apostles*, 212–13.

7. R. T. France, "The Worship of Jesus: A Neglected Factor in Christological Debate?" in *Christ the Lord: Studies in Christology Presented to Donald Guthrie*, ed. Harold H. Rowdon (Leicester, UK; Downers Grove, IL: InterVarsity Press, 1982), 30.

8. Murray J. Harris, *The Second Epistle to the Corinthians: A Commentary on the Greek Text*, NIGTC (Grand Rapids: Eerdmans; Milton Keynes, UK: Paternoster, 2005), 860.

9. Larry W. Hurtado, *Lord Jesus Christ: Devotion to Jesus in Earliest Christianity* (Grand Rapids: Eerdmans, 2003), 140.

10. These examples seem more relevant than texts asking God to act "for your name's sake" (Pss. 25:11; 31:3; 79:9), cited, e.g., in D. A. Carson, *The Gospel According to John* (Leicester, UK: InterVarsity Press; Grand Rapids: Eerdmans, 1991), 498.

11. E.g., F. F. Bruce, *The Gospel of John: Introduction, Exposition, and Notes* (Grand Rapids: Eerdmans, 1983), 301.

12. Most of the critical editions of the Greek New Testament in modern times, including the Westcott/Hort edition, the Nestle-Aland edition, and the United Bible Societies edition, include the word while noting the inferior reading that omits it. The UBS edition gives the reading

with *me* a rank of (B), which means that the editors regarded it as "nearly certain" to be correct. The so-called Majority Text edition places the word in brackets because it is lacking in a majority of manuscripts, most of which are medieval in origin. Thus, the NKJV, like the KJV, omits "me," while virtually all other modern translations (with the exception of the Jehovah's Witnesses' NWT) include it. The word *me* is found in early papyri from the second and third centuries (P⁶⁶ and probably P⁷⁵), the Vaticanus, Sinaiticus, and Washington codices of the fourth and fifth centuries, and many other manuscripts. It is omitted most significantly in the fifth-century Alexandrinus codex as well as in many later manuscripts. For a list of variant readings, see Reuben J. Swanson, ed., *New Testament Greek Manuscripts: John: Variant Readings Arranged in Horizontal Lines Against Codex Vaticanus* (Sheffield: Sheffield Academic Press; Pasadena, CA: William Carey International University Press, 1995), 202. See also the helpful analysis by James Stewart at http://www.forananswer.org/John/Jn14_14.htm.

13. Bruce, for example, who thinks the text originally did not contain the word *me*, agrees that the union of the Father and the Son means that we may address either of them in prayer (Bruce, *Gospel of John*, 301).

14. E.g., Matthew Black, "The Maranatha Invocation and Jude 14, 15 (1 Enoch 1:9)," in *Christ and Spirit in the New Testament*, ed. Barnabas Lindars and Stephen S. Smalley (Cambridge: Cambridge University Press, 1973), 189–96.

15. Joseph A. Fitzmyer, "New Testament *Kyrios* and *Maranatha* and Their Aramaic Background," in *To Advance the Gospel: New Testament Studies*, 2nd ed., Biblical Resource Series (Grand Rapids: Eerdmans; Livonia, MI: Dove Booksellers, 1998), 218–35.

16. Ben Witherington III, *The Many Faces of the Christ: The Christologies of the New Testament and Beyond*, Companions to the New Testament (New York: Crossroad, 1998), 75.

17. France, "Worship of Jesus," 30.

18. Fitzmyer, "New Testament *Kyrios* and *Maranatha*," 228–29; cf. J. L. Wu, "Liturgical Elements," in *Dictionary of Paul and His Letters*, ed. Gerald F. Hawthorne, Ralph P. Martin, and Daniel G. Reid (Downers Grove, IL: InterVarsity Press, 1993), 559–60; and see also Martin Hengel, *Studies in Early Christology* (Edinburgh: T & T Clark, 1995), 237.

19. The Didache is usually dated between about A.D. 90 and 110 (although

it may be even earlier). The book of Revelation is traditionally dated in the 90s, but a strong case can and has been made for dating it in the mid to late 60s.

Chapter 4: Sing to the Lord

1. The Trinitarian pattern is noted by R. T. France, "The Worship of Jesus: A Neglected Factor in Christological Debate?" in *Christ the Lord: Studies in Christology Presented to Donald Guthrie*, ed. Harold H. Rowdon (Leicester, UK; Downers Grove, IL: InterVarsity Press, 1982), 30. For a review of over sixty such "Trinitarian" passages in the New Testament, see Robert M. Bowman Jr., *Why You Should Believe in the Trinity* (Grand Rapids: Baker, 1989), 127–31.

2. This assumes that Ephesians was written by Paul about A.D. 60. On the authorship and date of Ephesians, see Harold W. Hoehner, introduction to *Ephesians: An Exegetical Commentary* (Grand Rapids: Baker, 2003).

3. James D. G. Dunn, "How Controversial Was Paul's Christology?" in *From Jesus to John: Essays on Jesus and New Testament Christology in Honour of Marinus de Jonge*, ed. Martinus C. De Boer, JSNTSup 84 (Sheffield: JSOT Press, 1993), 164.

4. G. K. Beale, *The Book of Revelation: A Commentary on the Greek Text*, NIGTC (Grand Rapids: Eerdmans; Milton Keynes, UK: Paternoster, 1999), 358. In the LXX there is one reference that uses the same expression *ōdēn kainēn* (Ps. 144:9 [143:9 LXX]); other psalms use synonymous expressions.

5. We do not claim that the song of Revelation 5:9–10 was derived from early Christian worship. It seems rather to have been the author's composition (deriving from his visionary experience). See David R. Carnegie, "Worthy Is the Lamb: The Hymns in Revelation," in *Christ the Lord: Studies in Christology Presented to Donald Guthrie*, ed. Harold H. Rowdon (Leicester, UK; Downers Grove, IL: InterVarsity Press, 1982), 243–47.

6. Martin Hengel, *Studies in Early Christology* (Edinburgh: T & T Clark, 1995), 277–78.

7. See Colin Brown, "Ernst Lohmeyer's *Kyrios Jesus*," in *Where Christology Began: Essays on Philippians 2*, ed. Ralph P. Martin and Brian J. Dodd (Louisville: Westminster John Knox, 1998), 7–9. Although Lohmeyer

viewed the line "death on a cross" as a Pauline insertion, we see no need to resort to that explanation, since hymns and psalms could have their arrangement "disrupted" for effect. In this and other respects, most scholars have not followed various aspects of Lohmeyer's interpretation of Philippians 2 (cf. Brown, "Ernst Lohmeyer's *Kyrios Jesus*," 10–12, 18).

8. It is difficult to say whether Pliny would have preferred "as to a God" or "as to a god" as an English rendering of his words *quasi deo*. The rendering "as to God" may be too specific, whereas "as to a god" may imply that Pliny thought Christians viewed Christ as a lesser deity. Either way, he testifies to the historical fact that Christians extended religious honors to Christ by singing hymns to him as a divine figure.

9. See A. N. Sherwin-White, *The Letters of Pliny: A Historical and Social Commentary*, 3rd ed. (Oxford: Clarendon, 1985), 691–710; Ralph P. Martin, *Carmen Christi: Philippians ii. 5–11 in recent interpretation and in the setting of early Christian Worship* (London: Cambridge University Press, 1967), 1–9; and Margaret Daly-Denton, "Singing Hymns to Christ as to a God (cf. Pliny *Ep.* X, 96)," in *The Jewish Roots of Christological Monotheism*, ed. Carey C. Newman, James R. Davila, and Gladys S. Lewis, Supplements to the *JSJ* 63 (Leiden: Brill, 1999), 277–92 (papers from the St. Andrews Conference on the Historical Origins of the Worship of Jesus).

10. Larry W. Hurtado, *Lord Jesus Christ: Devotion to Jesus in Earliest Christianity* (Grand Rapids: Eerdmans, 2003), 606–7, emphasis in original.

11. Eusebius, *Ecclesiastical History* 5.28.5, as quoted in Hengel, *Studies in Early Christology*, 247, emphasis in Hengel.

12. Quoted in Hengel, *Studies in Early Christology*, 244.

13. Ibid., 290.

Chapter 5: The Ultimate Reverence Package

1. Craig S. Keener, *The Gospel of John: A Commentary* (Peabody, MA: Hendrickson, 2003), 2:931.

2. We can see no justification for the NRSV rendering here, "in Christ Jesus you are all children of God through faith," which dissociates faith from Christ Jesus as its object. The prepositional phrase *en Christō ʾIēsou* follows immediately after the phrase *dia tēs pisteōs*.

Although the NRSV rendering is grammatically possible, it is not the most natural or plausible reading of the text.

3. E.g., John H. Elliott, *1 Peter: A New Translation with Introduction and Commentary*, AB 37B (New York: Doubleday, 2000), 624–25. For a detailed comparison of the two passages, see chapter 13.

4. These statements supplement rather than contradict Matthew 28:19, which speaks of baptizing new disciples "in the name of the Father and of the Son and of the Holy Spirit." Neither Matthew 28:19 nor the passages in Acts are specifying the words to say in a baptismal ceremony; the New Testament, in fact, contains no record of words spoken at a baptismal ceremony. In Matthew, just as much as in Acts, the focus of disciple making is commitment to Jesus Christ. Hence, in Matthew 28:18–20 those who believe are to recognize his universal authority (v. 18), become Jesus' disciples (v. 19a), be baptized in the Son's name as well as the Father's and the Holy Spirit's (v. 19b), observe all that Jesus taught (v. 20a), and live in the awareness of his presence (v. 20b).

5. See Larry W. Hurtado, *Lord Jesus Christ: Devotion to Jesus in Earliest Christianity* (Grand Rapids: Eerdmans, 2003), 146.

6. The one text that might be cited as an exception is Daniel 7:27, where the proper translation is disputed. Some versions read "serve and obey *him*" (NASB, NKJV, NIV), and others read "serve and obey *them*" (NRSV, ESV, NLT), that is, the "saints of the Most High" (ESV). The dispute arises from the Hebrew use of "serve and obey" with no pronoun following; thus the translators supply a pronoun to make for more idiomatic English. The Hebrew text refers earlier in the sentence, however, to "his kingdom" (*malkûtēʰ*), and both Greek versions of Daniel have "him" (*autō*), not "them," at the end of the verse. In the immediate context the antecedent for "his" and "him" would be "the Most High." Thus, Daniel 7:27 confirms that "service" (*pelach*) properly goes to God alone.

7. *Pelach* is translated "fear" (*phoboumetha*) in Daniel 3:17 LXX (but it is translated with "serve," *latreuō*, in Theodotion); in turn *latreuō* is used to translate "fear" (*dāhāl*) in Daniel 6:26 (6:27 in Greek). *Pelach* is translated with *douloō* in Theodotion at both Daniel 7:14 and 7:27; in the LXX it is translated with *latreuō* in Daniel 7:14 but with *hupotassō* in 7:27.

8. It is possible that Revelation 22:3 also uses *latreuō* with reference to Jesus: "The throne of God and of the Lamb will be in it, and his servants will worship [*latreuō*] him; they will see his face, and his name will be on their foreheads" (22:3–4). The term "servants" (*douloi*) in Revelation nearly always refers to servants of God (7:3; 10:7; 11:18; 15:3; 19:2, 5), including in the immediate context (22:6); on the other hand, 1:1 is ambiguous and 2:20 clearly refers to servants of Christ. Even if the service is here directed specifically to "God" as distinct from "the Lamb," it is doubtful that such a distinction is meant to be pressed, since God and the Lamb occupy the same throne.

9. Craig Keener, *A Commentary on the Gospel of Matthew* (Grand Rapids: Eerdmans, 1999), 330. Keener cites Genesis 22:2–12; Deuteronomy 13:6; 33:9; 2 Maccabees 7:22–23, additional ancient Jewish sources, and the Latin Stoic author Epictetus. He points out that the closest analogue in ancient sources to Jesus' statements, other than those about love for the Lord in the Old Testament, were oaths of allegiance to the Roman emperors and the empire.

10. Keener, *Gospel of John*, 2:974.

Chapter 6: Beyond Resemblance

1. John Piper, *Seeing and Savoring Jesus Christ* (Wheaton, IL: Crossway, 2004), 123.

2. Thomas C. Oden, *The Living God: Systematic Theology* (1987; reprint, Peabody, MA: Hendrickson, 1998), 1:35.

3. John Nolland, *The Gospel of Matthew: A Commentary on the Greek Text*, NIGTC (Grand Rapids: Eerdmans; Bletchley, UK: Paternoster, 2005), 790. Matthew 19:17 reports Jesus' comment as follows: "The good is one" or possibly "One is the good" (*heis estin ho agathos*). Mark 10:18 and Luke 18:19 read, "No one is good except one: God" (*oudeis agathos ei mē heis ho theos*). Mark and Luke also report Jesus asking, "Why do you call me good?" Jesus was not denying being good; he was pointing out that human beings are not good and therefore, since the young man who approached Jesus regarded him as a merely human "teacher," he should not have addressed him flatteringly as "good teacher" (Mark 10:17; Luke 18:18). If anything, Jesus' statement in context implies that Jesus is more than human, since Jesus goes on to summon the young man to *follow him* in order to be complete

(Matt. 19:18–21; Mark 10:19–21; Luke 18:20–22). Matthew's word-ing ("Why are you asking me about the good?") does not change the meaning; rather, on the assumption that Matthew's account is based on Mark, it avoids the possible misunderstanding that Jesus was de-nying being good. (All translations in this note are ours.) See further Simon J. Gathercole's recent study *The Preexistent Son: Recovering the Christologies of Matthew, Mark, and Luke* (Grand Rapids: Eerdmans, 2006), 73–74. On the question of whether Matthew has reworded Mark's version of Jesus' statement, see the cautious analysis of Peter M. Head, *Christology and the Synoptic Problem*, SNTSMS 94 (Cambridge: Cambridge University Press, 1997), 49–65. While in the end defend-ing Markan priority, Head does not think a definite case can be made for that position from this passage.

4. Wayne Grudem distinguishes between those attributes "that are *more shared* with us" (commonly called communicable) and those "that are *less shared* by us" (commonly called incommunicable). See Wayne Grudem, *Systematic Theology: An Introduction to Biblical Doctrine* (Leicester, UK: InterVarsity Press; Grand Rapids: Zondervan, 1994, 2000), 257. He favors using the traditional classification while keep-ing in mind that the two categories overlap.

5. Oden, *The Living God*, 1:36.

6. Johannes Louw and Eugene Nida, *Greek-English Lexicon of the New Testament: Based on Semantic Domains, Lexicon,* in BibleWorks 5.0. The word is simply the Greek word for God (*theos*) with an ending indicating nature or state (*-tēs*).

7. Admittedly, words ending in *-hood* also could be used to refer to all people collectively sharing the specified state, status, or nature. *Brotherhood,* for example, usually refers to the status of being broth-ers that is shared by a common group of people. The same was some-times true of the archaic suffix *-head,* which may explain why *Godhead* came to be understood to refer to the three persons of the Trinity col-lectively. But this is not what it meant in the KJV of Colossians 2:9.

8. We are not here addressing the question of what sort of false teach-ing, if any, Paul may have been combating in his epistle to the church in Colossae. The older view that Paul was opposing a sort of proto-Gnosticism has been widely abandoned in recent years. In any case, Paul was criticizing religious beliefs that sought divine power or

help from any source other than Jesus Christ. The pacesetting book on the subject is Clinton E. Arnold, *The Colossian Syncretism: The Interface Between Christianity and Folk Belief at Colossae*, WUNT 2.77 (Tübingen: Mohr, 1995; reprint, Grand Rapids: Baker, 1996).

9. Grammatically, the expression *pan to plērōma* ("all the fullness") can be construed as either nominative or accusative (the forms are identical). If *pan to plērōma* is accusative, then the subject is unstated. This reading is more or less required if we assume that the following clause ("and through him to reconcile all things," v. 20a) implies that the subject of the verb *eudokēsan* is the Father (as in the NASB). The subject of "reconcile" just two verses later, however, is Christ (v. 22; so also Eph. 2:16). If nominative, then "all the fullness" is the subject of *eudokēsan* ("was pleased"). This is how the NRSV construes the text ("For in him all the fullness of God was pleased to dwell"; see also the NASB marginal reading). The close parallel with Colossians 2:9, where the same expression *pan to plērōma* is the subject, supports this view, as does the fact that (at least in biblical Greek) whenever *eudokeō* is followed by an infinitive (such as *katoikēsai*) both have the same subject (Judg. 19:10, 25; 20:13; Pss. 40:13 [39:14 LXX]; 68:16 [67:17 LXX]; 1 Macc. 6:23; 14:41, 46–47; Luke 12:32; Rom. 15:26; 1 Cor. 1:21; 2 Cor. 5:8; Gal. 1:15; 1 Thess. 2:8; 3:1). Paul's meaning therefore seems to be that "all the fullness" of God chose to dwell in the incarnate Son. On this question, see further Murray J. Harris, *Colossians and Philemon*, EGGNT (Grand Rapids: Eerdmans, 1991), 49–50; and R. McL. Wilson, *A Critical and Exegetical Commentary on Colossians and Philemon*, ICC (London and New York: T & T Clark, 2005), 151–52, both of whom reach the conclusion affirmed here.

10. Harris, *Colossians and Philemon*, 99.

11. Noted briefly by Larry W. Hurtado, *Lord Jesus Christ: Devotion to Jesus in Earliest Christianity* (Grand Rapids: Eerdmans, 2003), 506; citing Christian Stettler, *Der Kolosserhymnus* (Tübingen: Mohr Siebeck, 2000), 252–59.

12. E.g., Greg Stafford, *Jehovah's Witnesses Defended: An Answer to Scholars and Critics*, 2nd ed. (Huntington Beach, CA: Elihu Books, 2000), 160.

13. Ibid., 159–60.

14. Colossians 2:9 indicates that God's fullness continues to dwell in the Son "bodily" after his resurrection and exaltation.

15. Wilson, *Colossians and Philemon*, 199.

16. For a thorough biblical critique of the belief that Jesus is the Father, see Gregory A. Boyd, *Oneness Pentecostals and the Trinity* (Grand Rapids: Baker, 1992).

17. On the meaning of *apaugasma*, see Paul Ellingworth, *The Epistle to the Hebrews: A Commentary on the Greek Text*, NIGTC (Grand Rapids: Eerdmans; Carlisle: Paternoster, 1993), 98–99; and Craig R. Koester, *Hebrews: A New Translation with Introduction and Commentary*, AB 36 (New York: Doubleday, 2001), 179–80. Both commentators agree that either meaning is possible.

18. David A. deSilva, *Perseverance in Gratitude: A Socio-Rhetorical Commentary on the Epistle "to the Hebrews"* (Grand Rapids: Eerdmans, 2000), 89.

Chapter 7: Jesus Existed Before He Was Born!

1. James D. G. Dunn, *Christology in the Making: A New Testament Inquiry into the Origins of the Doctrine of the Incarnation*, 2nd ed. (Grand Rapids: Eerdmans, 1996), 259 (emphasis Dunn's).

2. Ibid., 263–67.

3. Karl-Josef Kuschel, *Born Before All Time? The Dispute over Christ's Origin* (New York: Crossroad, 1992), 366.

4. James D. G. Dunn, "Christ, Adam, and Preexistence," in *Where Christology Began: Essays on Philippians 2*, ed. Ralph P. Martin and Brian J. Dodd (Louisville, KY: Westminster John Knox, 1998), 78–79.

5. Lincoln D. Hurst, "Christ, Adam, and Preexistence Revisited," in *Where Christology Began*, 84, emphasis in original.

6. Ibid., 84; citing G. B. Caird, *Paul's Letters from Prison* (Oxford: Oxford University Press, 1976), 121.

7. N. T. Wright, "*Harpagmos* and the Meaning of Philippians 2:5–11," *JTS* 37 (1986): 321–52 (348). The article was later reprinted in N. T. Wright's *The Climax of the Covenant: Christ and the Law in Pauline Theology* (Edinburgh: T & T Clark, 1991), 62–90.

8. See Dave Steenburg, "The Case Against the Synonymity of *morphē* and *eikōn*," *JSNT* 34 (1988): 77–86; Gerald F. Hawthorne, "In the Form of God and Equal with God (Philippians 2:6)," in *Where Christology Began*, 96–110; and Dennis W. Jowers, "The Meaning of *Morphē* in Philippians 2:6–7," *JETS* 49 (2006): 739–66.

9. This interpretation does not presuppose that the word "form" (*morphē*) is synonymous with "glory" (*doxa*). Rather, it presupposes the Jewish religious motif that God's "form" or external appearance as manifested in theophanies is also described as his "glory." In addition to the sources already cited, see Markus Bockmuehl, "'The Form of God' (Phil. 2.6): Variations on a Theme of Jewish Mysticism," *JTS* NS 48 (1997): 1–23. Jowers ("Meaning of *Morphē*") argues strongly that in this context *morphē* is synonymous with "essence" (*ousia*). Whether or not one agrees with this lexical conclusion, that Christ possessed God's form certainly entails or implies that he was, in essence, deity.

10. Some additional important treatments of Philippians 2:6–11 include the following: Ralph P. Martin, *A Hymn of Christ: Philippians ii.5–11 in Recent Interpretation and in the Setting of Early Christian Worship*, 3rd ed. (Downers Grove, IL: InterVarsity Press, 1997); C. F. D. Moule, "Further Reflexions on Philippians 2:5–11," in *Apostolic History and the Gospel: Biblical and Historical Essays Presented to F. F. Bruce on His 60th Birthday*, ed. W. Ward Gasque and Ralph P. Martin (Exeter: Paternoster Press, 1970), 264–76; Roy W. Hoover, "The HARPAGMOS Enigma: A Philological Solution," *Harvard Theological Review* 64 (1971): 95–119; Wright, "*Harpagmos* and the Meaning of Philippians 2:5–11"; Martin and Dodd, eds., *Where Christology Began*; Daniel B. Wallace, *Greek Grammar Beyond the Basics: An Exegetical Syntax of the New Testament* (Grand Rapids: Zondervan, 1996), 634–35; Denny Burk, "On the Articular Infinitive in Philippians 2:6: A Grammatical Note with Christological Implications," *TynB* 55 (2004): 253–74; Joseph H. Hellerman, *Reconstructing Honor in Roman Philippi*: Carmen Christi *as* Cursus Pudorum (Cambridge; New York: Cambridge University Press, 2005); and Gordon D. Fee, *Pauline Christology: An Exegetical-Theological Study* (Peabody, MA: Hendrickson, 2007), 372–401.

11. We proceed in this order on the assumption, broadly accepted by most biblical scholars, that at least some sayings of Jesus in the Synoptics derive from Jesus himself, that Paul's writings are basically the earliest of the New Testament writings, and that John's writings are among the latest of those writings. We, of course, view all of the New Testament writings as authoritative, all of the Synoptic sayings of Jesus as authentic, and the Gospel of John as a reliable source of information about Jesus. Still, we proceed in this order so as to show that, while

the later New Testament writings may have been more explicit on the point, the earlier sources also reflect a belief in the preexistence of Christ.

12. Emphasis in biblical quotations is ours. See Simon J. Gathercole's similar list in *The Preexistent Son: Recovering the Christologies of Matthew, Mark, and Luke* (Grand Rapids: Eerdmans, 2006), 84. Gathercole includes two utterances by demons directed to Jesus (Matt. 8:29; Mark 1:24) and two other sayings of Jesus not included here (Matt. 5:17; 10:35).

13. Douglas McCready, *He Came Down from Heaven: The Preexistence of Christ and the Christian Faith* (Downers Grove, IL: InterVarsity Press; Leicester, UK: Apollos, 2005), 117.

14. Even Gathercole, *Preexistent Son*, 110, concedes this claim.

15. Ibid., 113–47.

16. A recent study denying any implication of preexistence in these sayings is Aquila H. I. Lee, *From Messiah to Preexistent Son: Jesus' Self-Consciousness and Early Christian Exegesis of Messianic Psalms*, WUNT 2.192 (Tübingen: Mohr Siebeck, 2005), 182–201. Lee concludes "that in these sayings the emphasis falls on his God-given *mission* rather than on his transcendental *origin*" (199). But it is possible to agree with this assessment of the emphasis in Jesus' sayings while still recognizing in them the clear implication of preexistence.

17. Dunn, *Christology in the Making*, 47, emphasis in original; similarly Kuschel, *Born Before All Time?* 311–12.

18. Dunn, *Christology in the Making*, 48.

19. On the Old Testament background to Mark 1:9–11, see also Lee, *From Messiah to Preexistent Son*, 166–78.

20. In addition, Luke reports the apostle Paul explicitly quoting Psalm 2:7 in reference to Jesus' resurrection (Acts 13:33), without implying that Jesus became the Son only at his resurrection. The New Testament elsewhere consistently quotes Psalm 2:7 with reference to Jesus' resurrection (see also Heb. 1:5; 5:5), calling into question the claim that the Father's words at Jesus' baptism are an allusion to Psalm 2:7.

21. Dunn, *Christology in the Making*, 38–42. Gathercole observes with regard to the first point that Paul uses *exapostellō* ("send *forth*" or "send *out*") rather than the usual *apostellō* ("send"), which gives "a stronger impression" that the Son was sent from heaven (Gathercole, *Preexistent Son*, 29).

22. The clause "born of a woman" (*genomenon ek gunaikos*) is similar in wording and import to "born of the seed of David" (*genomenou ek spermatos Dauid*, Rom. 1:3) and "born in human likeness" (*en homoiōmati anthrōpōn genomenos*, Phil. 2:7). In both of those texts the human birth of Jesus appears to be contrasted with his true divine nature. See Larry W. Hurtado, *Lord Jesus Christ: Devotion to Jesus in Earliest Christianity* (Grand Rapids: Eerdmans, 2003), 324n. 170.

23. Often overlooked, but noted, for example, by Gathercole, *Preexistent Son*, 29.

24. Kuschel, *Born Before All Time?* 272–77.

25. Dunn, *Christology in the Making*, 39. The passage in question is Wisdom 9, in which Solomon prays that God will "send" (*exaposteilon*) wisdom (v. 10). "Who has learned your counsel, unless you have given wisdom and sent your holy spirit from on high?" (v. 17). The parallel of sending wisdom and the Spirit and Paul's use of *exaposteilen* (only in Gal. 4:4, 6) is striking, although arguably not enough to establish direct dependence. As Lee points out, the main difference is that in Wisdom 9 the sending of God's wisdom is a form of inspiration whereas in Galatians 4 the sending of God's Son refers to incarnation (Lee, *From Messiah to Preexistent Son*, 303).

26. Although Paul does not speak in Romans 8 of God "sending" the Holy Spirit (as in Gal. 4:6), he does go on in the rest of the chapter to speak of the Holy Spirit's work following up on the redemptive accomplishment of the Son (Rom. 8:4–6, 9–11, 13–16, 26–27).

27. John Murray, *The Epistle to the Romans: The English Text with Introduction, Notes, and Commentary*, NICNT (Grand Rapids: Eerdmans, 1959, 1965), 1:279.

28. Biblical scholars are widely agreed that Romans 8:3 at least implies a belief in the Son's preexistence; cf. McCready, *He Came Down from Heaven*, 95–97.

29. Ibid., 154.

30. In English we would express this idiomatically as "going back," as some translations read in John 13:3 (NASB; cf. "returning," NIV) and 16:28 (NIV). The idea of returning is there, even if we do not translate using *back*.

Chapter 8: Jesus Has Always Been There

1.   Simon J. Gathercole, *The Preexistent Son: Recovering the Christologies of Matthew, Mark, and Luke* (Grand Rapids: Eerdmans, 2006), 214 (original in italics).

2.   In Luke, Jesus says the same thing in a different context and attributes the saying to "the Wisdom of God" (Luke 11:49). This parallel has led some interpreters to understand Matthew 23 to be identifying Jesus as Wisdom. Wisdom motifs applied to Jesus in Matthew, however, are allusive at best. The one saying of Jesus in Matthew potentially identifying himself as Wisdom is his comment, "Yet wisdom is vindicated by her deeds" (Matt. 11:19b; see also Luke 7:35), but this saying in context appears to refer to the wisdom displayed by both John the Baptist and Jesus in their different ministries (Matt. 11:18–19a; Luke 7:33–34). Some caution is, therefore, in order in characterizing Matthew's presentation of Jesus as a "wisdom Christology." In Matthew, most, if not all, of the possible allusions to Christ as wisdom are likely the result of Matthew's presenting Jesus as "God with us" (Matt. 1:23 ESV). In Old Testament wisdom literature the personification of wisdom is a literary device for speaking of God himself acting in his wisdom among his people. Jesus' lament, for example, that the city of Jerusalem refused his help and would soon be abandoned to face judgment (Matt. 23:37–38) may be compared to Wisdom's lament that the city refused to listen to her and would be abandoned to its calamity (Prov. 1:20–33). This parallel has been noted, for example, by Ben Witherington III, *Matthew*, Smith & Helwys Bible Commentary (Macon, GA: Smith & Helwys, 2006), 19:434 (misprinted as Prov. 4:20–33). But wisdom in Proverbs 1 is a literary personification of God himself in his wisdom. Hence, "wisdom" offers to "pour out" her "spirit" on the repentant (v. 23 NASB; cf. Ezek. 39:29; Joel 2:28), laments that she called to them but they refused to answer (v. 24; cf. Isa. 65:12; 66:4; Jer. 7:13), and warns that when judgment comes they will call on her for help but she will not answer them (v. 28; cf. Jer. 11:11; Ezek. 8:18). In short, any "wisdom Christology" in Matthew is at most one aspect of its *divine* Christology.

3.   See Craig Keener, *A Commentary on the Gospel of Matthew* (Grand Rapids: Eerdmans, 1999), 558; and John Nolland, *The Gospel of Matthew: A Commentary on the Greek Text*, NIGTC (Grand Rapids:

Eerdmans; Bletchley, UK: Paternoster, 2005), 950–51, both of whom also cite an array of extracanonical Jewish sources demonstrating the currency of this metaphor in the New Testament period.

4. See further Gathercole, *Preexistent Son*, 210–21, for a detailed examination of the passage and recent views of its significance.

5. Emphasis in quote is ours. See further Anthony C. Thiselton, *First Epistle to the Corinthians: A Commentary on the Greek Text*, NIGTC (Grand Rapids: Eerdmans; Carlisle, UK: Paternoster, 2000), 726–30. On the significance of this passage for the preexistence of Christ, see also Gordon D. Fee, *Pauline Christology: An Exegetical-Theological Study* (Peabody, MA: Hendrickson, 2007), 94–98.

6. The reading "Christ" (*christon*) has the earliest, most diverse, and most numerous manuscript support (starting with P[46], dated about A.D. 200) and is also better attested by early translations into other languages (such as Coptic and Latin) and in other Christian writings dating from as early as the second century. It is followed by the KJV, NKJV, NLT, and NRSV, among others. The reading "Lord" (*kurion*) does have the support of two major codices from the fourth century (the Sinaiticus and Vaticanus), but the rest of its external support is comparatively quite weak. It is followed (surprisingly) most notably by the NIV and NASB. See further Thiselton, *First Epistle to the Corinthians*, 740; and especially Carroll D. Osburn, "The Text of 1 Corinthians 10:9," in *New Testament Textual Criticism: Its Significance for Exegesis: Essays in Honour of Bruce M. Metzger*, ed. Eldon Jay Epp and Gordon D. Fee (Oxford: Clarendon Press, 1981), 1–12.

7. K. L. McKay, "'I Am' in John's Gospel," *ExpTim* 107 (1996): 302–3.

8. This is our literal translation of the Greek. The Hebrew text has "you are God"; the Greek translation construed the Hebrew word *ʾēl* to mean "not" and put it with the next sentence. Both versions express, of course, that God (to whom the psalmist is speaking) is everlasting or eternal in his existence.

9. McKay has argued that the grammatical structure of John 8:58 employs a usage of the Greek present tense that he calls "extension from past" (K. L. McKay, *A New Syntax of the Verb in New Testament Greek: An Aspectual Approach* [New York: Peter Lang, 1994], 41–42). This use of the present is better known as the present of past action still in progress. On McKay's view, John 8:58 states only that Jesus has

been in existence since some time prior to Abraham's birth. Other grammarians disagree that the present-tense verb *eimi* ("is") in John 8:58 fits this category of usage; e.g., A. T. Robertson, *A Grammar of the Greek New Testament in the Light of Historical Research*, rev. ed. (Nashville: Broadman Press, 1931), 879; and Daniel B. Wallace, *Greek Grammar Beyond the Basics: An Exegetical Syntax of the New Testament* (Grand Rapids: Zondervan, 1996), 531n. 48. The question is complicated because grammarians have defined this usage in varying ways, with broader definitions more likely to encompass John 8:58 (cf. Wallace's comments in *Greek Grammar Beyond the Basics*, 519). However one classifies the usage of the present tense in John 8:58, the meaning goes beyond temporal antecedence, as the parallel with Psalm 89:2 (LXX) illustrates. See further Robert M. Bowman Jr., *Jehovah's Witnesses, Jesus Christ, and the Gospel of John* (Grand Rapids: Baker, 1989), 103–16. A debate on the exegesis and translation of the verse took place between Bowman and Jason BeDuhn (who is not a Jehovah's Witness) in 2004–2005 on the Evangelical and JW Theologies discussion list and is archived in its Files section (http://groups.yahoo.com/group/evangelicals_and_jws/files/).

10. Those favoring "Lord" as original include Richard Bauckham, *Jude and the Relatives of Jesus in the Early Church* (Edinburgh: T & T Clark, 1990), 307–12; Charles Landon, *A Text-Critical Study of the Epistle of Jude*, JSNTSup 135 (Sheffield: Sheffield Academic Press, 1996), 70–75; and Thomas Schreiner, *1, 2 Peter, Jude*, NAC (Nashville: Broadman & Holman, 2003), 37:443–45. Those favoring "Jesus" as original include Carroll D. Osburn, "The Text of Jude 5," *Bib* 62 (1981): 107–15; Jarl Fossum, "Kyrios Jesus as the Angel of the Lord in Jude 5–7," *NTS* 33 (1987): 226–43; Philipp Bartholomä, "Did Jesus Save the People Out of Egypt?—A Re-Examination of a Textual Problem in Jude 5," Center for the Study of New Testament Manuscripts (2006), online http://www.csntm.org/essays/PaperJude5.pdf; and Gathercole, *Pre-existent Son*, 36–41.

11. Not the earliest extant reading, though, which is *theos christos* ("God Christ"), attested in a papyrus dating from the third or fourth century (P⁷²). This is so far the only ancient manuscript containing this reading, which is why no one argues that it is the original reading. If

it were, of course, it would mean that Jude was explicitly affirming the preexistence of Christ as God!

12. According to a note written in the margin of a tenth-century Greek manuscript (number 1739), Origen quoted Jude 5 with the name "Jesus." This information may be taken into consideration only with due caution.

13. Bruce M. Metzger, *A Textual Commentary on the Greek New Testament*, 2nd ed. (Stuttgart: United Bible Societies, 1994), 657.

14. Douglas McCready, *He Came Down from Heaven: The Preexistence of Christ and the Christian Faith* (Downers Grove, IL: InterVarsity Press; Leicester, UK: Apollos, 2005), 84.

15. Emphasis in biblical quotation is ours. The Greek preposition *pro*, "before," occasionally expresses physical location ("in front of" doors or gates, Acts 12:6, 14; James 5:9) or priority of importance in the unqualified idiom "above all" (*pro pantōn*, James 5:12; 1 Peter 4:8). Everywhere else in the NT, including eleven other occurrences in Paul (Rom. 16:7; 1 Cor. 2:7; 4:5; 2 Cor. 12:2; Gal. 1:17; 2:12; 3:23; Eph. 1:4; 2 Tim. 1:9; 4:21; Titus 1:2), the word expresses temporal priority. There is, therefore, little doubt that such is its meaning in Colossians 1:17.

16. The word translated "worlds" in Hebrews 1:2 is *aiōnas*, "ages," and thus refers to the whole order of history, the world in all of its successive ages.

17. Hebrews also speaks of Christ as eternally preexistent when it speaks of Melchizedek as a type: "Without father, without mother, without genealogy, *having neither beginning of days nor end of life*, but resembling the Son of God, he remains a priest forever" (7:3, emphasis added). The author's argument treats the silence of the Genesis narrative as to Melchizedek's parentage, genealogical roots, birth, and death (cf. Gen. 14:18) as typologically representing the Son of God, who literally had no "beginning of days" and will have no "end of life." This understanding of Hebrews 7:3 fits with the teaching of the rest of the book (Heb. 1:2, 10–12; 13:8). See Jerome H. Neyrey, *Render to God: New Testament Understandings of the Divine* (Minneapolis: Fortress Press, 2004), 228–42.

Chapter 9: Jesus: The Right Stuff

1. We will discuss in part 4 (when we examine the *deeds* of God that Jesus does) just what role the Son played in the creation of the world.

2.   Murray J. Harris, *Colossians and Philemon*, EGGNT (Grand Rapids: Eerdmans, 1991), 44.

3.   "Further Enrichment of Understanding," *Watchtower*, October 15, 1950, 396.

4.   Jehovah's Witnesses typically argue that because the word *all* (e.g., 2 Tim. 1:15) does not necessarily mean "all without exception" and in other places can be glossed with the word "other" (e.g., Luke 21:29), adding *other* in Colossians 1:16–17 is justifiable. See, e.g., Rolf Furuli, *The Role of Theology and Bias in Bible Translation: With a Special Look at the* New World Translation *of Jehovah's Witnesses* (Huntington Beach, CA: Elihu Books, 1999), 253–54. The neuter plural *ta panta* ("all things"), however, means the totality or entirety, and in context refers to the whole of creation (Paul emphasizes the point by including created beings in heaven and on earth, visible and invisible, and so on). In Jewish usage in the context of creation, *ta panta* clearly referred to creation in its entirety (Gen. 1:31; Neh. 9:6; Job 8:3; Eccl. 3:11; 11:5; Jer. 10:16; 51:19 [28:19 LXX]; 3 Macc. 2:3; Wisdom 1:14; 9:1; Sirach 18:1; 23:20; Rom. 11:36; 1 Cor. 8:6; Eph. 3:9; Heb. 2:10; Rev. 4:11; cf. also *panta* without the article, Isa. 44:24; Sirach 43:33). When this expression *all things* is used in a cosmic context, it "belongs to the standard rhetoric of Jewish monotheism, in which it constantly refers, quite naturally, to the whole of the created reality from which God is absolutely distinguished as its Creator and Ruler" (Richard Bauckham, *God Crucified: Monotheism and Christology in the New Testament* [Grand Rapids: Eerdmans, 1999], 32). When Jehovah's Witnesses bring up texts using the words *ta panta* outside the context of creation, they are totally missing the point. Later, Furuli admits that it might have been better had the NWT omitted *other*, asserting that it would still have been clear from verse 15 that Christ was a created being (ibid., 261). Such a claim assumes that the expression "firstborn of all creation" *unambiguously* means that the Son was the first created being, which is certainly not the case.

5.   This text in Greek (Ps. 88:28 LXX) clearly stands behind Revelation 1:5 ("the firstborn of the dead, and the ruler of the kings of the earth"), proving that it played an important role in the early church's using the term "firstborn" in reference to Jesus Christ.

6.   In other contexts, God refers to Israel as his "firstborn" (Exod. 4:22)

or to Ephraim, one of the tribes of Israel, as his "firstborn" (Jer. 31:9). The latter passage recalls the narrative in Genesis in which Joseph's father, Israel, bestows the blessing belonging to the firstborn on Joseph's younger son, Ephraim (Gen. 48:8–20).

7. For the correlation of the description "heir of all things" in Hebrews 1:2 with the title "the firstborn" in 1:6, see the table on page 192.

8. The Bible rarely uses a partitive genitive after *firstborn*, and when it does, *firstborn* is always generic (referring to any person or animal fitting the description) and the genitive noun is a plural form modified by a possessive noun or pronoun (Exod. 13:15d; 34:20; Num. 3:40; Deut. 15:19c). In Colossians 1:15, "creation" is a singular noun (though it may be construed as a collective singular) and is not modified by a possessive noun or pronoun, and of course "firstborn" refers to only one person.

9. The noun form, *qinyan*, which means "acquisition" or "possession," occurs once, speaking of wisdom as something acquired (Prov. 4:7b). Proverbs 20:14 uses the word *qanah* to mean "buyer" in a mundane context.

10. The Septuagint also rendered the word *qanah* as "who created" (*hos ektisen*) in Genesis 14:19, 22 ("maker," NRSV; "Creator," NIV, NASB marg.), although several English versions have "possessor" instead (NASB, NKJV, ESV). In context, Abram is paying a tithe to Melchizedek, recognizing that everything Abram has really belongs to God, which suggests that *possessor* or *owner* may be closer to the intended connotation. In Genesis 4:1, Eve says that she "got" (*qanah*) her son Cain with God's help. Here translations vary considerably ("gotten," KJV, NASB, ESV; "acquired," NKJV; "brought forth," NIV; "produced," NRSV). Perhaps Eve's usage is similar to our English idiom "had" for giving birth to a child: Eve "had" Cain with God's help. In any case, these statements appear in a different book, written by a different author, living in a different century, as part of a different genre, and addressing a different topic than Proverbs 8:22. We should put more stock in how the book of Proverbs elsewhere uses *qanah* in reference to wisdom than in these isolated and contextually irrelevant occurrences.

11. The same ambiguity appears in translations of verse 23: "From everlasting I was established" (NASB); "Ages ago I was set up" (NRSV).

12. Note Proverbs 3:19–20 and the many parallels between Proverbs 3:13–26 and Proverbs 8:10–35.

13. Michael J. Svigel, "Christ as *Archē* in Revelation 3:14," *BSac* (2004): 215–31.

14. See the discussions of Revelation 3:14 in George Eldon Ladd, *A Commentary on the Revelation of John* (Grand Rapids: Eerdmans, 1972); Leon Morris, *The Book of Revelation: An Introduction and Commentary*, TNTC (Leicester, UK: InterVarsity Press; Grand Rapids: Eerdmans, 1987); and Robert H. Mounce, *The Book of Revelation*, NICNT, rev. ed. (Grand Rapids: Eerdmans, 1997).

15. G. K. Beale has observed that the Septuagint used both *archē* (about 75 times) and *archōn* (about 90 times) to translate the Hebrew word *rôsh* ("ruler"). See G. K. Beale, *The Book of Revelation: A Commentary on the Greek Text*, NIGTC (Grand Rapids: Eerdmans; Milton Keynes, UK: Paternoster, 1999), 298. Beale proposes a variation on the "ruler" interpretation, according to which Revelation 3:14 means that Christ is the beginning/ruler, or head, of the new creation (297–301). Beale's view allows the genitive "of God's creation" to be partitive, and for *archē* to be translated "beginning," since Christ is the first member of the new creation as well as its ruling head.

16. Greg Stafford, *Jehovah's Witnesses Defended: An Answer to Scholars and Critics*, 2nd ed. (Huntington Beach, CA: Elihu Books, 2000), 237–39.

17. None of Stafford's nine examples in the New Testament uses *archē* in reference to a person (Matt. 24:8; Mark 13:19; John 2:11; Phil. 4:15; Heb. 3:14; 5:12; 6:1; 7:3; 2 Peter 3:4). At most, four of his examples from the Greek Old Testament refer to a person. Of these, two translate the Hebrew idiom "the beginning of [one's] strength" as a description of one's firstborn offspring (*archē teknon*, Gen. 49:3; Deut. 21:17; compare the similar expressions in Pss. 78:51; 105:36; possibly also Jer. 49:35). Numbers 24:20, which Stafford also cites, refers to Amalek as the *archē* of the nations, but since Amalek was not the first nation chronologically, the meaning must be something like the chief or greatest of the nations (see also Amos 6:1). In Greek, Proverbs 8:22, which we have already discussed, says that God created wisdom *archēn hodōn autou*, "the beginning of his ways." This is Stafford's only useful example, but it supports his conclusion only if he can show that Revelation 3:14 is alluding to Proverbs 8:22. Beale

has shown, however, that Revelation 3:14 alludes to Isaiah 65:15–17
(Beale, *Book of Revelation*, 297–301).

18. See, e.g., "*rulers* of the day . . . *rulers* of the night" (Gen. 1:16); "the
head of the chief cupbearer . . . the *head* of the chief baker" (Gen.
40:20); "the *chiefs* of the fathers of the Levites" (Exod. 6:25); "the *head*
of all the assembly" (Num. 1:2; 26:2); "*head* of the nations" (Num.
24:20); "the *head* of the people" (1 Kings 21:9, 12); "in every *domin-*
ion of my kingdom" (Dan. 6:26; cf. 7:12); "the *chief* of the sons of
Ammon" (Dan. 11:41); "the *heads* of the nations" (Amos 6:1); "the
heads of the house of Jacob" (Mic. 3:1). (All translations are the authors' and are based on the Greek OT.) Note that these examples are
consistent with Beale's interpretation of *archē* in Revelation 3:14.

19. Thomas C. Oden, *The Living God: Systematic Theology* (1987; reprint,
Peabody, MA: Hendrickson, 1998), 1:110–14.

20. Theologians tend to use *immutability* in a technical sense to denote
the unchangeableness of God's ontological attributes, i.e., immutability means that God is unchangeably infinite spirit, omnipotent,
omnipresent, omniscient, and so forth. They usually speak of the unchangeableness of God's moral attributes as his *faithfulness*. The two
concepts, though, are inextricably linked: it is only because God is
unchangeably omnipotent and omniscient that he can guarantee the
fulfillment of his promises.

21. See further, chapter 15.

22. Gordon R. Lewis and Bruce A. Demarest, *Integrative Theology* (Grand
Rapids: Zondervan, 1996), 1:200.

Chapter 10: He's Got What It Takes

1. These statements do not mean that Christ divested himself of omnipotence or other divine attributes but that he refused to use them in a
self-glorifying, self-serving way (see our earlier discussion in chapter
7 of Phil. 2:6–8).

2. Some critics of the doctrine that Jesus is God incarnate argue that if
Jesus were God he would not need to have authority "given" to him.
This objection overlooks that Christ humbled himself by becoming a
man and dying on the cross (Phil. 2:6–8). In doing so, Christ took a
position of dependence on God the Father to exalt him (v. 9).

3. The incident reported in John is probably not the same incident re-

ported in Matthew and Luke. Both incidents occurred in Capernaum, both involving a boy at home sick and a man to whom Jesus spoke about the boy, and, in both, the boy was healed the same hour that Jesus spoke to the man. In John, however, the man is a royal official and the boy is his son, while in Matthew and Luke the man is a centurion and the boy is apparently his servant (although *pais* also could mean a son). Further, in Matthew and Luke's accounts, Jesus praises the centurion's faith, while in John's account Jesus chides the man's lack of faith. It seems likely, then, that John's account is of a separate, although similar incident.

4. The centurion's comment that he had servants who would go and carry out his orders (Matt. 8:9; Luke 7:8) might seem to imply that he thought Jesus could heal at a distance through intermediary agents (such as angels). The Gospels never report, however, Jesus' healing through angels, and Matthew's report that the servant was healed the same hour (Matt. 8:13) implies that the healing took place immediately. It is more likely that the centurion thought that Jesus could command the entity or force responsible for the sickness to leave the boy and would know that it was done without having to be there watching it happen. In any case, Jesus commends and rewards the centurion's confidence in him without endorsing whatever opinions about demons and sickness he may have held.

5. It is noteworthy that all four Gospels report such an incident of Jesus' healing a child at a distance, without ever being physically in the child's presence.

6. David K. Rupp, *Matthew's Emmanuel: Divine Presence and God's People in the First Gospel*, SNTSMS 90 (Cambridge: Cambridge University Press, 1996), 187.

7. *Pirqe Aboth* 3.3, trans. Charles Taylor (1897). We have modernized the spelling and added the bracketed reference.

8. Craig Keener, *A Commentary on the Gospel of Matthew* (Grand Rapids: Eerdmans, 1999), 455–56, who cites additional references from rabbinical sources. See also Joseph Sievers, "'Where Two or Three . . .': The Rabbinic Concept of Shekhinah and Matthew 18.20," in *Standing Before God: Studies in Prayer in Scriptures and in Tradition with Essays in Honor of John M. Österreicher*, ed. Asher Finkel and Lawrence Frizzell (New York: KTAV, 1981), 171–82; reprinted in *The Jewish*

Roots of Christian Liturgy, ed. Eugene J. Fisher (Mahwah, NJ: Paulist, 1990), 47–61. Kupp, while cautioning that the historical relationship between Matt. 18:20 and the rabbinic Shekinah sayings is uncertain, agrees that the latter illustrates that the former is concerned with the question of the divine presence (*Matthew's Emmanuel*, 192–96).

9. Cf. Genesis 28:15 LXX, *kai idou egō meta sou . . . ean poreuthēs* ("and behold, I [am] with you . . . wherever you go") with Matthew 28:19–20, *poreuthentes . . . kai idou egō meth' humōn eimi* ("Go . . . and behold, I am with you"). In context, God is assuring Jacob that he will be with him wherever he goes in order to ensure the fulfillment of his promise that in Jacob and his seed "all the families of the earth shall be blessed" (v. 14). The Great Commission represents the new covenant stage in the fulfillment of that promise, as Jesus' disciples go to "make disciples of all the nations" (Matt. 28:19 NASB).

10. Harold W. Hoehner, *Ephesians: An Exegetical Commentary* (Grand Rapids: Baker, 2003), 537.

11. See our discussion of this verse earlier in chapter 3, where we show that the "Lord" to whom they were praying was indeed the Lord Jesus.

12. See our discussion of this point later in part 4.

13. Christians understand Jesus' prophecy in these parallel passages (known as the Olivet Discourse) in different ways. It is clear that most, if not all, of the first part of the prophecy (Matt. 24:1–28; Mark 13:1–23; Luke 21:5–24) focuses on the fall of Jerusalem and the destruction of the temple, events that transpired in A.D. 70. Since these events occurred before Jesus' generation passed away, it is natural to understand his statement to that effect a few verses later (Matt. 23:36; 24:32–34; Mark 13:28–30; Luke 21:28–32) as referring to those events. The difficulty is that Christians traditionally understand the intervening section of the prophecy to refer to the still future Second Coming (Matt. 24:29–31; Mark 13:24–27; Luke 21:25–27). The simplest resolution to this difficulty is to view this intervening section as describing events that prefigure or anticipate the Second Coming, not the event of the Second Coming itself. The Son of Man appearing in heaven and "coming on the clouds of heaven" is an apocalyptic vision derived from the book of Daniel. It is not speaking about Christ coming back to earth but about his going to heaven after his resur-

rection to begin ruling as the exalted King (Dan. 7:13–14; cf. Matt. 16:27–28; 26:64). If this view is correct, Jesus was saying that when the temple was destroyed, people (perhaps specifically the Jewish people) would be confronted with the evidence that he really was the exalted Son of Man. The rest of the prophecy (Matt. 24:35–25:46; Mark 13:31–37; Luke 21:33–36) then looks beyond the first century to the Second Coming and the final judgment. An alternative view more or less turns this interpretation around, suggesting that much, if not all, of the prophecy looks forward to events culminating in the Second Coming, with the early sections of the prophecy having an anticipatory or partial fulfillment in the events of the first century. Either way, all Christians can agree that Jesus prophesied the destruction of the temple in A.D. 70.

14. The significance of these statements is often overstated. Growing in wisdom is not the same thing as growing in knowledge. Still, one presumes that as a child Christ went through a process of education—learning to read, for example. "Learning obedience" also is not gaining knowledge but rather experience, and, in context, experience specific to humanity. Hebrews 5:8 clearly does not mean that Jesus progressed from disobedience to obedience, since the same author had just asserted that Jesus never sinned (4:15). Rather, the point is that Jesus went through a process in which he experienced the height of obedience to God the Father under the most extreme circumstances.

15. It is possible that by "that day or hour" Jesus means the exact timing of the fall of Jerusalem and the destruction of the temple in A.D. 70. When Jesus mentions the "passing away" of heaven and earth, however, the prophecy appears to shift attention away from the local events in and around Jerusalem to the more distant future judgment coming on the whole world. Either way, the passage juxtaposes Jesus' divine foreknowledge of future events with the Son's lack of knowledge as to the precise timing of certain future events.

16. Kris J. Udd, "Only the Father Knows: A Response to Harold F. Carl," *JBS* 1.4 (October–December 2001), http://www.journalofbiblicalstudies .org/issue4.html.

17. Harold F. Carl, "Only the Father Knows: Historical and Evangelical Responses to Jesus' Eschatological Ignorance in Mark 13:32," *JBS* 1.3 (July–Sept. 2001), http://www.journalofbiblicalstudies.org/issue3

.html. This may be the dominant explanation in orthodox Christology, although the nonuse explanation enjoys significant support as well.

18. Richard Swinburne, *The Christian God* (Oxford: Oxford University Press, 1994), 203.

19. When the disciples asked the risen Jesus if it was then time for the kingdom to be restored to Israel—an event they associated with the end of the age—he replied, "It is not for you to know the times or periods that the Father has set by his own authority" (Acts 1:7). Here, Jesus did not disavow knowing the timing of the event in question, as he had before his death (Matt. 24:36; Mark 13:32). On the other hand, he did not actually claim to have that knowledge either, but again refers to the timing as a matter of the Father's prerogative.

Chapter 11: Name One

1. Note that it would be fallacious to reason from the biblical use of the word *name* to cover both proper names and titles, to the conceptual claim that there is no distinction between proper names and titles. Such reasoning would be an example of the "word-concept" fallacy.

2. For example, German capitalizes every noun, so the word for God is *Gott*, whether in English we would use *God* or *god*.

3. The argument is *not* merely that Jesus' name is theophoric (having a name of deity within it) and, therefore, he must be God. Obviously, many Jews had theophoric names, including the Old Testament figure of Joshua, whose name is just another form of the name we spell as Jesus. Indeed, the name Jesus was common in first-century Jewish circles. The point is that the angel does not say, as we might have expected, that *God* would save his people, but that *he*, Jesus, would do so. Note also that the text uses the pronoun *autos* ("he"), which is grammatically superfluous (because the third person singular is signaled by the verb's form), and places it in an emphatic position (first in the sentence). The result is a very strong emphasis on the word *autos*: "for *he himself* will save his people from their sins" (see NASB marg.). Thus, the angel assigns a special significance to Mary's son's having the name Jesus that would not apply to anyone else.

4. The Hebrew text contains only the four consonants YHWH; medieval scribes added points around the consonants to indicate the vowels. There is much uncertainty as to its precise pronunciation, however,

because Jews rarely or never pronounced the name for centuries. The conventional form in modern English scholarship is Yahweh, but the traditional English form, dating from many centuries ago, is Jehovah. Spelling and pronunciation seems not to matter in the least, however, since despite the significance of the name in the Old Testament, no concern is ever expressed about how it is spelled or pronounced.

5. The shortened form *Yah* (or *Jah*) appears four times in the expression *Hallelujah* (Rev. 19:1–6), which means "Praise Jehovah" (or, as often expressed in English, "Praise the Lord").

6. See also Acts 15:14, 17; Romans 9:17; 15:9; Hebrews 6:10; 13:15; James 5:10; Revelation 3:12.

7. See also Matthew 28:19; John 5:43; 10:25; Ephesians 3:15; Hebrews 2:12; Revelation 14:1.

8. It is true that the word *theos* (God) appears about 1,400 times in the New Testament and *patēr* (Father) for God appears about 250 times, while *ʾIēsous* (Jesus) appears about 900 times. References to Jesus, however, often use other names, notably *kurios* (Lord) and *christos* (Christ), as well as the names "Son," "Son of God," and "Son of Man" (which was Jesus' most common way of referring to himself). The word *kurios* occurs over 700 times (at least 500, possibly much more, of which refer to Jesus), and *christos* occurs over 500 times; the "Son" names total well over another 100. These common names for Jesus, then, occur more than 2,000 times in the New Testament, as compared to about 1,650 occurrences of *God* and *Father*. If we wish to compare the number of verses referring to God or to Jesus, the result is the same. *God* appears in about 1150 verses, *Father* (as a designation of God) in about 225 verses; accounting for overlap, there are about 1,300 verses referring to God as either "God" or "Father" or both. *Jesus* appears in about 875 verses, *Christ* in about 500 verses, *Lord* in reference to Jesus in at least 450 verses, and one of the "Son" names in more than 100 verses. After we eliminate any overlap by subtracting the 300-plus times when a verse uses more than one of these names, we still have over 1,600 verses referring to Jesus. Even these numbers do not tell the whole story. We have not counted the number of times the New Testament uses pronouns to refer to Jesus (it is much more often than similar references to "God the Father") or the many other ways in which the texts identify Jesus.

9. This does not mean that the Jewish exorcists thought Jesus was God. Some exorcists of the period apparently appealed to the name of deceased men of reputed power over demons, such as Solomon, when performing exorcisms. Exorcists (whether Jewish or pagan) of the period who made such appeals, however, typically followed a "magical" model of exorcism, naming a variety of deities and other spirits over the possessed person. Christians, on the other hand, would simply invoke Jesus' name, treating his name as unique and sufficient. See Larry W. Hurtado, *Lord Jesus Christ: Devotion to Jesus in Earliest Christianity* (Grand Rapids: Eerdmans, 2003), 203–4.

10. The translations of these two verses are ours, to make clear the connection between them. *Megalunthēsometha* is future passive first person plural, while *emegaluneto* is imperfect passive third person singular, of the same verb *megalunō*.

11. F. F. Bruce, *The Acts of the Apostles: The Greek Text with Introduction and Commentary*, 3rd rev. and enlarged ed. (Grand Rapids: Eerdmans; Leicester, UK: Apollos, 1990), 412.

12. In Matthew, Jesus told his disciples to baptize "into [*eis*] the name of the Father and the Son and the Holy Spirit" (Matt. 28:19, literal translation). This statement does not contradict the references to baptism "into" the name of Jesus Christ, since none of the texts is specifying a baptismal formula or a set of words for use in the baptismal rite.

13. Lars Hartman, *"Into the Name of the Lord Jesus": Baptism in the Early Church* (Edinburgh: T & T Clark, 1997), 42; see also Hurtado, *Lord Jesus Christ*, 143–44.

14. Paul's statement that the Israelites, in crossing the Red Sea, were "baptized into Moses" (1 Cor. 10:2) treats Moses as a type of Christ. As Hurtado points out (*Lord Jesus Christ*, 202), what Paul says does not reflect any Jewish practice of invoking Moses' name in a religious rite or even any notion of Israelites as having a special relationship with Moses.

15. The Greek Old Testament spoke of ritual acts of blessing performed "in" (1 Chron. 16:2, 8) or "on" (Deut. 10:8; cf. 17:12; 18:5; 21:5; 1 Chron. 23:13) the name of Jehovah.

16. We will have more to say about this passage when we discuss the name "Lord" in chapter 13. Note also Paul's statement that Christians

were washed, sanctified, and justified "in the name of the Lord Jesus
Christ" (1 Cor. 6:11).

17. Paul's pre-Christian attitude toward the Christian reverence for Jesus'
name was apparently common among Jews of the time. The Jews in
Corinth took Paul before the proconsul Gallio, complaining that Paul
was "persuading people to worship God in ways that are contrary to
the law" (Acts 18:13). Gallio threw the case out, saying that it involved
"questions about words and names and your own law" (v. 15). His
reference to "names" likely implies that the Jews criticized Paul for
introducing the name of Jesus into the worship of God.

18. For other expressions of the exalted place of Jesus' name, see Matthew
18:5, 20; 24:5; Mark 6:14; 9:41; John 3:18; 14:13–14, 26; 15:16; 16:23–
26; Acts 8:12; Romans 1:5; 1 Corinthians 1:2, 10; Ephesians 5:20;
2 Thessalonians 1:12; 3:6; Hebrews 1:4; James 2:7; 5:14.

Chapter 12: Immanuel: God with Us

1. Allan A. MacRae, "ʿlm" in *The Theological Wordbook of the Old
Testament*, ed. R. Laird Harris, Gleason L. Archer Jr., and Bruce K.
Waltke (Chicago: Moody Press, 1980), 2:672.

2. Note that the word *sign* by itself does not necessarily denote a miracle
(cf. Isa. 8:18); it is the purpose of the sign and the way the sign is described that indicate a miracle is meant.

3. We take the view that the eighth-century prophet Isaiah authored
the entire book, but our argument would not be undermined by the
common view in modern scholarship that Isaiah 40–66 originated from after the Babylonian exile. Whoever put the book together
clearly expected readers to view Isaiah 40–66 in light of the earlier
chapters. Classic defenses of Isaiah's authorship of the whole book include Oswald T. Allis, *The Unity of Isaiah* (Philadelphia: Presbyterian
& Reformed, 1950); and Edward J. Young, *Who Wrote Isaiah?* (Grand
Rapids: Eerdmans, 1957). See also the discussion of this question in
Gleason L. Archer Jr., *A Survey of Old Testament Introduction*, rev. ed.
(Chicago: Moody Press, 1994), 363–90.

4. Our assumption here—backed in recent decades by a mountain of
research by many scholars—is that the prologue (John 1:1–18), like
the New Testament in general, is steeped in Old Testament religious
and theological motifs. The trend in Johannine studies definitely has

moved away from the practice of trying to interpret the prologue
(especially the Logos) primarily in terms of Platonic, Stoic, or other
Hellenistic philosophies. On the Jewish and specifically the Old
Testament context of John, see especially Anthony Tyrrell Hanson, *The
Prophetic Gospel: A Study of John and the Old Testament* (Edinburgh:
T & T Clark, 1991); and Claus Westermann, *The Gospel of John in the
Light of the Old Testament*, trans. Siegfried S. Schatzmann (Peabody,
MA: Hendrickson, 1998). The relevant literature on the Old Testament
background of the prologue alone is voluminous: see especially
Craig A. Evans, *Word and Glory: On the Exegetical and Theological
Background of John's Prologue*, JSNTSup 89 (Sheffield: JSOT Press,
1993).

5.   The imperfect *ēn* in this context has, for two reasons, the nuance of
"was already existing" (cf. NLT, "already existed"). The first is the apparently studied contrast between *ēn* and *egeneto* ("became," "came
to be," a key word appearing 21 times in the creation narrative in Gen.
1:1–2:4) in the Prologue (cf. John 1:1–4, 6, 8–10, 14–15, 17). The second reason is the context of existing "in the beginning."

6.   John's statement that the Word "dwelt [*eskēnōsen*] among us, and we
saw His glory [*doxan*], glory as of the only begotten of the Father,
full [*plērēs*] of grace and truth" (John 1:14 NASB) appears to allude
to the statement repeated in Exodus 40:34–35, "the glory [*doxēs*] of
the LORD filled [*eplēsthē*] the tabernacle [*skēnē*]." See also Numbers
14:10–11; and Psalm 26:8.

7.   Psalm 74:7 bemoans the fact that Israel's enemies had "desecrated the
dwelling place [*skēnōma*] of your name." The possible close association between God's "name" and his "word" is highly suggestive here.
The psalmist also noted that God once abandoned his tabernacle at
Shiloh, "the tent that he had set up among men [*kataskēnōsen en an-
thrōpois*]" (Ps. 78:60 NIV). The book of 2 Maccabees includes a prayer
thanking God that he was pleased for there "to become [*genesthai*] a
temple for your dwelling among us [*skēnōseōs en hēmin*]" (2 Macc.
14:35). Compare John's statement that the Word "became [*egeneto*,
another form of *genesthai*] flesh, and dwelt among us [*eskēnōsen en
hēmin*], and we saw His glory [*doxan*]" (John 1:14 NASB).

8.   Notice that John 1:14–18 contains at least four allusions to Exodus
33–34, confirming the importance of that passage for understanding

John's prologue. See further Alan R. Kerr, *The Temple of Jesus' Body: The Temple Theme in the Gospel of John*, JSNTSup 220 (New York and London: Sheffield Academic Press, 2002), 117–26.

9. James Moffatt, *A New Translation of the Bible, Containing the Old and New Testaments*, rev. ed. (1926; reprint, Grand Rapids: Kregel, 1995); and Edgar J. Goodspeed, *The New Testament: An American Translation* (Chicago: University of Chicago Press, 1923).

10. For additional examples, see Robert M. Bowman Jr., *Jehovah's Witnesses, Jesus Christ, and the Gospel of John* (Grand Rapids: Baker, 1989), 135–37.

11. Studies reaching orthodox conclusions on John 1:1 include Bowman, *Jehovah's Witnesses, Jesus Christ, and the Gospel of John*, 17–84; Murray J. Harris, *Jesus as God: The New Testament Use of Theos in Reference to Jesus* (Grand Rapids: Baker, 1992), 51–71; and Donald E. Hartley, "Revisiting the Colwell Construction in the Light of Mass/Count Nouns," Biblical Studies Foundation (1998), http://www.bible.org/studies/nt/topics/colwell.htm. On the use of the article in Greek, see also Daniel B. Wallace, *Greek Grammar Beyond the Basics: An Exegetical Syntax of the New Testament* (Grand Rapids: Zondervan, 1996), 206–70. Two thoughtful attempts to defend the Jehovah's Witnesses' translation of John 1:1 are Rolf Furuli, *The Role of Theology and Bias in Bible Translation: With a Special Look at the New World Translation of Jehovah's Witnesses* (Huntington Beach, CA: Elihu Books, 1999), 199–229; and Greg Stafford, *Jehovah's Witnesses Defended: An Answer to Scholars and Critics*, 2nd ed. (Huntington Beach, Calif.: Elihu Books, 2000), 305–66.

12. One of us argued this point in a book published in 1989; see Bowman, *Jehovah's Witnesses, Jesus Christ, and the Gospel of John*, especially 60–61. Daniel B. Wallace made the same point in another way in an unpublished paper titled, "The Implications of an Indefinite *Theos* in John 1:1c," presented at the 1999 annual meeting of the Evangelical Theological Society (in Danvers, MA).

13. Modern scholars have almost unanimously abandoned the older translation of *monogenēs* as "only begotten." Ancient writers did not use the word to denote that a child was the only one who was "begotten" or procreated by the parent (although in some occurrences, of course, that also happened to be the case), but rather to denote that the child stood

in a special, unique relationship to the parent. Indeed, sometimes the word in context had nothing to do with children at all (e.g., Wisdom 7:22). For this reason, some modern translations render the word as "only" (ESV) or "the One and Only" (NIV) or the like. In the immediate context in John 1:18, however, the idea of sonship is clearly present ("who is close to the Father's heart"; see also v. 14), as it is elsewhere when John uses it in reference to Christ (John 3:16, 18; 1 John 4:9).

14.   The question of how to translate *monogenēs theos* is a vexing one. The main options are "the only God" (ESV), "God the One and Only" (NIV), "the only begotten God" (NASB), and "God the only Son" (NRSV). These diverse renderings reflect disagreement on two questions. First, does *monogenēs* connote sonship in this text (NASB and NRSV, yes; ESV and NIV, no)? We agree that it probably does (see previous note). Second, does the text here use *monogenēs* substantivally, that is, like a noun (NIV, NRSV), or adjectivally (ESV, NASB)? Either is grammatically possible. John has just used *monogenēs* substantivally, however, in verse 14 ("glory as of the only Son [*monogenous*] from the Father," ESV). Furthermore, at least in biblical occurrences (including the Apocrypha), *monogenēs* functions adjectivally when qualifying the nouns *huios*, "son," or *thugatēr*, "daughter" (Tobit 6:11; Luke 7:12; 8:42; John 3:16, 18; 1 John 4:9). Otherwise, *monogenēs* usually functions substantivally (Judg. 11:34; Tobit 3:15; 8:17; Pss. 22:20; 35:17; John 1:14; Heb. 11:17; Ps. 25:16 and Wisdom 7:22 are exceptions). When used substantivally, *monogenēs* typically (although not always) means an only or unique child. We think it most likely, then, especially in light of John 1:14, that *monogenēs* in John 1:18 connotes sonship and that it functions substantivally. This means that *monogenēs* and *theos* are in apposition, so that the whole expression should be translated either "God the only Son" (NRSV) or something equivalent, such as "the only Son, who is God." For the latter translation, see Harris, *Jesus as God*, 88–92.

15.   Bruce M. Metzger, *A Textual Commentary on the Greek New Testament*, 2nd ed. (Stuttgart: United Bible Societies, 1994), 169–70 (which notes one dissent from its five-member committee, Allen Wikgren). Two major contemporary English versions that do not accept this conclusion are the NKJV ("only begotten Son") and the HCSB ("the only Son"). Bart Ehrman also has argued against the reading

monogenēs theos, on the grounds that this wording could only mean "the unique God," which in the context of the Gospel of John is unthinkable. See Bart D. Ehrman, *The Orthodox Corruption of Scripture: The Effect of Early Christological Controversies on the Text of the New Testament* (New York: Oxford University Press, 1993), 81, and idem, *Misquoting Jesus: The Story Behind Who Changed the Bible and Why* (San Francisco: HarperSanFrancisco, 2005), 161–62, and the response in J. Ed Komoszewski, M. James Sawyer, and Daniel B. Wallace, *Reinventing Jesus: How Contemporary Skeptics Miss the Real Jesus and Mislead Popular Culture* (Grand Rapids: Kregel, 2006), 290–93.

16. According to most of the manuscripts, although there is some early support for the article before *theos* in John 1:18 (P⁷⁵). See the discussion in Harris, *Jesus as God*, 77–78.

17. Harris, *Jesus as God*, 102.

18. In recognizing the end of chapter 20 as the climax of the Gospel, we are not implying that the Gospel ever circulated without chapter 21. Rather, chapter 21 is an epilogue, balancing the Gospel's prologue (1:1–18), resolving certain themes that arise in the body of the Gospel, and identifying the author as the beloved disciple. See Andreas J. Köstenberger, *John*, BECNT (Grand Rapids: Baker, 2004), 583–86.

19. Harris, *Jesus as God*, 110; see his footnotes for extensive references.

20. The introductory formula "he answered and said" occurs frequently in the Old Testament (mostly in the books of Samuel and Kings), twice in Luke (13:15; 17:20), and nowhere else in the New Testament outside the Gospel of John.

21. One of these creative interpretations is that Thomas directed his words "My Lord" to Jesus but the words "my God" to the Father. A recent advocate of this view is Margaret Davies, *Rhetoric and Reference in the Fourth Gospel*, JSNTSup 69 (Sheffield: Sheffield Academic Press, 1992), 125–26. Davies claims that this interpretation "actually makes much better sense in the context of the Fourth Gospel." John already has prepared his readers for Thomas's confession, however, by calling Jesus "God" twice in the prologue (1:1, 18). Davies's view simply does not account for John's introducing Thomas's words as addressed directly to Jesus.

22. See also "my King and my God" (*ho basileus mou kai ho theos mou*,

Pss. 5:2 [5:3 LXX] and 84:3 [83:4 LXX]). Some critics of the traditional interpretation argue that Thomas's words are not directed
to Jesus, because in biblical Greek, speakers addressing someone as
"Lord" usually use the vocative case (*kurie*) instead of the nominative case (*kurios*). The examples from the Psalms, however, show this
argument to be fallacious. Although the vocative *kurie* frequently appears in biblical Greek, the vocative *Theé* for "God" is very rare (occurring in the LXX only in Judg. 16:28; 21:3; 2 Kings [2 Sam. MT]
7:25; Ezek. 4:14; and in the New Testament only in Matt. 27:46) and is
never modified by *mou* (my) or any other pronoun. Instead, we find
the nominative form *theos* as occurring commonly in direct address
(over a hundred times in the Psalms; for the New Testament, see, e.g.,
Mark 15:34; Luke 18:11, 13). The use of the nominative *kurios* is thus
easily explained as influenced by the nominative form of *theos* in the
same expression.

23. Jesus' response to Thomas's confession is instructive: he chided him
not for what he said but for insisting on seeing before he would believe (John 20:29).

24. D. A. Carson, *The Gospel According to John* (Leicester, UK: InterVarsity
Press; Grand Rapids: Eerdmans, 1991), 344.

25. Murray J. Harris, *3 Crucial Questions About Jesus* (Grand Rapids:
Baker, 1994), 98–99.

26. One possible reference to Jesus as God that we will not discuss here is
1 John 5:20. For the view that "God" in this text refers to the Father,
see Harris, *Jesus as God*, 239–53.

27. R. T. France, "The Worship of Jesus: A Neglected Factor in Christological Debate?" *Vox Evangelica* 12 (1981): 25.

28. Somewhat surprisingly, Murray Harris, in his excellent book *Jesus as
God*, comes down in favor of the NRSV rendering, concluding that "it
remains unlikely, although not impossible, that in Acts 20:28 *ho theos*
denotes Jesus" (141, cf. 137–41).

29. Technically, this verbal arrangement (article + noun + article + adjective) is known as the second attributive position and is universally recognized in the study of Greek grammar; see Wallace, *Greek
Grammar Beyond the Basics*, 306–7.

30. The first scholars to propose the alternate translation "the blood of
his own" appear to have been J. A. Bengel and F. J. A. Hort; see Harris,

Jesus as God, 139; and Charles F. DeVine, "The 'Blood of God' in Acts 20:28," *CBQ* 9 (1947): 405.

31. This does not mean that everyone was perfectly comfortable with the text's speaking of God's own blood, since early in church history copyists started changing "church of God" to "church of the Lord." The copyist or copyists who introduced this reading obviously understood *tou haimatos tou idiou* to mean "his own blood" but thought that it was more acceptable to speak of the Lord's blood than of God's. There is a near consensus today that "God" was the original wording (see Metzger, *Textual Commentary on the New Testament*, 425–27; Harris, *Jesus as God*, 134–36). Incidentally, if Acts 20:28 did refer to Jesus by using the expression "the church of the Lord," this would be a strong affirmation of his deity, since that expression comes directly from the Old Testament as a description of the congregation of YHWH, or Jehovah (Deut. 23:2–3, 8; 1 Chron. 28:8; Mic. 2:5).

32. "If you were of the world, the world would love its own [*to idion*]" (John 15:19 NASB). Here *to idion* is a generic singular, referring not to a specific person but to anyone who was of the world. This usage is hardly comparable to the proposed substantival use in Acts 20:28. There are a few clear examples of the plural used in reference to persons (John 1:11; Acts 4:23; 24:23; possibly John 13:1; 1 Tim. 5:8).

33. Nigel Turner, *Grammatical Insights into the New Testament* (Edinburgh: T & T Clark, 1965), 14–15.

34. DeVine, "The 'Blood of God' in Acts 20:28," 405.

35. See Harris, *Jesus as God*, 150–51, for a table laying out nine options.

36. Translations that render Romans 9:5cd as a separate sentence include the NEB and REB; the RSV (but not the NRSV), and the Good News Translation (1992).

37. The New Life Version (1969) translates Romans 9:5d as a separate sentence; this rendering is also given as an alternative in marginal notes in the NEB, REB, and NIV.

38. The NASB, NIV, NRSV, NKJV, HCSB, and NET are among the many modern versions that translate Romans 9:5 as referring to Christ as "God."

39. For more on Romans 9:5, see Harris, *Jesus as God*, 143–72; Bruce M. Metzger, "The Punctuation of Romans 9:5," in *Christ and the Spirit in the New Testament: Essays in Honour of Charles Francis Digby Moule*,

ed. Barnabas Lindars and Stephen S. Smalley (Cambridge: Cambridge University Press, 1973), 95–112. For a recent dissent, see Gordon D. Fee, *Pauline Christology: An Exegetical-Theological Study* (Peabody, MA: Hendrickson, 2007), 272–77. Fee's primary objection to the view that Paul calls Jesus "God" in Romans 9:5 is his understanding that Paul consistently uses *God* for the Father and *Lord* for Jesus the Son. On this question, see below on Titus 2:13.

40.   It may be worth noting that if Paul called Jesus "God" in Acts 20:28, as we have argued he did, that speech came just a few weeks after he would have finished writing the epistle to the Romans from Corinth (see Rom. 15:25–27; 16:1; Acts 20:2–3).

41.   Harris, *Jesus as God*, 191.

42.   Ibid., 192–96, 203–4.

43.   Peter modeled this way of interpreting the Psalms as messianic when he argued that Psalm 16, which in its original context was a psalm of David to thank God for rescuing him from death, actually looked forward to the death and resurrection of David's descendant, the Messiah (Acts 2:25–31).

44.   On the Pauline origin of Titus and the epistles to Timothy, see Philip H. Towner, *The Letters to Timothy and Titus* (Cambridge; Grand Rapids: Eerdmans, 2006), 9–88. The question has some indirect bearing on our subject, since one commonly given reason for denying that Romans 9:5 calls Jesus "God" is that it would be the only such instance in Paul's writings. There are, in fact, potentially three statements by Paul that explicitly call Jesus "God": Romans 9:5 (in a letter that everyone agrees came from Paul); Titus 2:13; and Acts 20:28 (in a speech of Paul as reported by Luke). Even those scholars who dispute that Paul wrote Titus or that Luke records what Paul actually said generally agree that Titus and Acts both represent a broadly "Pauline" understanding of Christ.

45.   To see that only one person is actually meant in Titus 2:13, one should omit not only the bracketed *the* but also the word *of* that precedes it in the NWT; thus, "of the great God and Savior of us, Christ Jesus." There is no separate Greek word translated "of"; rather, Greek inflects (spells differently) all of the nouns, adjectives, and articles that stand in the same grammatical position or relation in the sentence. Translators may, of course, use *of* where appropriate (as at the begin-

ning of the phrase in question) but should not do so where it misleadingly implies a separate person. It would be incorrect, for example, to translate 2 Peter 1:11 (which is grammatically parallel to Titus 2:13) "the eternal kingdom of our Lord and *of the* Savior Jesus Christ."

46. The explanation of the rule given here is not a formal, technical definition and does not delve into all of the details necessary to establish the validity of the rule. We also should point out that, like all "rules" in grammar or language, Sharp's rule is a descriptive observation of what is normal or customary in ancient Greek, not a prescriptive rule that Greek writers consciously accepted or to which they invariably adhered. As a valid general observation, though, Sharp's rule, along with other contextual factors, should be taken into consideration when interpreting the text. On Granville Sharp, see Daniel B. Wallace, "Granville Sharp: A Model of Evangelical Scholarship and Social Activism," *JETS* 41 (1998): 591–613. For a defense of Sharp's rule, see Robert M. Bowman Jr., "Sharp's Rules and Antitrinitarian Theologies: A Defense of Granville Sharp's Argument for the Deity of Christ," at http://www.biblicalapologetics.net/NTStudies/Sharps_Rule.pdf. See also Daniel B. Wallace, *Greek Grammar Beyond the Basics*, 270–90; and idem, *Granville Sharp's Canon and Its Kin: Semantics and Significance* (New York: Peter Lang, 2007).

47. We have translated these phrases literally; the two nouns connected by *kai* are shown in italics.

48. We can touch on only some of the evidence here. See Bowman, "Sharp's Rules and Antitrinitarian Theologies," 27–41; Harris, *Jesus as God*, 173–85, 229–38; and I. Howard Marshall, *A Critical and Exegetical Commentary on the Pastoral Epistles*, in collaboration with Philip H. Towner, ICC (Edinburgh: T & T Clark, 1999), 272–82.

49. Fee, *Pauline Christology*, 440–48.

50. No other epistle of Paul, not even the very short Philemon, uses *kurios* for Jesus less than five times. Paul uses *sōtēr* for Jesus outside Titus only twice (Phil. 3:20; 2 Tim. 1:10).

51. Harris, *Jesus as God*, 177.

52. Fee acknowledges this to be an "obvious difficulty" for his view, but claims, mistakenly, that it "is the only difficulty" (Fee, *Pauline Christology*, 444n. 86).

53. When Paul speaks of God's "grace" or his "goodness and love"

appearing, he uses the related verb *epephanē* (Titus 2:11; 3:4), not the noun *epiphaneia*.

54. Fee asserts that such a usage of "the glory" adjectivally to mean "glorious" is "out of sync with Paul's usage elsewhere" (Fee, *Pauline Christology*, 443). In light of the dozen examples of this usage in Paul, Fee's statement would seem to be mistaken.

55. Richard J. Bauckham, *Jude, 2 Peter*, WBC 50 (Waco, TX: Word, 1983), 168.

56. There is some uncertainty about whether "our" (*hēmōn*) appears in 2 Peter 2:20, and if so, where. This textual variant does not affect the argument.

Chapter 13: He Is Lord

1. See chapter 11 on the form and significance of the name YHWH in the Old Testament.

2. To be precise, although angels are apparently called "gods" in certain contexts (e.g., Ps. 82:1, 6), the Old Testament insists emphatically that YHWH is the only "true God" (2 Chron. 15:3; Jer. 10:10), the only being properly worshiped and served as one's God. YHWH alone is identified as "God Most High" (Gen. 14:22; Pss. 7:17; 47:2; 83:18; 97:9). The Church of Jesus Christ of Latter-day Saints (popularly called Mormons), on the other hand, teaches that "Jehovah" is the name of the Son, Jesus Christ, who is to be distinguished from "Elohim," the name of God the Father. Recently, they have received some support for this view from Margaret Barker, especially in her book *The Great Angel: A Study of Israel's Second God* (Louisville: Westminster/John Knox Press, 1992). Although Barker is reportedly a Methodist, she has spoken at LDS conferences in support of some of their beliefs. Her theory is that in ancient Israelite religion "there was a High God and several Sons of God, one of whom was Yahweh," and that the New Testament identifies Jesus as that Yahweh, not as the High God (ibid., 3). She argues that monotheism was imposed on the OT, beginning with the so-called Deuteronomistic reform and continuing during the Babylonian exile. This argument implies that the OT with which the NT writers would have been familiar would have been monotheistic— as indeed the evidence from the NT itself proves. Yet Barker argues that the NT writers held to the earlier belief in a High God and Yahweh as

one of the Sons of God! The assumption throughout the NT is, in fact, quite otherwise: it assumes the truth of the "Deuteronomistic" claim that the Lord (YHWH) is the only true God (Deut. 6:4; Mark 12:29–34; cf. Rom. 3:30; Gal. 3:20; James 2:19). Barker's theory is at any rate of no use to Mormon theology, which asserts that the only proper object of worship is God the Father—despite the fact that throughout the OT, YHWH (Jehovah) is the only proper object of worship. On the importance of Barker's theories to Mormon scholarship, see Kevin Christensen, "Paradigms Regained: A Survey of Margaret Barker's Scholarship and Its Significance for Mormon Studies," *FARMS Occasional Papers* 2 (2001): 1–94. Relevant critiques of Barker and LDS theology include Paul Owen, "Monotheism, Mormonism, and the New Testament Witness," in *The New Mormon Challenge: Responding to the Latest Defenses of a Fast-Growing Movement,* ed. Francis J. Beckwith, Carl Mosser, and Paul Owen (Grand Rapids: Zondervan, 2002), 271–314; Matthew A. Paulsen, *Breaking the Mormon Code: A Critique of Mormon Scholarship Regarding Classical Christian Theology and the Book of Mormon* (Livermore, CA: WingSpan Press), especially 93–97. On Jewish monotheism, see especially Larry W. Hurtado, *Lord Jesus Christ: Devotion to Jesus in Earliest Christianity* (Grand Rapids: Eerdmans, 2003), 29–48; and Richard Bauckham, *God Crucified: Monotheism and Christology in the New Testament* (Grand Rapids: Eerdmans, 1999), 1–22.

3. Documentation from the Dead Sea Scrolls shows that this practice of avoiding speaking the name Yahweh aloud dated back to at least the second century B.C., and there are reasons to think it originated even earlier. See P. W. Skehan, "The Divine Name at Qumran, in the Masada Scroll, and in the Septuagint," *BIOSCS* 13 (1980): 14–44. On the factors that led to this development, see Sean M. McDonough, *YHWH at Patmos: Rev. 1:4 in Its Hellenistic and Early Jewish Setting,* WUNT 2.107 (Tübingen: Mohr Siebeck, 1999), 58–116, esp. 111–16.

4. Albert Pietersma, "Kyrios or Tetragram: A Renewed Quest for the Original LXX," in *De Septuaginta: Studies in Honour of John William Wevers on His Sixty-fifth Birthday,* ed. Albert Pietersma and Claude Cox (Mississauga, ON: Benben Publications, 1984), 85–101. See also Skehan, "Divine Name at Qumran," for additional lines of evidence showing at the least that the Christian practice of substituting *kurios*

for YHWH in the Greek Old Testament had its roots in Jewish scribal practices. See also D. R. deLacey, "'One Lord' in Pauline Christology," in *Christ the Lord: Studies in Christology Presented to Donald Guthrie*, ed. Harold H. Rowdon (Leicester, UK; Downers Grove, IL: InterVarsity Press, 1982), 191–94; and McDonough, *YHWH at Patmos*, 58–61.

5. See especially Josephus, *Jewish Antiquities* 2.12.4; 20.4.2; and idem, *Jewish War* 5.5.7. Josephus more frequently used the synonym *despotēs* (Master) in place of the tetragram.

6. The key New Testament papyri here are P⁴⁶ and P⁶⁶, both of which use "Lord" (*kurios*) in quotations from the Old Testament. Kurt Aland and Barbara Aland in 1989 dated both of these papyri to about A.D. 200 (*The Text of the New Testament*, trans. Erroll F. Rhodes, 2nd ed. [Grand Rapids: Eerdmans; Leiden: Brill, 1989], 57, 99–100), a date that is still widely cited. Young Kyu Kim, however, in a 1988 article (apparently not consulted for the Alands' 1989 publication) dates P⁴⁶ to the period A.D. 70–90 ("Paleographical Dating of P46 to the Later First Century," *Bib* 69 [1988]: 248–61). P. W. Comfort and D. P. Barrett in 1999 dated both P⁴⁶ and P⁶⁶ slightly later, to about A.D. 98–138 (*The Complete Text of the Earliest New Testament Manuscripts* [Grand Rapids: Baker, 1999], 195–97). Greg Stafford, *Jehovah's Witnesses Defended: An Answer to Scholars and Critics*, 2nd ed. (Huntington Beach, CA: Elihu Books, 2000), 18n. 40, cites all of these studies, although he argues that the papyri are late enough that the tetragram may have stood originally in the New Testament and later was replaced by *kurios*.

7. For an excellent introduction to the study of the reliability of the NT text, see J. Ed Komoszewski, M. James Sawyer, and Daniel B. Wallace, *Reinventing Jesus: How Contemporary Skeptics Miss the Real Jesus and Mislead Popular Culture* (Grand Rapids: Kregel, 2006), 53–117.

8. David Trobisch, *The First Edition of the New Testament* (New York: Oxford University Press, 2000), has argued that most or all of the extant NT manuscripts go back to a "canonical edition" that included all 27 books and in which certain aspects of the text were fixed. Even Trobisch acknowledges, however, that the success of this hypothetical edition would not have depended "on an authoritative decision of the church" (106). In any case, there are serious weaknesses in Trobisch's theory. For an overall positive review that points out some of the problems, see Jason T. Larson's review in *TC: A Journal*

of Biblical Textual Criticism 6 (2001), http://rosetta.reltech.org/TC/
vol06/Trobisch2001rev.html (accessed January 13, 2007).

9. For the religion's official explanation and a complete list of the af-
fected texts, see *New World Translation of the Holy Scriptures: With
References* (Brooklyn: Watchtower Bible and Tract Society, 1984),
1561–66. For more sophisticated defenses of the practice, see Stafford,
Jehovah's Witnesses Defended, 12–52; and Rolf Furuli, *The Role of
Theology and Bias in Bible Translation: With a Special Look at the New
World Translation of Jehovah's Witnesses* (Huntington Beach, CA:
Elihu Books, 1999), 152–97. For a critique of the religion's views on
the divine name, see Robert M. Bowman Jr., *Understanding Jehovah's
Witnesses: Why They Read the Bible the Way They Do* (Grand Rapids:
Baker, 1991), 109–22.

10. George Howard, "The Tetragram and the New Testament," *JBL* 96
(1977): 63–83; idem, "The Name of God in the New Testament," in
*Approaches to the Bible: The Best of Bible Review, Volume I: Composition,
Transmission and Language,* ed. Harvey Mintoff (Washington, DC:
Biblical Archaeology Society, 1994), 246–52; Trobisch, *First Edition
of the New Testament,* 66–67. See the criticisms of Howard's view in
McDonough, *YHWH at Patmos,* 60–61, 97–98.

11. Howard, "Name of God in the New Testament," 252.

12. See Carl Judson Davis, *The Name and Way of the Lord: Old Testament
Themes, New Testament Christology,* JSNTSup 129 (Sheffield, England:
Sheffield Academic Press, 1989), esp. 61–102. Davis shows that the
Gospel writers understood Isaiah 40:3 to be speaking of a "new exo-
dus" in which God's presence would come to bring salvation, and that
this promise was fulfilled in the coming of Jesus.

13. Were we to take seriously the hypothesis of an original New Testament
text containing the tetragram, Matthew 7:21–22 would be a clear can-
didate for "restoring" the divine name YHWH, since the doubled *kurie kurie* evidently originated from Greek-speaking Jews translating
"Lord YHWH" and "YHWH Lord."

14. That Matthew quotes verses both before and after this one (Ps.
118:22–23, 26) later in the Gospel (Matt. 21:9, 42) confirms that the
allusion to Psalm 118:25 in Matthew 8:25 and 14:30 is real.

15. See chapter 3 for the evidence that the "Lord" to whom the disciples
prayed was Jesus.

16. When Peter refers to Jesus' own teaching as "the word of the Lord" (Acts 11:16), "word" in Greek is *rhēma*, whereas in the expression "the word of the Lord," referring to the apostles' message about Jesus, "word" in Greek is *logos*.

17. In the Septuagint, the expression "the word of the LORD" nearly always uses *kuriou* (LORD) without the article (although see Ps. 33:4, 6, where the expression refers to the creative word of God). This is probably because the Septuagint uses *kuriou* in these passages in place of the tetragram as if it were a proper name. In Acts, the expression "the word of the Lord" always uses the article with *kuriou*, likely because Acts is not translating a Hebrew text or quoting the Old Testament. Nevertheless, the expression in Acts is both linguistically and conceptually parallel to its counterpart in the Old Testament. The Lord Jesus is the cosmic, heavenly "Lord" who is the authoritative source and focal point of the apostolic "word."

18. See further, Darrell L. Bock, *Proclamation from Prophecy and Pattern: Lucan Old Testament Christology*, JSNTSup 12 (Sheffield: JSOT Press, 1987), 181–86; and H. Douglas Buckwalter, *The Character and Purpose of Luke's Christology*, SNTSMS 89 (Cambridge and New York: Cambridge University Press, 1996), 182–86.

19. Although also not attempting to discuss every relevant text, an excellent published dissertation on this topic is David B. Capes, *Old Testament Yahweh Texts in Paul's Christology*, WUNT 2.47 (Tübingen: Mohr, 1992). Gordon D. Fee does review every Pauline reference to Jesus as "Lord" in *Pauline Christology: An Exegetical-Theological Study* (Peabody, MA: Hendrickson, 2007).

20. But not always: Paul can also call Jesus "God," as apparently he did in the previous chapter (Rom. 9:5; cf. Titus 2:13; see our discussion of these texts in chapter 12).

21. The word *kurios* actually appears only once in verse 12; *ho gar autos kurios pantōn* can be translated, "for the same [one] is Lord of all," or "for the same Lord is [Lord] of all" (as most translations do), or possibly "for the same Lord over all is . . ." (as in the NKJV). Regardless, Paul's train of thought is essentially unaffected.

22. The NWT renders *kurios* as "Jehovah" in Romans 10:13 but not in Romans 10:9 and 12, thereby differentiating the Lord Jesus from Jehovah. There is no textual support, however, for such a change (as

we have already explained), and doing so disrupts Paul's line of argument from verses 9–12 to verse 13. This passage, then, provides strong internal evidence against the theory that the New Testament writings originally contained the tetragram in such verses as Romans 10:13. See also Capes, *Old Testament Yahweh Texts*, 116–23; and McDonough, *YHWH at Patmos*, 61.

23. On Jesus as "Lord" in 1 Corinthians, see Fee, *Pauline Christology*, 88–94, 120–42.

24. Cf. Capes, *Old Testament Yahweh Texts*, 83–84; Fee, *Pauline Christology*, 568–69.

25. Note that in these and many other references to Jesus as "Lord" in Paul's writings, it really does not matter whether the New Testament originally contained the tetragram or not, since Paul's language clearly refers to Jesus as if he were YHWH.

26. See Capes, *Old Testament Yahweh Texts*, 130–36.

27. First Corinthians 2:16 is a key text in the argument that the New Testament originally contained the tetragram. The reason is that a weakly attested variant reading has "but we have the mind of the Lord." (This reading is attested in the fourth-century Codex Vaticanus, citations from the late fourth-century theologians Ambrosiaster and Pelagius, in four Greek manuscripts from the sixth through the eleventh centuries, and a few Old Latin manuscripts.) Howard ("Tetragram and the New Testament," 80) argues that the best explanation for the variant is that the text originally said, "For who has known the mind of YHWH . . . but we have the mind of the Lord," with "Lord" being "a secondary reference" to YHWH. He theorizes that after YHWH was changed to "Lord" the second occurrence of "Lord" was changed to "Christ." Stafford (*Jehovah's Witnesses Defended*, 28n. 63) takes a similar view, although he thinks that in the original text Paul distinguished YHWH from the Lord (Jesus). Using a weakly attested reading, however, to support emending the text to say something for which we have no manuscript attestation at all is really an indefensible text-critical method, especially when the best-attested reading makes sense as it stands. Such is the case here. Cf. Capes, *Old Testament Yahweh Texts*, 136–40.

28. Similarly Capes, *Old Testament Yahweh Texts*, 149–51.

29. Paul uses a different verb for "love" (*philei*) than the verb found in

the Greek Septuagint of Deuteronomy 6:5 (*agapēseis*), but the idea is still the same. On the fallacy of trying to distinguish sharply between these two verbs, see D. A. Carson, *Exegetical Fallacies* (Grand Rapids: Baker, 1984), 28, 31–32, 51–54.

30. Other allusions to the Shema in the Gospels include Mark 2:7; 10:18; cf. Matthew 19:17; Luke 5:21.

31. See also Romans 16:27; 1 Timothy 1:17; 6:15–16; Jude 25.

32. See further deLacey, "'One Lord' in Pauline Christology," 195–203.

33. Translation by Lancelot C. L. Brenton, *Septuagint Version of the Old Testament with an English Translation* (London: Samuel Bagster, 1870). Available online at Christian Classic Ethereal Library, http://www.ccel.org/ccel/brenton/lxx.html.

34. Capes, *Old Testament Yahweh Texts*, 159, who presents a similar table comparing Isaiah 45:23 LXX with Philippians 2:10–11.

35. See Moisés Silva, *Philippians*, 2nd ed., BECNT (Grand Rapids: Baker, 2005), 109–11.

36. Compare *egeusasthe hoti chrēstos ho kurios* (1 Peter 2:3) with *geusasthe . . . hoti chrēstos ho kurios* (Ps. 34:8 [33:9 LXX]). There is an interesting play on words here: the Greek word for "good" (*chrēstos*) is a homonym of the Greek word for "Christ" (*christos*). Some scribes occasionally even wrote *christos* here by mistake.

37. Translations in this table are ours.

38. An interesting textual variant is found here in 1 Peter 3:15. Many of the later Greek manuscripts read *kurion de ton theon hagiasate* ("but regard as holy the Lord God") here instead of *kurion de ton christon hagiasate* ("but regard as holy Christ the Lord"). The KJV and NKJV follow this later variant, whereas other modern versions do not. But George Howard argues, "The reading *Christon*, though better attested, is probably secondary, if we suppose that the Tetragram stood in the original citation. In that case the original text would have read: [*YHWH*] *de ton theon hagiasate*. The author would hardly have written *Christon* since that would have identified Christ with *Yhwh*" (Howard, "Tetragram and the New Testament," 81). Howard's argument begs the question theologically as well as appealing to an inferior variant reading to establish a nonexistent variant reading. It also fails to take into account 1 Peter 2:3, where Peter already has identified Christ as the Lord YHWH.

Chapter 14: Jesus Is It from *A* to *Z*

1. We should not try to force the details of Jesus' parables into a systematic theological framework. Thus, it would be a mistake to reason that the "wedding guests" (disciples) are to be distinguished from the "bride" (the church). Jesus portrays his disciples as wedding guests rather than as the bride because it better served his message—that some of his professed followers would prove faithful while others did not.

2. Payne notes that twenty of Jesus' recorded parables ascribe to him imagery used of God in the Old Testament. In addition to the imagery of the bridegroom, Payne suggests that images implying the deity of Christ include sower, director of the harvest, father, giver of forgiveness, vineyard owner, shepherd, rock, lord, and king. Philip B. Payne, "Jesus' Implicit Claim to Deity in His Parables," *TrinJ* 2.1 (1981): 3–23.

3. We do not deny, of course, that the redeemed will live in a glorious place. On the New Jerusalem as a symbolic vision of the church, see Kenneth D. Boa and Robert M. Bowman Jr., *Sense and Nonsense About Heaven and Hell* (Grand Rapids: Zondervan, 2007), chap. 17.

4. See also "the Lord of lords," Psalm 135:26 in the Greek OT (136:26 according to the usual citation, though not in the Hebrew or English Bibles, which have "the God of heaven"). The closest parallel in the NT is Paul's description of God as "the blessed and only Sovereign, the King of kings and Lord of lords" (1 Tim. 6:15; literally, "the King of those who are kings and Lord of those who are lords," using the participles *basileuontōn* and *kurieuontōn*). It is grammatically unlikely, although possible, that the description refers to Jesus Christ (mentioned in the preceding clause). It is also theologically unlikely, since Paul goes on to describe this King and Lord as one "whom no one has ever seen or can see" (v. 16b; cf. John 1:18).

5. On the connections between Revelation 17:14 and Daniel 4:37 LXX, see further G. K. Beale, *The Book of Revelation: A Commentary on the Greek Text*, NIGTC (Grand Rapids: Eerdmans; Milton Keynes, UK: Paternoster, 1999), 881. Evidently, Nebuchadnezzar had the reputation of being the greatest of all kings; even Ezekiel's prophecy of the Babylonian conquest of Tyre refers to Nebuchadnezzar as "king of kings" (Ezek. 26:7). Daniel, in an earlier passage, calls Nebuchadnezzar

"king of kings" (Dan. 2:37), and in some Greek versions, "king of kings and of lords" (Dan. 3:2). These courtly honorific titles, however, merely set up the reader to discover, along with Nebuchadnezzar himself, that God is the real King of kings and Lord of lords, that full title being reserved for God alone (see Nebuchadnezzar's first acknowledgment that Daniel's God is "God of gods and Lord of kings," Dan. 2:47). It is also interesting to note that the Persian ruler Artaxerxes, more than a century after Nebuchadnezzar, also fancied himself as "king of kings" (Ezra 7:12). Devout Jews knew better!

6. John does not apply the expression "God of gods" to Jesus, not because he thinks of Jesus as *less* than God, but because the early church customarily used the divine name *God* for the Father and the divine name *Lord* for Jesus (e.g., 1 Cor. 8:6; see chapter 13).

7. See chapter 13 for the evidence that Titus 2:13 and 2 Peter 1:1 call Jesus "God."

8. Larry W. Hurtado, *Lord Jesus Christ: Devotion to Jesus in Earliest Christianity* (Grand Rapids: Eerdmans, 2003), 515–16.

9. Cf. Sean M. McDonough, *YHWH at Patmos: Rev. 1:4 in Its Hellenistic and Early Jewish Setting*, WUNT 2.107 (Tübingen: Mohr Siebeck, 1999), 131–37.

10. The words *I AM WHO I AM* also function as an interpretation of the significance of the Hebrew YHWH. Whether or not YHWH (*Yahweh?*) derives etymologically from EHYEH, Exodus 3:14–15 makes a meaningful association between the two: "He said further, 'Thus you shall say to the Israelites, "I AM [EHYEH] has sent me to you. . . . The LORD [YHWH] . . . has sent me to you." Semantically, EHYEH means "I am" or "I will be," and is thus what God says about himself. The text implies that YHWH means something like "He is" or "He will be," and is thus what human beings are to say about God. See McDonough, *YHWH at Patmos*, 134.

11. On this subject, see David Mark Ball, *"I Am" in John's Gospel: Literary Function, Background and Theological Implications*, JSNTSup 124 (Sheffield: Sheffield Academic Press, 1996), esp. 177–203; and Catrin H. Williams, *I am He: The Interpretation of ʾĀni Hû in Jewish and Early Christian Literature*, WUNT 2.113 (Tübingen: Mohr Siebeck, 2000), 255–308.

12. All translations in this table are the authors'.

13. Hebrews 12:2 contains an expression for Jesus, "the pioneer and per-fecter [*archēgon kai teleiōtēn*] of our faith," which is similar to "the beginning and the end" (*hē archē kai to telos*).

14. There certainly is no indication that the speaker changes between Revelation 22:12 and 22:13. So, rightly, Peter R. Carrell, *Jesus and the Angels: Angelology and the Christology of the Apocalypse of John* SNTSMS 95 (Cambridge: Cambridge University Press, 1997), 116.

15. On Revelation 1:4 and related titles in the book, including in Revelation 1:17–18, see McDonough, *YHWH at Patmos*, 195–231.

16. The Greek reads, *egō eimi ho prōtos kai ho eschatos kai ho zōn*. The verse division, which places *kai ho zōn* at the beginning of verse 18, is extremely misleading.

17. The Greek is identical in these two occurrences: *ho ōn kai ho ēn kai ho erchomenos* (Rev. 1:4, 8). Revelation 4:8 has the same title but re-verses the first two elements: *ho ēn kai ho ōn kai ho erchomenos* ("the one who was and the one who is and the one who is coming"). In two other passages Revelation uses the same title in a two-part form, *ho ōn kai ho ēn* ("the one who is and the one who was," 11:17; 16:5). Other than in Exodus 3:14, Revelation is the only book of the Bible to use *ho ōn* absolutely (i.e., without some sort of predicate, such as an adjec-tive or prepositional phrase following the verb) to express existence.

18. As we mentioned in our discussion of Jesus' divine attribute of im-mutability, God's unchangeableness does not prevent him from being involved in our lives or from caring about what happens in the ever-changing world. The Incarnation is simply the definitive instance of God's immanent engagement in his own creation.

19. The title evidently derives from Psalm 118:26, which all four Gospels quote. Only one other OT text uses the words *ho erchomenos*, and it is clearly a nontheological use (2 Sam. 2:23). The NT never uses the expression with reference to the Father and only rarely in any context uses it of anyone other than Jesus (Luke 6:47; John 6:35; 2 Cor. 11:4).

Chapter 15: Meet Your Maker

1. One biblical text *may* refer to angels ("the sons of God") existing at the time God created the physical universe: "Where were you when I laid the foundation of the earth? Tell me, if you have understand-ing. Who determined its measurements—surely you know! Or who

stretched the line upon it? On what were its bases sunk, or who laid its cornerstone, when the morning stars sang together and all the sons of God shouted for joy?" (Job 38:4–7 ESV). This text does *not* say, however, that the angels existed before God began making the physical universe. The statement that "the morning stars sang together" probably refers to the beginning of their existence (cf. Gen. 1:14–19); the angels' shouting for joy, therefore, likely refers also to their first cry of joy at being created. If this is correct, the implication is that God created the angels at some point during the process of forming the universe.

2. Greg Stafford, *Jehovah's Witnesses Defended: An Answer to Scholars and Critics*, 2nd ed. (Huntington Beach, CA: Elihu Books, 2000), 324.

3. Richard Bauckham, *God Crucified: Monotheism and Christology in the New Testament* (Grand Rapids: Eerdmans, 1999), 11–12. In a footnote, Bauckham observes that the only partial exception to this generalization is that some Jews, such as Philo, held (based on the plural pronouns in Gen. 1:26) that "subordinate co-workers of God" participated in the creation of the first human beings (ibid., 12n. 12).

4. Francis J. Beckwith, "Of Logic and Lordship: The Validity of a Categorical Syllogism Supporting Christ's Deity," *JETS* 29 (1986): 429–30.

5. Robert M. Grant, *Gods and the One God*, Library of Early Christianity 1, ed. Wayne A. Meeks (Philadelphia: Westminster Press, 1986), 112. Greg Stafford cites this statement with approval (*Jehovah's Witnesses Defended*, 201).

6. *Should You Believe in the Trinity?* (Brooklyn: Watchtower Bible and Tract Society, 1989), 7. This publication is also available online at http://www.watchtower.org/e/ti/article_05.htm (accessed February 4, 2007).

7. Bauckham, *God Crucified*, 38.

8. Most English translations render the last prepositional phrase, *eis auton*, "to him," although they translate the same phrase as "for him" in 1 Corinthians 8:6. Both renderings express in different ways the idea that all things exist, having God as their purpose or goal.

9. Thomas Schreiner, *Romans*, BECNT (Grand Rapids: Baker, 1998), 637–38.

10. Bauckham, *God Crucified*, 39. Bauckham's point does not presuppose

that Paul derived his language directly from Aristotelian philosophy. The Greek philosophical distinction of different types of causation was common in Hellenistic culture and was familiar to Greek-speaking Jews. Those Jews, including Paul, adapted the language distinguishing different types of causation to their own theistic worldview. Thus, whereas the Greeks sometimes used the preposition *ek* or *ex* to express the material cause (e.g., a statue was made "out of" bronze), in Paul it expresses the efficient cause (since Paul, of course, was no pantheist). See Eduard Lohse, *Colossians and Philemon*, trans. William R. Poehlmann and Robert J. Karris, Hermeneia (Philadelphia: Fortress Press, 1971), 49–50; and Vincent A. Pizzuto, *A Cosmic Leap of Faith: An Authorial, Structural, and Theological Investigation of the Cosmic Christology in Col 1:15–20*, Contributions to Biblical Exegesis and Theology 41 (Leuven: Peeters, 2006), 177.

11. Bauckham, *God Crucified*, 39.

12. Similarly, one should not infer that the Father is not the "one Lord" (which would mean that the Father is not Jehovah), nor that Jesus Christ is not the "one God."

13. Commentators have offered a variety of explanations of the phrase *en autō*. Perhaps it is best to see it as an application of Paul's common expression "in Christ" (and equivalents), which typically conveys the idea of unity with Christ in salvation (Col. 1:2, 14, 28; 2:3, 6–7, 10–12). The idea, then, may be that all things were created, having Christ as their unifying agent.

14. The phrase *di' hon* is translated "for whom" because *hon* is accusative, and *dia* followed by the accusative means "for, on account of, because of." Thus, *di' hon* here is another way of expressing the "final cause" or idea of God as the goal of all things. The same preposition followed by the genitive (*di' hou*) means "through" or "by means of"; this is the usage familiar in John 1:3, 10; 1 Corinthians 8:6b; Colossians 1:16; and Hebrews 1:2.

15. "But since this prep. [*dia*] + gen. can express ultimate cause (e.g., Rom. 11:36) as well as intermediate agency, there may be no special emphasis on Christ's mediatorial or cooperative role in creation." Murray J. Harris, *Colossians and Philemon*, EGGNT (Grand Rapids: Eerdmans, 1991), 46.

16. Some sort of "economic" distinction between the roles of the Father

and the Son (as well as of the Holy Spirit) in the work of Creation is
consistent with both Scripture and the historic doctrine of the Trinity.
All we are insisting here is that any such distinction falls short of implying that the Son performs an *inferior* role. Still, it does seem to us
that the New Testament does not provide compelling evidence for
hard and fast distinctions in the roles of the Father and the Son in
creation.

17. Stafford, *Jehovah's Witnesses Defended*, 171.
18. *Reasoning from the Scriptures* (Brooklyn: Watchtower Bible and Tract
    Society, 1989), 414, quoted in Stafford, *Jehovah's Witnesses Defended*,
    172–73.
19. We should point out that the Jehovah's Witnesses' interpretation of
    Hebrews 1:8–9 assumes their translation of verse 8, "God is your
    throne" (NWT). If Psalm 45:6 (quoted in Heb. 1:8) says, "Your throne,
    O God," then in fact the text looks beyond Solomon, who only typi-
    fied Christ, to the divine Son who truly is God. On Psalm 45:6 and
    Hebrews 1:8, see chapter 13.

Chapter 16: He's Got the Whole World in His Hands

1. See Thomas C. Oden, *The Living God: Systematic Theology, Volume
   One* (1987; reprint, Peabody, MA: Hendrickson, 1998), 270–315, for a
   careful definition and defense of the doctrine of divine providence.
2. Psalm 104 attributes God's creative and providential works to his wisdom (v. 24) and to his Spirit (v. 30), here understood as aspects of
   his own divine being. In the light of the NT, however, in which Jesus
   Christ is God's Word and Wisdom (John 1:1, 14; 1 Cor. 1:30; etc.), it
   is reasonable to see in this passage an anticipation of the doctrine of
   the Trinity.
3. The argument here is not that the aorist always denotes a one-time
   past event or that the perfect cannot express simple past action. Such
   a way of handling Greek tenses is widely understood to be inade-
   quate. See Daniel B. Wallace, *Greek Grammar Beyond the Basics: An
   Exegetical Syntax of the New Testament* (Grand Rapids: Zondervan,
   1996), 494–512, 554–65, 572–82. The argument, rather, is that Paul's
   shift from the aorist to the perfect in this context is best explained as
   indicating a shift in nuance.
4. Margaret Y. MacDonald, *Colossians and Philemon*, Sacra Pagina 17, ed.

Daniel J. Harrington (Collegeville, MN: Liturgical Press—A Michael Glazier Book, 2000), 60. Similarly, Murray J. Harris, *Colossians and Philemon*, EGGNT (Grand Rapids: Eerdmans, 1991), 45; and Eduard Lohse, *Colossians and Philemon*, trans. William R. Poehlmann and Robert J. Karris, Hermeneia (Philadelphia: Fortress Press, 1971), 49.

5. Compare the reference to "that which holds all things together" (*to sunechon*, Wisdom 1:7), probably referring to God in his wise omniscience, closely associated with "the spirit of the Lord." In context, the writer is saying that God knows everyone's hearts and in his wisdom will judge them for whatever they say (vv. 5–8).

6. The Greek word *sugkeitai* ("holds together") in context is roughly synonymous with both *pherōn* in Hebrews 1:3 and *sunestēken* in Colossians 1:17. Sirach is also called Ecclesiasticus (not to be confused with Ecclesiastes).

7. Paul's statement in Acts 17:28a may, in turn, derive from or allude to a pagan Greek writer, although the evidence for this is inconclusive (whereas Paul states explicitly that v. 28b is a quote from a Greek poet). See F. F. Bruce, *The Acts of the Apostles: The Greek Text with Introduction and Commentary*, 3rd rev. and enlarged ed. (Grand Rapids: Eerdmans; Leicester, UK: Apollos, 1990), 384–85.

8. This is almost certainly what John 1:9 means; that is, what John says is not that the true light "enlightens everyone coming into the world" but that "there was the true light, which enlightens every human being, coming into the world" (literal translation). See Craig S. Keener, *The Gospel of John: A Commentary* (Peabody, MA: Hendrickson, 2003), 1:393–95.

9. Cf. Jerome H. Neyrey, *Render to God: New Testament Understandings of the Divine* (Minneapolis: Fortress, 2004), 214. He cites Philo, *De Cherubim* 88–89; *Legatio ad Gaium* 1.5; and two texts from the Mishnah, *Rabba Genesis* 11.10 and *Rabba Exodus* 30.6, as illustrative of the Jewishness of this point.

10. Graham H. Twelftree, *Jesus the Miracle Worker: A Historical and Theological Study* (Downers Grove, IL: InterVarsity Press, 1999), 253–57.

11. It is worth noting that, in contrast to reporting Jesus' many miracles, the Gospels report none performed by John the Baptist (cf. John 10:41, which states plainly that John did none). This lack of reported

miracles for John is actually surprising given that the Gospels refer to him as a latter-day Elijah (Matt. 11:14; 17:10–13; Mark 9:11–13; Luke 1:17; cf. Mal. 4:5–6). In John 1:19–28, John the Baptist denies being Elijah, likely because those inquiring associated certain false expectations with Malachi's prophecy, perhaps even including miracles of judgment akin to Elijah's famous encounter with the prophets of Baal (1 Kings 18:17–40). In any case, the fact that the Gospels report no miracles through John evinces a restraint inconsistent with the supposition that their accounts of Jesus' miracles are pious fictions.

12. Twelftree, *Jesus the Miracle Worker*, 345, emphasis in original.

13. Werner Kahl, *New Testament Miracle Stories in Their Religious-Historical Setting: A Religionsgeschichtliche Comparison from a Structural Perspective*, FRLANT 163 (Göttingen: Vanderhoeck & Ruprecht, 1994), 76; cited in Eric Eve, *The Jewish Context of Jesus' Miracles*, JSNTSup 231 (London and New York: Sheffield Academic Press, 2002), 15.

14. Eve, *Jewish Context of Jesus' Miracles*, 16.

15. Geza Vermes, *Jesus the Jew: A Historian's Reading of the Gospels* (Minneapolis: Augsburg Fortress, 1981), 58–82. For a critique of this book, see Craig A. Evans, *Jesus and His Contemporaries*, AGJU 25 (Leiden: Brill Academic, 2001), 227–43.

16. Eve, *Jewish Context of Jesus' Miracles*, 273–87.

17. Ibid., 285.

18. Ibid., 289; see 287–95.

19. Ibid., 295.

20. Note that the claim we are making is not that Jesus never prayed prior to performing a miracle but that Jesus apparently never petitioned the Father to perform a miracle. In Mark 7:34, Jesus looked up to heaven and sighed before healing, suggesting some sort of communion with the Father but not a petitionary prayer. Regarding John 11:41–42, the neo-orthodox scholar Rudolf Bultmann commented, "Jesus directs his gaze to heaven for prayer, but he utters no request; he gives thanks for the hearing already granted (v. 41). It thus appears that the Son of God does not need to make a request in prayer; and precisely this appears to be stressed in v. 42; since the Son is constantly sure of the Father's hearing, he never needs to make requests; if he prayed on this occasion it was only for the sake of the people present, 'that they

might grasp faith' that God sent him" (Rudolf Bultmann, *The Gospel of John: A Commentary*, trans. G. R. Beasley-Murray, R. W. N. Hoare, and J. K. Riches [Philadelphia: Westminster Press, 1971], 407–8; quoted in Craig L. Blomberg, *The Historical Reliability of John's Gospel: Issues and Commentary* [Downers Grove, IL: InterVarsity Press, 2001], 170n. 250). By thanking the Father for always hearing him, Jesus "demonstrates that his work is done in concert with God's will, for he never acts autonomously" (Gary M. Burge, *John*, NIV Application Commentary [Grand Rapids: Zondervan, 2000], 319–20).

21. R. T. France, *The Gospel of Mark: A Commentary on the Greek Text*, NIGTC (Grand Rapids: Eerdmans; Carlisle: Paternoster, 2002), 370.

22. Literally, Luke writes, "And the power of the Lord was for him to heal [*eis to iasthai auton*]" (Luke 5:17). Grammatically, "him" (*auton*) could simply refer to "the Lord," or it could refer to Jesus as one to whom someone else, the Lord, had made his power available. The latter view has possible support in that earlier in Luke, Jesus applies to himself the statement in Isaiah 61:1–2 that "the Spirit of the Lord" was upon him, sending him to give sight to the blind and perform other divine works (Luke 4:18–21). In the immediate context, however, Jesus is himself the miracle-working "Lord" (Luke 5:8, 12; cf. 7:13, 19). In Luke's understanding, both thoughts are probably true: Jesus is himself the Lord exercising his divine power, and he also is the Messiah "anointed" by God with the power of the Spirit (see also Luke 4:14; Acts 2:22; 3:12–16; 4:7–12; 10:38).

23. For more on these passages, see Robert M. Bowman Jr., *The Word-Faith Controversy: Understanding the Health and Wealth Gospel* (Grand Rapids: Baker, 2001), 107–9, 196–97.

24. See chapter 10 for a discussion of how these miracles reveal Christ's omnipresence.

25. The word *epeskepsato* ("looked favorably on") can also be translated "visited" (NASB); while the townspeople presumably did not think or realize that Jesus was God, Luke may have worded his quotation of their response to allow for that deeper significance.

26. See especially William Richard Stegner, "Jesus' Walking on the Water: Mark 6:45–52," in *The Gospels and the Scriptures of Israel*, ed. Craig A. Evans and W. Richard Stegner, JSNTSup 104; Studies in Scripture in Early Judaism and Christianity 3 (Sheffield, UK: Sheffield Academic

Press, 1994), 212–34; and Roger David Aus, *"Caught in the Act,"* *Walking on the Sea, and the Release of Barabbas Revisited,* South Florida Studies in the History of Judaism 157 (Atlanta: Scholars Press, 1998), 51–133. Both Stegner and Aus conclude that the story is a pious fiction created from the Red Sea crossing narrative in Exodus. The parallels between the two accounts are suggestive, but they are too indirect to explain the *origin* of the Gospel miracle account. For some cautious comments on the historicity of the miracle, see Twelftree, *Jesus the Miracle Worker,* 320–22.

27. It is odd, if Mark were creating (or repeating) a pious fiction deliberately echoing the Exodus account, that he did not just say that the wind was out of the east.

28. Eve, *Jewish Context of Jesus' Miracles,* 384.

Chapter 17: The Way, the Truth, and the Life

1. Mary Baker Eddy, *Science and Health with Key to the Scriptures* (Boston: Writings of Mary Baker Eddy, 2000), 288:29–30. (*Science and Health,* originally published in 1875, functions as a scriptural text for Christian Science; the citation refers to page number and lines from the official edition.) Eddy's misunderstanding of biblical language for Jesus is evident from her use of the terms *Christ* and *Messiah* as if they had different meanings. *Christ* is simply an Anglicized form of the Greek *Christos,* meaning "anointed one," which the NT uses to translate the Hebrew *mashiach* (which is Anglicized as "Messiah"), also meaning "anointed one."

2. Levi H. Dowling, *The Aquarian Gospel of Jesus the Christ* (Kila, MT: Kessinger Publishing, 2003), 26:23–24 (see also 120:33–34). It is hard to believe that anyone takes this twentieth-century fiction seriously while disparaging the New Testament Gospels because they were written in the mid- to late first century! Yet the *Aquarian Gospel* had a significant impact in the development of what came to be known as the New Age movement.

3. Since we do not find this terminology in any of the epistles, it most likely goes back to the early church, just as Luke says it does.

4. See Gary R. Habermas and Michael R. Licona, *The Case for the Resurrection of Jesus* (Grand Rapids: Kregel, 2004).

5. Although created angels are heavenly, supernatural beings and might

be the agents of God's physical deliverance, the Bible never designates them as saviors. In Genesis 48:16 "the angel who has redeemed me from all harm" is probably a reference to the mysterious "angel of YHWH" (note the parallel references to God in v. 15), whom the OT calls both YHWH and God. A good case exists for viewing this figure as the preincarnate Son of God. See further Kenneth D. Boa and Robert M. Bowman Jr., *Sense and Nonsense About Angels and Demons* (Grand Rapids: Zondervan, 2007), chap. 10. Likewise, "the angel of His presence" who "saved them" in Isaiah 63:9 (NASB, if that wording is correct) is a reference to the Lord. Isaiah has just said that the Lord "became their savior" (v. 8), and he goes on to say that, although the Lord mercifully redeemed them, they grieved his Holy Spirit (vv. 9–10). (The NRSV, unlike most English versions, follows the LXX at this point: "It was no messenger or angel but his presence that saved them.")

6. On Titus 2:13 and 2 Peter 1:1, see chapter 12.

7. Joel Marcus, "Authority to Forgive Sins upon the Earth: The *Shema* in the Gospel of Mark," in *The Gospels and the Scriptures of Israel*, ed. Craig A. Evans and W. Richard Stegner, JSNTSup 104; Studies in Scripture in Early Judaism and Christianity 3 (Sheffield: Sheffield Academic Press, 1994), 196–211. Marcus needlessly presupposes that the historical Jesus did not claim to forgive sins (199).

8. Cf. Rikki E. Watts, *Isaiah's New Exodus and Mark*, WUNT 2.88 (Tübingen: Mohr Siebeck, 1997). Watts notes that in the context of the Gospel of Mark, "The miracles of Jesus are not only evidence pointing to Yahweh's coming as a mighty Warrior waging war against his people's oppressors but are also genuine expressions of his compassion as shepherd of his people (1:41; 6:34; 8:2; cf. Isa. 40:1, 10f.; 49:10, 13, 15; 51:3; 54:7f.)" (181).

9. The sense of the word *rabbi* was "master," but it came to be used as a term for a teacher or scholar in Judaism who instructed others in the Torah. Thus, in some contexts in which human beings address Jesus as "Lord" in the Gospels, it is possible that the original-language term used was *Rabbi* (e.g., Matt. 8:21). The Gospel writers, however, understand in retrospect that Jesus was much more than a rabbi, something those disciples eventually learned for themselves. In later Judaism after the fall of Jerusalem in A.D. 70, the position of rabbi became much more formalized or institutionalized.

10. On the similarity of Jesus' teaching style (including his parables) to that of the rabbis, see Craig A. Evans, *Jesus and His Contemporaries,* 25 (Leiden: Brill Academic, 2001), 251–97.

11. It appears that the categories of rabbis and scribes were overlapping: some rabbis were scribes, and some scribes were rabbis. The terms seem to have been used informally, without any precise or technical definition. Historians are not even entirely certain whether the scribes were aligned primarily with the Pharisees or with the Sadducees, although it seems that both factions had their scribes. See Oskar Skarsaune, *In the Shadow of the Temple: Jewish Influences on Early Christianity* (Downers Grove, IL: InterVarsity Press, 2002), 100, 107–9.

12. Quoted in John Nolland, *The Gospel of Matthew: A Commentary on the Greek Text,* NIGTC (Grand Rapids: Eerdmans; Bletchley, UK: Paternoster, 2005), 346n. 542.

13. Note that Jesus is not setting aside the Old Testament; he explicitly denies doing that (Matt. 5:17–18). Rather, he is setting aside the tradition of oral interpretations of the Old Testament that in Jewish teaching were already in his day beginning to overshadow the Scriptures. That process became even more pronounced after the fall of Jerusalem, leading eventually to the formation of the Talmud, which is the authoritative text for Orthodox Judaism to this day.

14. We may put the frequency with which Jesus uses this introductory expression "I say to you" in context by noting that roughly 1,700 verses of the Gospels contain sayings of Jesus. Thus, Jesus uses the words "I say to you" about once every twelve verses.

15. The number is 75 if we include Matthew 18:19, where some manuscripts omit "Amen." In the Gospel of John, these sayings begin "Amen, Amen."

16. Klyne R. Snodgrass, "Amen," in *Baker Encyclopedia of the Bible,* ed. Walter A. Elwell (Grand Rapids: Baker, 1988), 1:69.

17. Ben Witherington III, *The Christology of Jesus* (Minneapolis: Fortress, 1990), 188–89.

18. This aspect of rabbinical Judaism continues to this day in Orthodox Judaism, as a recent news story about "Keeping Appliances Kosher" illustrates (National Public Radio, February 11, 2007, at http://www.npr.org/templates/story/story.php?storyId=7348576). It turns out

that a light bulb coming on when a refrigerator door is opened is considered "work," and for this reason some manufacturers sell refrigerators with technology that automatically prevents the light from coming on during the Sabbath.

19. Peter W. Ensor, *Jesus and His "Works": The Johannine Sayings in Historical Perspective*, WUNT 2.85 (Tübingen: Mohr Siebeck, 1996), 190. Ensor is speaking of the Gospel of John (especially 5:17), but his statements apply to the other Gospels as well.

20. Robert H. Gundry, *Jesus the Word According to John the Sectarian: A Paleofundamentalist Manifesto for Contemporary Evangelicalism, Especially Its Elites, in North America* (Grand Rapids: Eerdmans, 2001), 1–50, 97–100.

21. Characteristically, Jesus exalts the Father above himself (see also John 10:29; 14:28), seeing his mission as that of glorifying the Father by accomplishing his work (4:34; 17:4). Jesus' statement in John 17:3 distinguishes himself from the Father (to whom he is speaking in prayer), but grammatically it does not *deny* that Jesus is also the true God. That Jesus is himself God is affirmed three times in the Gospel (1:1, 18; 20:28; see above, chap. 12).

22. The only Pauline salutations that do not attribute grace and peace to Christ are Colossians 1:2, which attributes them only to the Father, and 1 Thessalonians 1:1, which does not attribute them to any specified source. The epistles to Timothy add "mercy" to the blessings that come from "God the Father and Christ Jesus our Lord" (1 Tim. 1:2; 2 Tim. 1:2). Other NT books contain similar salutations attributing grace and peace to both Father and Son (2 John 3; Rev. 1:4; cf. 2 Peter 1:2).

23. Critics often claim that John's account in John 20:22 contradicts Luke's account in Acts 2, but there is no reason why both cannot be true. John reports Jesus imparting the Spirit to his disciples as an act of commissioning them to be his representatives after he physically leaves them (John 20:21–23). Luke reports Jesus' imparting to his disciples the baptizing fullness of the Spirit with powerful manifestations as an act of empowering them to begin their public ministry of witness to Jesus (Acts 2:1–36).

24. Max Turner, "The Spirit of Christ and 'Divine' Christology," in *Jesus of Nazareth: Lord and Christ: Essays on the Historical Jesus and New*

Testament Christology, ed. Joel B. Green and Max Turner (Grand Rapids: Eerdmans; Carlisle: Paternoster, 1994), 413–36, esp. 423, emphasis in original.

25. Mehrdad Fatehi, *The Spirit's Relation to the Risen Lord in Paul: An Examination of Its Christological Implications,* WUNT 2.128 (Tübingen: Mohr Siebeck, 2000), 322.

26. Ibid., 331.

Chapter 18: Here Comes the Judge

1. See Kenneth D. Boa and Robert M. Bowman Jr., *Sense and Nonsense About Heaven and Hell* (Grand Rapids: Zondervan, 2007), chaps. 7–8.

2. Ibid., chap. 17.

3. Andrew C. Brunson, *Psalm 118 in the Gospel of John: An Intertextual Study on the New Exodus Pattern in the Theology of John,* WUNT 2.148 (Tübingen: Mohr Siebeck, 2003), 388.

4. The NET italicizes "bear the sins of many" because it alludes to Isaiah 53:12.

5. Andrew Y. Lau, *Manifest in Flesh: The Epiphany Christology of the Pastoral Epistles,* WUNT 2.86 (Tübingen: Mohr [Siebeck], 1996), 248, emphasis in original.

6. As Craig Keener points out, Jesus' statement also alludes to Psalm 95:7, which affirms that God's people are "the sheep of his hand" and urges Israel to "listen to his voice" (cf. John 10:27–28 NASB, "My sheep hear My voice . . . and no one will snatch them out of My hand"). See Craig S. Keener, *The Gospel of John: A Commentary* (Peabody, MA: Hendrickson, 2003), 1:825.

7. That is, Psalm 61:13 in the Greek text. It seems likely to be significant that both parts of Jesus' statement in Revelation 2:23 allude to Proverbs 24:12.

Chapter 19: Jesus Takes the Stand

1. Anonymous story, published on over a dozen Web sites on the Internet.

2. Note that John does not actually record the interrogation before the Sanhedrin but simply mentions that Jesus had been taken to Caiaphas and then to Pilate. This may be because John assumed some familiarity with the Synoptic Gospels (Matthew, Mark, and Luke), but more

likely he simply assumed familiarity with the "Passion Narrative," the basic story line of Jesus' last supper, arrest, trials, execution, and burial, which many biblical scholars believe existed at least as a well-defined oral tradition prior to the publication of the Gospels. See Craig S. Keener, *The Gospel of John: A Commentary* (Peabody, MA: Hendrickson, 2003), 1:40–47; 2:1067–73.

3. See Darrell L. Bock, *Blasphemy and Exaltation in Judaism: The Charge against Jesus in Mark 14:53–65* (Grand Rapids: Baker, 2000), 189–95. As will become obvious, we are significantly indebted to Bock for our understanding of this subject.

4. We focus on Mark's account here (although the accounts in Matthew and Luke are quite similar at this point) for sake of simplicity and because biblical scholars (both conservative and liberal) generally agree that Mark's Gospel was probably written first. This passage in Mark, then, is a strategic text because it shows that belief in Christ's deity can be traced to the earliest documents and even back to Jesus himself.

5. The accusation apparently was a conflation of two or more statements that Jesus had made. One was Jesus' prediction that the temple would be destroyed (Mark 13:2). Another was Jesus' enigmatic saying, "Destroy this temple, and in three days I will raise it up" (John 2:19), which according to John was a prediction of Jesus' death and resurrection (vv. 20–22). The conflation of these statements may explain why the witnesses were unable to agree on what Jesus had said.

6. So Bock, *Blasphemy and Exaltation in Judaism*, 230–31.

7. The Greek text has *kai* before *hoti* ("because"), but most interpreters seem to agree that *kai* in this context means something like "even" or "that is"; hence, it is left untranslated in several versions (e.g., ESV, NET, NIV, NRSV). Thus, there is only one reason given for the threat of stoning, not two. Jesus' response confirms that blasphemy is the only reason given (10:34–38).

8. Given this pervasive evidence from the context of John 10:33, we can rule out with a high degree of confidence the translation "make yourself to be a god" (NWT). Such a translation may be grammatically possible, but it is not contextually plausible.

9. Our argument here is not that if Jesus' Jewish critics thought he was claiming equality with God, then he must, in fact, have been making such a claim. We are simply documenting that this is what they

repeatedly understood to be the import of Jesus' statements. The case for concluding that Jesus claimed equality or parity with God rests on what Jesus himself said in context and in light of the Old Testament. When Jesus responds to such accusations of blasphemy, he humbly emphasizes that he makes no claim to operate as a divine being *independent of the Father*, while at the same time repeating his claim to exercise the prerogatives and do the deeds of God (John 5:19–26; 10:36–38). The fact that after all these confrontations his opponents still understood him to be making blasphemous claims confirms that Jesus was, indeed, claiming equality with God.

10. Noted by Bock, *Blasphemy and Exaltation in Judaism*, 185.
11. Ibid., 188.

Chapter 20: God's Right-hand Man

1. See the similar table in J. Ed Komoszewski, M. James Sawyer, and Daniel B. Wallace, *Reinventing Jesus: How Contemporary Skeptics Miss the Real Jesus and Mislead Popular Culture* (Grand Rapids: Kregel, 2006), 178.
2. Darrell L. Bock, *Blasphemy and Exaltation in Judaism: The Charge Against Jesus in Mark 14:53–65* (Grand Rapids: Baker, 2000), 231.
3. That Jesus was "the son of David" is affirmed by sympathetic figures elsewhere in Mark (10:47–48; 11:10) and nowhere denied. Both Matthew and Luke include the account in which Jesus asks how the Messiah can be David's Lord (Matt. 22:42–45; Luke 20:41–44), evidently seeing this question as in no way undermining the claim that Jesus as the Messiah was a descendant of David (Matt. 1:1, 6, 17, 20; Luke 1:27, 32, 69; 2:4, 11; 3:31).
4. What follows in the rest of this paragraph and in the next is essentially repeated from Komoszewski, Sawyer, and Wallace, *Reinventing Jesus*, 178.
5. Josephus *Antiquities* 3.181–87, cited in Bock, *Blasphemy and Exaltation in Judaism*, 54.
6. Darrell L. Bock, *Jesus According to Scripture: Restoring the Portrait from the Gospels* (Grand Rapids: Baker, 2002), 375.
7. Cf. E. Earle Ellis, "Deity-Christology in Mark 14:58," in *Jesus of Nazareth: Lord and Christ: Essays on the Historical Jesus and New Testament Christology*, ed. Joel B. Green and Max Turner (Grand

Rapids: Eerdmans; Carlisle: Paternoster, 1994), 196–97. It is interesting to note that Ezekiel and Daniel, on the traditional, conservative view, wrote during the same period (i.e., during the Babylonian
exile). Some biblical scholars, who accept the view that Daniel was
written in the second century B.C., suggest that Daniel 7:13 is actually dependent on Ezekiel 1:26, e.g., David E. Aune, *Revelation 1–5*,
WBC 52a (Nashville: Nelson Reference, 1997), 92. For a defense of
the sixth-century origin of the book of Daniel, see Gleason L. Archer
Jr., *A Survey of Old Testament Introduction*, rev. ed. (Chicago: Moody
Press, 1994), 421–48.

8. Bock, *Jesus According to Scripture*, 345–46.

9. Some biblical scholars question whether Jesus ever used this title of
himself. The designation "Son of Man" was not used, however, in the
New Testament as part of the church's own way of speaking about
Jesus. Other than on the lips of Jesus, he is so designated only in
Acts 7:56 (Stephen's vision prior to his stoning) and Revelation 1:13
(John's initial vision). The Son of Man sayings of Jesus, then, pass a
stringent test of authenticity (the so-called criterion of dissimilarity):
if a saying of Jesus is unlikely to have been worded as it is by the early
church, then we may infer that Jesus probably said it. (The reverse,
though, is not a valid argument: from the fact that the early church
would be comfortable wording something as it appears in a Gospel
saying, it does *not* follow that Jesus *didn't* say it.)

10. Bock, *Blasphemy and Exaltation in Judaism*, 209. We wish to stress
that, while the high priest and the rest of the Sanhedrin were no doubt
highly offended at Jesus' implicit repudiation of their authority, the
actual blasphemy for which they found him deserving of death was
his claim that he was, as the unique Son of God, on the same level as
God (Mark 14:61–64; John 19:7). Insulting the religious leaders could
itself be judged technically as blasphemy; the consistent report of the
Gospels, however, is that the leaders' main basis for accusing Jesus of
blasphemy was that he claimed the stature and prerogatives of God
(see also our earlier discussion of Mark 2:7; John 5:17–18; 8:58–59;
10:33).

11. Martin Hengel, *Studies in Early Christology* (Edinburgh: T & T Clark,
1995), 155.

12. Ibid., 180.

13. This statement *by itself* does not prove the deity of the Messiah, since in John 7:24, Jesus urges this standard of judgment for human beings.
14. Hengel, *Studies in Early Christology*, 180.
15. See Bock, *Blasphemy and Exaltation in Judaism*, 98–99, 145–46.
16. Jerusalem Talmud, *Ta'anith* 2.1 65b, quoted in Hengel, *Studies in Early Christology*, 181. Bock dates the saying to about A.D. 300 (*Blasphemy and Exaltation in Judaism*, 204).
17. For surveys of these figures (from differing scholarly perspectives), see Larry W. Hurtado, *One God, One Lord: Early Christian Doctrine and Ancient Jewish Monotheism* (London: SCM Press, 1988), esp. chaps. 3–4; Bock, *Blasphemy and Exaltation in Judaism*, 113–83; Charles A. Gieschen, *Angelomorphic Christology: Antecedents and Early Evidence*, AGJU 42 (Leiden and Boston: Brill, 1998), 124–83; and Timo Eskola, *Messiah and the Throne: Jewish Merkabah Mysticism and Early Christian Exaltation Discourse*, WUNT 2.142 (Tübingen: Mohr Siebeck, 2001), 65–123. In addition, some precedent for the exalted Christology of the New Testament is often sought in divine "hypostases," that is, personified attributes of God (such as his name, glory, word, power, and especially wisdom) that seem to be treated as if they function as divine persons distinct from God. On these, see, e.g., Hurtado, *One God, One Lord*, chap. 2; and Gieschen, *Angelomorphic Christology*, 70–123. We have commented earlier in this book on some of these topics, especially wisdom. Here we would simply make three points. First, if the New Testament identifies Jesus as the incarnation of a divine "hypostasis," that is essentially the same thing as identifying him as God incarnate. Second, a divine hypostasis, per se, would not be *exalted* to sit on God's throne at his right hand. The scandal of the Christian position is that it claims that a *human being* was exalted to rule over all creation from the throne of God. Third, the dominant "model" of New Testament Christology is not glory-Christology, or wisdom-Christology, or even word-Christology, but Son-Christology. That is, the dominant model of Christology in the New Testament is the narrative that God the Father sent his divine Son into the world to redeem us from sin by dying on the cross, after which he rose from the dead and was exalted to the right hand of God.
18. As quoted in Eskola, *Messiah and the Throne*, 87–88. There is some

dispute about the word translated "raise up" (*exanistēmi*), which
some interpreters think could mean "remove" or "overthrow."

19. Pieter W. van der Horst, "Moses' Throne Vision in Ezekiel the
    Dramatist," *JJS* 34 (1983): 21–29, esp. 25; reprinted in *Essays of the
    Jewish World of Early Christianity*, NTOA 14 (Fribourg-Göttingen:
    Universitätsverlag—Vandenhoeck & Ruprecht, 1990), 63–71, esp. 67;
    David Aune, *Revelation 1–5*, 262; likewise Gieschen, *Angelomorphic
    Christology*, 164–65; and others.
20. Hengel, *Studies in Early Christology*, 191.
21. See also 1 Enoch 43:1–4, where stars are part of a parabolic vision
    representing the holy ones who live on the earth and believe in the
    Lord of Spirits.
22. Richard Bauckham, "The Throne of God and the Worship of Jesus," in
    The Jewish Roots of Christological Monotheism, ed. Carey C. Newman,
    James R. Davila, and Gladys S. Lewis, Supplements to the *JSJ* 63
    (Leiden: Brill, 1999), 55 (citing *Jubilees* 1:4).
23. Contra, e.g., Eskola, *Messiah and the Throne*, 88.
24. Ibid., 366; cf. 90.
25. Bock, *Blasphemy and Exaltation in Judaism*, 144; see his discussion,
    141–44; likewise Bauckham, "Throne of God and the Worship of
    Jesus," 55–57. Noting that in the vision, Moses sits on God's throne in
    his place (not with him), Bauckham concludes, "The dream depicts
    Moses quite literally as God, but the meaning of the dream is not its
    literal meaning" (57). Thus, *in his dream* Moses has God's attribute
    of omniscience, receives God's honor of worship, and occupies God's
    seat on the divine throne, but when he wakes up, Moses is still just
    another human servant of God.
26. We know 1 Enoch primarily from a handful of copies of an Ethiopic
    translation dating from the fifteenth century A.D., generally regarded
    as based on a Greek translation from an original Aramaic. Scholars
    date the five parts of the book to different centuries, and no clear
    consensus has emerged in this matter. The relevant part of the book
    (1 Enoch 37–71) has been dated as early as the first century B.C. and
    as late as the third century A.D., although most scholars prefer a date
    before the end of the first century A.D. "No fragments of these chap-
    ters have been found at Qumran, and some think their original lan-
    guage was Hebrew, not Aramaic" (James C. VanderKam, "The Enoch

Literature" [1997], http://www.st-andrews.ac.uk/~www_sd/enoch
.html). It is ironic that many people feel free to draw sweeping conclusions from material that we have only in the form of a translation
of a translation, that is attested by just a handful of manuscript copies
dating about fifteen centuries after the original, and that is written
in the name of someone who had been dead for millennia, while at
the same time they look askance at the New Testament writings, for
which we have thousands of manuscripts in the original language,
some dating to within a few decades of the originals, and which were
written in the same century as its main figures.

27. Hengel, *Studies in Early Christology*, 188.
28. So Bauckham, "Throne of God and the Worship of Jesus," 60n. 32.
    Hengel's argument for direct dependence of Matthew on 1 Enoch as-
    sumes a date for Matthew toward the end of the first century (which
    many conservative scholars dispute) as well as a pre-A.D. 70 date for
    Enoch (which is widely, although not universally, accepted). It also as-
    sumes that Matthew is not reporting Jesus' own teaching. If Jesus spoke
    of himself as the Son of Man who would sit on the throne of his glory,
    and if 1 Enoch 37–71 dates from before Jesus, it may be, of course, that
    Jesus derived the term from 1 Enoch. There are a lot of suppositions
    on all sides of this question; again, caution seems to be in order.
29. In Testament of Job 33:3, Job says, "My throne is in the upper world,
    and its splendor and majesty come from the right hand of the Father."
    This is not the same thing as claiming to sit on God's throne at his right
    hand. For an English translation of Testament of Job, see Rudolf P.
    Spittler, "Testament of Job," in *Old Testament Pseudepigrapha*, ed.
    J. H. Charlesworth (Garden City, NY: Doubleday, 1983), 1:829–68.
30. Bock, *Blasphemy and Exaltation in Judaism*, 162.
31. Ibid., 203.
32. Eskola, *Messiah and the Throne*, 332–33, emphasis in original.
33. Bauckham, "Throne of God and the Worship of Jesus," 64.

Chapter 21: Jesus Takes His Seat

1. Richard Bauckham, *God Crucified: Monotheism and Christology in the
   New Testament* (Grand Rapids: Eerdmans, 1999), 31–32. Bauckham
   cites Isaiah 44:24; Jeremiah 10:16; 51:19; and numerous texts from
   Apocryphal and other intertestamental Jewish literature.

2. Note that all emphasis in biblical quotations in the conclusion is ours.
3. Richard Bauckham, "The Throne of God and the Worship of Jesus," in *The Jewish Roots of Christological Monotheism*, ed. Carey C. Newman, James R. Davila, and Gladys S. Lewis, Supplements to the *JSJ* 63 (Leiden: Brill, 1999), 52.
4. Bauckham, *God Crucified*, 32.
5. Martin Hengel, *Studies in Early Christology* (Edinburgh: T & T Clark, 1995), 225.
6. NIV, NASB, and HCSB translate "will serve him." NRSV and NET have "will worship him." The Greek word here, *latreusousin*, means to render religious devotion or service to someone.
7. According to Gregory K. Beale, the singular pronoun "likely does not refer only to God or only to the Lamb. The two are conceived so much as a unity that the singular pronoun can refer to both. . . . Such statements . . . were among those that gave rise to later trinitarian formulas" (G. K. Beale, *The Book of Revelation: A Commentary on the Greek Text*, NIGTC [Grand Rapids: Eerdmans; Milton Keynes, UK: Paternoster, 1999], 1113). Similarly, Revelation 11:15 speaks of "the kingdom of our Lord and of his Messiah," yet states "*he* will reign forever."
8. Hengel, *Studies in Early Christology*, 189.
9. Ibid., 142; similarly 149: "One must interpret the sitting at the right hand in relation to Christ as 'on the right side of the throne . . . ,' that is, the resurrected Christ sat to the right beside God himself on the 'throne of glory.'"
10. Henry Barclay Swete, *The Apocalypse of St John*, 2nd ed. (London: Macmillan, 1907), 127; cited in Richard Bauckham, "The Worship of Jesus in Apocalyptic Christianity," *NTS* 27 (1981): 322–41 (330).
11. Bauckham, "Worship of Jesus in Apocalyptic Christianity," 335.
12. Richard Bauckham, "The Worship of Jesus in Philippians 2:9–11," in *Where Christology Began: Essays on Philippians 2*, ed. Ralph P. Martin and Brian J. Dodd (Louisville: Westminster John Knox, 1998), 131.

Conclusion: The Case for the Deity of Christ

1. Richard Bauckham, *God Crucified: Monotheism and Christology in the New Testament* (Grand Rapids: Eerdmans, 1999), 26.
2. See Bauckham's elaboration of these four lines of evidence in ibid., 28–40.

3. Ibid., 40–42.

4. Charles A. Gieschen, *Angelomorphic Christology: Antecedents and Early Evidence*, AGJU 42 (Leiden and Boston: Brill, 1998), 30–31. Gieschen presents these five criteria as ways of recognizing the divinity of an "angelomorphic" figure, meaning one depicted with angelic forms or functions, although not necessarily a member of the ranks of created angels. Gieschen's contention is that the NT exhibits an "angelomorphic Christology" that nevertheless also affirms Christ's full divinity. He argues that such "angelomorphic" aspects of early Christology derive ultimately from the OT traditions of the "angel of the Lord," understood as a manifestation of God (i.e., a *theophany*). It is beyond our purpose here to assess the merits of such an angelomorphic model of early Christology. As Gieschen defines it, such a model is more or less compatible with an affirmation of the deity of Christ. We would simply stress that, in NT teaching about Christ, whatever angelomorphic elements or traditions may be detected play a secondary role. The dominant, *defining* motifs of NT Christology portray Christ as the divine Lord and incarnate Son.

5. Ibid., 31–33. We have rearranged Gieschen's five criteria to parallel in order our five lines of evidence.

6. Timo Eskola, *Messiah and the Throne: Jewish Merkabah Mysticism and Early Christian Exaltation Discourse*, WUNT 2.142 (Tübingen: Mohr Siebeck, 2001), 145. Eskola comments that "the criterion of divine veneration" might be helpful in theory, but does not clearly apply in Jewish literature about angels and exalted human beings.

7. Ibid., 139–42, esp. 142.

8. Ibid., 139.

9. Cf. P. G. Davis, "Divine Agents, Mediators, and New Testament Christology," *JTS* 45 (1994): 479–503, who classifies various figures according to whether they act on God's behalf in the past, present, or future. See also James R. Davila, "Of Methodology, Monotheism and Metatron: Introductory Reflections on Divine Mediators and the Origins of the Worship of Jesus," in *The Jewish Roots of Christological Monotheism*, ed. Carey C. Newman, James R. Davila, and Gladys S. Lewis, Supplements to the *JSJ* 63 (Leiden: Brill, 1999), 6–7.

10. Eskola, *Messiah and the Throne*, 144.

11. There is, of course, nothing unique about the nature or attributes of

a president. If, however, the person claiming to be the president is at least thirty-five years old and is a natural-born citizen of the United States, his attributes are at least consistent with his claim.

12. Formed by combining a word for "exalt" with a preposition meaning "above." For the translation "super-exalted," see Markus Bockmuehl, *The Epistle to the Philippians*, Black's New Testament Commentary (Peabody, MA: Hendrickson, 1998), 141.

13. Richard Bauckham, "Paul's Christology of Divine Identity" (paper presented at the annual meeting of the Society of Biblical Literature, Toronto, Canada, November 25, 2002), 14. Available online at http://www.foranswer.org/Top_JW/Richard_Bauckham.pdf.

14. Larry W. Hurtado, *At the Origins of Christian Worship: The Context and Character of Earliest Christian Devotion* (Grand Rapids: Eerdmans, 1999), 97, emphasis added.

15. N. T. Wright, *What Saint Paul Really Said: Was Paul of Tarsus the Real Founder of Christianity?* (Grand Rapids: Eerdmans, 1997), 68.

RECOMMENDED RESOURCES

Bauckham, Richard. *God Crucified: Monotheism and Christology in the New Testament*. Grand Rapids: Eerdmans, 1999.

Bock, Darrell L. *Blasphemy and Exaltation in Judaism: The Charge Against Jesus in Mark 14:53–65*. Grand Rapids: Baker, 2000.

Evans, Craig A. *Fabricating Jesus: How Modern Scholars Distort the Gospels*. Downers Grove, IL: InterVarsity Press, 2006.

Fee, Gordon D. *Pauline Christology: An Exegetical-Theological Study*. Peabody, MA: Hendrickson, 2007.

Gathercole, Simon J. *The Preexistent Son: Recovering the Christologies of Matthew, Mark, and Luke*. Grand Rapids: Eerdmans, 2006.

Green, Joel B., and Max Turner, eds. *Jesus of Nazareth: Lord and Christ: Essays on the Historical Jesus and New Testament Christology*. Grand Rapids: Eerdmans; Carlisle: Paternoster, 1994.

Harris, Murray J. *Jesus as God: The New Testament Use of* Theos *in Reference to Jesus*. Grand Rapids: Baker, 1992.

———. *3 Crucial Questions About Jesus*. Grand Rapids: Baker, 1994.

Hengel, Martin. *Studies in Early Christology*. Edinburgh: T & T Clark, 1995.

Hurtado, Larry W. *Lord Jesus Christ: Devotion to Jesus in Earliest Christianity*. Grand Rapids: Eerdmans, 2003.

Komoszewski, J. Ed, M. James Sawyer, and Daniel B. Wallace. *Reinventing Jesus: How Contemporary Skeptics Miss the Real Jesus and Mislead Popular Culture*. Grand Rapids: Kregel, 2006.

Longenecker, Richard N., ed. *Contours of Christology in the New Testament*. Grand Rapids: Eerdmans, 2005.

Piper, John. *Seeing and Savoring Jesus Christ*. Wheaton, IL: Crossway Books, 2004.

Rowdon, Harold H., ed. *Christ the Lord: Studies in Christology Presented to Donald Guthrie*. Leicester, UK; Downers Grove, IL: InterVarsity Press, 1982.

Witherington, Ben, III. *The Many Faces of the Christ: The Christologies of the New Testament and Beyond*. Companions to the New Testament. New York: Crossroad, 1998.

SCRIPTURE INDEX

Page references in which a biblical text is given significant explanation are shown in bold type.

OLD TESTAMENT

GENESIS

EXODUS

PROVERBS

ECCLESIASTES

Jeremiah

Lamentations

Ezekiel

John

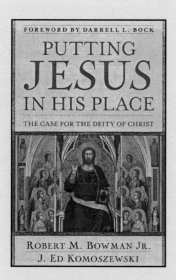